Mark Twain

at the *Buffalo Express*

Mark Twain

at the *Buffalo Express*

Articles and Sketches by
America's
Favorite Humorist

Mark Twain

Edited by

Joseph B. McCullough and Janice McIntire-Strasburg

NORTHERN ILLINOIS

UNIVERSITY

PRESS

DeKalb 2000

Library of Congress Cataloging-in-Publication Data

Twain, Mark, 1835–1910

    Mark Twain at the Buffalo express : articles

and sketches by America's favorite humorist /

Mark Twain ; edited by Joseph B. McCullough

and Janice McIntire-Strasburg.

    p.   cm.

Includes bibliographical references and index.

ISBN 0-87580-585-X (paperback)

(acid-free paper)

1. Humorous stories, American—New York

(State)—Buffalo. 2. United States—

History—1865–1898—Sources.

3. Editorials—New York (State)—Buffalo.

I. McCullough, Joseph B. II. McIntire-Strasburg,

Janice. III. Buffalo express. IV. Title.

PS1303.M325 1999

814'.4—dc21

99-20031 CIP

Cover photograph courtesy of the

Buffalo and Erie County Historical Society

Contents

Preface   ix   *Note to the Text*   xi   *Introduction*   xiii

PART I / SETTLING IN TO EDITORIAL DUTIES
August 1869–October 1869

"Salutatory"   5

Removal of the Capital   7

Lady Byron—Mrs. Stowe's Revelations   8

Inspired Humor   9

The "Monopoly" Speaks   11

A Day at Niagara   12

Uncriminal Victims   18

The Byron Scandal   19

[A Fine Old Man]   21

Only a Nigger   22

English Festivities   23

The Prodigal Son Returns   28

The Byron Scandal   29

The Byron Question   30

Journalism in Tennessee   31

More Byron Scandal   37

Butler on the Byron Scandal   38

The Last Words of Great Men   44

Personal   47

"Mr. and Mrs. Byron"   47

The Gates Ajar   51

The "Wild Man"   53

Rev. H. W. Beecher   56

The Ticket — Explanation   59

Engineer Griffin   60

The Latest Novelty   62

PART II / LIGHTING OUT FOR THE LECTURE CIRCUIT
October 1869–January 1870

Around the World: Letter No. 1   67

Mark Twain: His Greetings to the California Pioneers   71

The Legend of the Capitoline Venus   73

Around the World: Letter No. 2   78

The Paraguay Puzzle   84

A Good Letter   86

Hanging to Slow Music   88

Around the World: Letter No. 3   89

Civilized Brutality   93

Browsing Around   95

The Richardson Murder   101

Browsing Around   102

The Law of Divorce   107

Around the World: Letter No. 4   108

Around the World: Letter No. 5   112

Ye Cuban Patriot   117

An Indignant Rebuke   120

The Hyenas   121

An Awful — Terrible Medieval Romance   123

Mrs. Stowe's Vindication   129

Around the World: Letter No. 6   130

A Ghost Story   134

Around the World: Letter No. 7   140

Around the World: Letter No. 8   144

PART III / BACK TO BUFFALO
February 1870–May 1870

Nasby's Lecture   153

Anson Burlingame   153

The Blondes   157

Personal   159

More Wisdom   159

"A Big Thing"   161

A Mysterious Visit   166

Literary Guide to *Williams & Packard's System of Penmanship*   170

The Facts in the Great Land Slide Case   172

Mark Twain on Agriculture   176

The New Crime   177

The Story of the Good Little Boy Who Did Not Prosper   182

Curious Dream   186

Curious Dream, Conclusion   191

Murder and Insanity   194

PART IV / PERSONAL TROUBLES AND RUMORS OF WAR
May 1870–October 1870

Personal   199

Our Precious Lunatic   204

Street Sprinkling   207

More Distinction   208

How Higgins Gently Broke the News   210

Buffalo Female Academy   211

The Editorial Office Bore   215

How I Edited an Agricultural Paper   217

The European War!!!   222

Obituary   224

To the Reader   227

At the President's Reception   229

Curious Relic for Sale   233

Mark Twain: His Map and Fortifications of Paris   238

PART V / THE LAST DAYS OF JOURNALISM
October 1870–January 1871

On Riley—Newspaper Correspondent   243

The Libel Suit   246

A Reminiscence of the Back Settlements   248

A General Reply   250

Running for Governor   254

My Watch—An Instructive Little Tale   259

An Entertaining Article   262

Dogberry in Washington   266

War and "Wittles"   268

The Facts in the Case of George Fisher, Deceased   270

"Waiting for the Verdict"   276

A Sad, Sad Business   277

Mean People   280

The Danger of Lying in Bed   281

Notes   285   *Index*   307

Preface

Seeking to impress his fiancée, Olivia Langdon, with a stable income and a settled lifestyle, in 1869 Mark Twain decided upon a career in newspapers and bought part interest in the *Buffalo Express.* Twain spent only eighteen months in Buffalo, but this pivotal period in his life marked his transition from sometime journalist to celebrated author and storyteller. This collection presents for the first time all of Twain's signed pieces for the *Express,* as well as thirty-seven unsigned editorials that can now be identified with certainty as his. These articles and sketches rival Twain's finest humor and social criticism and allow renewed appreciation for the talents of this American literary figure on the threshold of literary fame.

We have incurred many debts in the preparation of this volume. We wish especially to thank Louis J. Budd, James B. Duke Professor Emeritus, Duke University, and Victor Doyno, Professor of English, State University of New York at Buffalo, for their encouragement and many useful suggestions, which they offered through a close reading of the manuscript. Their suggestions not only improved the manuscript considerably but also prevented several embarrassing errors from finding their way into the final edition.

Our deep gratitude to Edgar M. Branch, whose encouragement to undertake this project over twenty-five years ago cannot be underestimated. We also wish to thank Robert H. Hirst and the staff at the Mark Twain Project, University of California, Berkeley, for their invaluable assistance throughout this project. We would also like to acknowledge the support and the invaluable assistance of William H. Loos, Curator, Gosvenor Rare Book Room, Buffalo and Erie County Public Library, in supplying useful materials, and to thank the staff in the library at the University of Nevada, Las Vegas, for going well beyond the call of duty.

In addition, we are grateful to the Mark Twain Archives, Elmira College, and the Bancroft Library, University of California, Berkeley, for permission to reprint the photographs used in this volume. We also wish to thank the Research Council and the Foundation of the University of Nevada, Las Vegas, for generous assistance to Joseph

McCullough for travel to research collections and for other support, as well as Mary Alice Wolf and James and the folks at System Computing Services at the University of Nevada, Las Vegas.

Finally, Joe McCullough would like to thank his mother, whose support and encouragement never wavered, and Judy, who cheerfully endured yet one more Mark Twain story. Jan McIntire-Strasburg would like to thank her parents, who early taught the value of persistence, her husband, Jeff, and her children, Matt, Beth, and Katie, without whose patience and loving support this project might never have been completed.

Note to the Text

The articles and sketches in this volume were edited from a microfilm of the original printing of the *Buffalo Express,* since printed copies of the newspaper no longer exist. All of Twain's writings for the *Express* have been arranged chronologically as they appeared in the *Express,* with the exception of Twain's "Salutatory," which, while not being Twain's first contribution to the newspaper, more logically opens the volume. We have also grouped the pieces according to discernable biographical moments. The notes identify people and places not readily found in a desk dictionary and draw extensively from Mark Twain's letters to provide material relevant to the texts or to present evidence supporting attribution. We have used the *Galaxy* magazine as copy-text for those sketches that Twain published simultaneously in both the *Express* and the *Galaxy,* since the latter carries more authority.

Only occasionally were there difficulties separating authorial intention from typographical accident. The editing has been conservative, and original spelling and punctuation have been changed only in the case of obvious errors. Variant spellings, if once acceptable, have been retained (for example, "ancle" for "ankle"), as have hyphenations such as "to-day" and "birth-day." We have also reproduced the spelling of words that Twain renders in the texts in more than one way (for example, "grave stone," "grave-stone," and "gravestone," or "by and bye" and "bye and bye"). Misspellings that occur as a result of missing, dropped, transposed, or doubled letters have been emended. In the case of doubled words such as "give give," we have dropped the duplication. The exceptions to this principle are "that that," in its relative/demonstrative construction (one that Twain uses often), "to to," and other prepositional phrases that retain a specific meaning and sense. Missing punctuation marks at the obvious end of a sentence where space is left in the text for them or punctuation marks that have been obscured by copy quality have been supplied.

Since it would be impractical to column print the sketches as they occurred in the newspaper, the sketches have been reformatted for this volume. The original titles of each sketch have been retained but also restyled for this volume. Also, we have regularized the placement of Twain's signature for this volume. In the early sketches, Twain supplied a title for each piece, with his signature at the end. Most of the later sketches, however, bear the heading [FROM MARK TWAIN] above the title, probably to call attention to Twain's authorship for the readers. For consistency, we have moved his name to the end of these sketches. A complete list of emendations is available from the editors.

Introduction

By any measure, Mark Twain is an American icon in both literature and popular culture. In the latter half of the twentieth century,
the Mark Twain image has nearly subsumed its creator, Samuel
Langhorne Clemens. Now Mark Twain cigars and tobacco, ice cream
parlors and pizzerias, banks, and streets blanket America. Twain's familiar white shock of hair, bushy mustache, white suit, and cigar have
become endorsements for everything from cemetery plots to investment houses. Where the image of Twain himself appears unwar-
ranted, major characters from his most famous novels—Tom Sawyer,
Huck Finn, and Becky Thatcher—lend their names to hotel suites,
river boats, or painting companies. Advertisers use maxims that have
been attributed, accurately or otherwise, to Mark Twain to sell services as diverse as dry cleaning and investment instruments.[1] Because the name Mark Twain has become so familiar, it is difficult to
recall the man who wrote sketches for the *Buffalo Express* between
August 1869 and January 1871. That Mark Twain was in his middle
thirties; a rolling stone with a knack for spinning a tall tale, hoax, or
burlesque yarn; a naive traveler given to exaggerated descriptions of
Old World Europe through the eyes of a brash and oftentimes crass
American. The bestseller status of *The Innocents Abroad* was then
still six months away, but "Jim Smiley's Jumping Frog" and the *Alta
California* letters had already brought a certain degree of fame to this
young man. He was known then as a wild Washoe Zephyr—Nevada's
name for the wind that blows down from the mountains, disheveling
everything in its path—yet encased in this young man's imagination
was the fully realized image of the future "Mark Twain" who would
shape popular culture.

In many ways, the years between 1869 and 1871 were the best of
times and the worst of times for Samuel Clemens. Prior to August
1869, he had spent fully half of his life traveling both east and west as
a typesetter, journalist, river boat captain, prospector, and finally
travel writer and lecturer. After completing a tour onboard the
Quaker City, he contracted with Elisha Bliss at the American Publishing Company to complete a manuscript of *Innocents Abroad* from his

Alta California letters and such new material as he deemed necessary, and then he embarked upon a lecture circuit in San Francisco and other points West. In the fall of 1868 and early 1869 he lectured in the East and Midwest on "A Vandal Abroad" while working on his manuscript. Though he protested in a letter to his family on June 4, 1869, "I have earned just eighty dollars by my pen—two little magazine squibs & one newspaper letter—altogether the idlest, laziest, 14 months of my life," Twain was by most accounts a quite busy and industrious man, even if he was not writing any new material.

Twain claims in the same letter that part of the reason for his supposed "idleness" was his inclination to court Olivia Langdon at the expense of all else. He had met Olivia in November 1867 under the auspices of her brother, Charles, whom Twain had met aboard the *Quaker City*. Twain paid a long postponed visit to the family at Elmira in August 1868, after which he embarked upon a campaign of letters and personal reformation to deserve, earn, and win her hand in marriage. Olivia Langdon provisionally accepted his proposal by Thanksgiving of 1868, and the engagement became official on February 4, 1869. With his formal acceptance as Olivia's future husband, Twain urgently felt the need for a settled, permanent position in life that he did not believe he could earn by his pen alone. In his December 12, 1867, letter to Mary Fairbanks, his friend and companion from the *Quaker City* excursion, he commented, "I am as good an economist as anyone, but I can't turn an inkstand into Aladdin's lamp." He judged that lecturing was also unsatisfactory; his letters to Olivia at the time indicate a desire to end his traveling days and to settle into a permanent home where he could provide them both with the comfort and the security she was enjoying at the Langdon residence.

With these qualifications in mind, Twain set about negotiating for an editorial interest in several newspapers. His first choice was the *Cleveland Herald*. He hoped that Mary Fairbanks would be able to exert some influence on his behalf with her husband, Abel Fairbanks, one of the *Herald*'s owners, thereby helping Twain to secure an interest in the paper and to establish himself and his future wife in Cleveland. During the intervening months of negotiation, the purchase amount fluctuated between one-eighth and one-quarter interest in the paper. But the *Herald* owners were apparently slow to close negotiations, and Twain began looking elsewhere.

Twain approached the owners of the *Hartford Courant* about purchasing one-third interest of the newspaper. The city of Hartford

Mark Twain, in his new status as part owner of the *Buffalo Express*. (Buffalo and Erie County Historical Society)

Olivia Langdon, Twain's future bride. (The Mark Twain Project, Bancroft Library)

The Twain home in Buffalo. (The Mark Twain Project, Bancroft Library)

Jervis Langdon loaned his prospective son-in-law half the $25,000 required to purchase one-third of the *Buffalo Express*. (Mark Twain Archives, Center for Mark Twain Studies, Elmira College)

MARK TWAIN

WRITES FOR

THE GALAXY

FREQUENTLY.

IT IS THE BEST AMERICAN MAGAZINE.

No Family can Afford to do Without it.

IT GIVES MORE GOOD AND ATTRACTIVE READING MATTER
FOR THE MONEY THAN ANY OTHER PERIODICAL
OR BOOK PUBLISHED IN THIS COUNTRY.

The Leading Newspapers pronounce

THE GALAXY

The Best and Most Ably-Edited American Magazine.

THE GALAXY MEETS THE WANTS OF EVERY MEMBER OF THE FAMILY.

It contains Thoughtful Articles by our Ablest Writers.
It contains Sketches of Life and Adventure.
It has Serial Stories by our best Novelists.
It has Short Stories in Each Number.
It has Humorous Articles by Mark Twain in Each Number, which are a constant source of delight to the public.
In Each Number is a Complete Review of the World of Literature.

NOW IS THE TIME TO SUBSCRIBE FOR 1871.

TERMS OF THE GALAXY.—$4 per year; Single Copies, 35 cents each.
CLUBBING TERMS.—The Galaxy and Harper's Weekly or Bazar, or Appleton's Journal, sent to one address for a year for $6. The regular price is $8. The Galaxy and Every Saturday for $7; regular price, $9. With Our Young Folks, or American Agriculturist, $4.50; regular price, $5.50. With Littell's Living Age, $10; regular price, $12.

SHELDON & CO., *New York.*

Advertisement highlighting Twain's contributions to *The Galaxy*, where many of Twain's articles for the *Buffalo Express* also appeared.

Twain continued to lecture throughout the country while at the *Buffalo Express*. This 1873 depiction captures his perplexed and bemused speaking persona.

would have been an ideal place for Twain to settle. First, Twain's future father-in-law, Jervis Langdon, had personal and financial ties there through the Beechers. Second, Hartford, a progressive town, was the home of Twain's publisher at the time, Elisha Bliss. However, even with the added influence of Joseph Twitchell on Twain's behalf, the owners, Joseph Hawley and Charles Dudley Warner, gave Twain's offer a cool reception. At that time, Twain was still reading proof on *Innocents Abroad* and the *Courant*'s co-owners "saw themselves negotiating with the latter-day Wild Humorist of the Pacific Slope, not the figure of wide renown and acclaim Mark Twain soon became."[2] Hawley and Warner would later regret their early rejection of Twain; after the reception of *Innocents Abroad* six months later, the Hartford editors tried to reopen negotiations with Twain, but by then he and Olivia had already settled upon Buffalo as their home. While awaiting the final outcome of these two transactions, Twain met Petroleum V. Nasby (David Ross Locke), who suggested that Twain join him at the *Toledo Blade,* but apparently the author never entertained any serious notions of settling there. When negotiations seemed stalemated at both the *Herald* and the *Courant,* Twain made a half-hearted attempt to buy into the *Springfield Republican* in Massachusetts, but his attempt was rejected out of hand by the editor, Samuel Bowles.

In the end, it was Jervis Langdon who finally decided the issue, finding Twain an editorship at the *Buffalo Express* and advancing him $12,500, one-half of the buy-in price of $25,000. The *Express* was a Republican-oriented daily newspaper established in 1846 by Alman M. Clapp. The loan from Jervis Langdon enabled Twain to purchase one-third interest in the paper from Thomas A. Kennett. In early August 1869 the bottom had fallen out of negotiations with the *Herald;* within two weeks similar negotiations with the *Buffalo Express* were complete. His partners were George H. Selkirk, who handled most business matters, and Josephus Nelson Larned, the paper's political editor.

The *Buffalo Express* occupied a four-story brick building at 14 East Swan Street, located just a few steps from a boardinghouse in which Twain lodged. Although his editorial duties were only vaguely defined, Twain actively assumed his post as managing editor on August 15, 1869. Evidently, he immediately threw himself into his new responsibilities. John Harrison Mills, an artist on the editorial staff of the paper in 1869, later wrote: "I cannot remember that there was any delay in getting down to his work. I think within five minutes the new editor had assumed the easy look of one entirely at home, pencil in hand and a

clutch of paper before him, with an air of preoccupation, as of one intent on a task delayed."[3] Earl D. Berry, an *Express* reporter and subsequent city editor, remembered Twain's arrival differently:

> "Is this the editorial room of The Buffalo Express?"
>
> "It is," responded a chorus of voices.
>
> "Are you sure that this is the editorial room of The Buffalo Express?"
>
> "Certainly, what can we do for you?"—and one or two chair occupants
> made inviting gestures for the stranger to enter the room.
>
> There was a brief pause and then Samuel L. Clemens stepped across
> the threshold, and with cold and biting emphasis drawled: "Well, if this
> is the editorial room of The Buffalo Express I think that I ought to have
> a seat, for I am the editor."
>
> Of course, the enlightened politicians were effusive in their greetings
> and each one tried to express his appreciation of "Mark Twain's little
> joke," but the new editor frowned them down and· made no bones of let-
> ting them know that the nature of his work made it desirable that he be
> alone. Mark Twain and the politicians never affiliated.[4]

Although Clemens's first sketch signed as Mark Twain did not appear in the paper until August 21, 1869, he apparently began "re-
training" reporters, making changes in the paper's appearance, and
writing or collaborating on unsigned material, in particular contributing several items to a "People and Things" column. He also likely
wrote four unsigned editorials prior to August 21: "Removal of the
Capital" (August 17, 1869), "Lady Byron—Mrs. Stowe's Revelations"
(August 18, 1869), "Inspired Humor" (August 19, 1869), and "The 'Monopoly' Speaks" (August 20, 1869). Twain seems to have written "The
'Monopoly' Speaks" in order to please Jervis Langdon, his benefactor
and future father-in-law and the owner of one of four coal companies
that supplied virtually all of Buffalo's coal and had united to form the
Anthracite Coal Association. In a letter to Olivia Langdon (August 19,
1869), Twain describes his first days at the *Express:*

> My child, I believe you'll have to be obeyed at last—I don't see any easy
> way around it without having your fingers in my hair. And so at this mo-
> ment I slash from this morning's paper everything of mine that is in it. Of
> course it don't take ten or twelve hours to write those twenty or thirty
> pages of MS., dearie, but it takes a deal of time to skim through a large
> pile of exchanges, because one gets interested every now and then & stops

to read a while if the article looks as if it might be a good thing to copy. And then one is interrupted a good deal by visitors—& there is proof-reading to do, & a great many little things that use up time—but it is an easy, pleasant, *delightful* situation, & I never liked anything better. I am grateful to Mr. Langdon for thinking of Buffalo with his cool head when we couldn't think of any place but Cleveland with our hot ones. [Before I forget it, tell him I got his dispatch yesterday, but of course I never could have needed it, for I think Slee would not dare to write and print articles over his name, and I am particularly sure *I* wouldn't.] So you see, with all my work I do very little that is visible to the naked eye, & certainly not enough, visible or invisible, to hurt me. I am simply working late at night in these first days until I get the reporters accustomed & habituated to doing things my way,—after that, a very little watching will keep them up to the mark. I simply want to educate them to modify the adjectives, curtail their philosophical reflections & leave out the slang. I have been consulting with the foreman of the news room for two days, & getting *him* drilled as to how I want the type-setting done—& this morning he has got my plan into full operation, & the paper is vastly improved in appearance. I have annihilated all the glaring thunder-&-lightning headings over the telegraphic news & made that department look quiet and respectable.

In the *Express*'s official announcement about Twain's arrival as editor, the paper stated: "As we speak now in advance of his occupation of the chair in which he will seat himself with us a few days hence, we can properly indulge these congratulations and confess the pride that we feel in identifying the celebrity of the name and popularity of the writings of 'Mark Twain' with the *Express*." On August 21, 1869, Twain's "Salutatory" and his first signed sketch, "A Day at Niagara," appeared in the paper. Almost every Saturday one of his signed articles made its appearance. Determining conclusively that unsigned pieces were written wholly or partially by Twain is sometimes difficult, given his association with Josephus Larned, the paper's political editor. In a letter to Olivia Langdon on August 21, 1869, only days after assuming his editorial duties, Twain described his daily routine:

Larned & I sit upon opposite sides of the same table & it is exceedingly convenient—for if you will remember, you sometimes write till you reach the middle of a subject & then run hard aground—you know what you *want* to say, but for the life of you you can't say—your ideas & your words get thick & sluggish & you are vanquished. So occasionally, after

biting our nails & scratching our heads awhile, we just reach over &
swap manuscript—& then we scribble away without the least trouble,
he finishing my article & I his. Some of our patch-work editorials of this
kind are all the better for the new life they get by crossing the breed.

Mark Twain had transformed himself from a vagabond travel
writer and lecturer to a "settled" man with a solid financial interest,
though even his new readers caught a glimpse of the old Twain in his
opening remarks to his "Salutatory": "I shall always confine myself to
the truth, except when it is attended with inconvenience." Though he
now had a full-time job, the only articles that Clemens regularly
signed as Mark Twain appeared on Saturdays. By 25 September he
had published six such pieces on Saturday, receiving $25 for each
sketch. Of the first six Saturday articles, all but the fourth and sixth
were published with crudely drawn illustrations prepared by John
Harrison Mills. All subsequent sketches were not illustrated.[5]

It is impossible to know ultimately how much Samuel Clemens
contributed to the *Express* during his association with the paper. Several years ago Irving S. Underhill, bibliographer and personal friend
of Mark Twain, together with Willard S. Morse and George Hiram
Brownell, began to compile a list of Twain's contributions to the *Express*. Their investigation was never completed, and while other bibli-
ographers have emended or added to their unpublished findings,
Twain's complete *Express* contributions still remain one of the most
unsettled areas of Twain scholarship.[6]

During his year and a half as part owner and editor, Clemens contributed over sixty humorous articles and sketches signed as Mark
Twain. Many of these he eventually reprinted, often in revised form,
notably in *Sketches, New and Old* (1875) and in *Roughing It* (1872).
About one-fourth of them were never reprinted. He continued to write
editorials, sometimes in collaboration with Josephus Larned, as well
as to supply items to the "People and Things" column. Details pointing
to Twain's authorship are the literary style of the thirty-seven unsigned editorials included in this edition; the choice of current topics;
external evidence, such as Twain's acknowledgment of authorship of
specific unsigned editorials in personal letters; and a correction of one
word in Twain's hand in one of the pieces ("Inspired Humor"). Annotations for individual unsigned editorials often include evidence sub-
stantiating attribution.

Ample evidence exists that Twain also contributed additional items

to the "People and Things" column, though most of these contributions
are brief and negligible and therefore do not appear in this collection.
Except for "A Fine Old Man" (August 25, 1869), the issue of authorship is unclear. Trying to determine which items were supplied by
Twain and which were supplied by Larned remains largely speculative. Because Twain later included "A Fine Old Man" under his own
name in *Sketches, New and Old,* however, it seems appropriate for it
to be included here.

A more difficult problem of authorship arises with respect to the
many sketches signed as Hy Slocum and the seven sketches and one
poem signed as Carl Byng—all of which have been attributed by some
scholars to Mark Twain, despite Twain's repeated denial of authorship
of these writings.[7] Even though many Slocum pieces appeared in the
Express during Twain's connection with the paper, external considerations, such as the appearance of the first four Slocum items in the *Express* long before Twain's arrival in Buffalo, together with internal evidence indicating significant differences from items signed by Twain,
definitively argue against Twain authorship. While there is some justification for disregarding Twain's repudiation of the Byng pieces, arguments for attribution of the Byng material to Twain remain too speculative to justify inclusion in this edition. In all likelihood, the pieces
signed as Hy Slocum and Carl Byng were probably written by a still
unidentified humorist or humorists influenced by Twain.

Characteristically, Twain began his settled, permanent life in Buffalo by striking out on a lecture tour scheduled through James Red-
path's Lyceum. Within two weeks of writing his first sketch for the
Express, Twain had already agreed to a speaking tour that began on
November 1, 1869. The tour started in Pittsburgh, took him through
Pennsylvania, Rhode Island, Connecticut, Massachusetts, and New
York, and ended on January 20, 1870, near Elmira. Twain then had
one week to rest up and prepare for his wedding to Olivia on 2 February. For this season, Twain chose to entitle his lecture "Our Fellow
Savages in the Sandwich Islands," a departure from the previous
year's lecture, which was entitled "A Vandal Abroad."

The lectures were well received, for the most part, as evidenced by a
review in the *Boston Evening Transcript* on November 11, 1869, which
was later reprinted in the *Express,* but Twain's letters to Olivia and
others during that time indicate that he was travel weary and looking
forward to returning to Elmira and eventually to Buffalo. The lecture
tour and the sales of *Innocents Abroad* were sufficiently lucrative,

however, that Twain was able to retire $15,000 of debt and still retain about $3,000 on hand. While on tour, Twain managed to make frequent contributions to the *Express* by mail, including several "Around the World" sketches, two of which he entitled "Browsing Around" and "An Awful—Terrible Medieval Romance." The latter of these articles was later reprinted as *A Burlesque Autobiography* (1871). Occasionally, as in the case of "A Good Letter" (November 10, 1869), Twain recycled earlier material. "A Good Letter," which derives from his Western days, is merely a partial reprinting of a sketch published in 1866 (see notes to the sketch for a discussion of the sketch's publishing history).

After his marriage to Olivia took place on February 2, 1870, the two settled into a splendid home—a gift to the newlyweds from Twain's father-in-law—at 472 Delaware Street. Their happiness was short-lived, however, because in the summer of 1870 Jervis Langdon was diagnosed with cancer of the stomach. The Clemenses spent May in Elmira nursing Livy's father and canceled a trip to Europe that they had planned for their family that summer. Twain began to publish less and less in the *Express* as the constraints of a sickbed gnawed at his time and energy. The pieces that appeared during that time were inevitably those published in the *Galaxy* "Memoranda." Langdon appeared to be recovering in July, and so Twain made a trip to Washington, during which time he met with President Grant and signed a contract with Elisha Bliss for the book that would later become *Roughing It*. Langdon's recovery was brief, however. After suffering several setbacks, Olivia's father and Twain's friend and benefactor, Jervis Langdon, died on August 6, 1870.

Her father's illness and eventual death had exacerbated Olivia's own frail health; she was pregnant with their first child, and Twain spent the months following Jervis Langdon's death nursing her and awaiting the birth of their son, Langdon, who was born prematurely on November 7, 1870. Although these family matters consumed much of his time, Twain had further committed himself to finishing the "big book" (*Roughing It*) by January, his monthly column for the *Galaxy*, his *Buffalo Express* obligations, a collection of sketches (finally published in 1875 as *Sketches, New and Old*), and a book (which was ultimately never written) on the South African diamond mines based on data collected by John Henry Riley, a friend from his California days. For this latter project, Riley was to travel to South Africa, where a diamond frenzy similar to the Gold Rush days in Nevada was in progress, and send letters to Twain while he acquired a fortune in diamonds. Twain would write the book, and Riley would keep the diamonds. Unfortunately, by the time Riley was ready to supply Twain with material, Twain was fully engaged in the illnesses and deaths that marked his last days with the *Express*. Twain put Riley off with excuses, and Riley contracted peritonitis from his trip and died before Twain could devote any time to the project. Moreover, to add to the Clemens family's woes, one of Olivia's friends, Emma Nye, who had come to stay with them after Livy's father's death, contracted typhoid fever and died at the family residence. Progress on *Roughing It* had come to a standstill, and Twain barely kept up his commitments to the *Galaxy* and the *Express*. Livy remained bedridden through the winter, and in March 1871 the family retired to Elmira, where young Langdon died at the age of eighteen months. In later years, Twain described this time as "the blackest, the gloomiest, the most wretched"[8] of his life. During this time the Delaware Avenue house in Buffalo went on the market. It was advertised for sale on the front page of the *Express* for six months and finally sold in December for $19,000, a thousand dollars less than Jervis Langdon had paid for it the previous year. Twain also lost money on his interest in the *Express* when he sold it in August 1871 to Colonel George F. Selkirk for $10,000 less than he had paid for it.

After Buffalo, Twain closed the book on his journalistic career. He moved his family to Hartford, Connecticut, and began a full-time "literary" career made possible by the popularity of *Innocents Abroad,* which had already elevated him to the status of a folk hero. Mark Twain's post-*Express* writing demonstrates unparalleled literary success as a novelist, as evidenced by such works as *The Adventures of Tom Sawyer*, *Adventures of Huckleberry Finn*, and *A Connecticut Yankee in King Arthur's Court*, and his continued success in the genre of travel books (*Roughing It* and *Following the Equator*). These later years also established Twain as a lecturer, political pundit, and cultural icon. One of his major contributions to American literature, one that he clearly debuts and develops in these early sketches, is his experimentation and refinement of American humor. These short works appropriate the existing conventions of late nineteenth-century humor and modify those conventions to his own personal literary specifications and purposes.

. . .

In his landmark study, *Native American Humor,* Walter Blair argues that Twain represents the "climax to a consideration of American humor."[9] While any definitive classification of the genre of humor eludes scholars, it is most often characterized by its subject matter and technique. American humor in its earliest forms did not differ greatly from its British counterpart. In the eighteenth century, American humorists broke with British writers when they began to develop a general perception of the elements that differentiated America from Britain in custom, situation, and character. Later, American humorists created or modified existing techniques that allowed for extensive treatment of the material. Tracing this inclination in American humor, scholars note a rise in realistic portrayal, although that "realism" was most often applied to characterizations, whereas the subject matter might involve extensive use of hyperbole. The situations might be exaggerated, but the vernacular and descriptions are realistic.

Another device that contributed to the rise of humorous writing was the detachment of the narrator and the reader from the tale. While this was hardly a new or innovative technique at the time, it fit well with the topics humorists wished to portray. It allowed readers to laugh at the characters yet retain their own superiority. This detachment was most often achieved by constructing a framed narration in which the speaker appears as a "Self-Controlled Gentleman" relating a humorous account of a situation he has seen, heard of, or experienced in his travels. The story is often anecdotal, based on the assumption that such things cannot or do not occur anymore, or affords a quaint glimpse of life in America's backwater frontier towns, and it takes the form of the burlesque, the tall tale, and the hoax. The sense of detachment is enhanced by use of genuine vernacular from either the Southwest or Southeast; in any of the above forms the story depicts vernacular characters somehow gaining the upper hand over more educated, sophisticated characters.

Twain borrows heavily from this model in his sketches and tales, although he quickly modifies the original format to suit his narrational purposes. The earliest piece in which Twain plies this tradition is "The Dandy Frightening the Squatter," written in the 1850s. Twain's use of the tradition culminates in "Jim Smiley's Jumping Frog," written in 1864. Even as early as "Jim Smiley's Jumping Frog," the story that first brought him national attention, Twain was altering the structure and the style to fit his own peculiar vision of humor and the frame tale. Readers expect Simon Wheeler to get his comeuppance, and he is, indeed, gulled by the stranger; but the self-controlled and well-educated narrator has been conned into listening to a long, rambling, disconnected tale concerning a man about whom he has not even inquired. Moreover, he speculates that the friend who recommended Wheeler in the first place was an accessory in the deceit. In addition, the reader has been deceived along with the narrator. As an author of humor, Twain often manipulates the form, use of vernacular, and narration of the traditional humorous story to shift the distance between the characters, the narrator, and the reader, thereby creating a "new" version of an older model. He provokes laughter in the burlesque, the tall tale, and the hoax, but he also presents more sophisticated satire as a framework for social commentary. The progression from his earliest sketches to the later ones clearly indicates a shift from broader, slapstick humor to a more refined, language-based treatment.

The majority of the signed sketches Twain wrote for the *Express* were burlesques, often frame tales further complicated by added elements of the tall tale and/or the hoax. The humor is broad, reliant on elements of slapstick, and the laughter is most often at the expense of the Mark Twain persona. Twain's style would have been familiar to, and even expected by, his reading public, primed as they were by "Jim Smiley's Jumping Frog" and the *Quaker City* letters. The earliest of the sketches, "A Day at Niagara" and "English Festivities," make use of a hard-drinking, card-playing "bad boy" image of Mark Twain but are complicated by his criticism of the commercialization of Niagara Falls and the nearly constant celebration of birthdays by the then quite large Royal Family. Laughter at the expense of the bumbling, ignorant narrator also appears in later sketches. In "A Mysterious Visit," the narrator's foolish attempt to expose a stranger's occupation by revealing the lucrative nature of his own job backfires when the stranger turns out to be an agent of the Internal Revenue Department. He uses the naive persona again in "At the President's Reception." This time he dons the persona of a backwoods Western bumpkin who holds up the presidential reception line to discuss Nevadan James Nye's political savvy and to school the gentleman behind him in proper reception etiquette. These sketches constitute what readers of the time might have considered typical Twain.

Several of the burlesques, however, depart from the tradition of making the ignorant narrator the butt of the joke. In "Browsing Around: Back from Yurrup," the narrator, also Twain, acquires a note of sophistication missing from the previously mentioned sketches. Here, the narrator adopts the persona of the seasoned traveler and lecturer who is annoyed by a family of American travelers returning from Europe. They scoff at everything American while at the same time they reveal their ignorance about European custom, art, and culture. The same is true of "The Facts in the Great Land Slide Case." This sketch relies for its humor on a sophisticated Eastern lawyer who is ultimately gulled by his less well-educated Western neighbors. The burlesques represented in the *Express* material evolve from Twain's slapstick humor into a progressively more sophisticated humor, depending less on the foolish excesses of the narrator and more on diction, understatement, and contrast.

Twain made use of the same burlesque/tall-tale technique in order to criticize the sensational journalism of his day. Twain himself participated to some extent in these journalistic practices while writing for the *Virginia City Territorial Enterprise* and the California papers the *Alta,* the *Union,* and the *San Francisco Morning Call.* Most notable among his own literary "hoaxes" are the sketches "The Petrified Man" and "My Bloody Massacre," the latter of which he later discussed and reprinted in the *Galaxy* and in the 1875 sketch book. These sketches served as Twain's proof that "to write a burlesque so wild that its pretended facts will not be accepted in perfect good faith by somebody, is very nearly an impossible thing to do."[10] Aside from the inherent humor in these sketches, Jeffrey Steinbrink suggests that Twain wished to instruct his readers in proper reading methods. By creating more sophisticated readers, Twain might have hoped to pave the way for the sometimes subtle humor of his own work.[11] While this may well have been the end result, it is likely that Twain's "statement" in these sketches was intended as moralistic. His impatience seems reserved for strictly sensational journalism—sensationalism as a method of boosting circulation—presupposing as it does the general public's hunger for scandal and private information about public figures; his contempt seems directed toward the ignorance of editors in general. Sensationalism ought to be the province of the writer of humor—it ought not to become the standard for everyday journalistic writing.

"Journalism in Tennessee" criticizes the rhetorical style, in the form of inflammatory language, employed by Southwestern journalists; it makes use of the Twain persona and physical humor. The editor of the *Morning Glory and Johnson County War Whoop* is described as a man twenty years out of date in his dress who pulls at his hair in search of proper wording for his articles. "Milquetoast" journalism gives him "the fan-tods." Twain's fictional editor's office is a shambles of exploded stove and broken furniture and windows; in addition, the post of associate editor leaves Twain mortally wounded in the wake of one day's work. He is alternately shot, hand-grenaded, brickbatted, horsewhipped, and scalped in the course of the afternoon.

Eastern papers fare no better in Twain's estimation. These become the butt of his satire in "The 'Wild Man.'" The Wild Man agrees to speak to Twain (the reporter) only because he is a member of the press. In the course of the "interview," he claims to be coeval with the Creation and credits himself with a major role in the most sensational events in history, from the Flood to local robberies, for the purpose of creating stories and raising the circulation of newspapers as various as the *Cleveland Herald* and the *New York Tribune*. When readers reach the end of the sketch, the being's name, SENSATION, comes as no surprise. "Rev. H. W. Beecher," roasts Henry Ward Beecher but additionally comments on the newspaper-reading public's desire to know all the private foibles and eccentricities of public men. Twain intentionally overstates Beecher's habits, using sensational language to create sensation where none actually exists.

Two later sketches, "To the Reader," which contains his Map of Paris, and "The European War," clearly demonstrate that journalists, in their desire to get the story out and "scoop" rival papers, often present news that has yet to happen and in the process whip the reading public into a frenzy and create a tempest in a teapot. American newspapers were crammed with maps depicting places of which general readers had only the vaguest notion. The maps' intentions to clarify European positions merely confused most readers, as does Twain's "burlesque" map. Its date of publication (September 17, 1870) predates Bismarck's siege by two days. The "European War" sketch consists of sets of glaring headlines containing numerous exclamation points and large, bold fonts but little hard news. The "news" consists of "no battle yet." The Franco-Prussian War turned out to be considerably more significant than Twain's sketches imply, but the satire on journalism contained in the sketches is legitimate nonetheless.[12]

Likewise, the satire of "Ye Cuban Patriot" reviles both sides of the then current Cuban conflict. Editors and journalists tended to slant their coverage of the conflict in favor of the rebels, a traditional American stance against colonizers at the time. Twain believed that the rebels committed atrocities every bit as vile as the Spaniards did and that the only persons who suffered were those who traditionally did so, the common men and slaves. The conditions in the American South were similar, but more one-sided. The sketch, however, reserves some of its bite for journalists who rush to publicize each heinous act with purple prose in praise of its perpetrators.

Twain comments on the relative intelligence of editors about their subject matter in "How I Edited an Agricultural Paper." Twain himself, as narrator, becomes the substitute editor of an agricultural paper, a subject about which he knows nothing. This becomes clear when he describes turnips being shaken out of trees and the guano as a fine bird. The erstwhile substitute becomes irate when he is criticized by the returning editor, and he states, "I tell you, I have been in the editorial business going on fourteen years, and it's the first time I ever heard of a man's having to know anything in order to edit a newspaper." The comment on editorial intelligence here seems clear: in the newspaper business, circulation numbers figure more prominently than does accuracy. In the sketch's final paragraphs, Twain takes on the particular ignorance of editors in the role of drama and literary critics. He states, "The less a man knows, the bigger noise he makes and the higher the salary he commands."

Related sketches with journalism as their general theme demonstrate Twain's growing frustration with his editorial duties. "The Editorial Office Bore" depicts a hard-working editor whose attendance to the duties of his occupation is constantly thwarted by hangers-on in the office, people who take up space, talk politics, smoke cigars, and loiter about. These "bores" shoulder some of the blame for the lack of journalistic excellence found in newspapers of the day. The sketch airs one of the complaints Twain makes to Mary Fairbanks in his March 22 and 24, 1870, letters that weekly journalism stifles creativity: "People who write every week *write themselves out,* and tire the public, too, before long."

Two other sketches of March 1870 that were not published and therefore are not included here address a similar disillusionment with journalism. The first, "A Wail," is similar in nature to "Journalism in Tennessee," except in time frame. The narrator has clearly shouldered his editorial duties for much longer than the single day of the earlier sketch. Where the persona in "Journalism in Tennessee" "assumes the perspective of the tenderfoot or innocent who wanders into the world of adult and altogether savage responsibility," the narrator in "A Wail," a more seasoned, veteran editor, must accept the consequences "not only of his own actions but also those of his associates, and . . . suffer accordingly."[13] In conjunction, the two sketches, one published in the *Express* and the other unpublished, mirror the tenderfoot-veteran structure Twain would later make use of in

Roughing It. The novice editor of "Journalism in Tennessee" is similar in style to and serves a similar function as the naive younger narrator who relates the early chapters of *Roughing It,* while the seasoned, disillusioned veteran editor of "A Wail" can be seen as a representation of the veteran old timer who appropriates the narration in the later chapters. "A Wail" complains about the drivel of sentimentality published in the newspaper and attributed to the narrator as well as about the ignorance of the reading public displayed by their preference for such writing.

The second unpublished sketch is entitled "A Protest." It appears to be written around the same time, and it may perhaps be a revision of "A Wail." Its opening is more pointed and makes less effort to mask Twain behind the persona: "I wish to protest, mildly but firmly against being called upon to bear all & single, the promiscuous, manifold & miscellaneous sins of the BUFFALO EXPRESS."[14] Clearly, Twain's interest in journalism was waning at this point in his editorial career; this fact probably played a major role in his decision to accept the *Galaxy* "Memoranda" column proposed by its editor, Francis P. Church. In the same letter to Mary Fairbanks quoted above, Twain envisions the column as a place for his more "fine-spun" work. Steinbrink notes that the *Galaxy* material shows little change from the *Express* sketches and that, indeed, much of what Twain wrote thereafter did double duty in both publications; however, these later sketches do tend to demonstrate a slightly more sophisticated use of humor, persona, diction, and dialect. Circumstances in Twain's personal life at this time—the illness and death of Jervis Langdon and Emma Nye, combined with Livy's pregnancy and illness—probably did not allow him the luxury of writing for two audiences, as he had intended.

Twain's sketches that in one way or another deal with hoaxes present a similar thematic thread. His stance in these sketches vacillates between criticism of journalists for perpetuating hoaxes upon an unwitting public and contempt for the public gullibility that makes the tricks possible. In his work for the *Territorial Enterprise* Twain himself had published two notorious hoaxes, "Petrified Man" and "Bloody Massacre," sketches that were picked up by other papers as fact and that consequently created a flurry of journalistic animosity at the time. He defended himself then, and later in his "Memoranda" column for the *Galaxy,* by stating that a careful reading of the "facts" would have proved the stories to be hoaxes. His earliest *Express* hoax sketch, "The Legend of the Capitoline Venus," appeared on October

23, 1869. In the sketch, a starving sculptor in Italy, despairing of earning a sufficient amount of money to woo his sweetheart, trusts his fortunes to "John Smitthe," an unscrupulous friend. Smitthe takes the young man's beautiful but unsalable sculpture of a young woman, titled "America," smashes it with a hammer, buries it in the Campagna for five months, then unearths and sells it as a rare antiquity to the Italian government for four million francs. The young man's fortune is thus made, with no one but the sculptor and his friend the wiser. In the final paragraph, Twain issues a warning to the reading public that if they "read about gigantic Petrified Men being dug up near Syracuse in the State of New York, keep your own counsel,—and if the Barnum that buried them there offers to sell to you at an enormous sum, don't you buy. Send him to the Pope!" Twain was clearly referring to the Cardiff Giant, a hoax then making the rounds of upstate New York. His caveat to the public exhorts them not to believe everything they see or read and implies that if they are taken in by such a con, then they get only what they deserve.

"A Ghost Story" can be read as a companion piece to "Capitoline Venus," from the perspective of the hoax itself. The tale begins as a ghost story complete with haunted old house, rattling chains, and spectral apparitions. Twain, as narrator, is at first frightened by the apparition, but he relaxes considerably when he discerns that the "ghost" is the Cardiff Giant mentioned in his conclusion to the "Capitoline Venus" sketch. The sketch retains Twain's penchant for slapstick, as the ghostly giant breaks everything it attempts to sit on and makes off with the narrator's blanket. Its denouement, however, suggests that the potential power of a hoax is so strong that it can, in fact, fool even the personalities involved in it. Twain's ghost has been haunting a plaster cast of itself, and it retreats ignominiously after having been itself "taken in" by the hoax's perpetrators.

Twain profits from the humoristic and literary mileage he achieves in the "Capitoline Venus" sketch—the hoax winds up costing the Pope plenty, but none of the principles involved seem overly concerned about this fact. In contrast, Twain's hoaxes in the *Enterprise* greatly embarrassed the newspapers and the reading public who were taken in by them, though in the end nothing but pride was lost. In later sketches, however, Twain reserves his most biting criticism for those hoaxes designed to bilk either the public or the government and that cause them to invest money in unprofitable schemes. "'A Big Thing,'" published on March 12, 1870, attempts to debunk an article announcing the "richest silver mine in the world in Kentucky." The original article appears to be no more than an advertisement designed to induce the public to buy interests in the mine on shares. Twain proceeds to take the article apart word by word and line by line, thus deconstructing the hoax. The sketch becomes a rant that recounts Twain's own experience in Nevada, where thousands of "feet" of worthless mines were sold to both seasoned and inexperienced prospectors alike. He concludes with another sarcastic comment aimed at the journalist responsible for publicizing the hoax: "Finally—and without meaning any impertinence or any offence—I wish to ask the Louisville reporter the old familiar question, so common among reporters in the mines: 'How many 'feet' did the doctor give you?' . . . We always got 'feet' in Nevada, for whooping about a Nearly-Pure-Silver-National-Debt-Liquidator in this gushing way."

"The Facts in the Case of George Fisher, Deceased" centrally involves not a hoax but a "swindle." This major sketch, which Twain later called "a wild extravaganza," reports attempts to defraud the government out of reimbursement money for the loss of George Fisher's farm during an Indian battle. Twain begins the sketch by stating that the facts contained in it are "history"—that is, objective facts not open to conjecture—then he traces the development of the Fisher case, in which the government pays out the fantastic sum of $133,323.18 in damages when none are actually owed. Twain targets the responsible parties for this hoax, the greedy descendants of Fisher and the very ignorant members of Congress who are deceived into making the allocations in the first place or who unscrupulously collect fees for their services to push the appropriation through Congress.

Twain's criticism of the swindle might at first glance seem hypocritical when one considers his earlier Western journalistic practices. In analyzing the progression of his treatment of this topic, however, it seems clear that he considers his own hoaxes, in and of themselves, to be the harmless province of humor, with "harmless" being the key word. He considers the hoax purely for the purpose of entertaining the public, as long as it costs those reading it nothing more than private embarrassment at their own gullibility. However, when swindles are used for the financial gain of its perpetrators, resulting in financial losses to private individuals or the federal government, they overstep the bounds of entertainment and become public menaces. This reading seems particularly apt when one considers the hoaxes that appear in the *Express*. Twain's Map of Paris and its subsequent "endorsements" by Sherman, Grant, and other famous people is clearly a hoax, but its very design declares itself so. It invites readers to laugh along with Twain, instead of him laughing at their expense.

The only *Express* hoax that actually gulls his readers appears in the sketch "An Entertaining Article," which purports to reprint a review of *Innocents Abroad* from the London *Saturday Review* of October 8, 1870. It was also printed in the December 1870 issue of the *Galaxy* and was apparently so successful a hoax that none of the commentators on it bothered to consult the original article. He followed up "An Entertaining Article" with "A Sad, Sad Business," a sketch in which he reveals the hoax, in the *Express* on December 24, 1870, and in January's *Galaxy*.[15] In these two sketches in particular, and in his exposés of the hoaxes in the earlier sketches, Twain privileges his readers with his interpretation of the terms under which the hoax is an acceptable form of satire. His treatment of the bogus review of his own book permits his general readers, and writers dependent upon the opinion of literary critics for their livelihood, to laugh at the expense of an obtuse critic who completely misinterprets the humor of *Innocents Abroad*. "An Entertaining Article" and "A Sad, Sad Business" reprimand literary critics who, through their misreading of the text, misinform the public and do the humorist injustice in their reviews.

Although Twain ran the risk of offending his Eastern critics, no one sustains any lasting damage at the expense of his humor. At the same time, however, the two sketches, read in tandem, demonstrate the dangers of trusting too fully in the printed word without substantiation or research. Too often, the reading public becomes complacent, acquiescing to journalists' stories without holding them accountable for intentional or unintentional falsifications in print. Twain takes up this same issue in three of his unsigned editorials, "The Libel Suit," "The Hyenas," and "An Indignant Rebuke." "The Libel Suit" refers to a suit filed against the *Buffalo Commercial Advertiser* by D. S. Bennett, a Buffalo businessman and then recently elected congressman accused of fraudulent loan practices. The other two take the *Albany Argus* to task for maligning Edwin M. Stanton after his death on December 24, 1869. For those readers who place too much faith in the printed word, these pieces are intended as a warning.

The "Around the World" sketches that appear in the *Express* from October 16, 1869, to March 5, 1870, represent Twain's only sustained series published during his stint as editor. The idea for the series stemmed from an around-the-world trip planned by Twain's brother-in-law, Charles Langdon, and Professor Darius R. Ford, a professor of physics at Elmira College and sometime tutor for Olivia Langdon Clemens. Twain proposed that Professor Ford send back from the trip informative, chatty letters similar to those Twain wrote for the *Alta* on the *Quaker City* pilgrimage and subsequently published as *Innocents Abroad*. Twain would then edit and polish them, and publish them as a regular column in the *Express* and other papers as well. His original plan was to accumulate at least fifty letters, publishing no more than ten in any one newspaper.

The two were to travel across the country by rail and then take a ship to Japan, where the official journey was to begin. Since the overland and ocean journeys were long and time-consuming, Twain began the series himself, culling his Western memories in order to create "letters" until he could receive Ford's letters. Ironically—and quite inconveniently for Twain, as it turned out—Professor Ford was a less than prolific writer of travel letters. He supplied only two in six months, and Twain became impatient with the series. He canceled it after the first eight letters, although he did publish the two Ford wrote, signing them D.R.F. and eliminating the "[FROM MARK TWAIN]" standard that customarily appeared above his own "Around the World" letters. For this edition, we are not including two letters, numbers nine and ten, since they were written exclusively by Ford. In a letter to Jervis Langdon dated March 27, 1870, Twain stated:

> I have given up Prof. Ford, & shall discontinue the "Round the World" letters—have done it. The Prof. has now been 6 months writing 2 little letters, & I ten—making 12 in all. If they continue their trip 18 months, as they propose, the Prof. will succeed in grinding out a grand total of 6 letters, if he keeps at his present vigor. So I shall quietly drop the "Round the World" business.

In one sense this collaborative series was a failure, but the "Around the World" series did, however, serve as the testing ground for a number of sketches and other material gleaned from Twain's Western years. Letter number two consists of a burlesque of inflation rates in war-ravaged Haiti. Twain, the narrator, and his companion flee the country as a result of their ignorance of inflation and exchange rates, leaving their baggage and purchases behind. The remainder of the

letters all consist of Western material that the author later mined
and refined for use in composing *Roughing It.* Letter one sets up the
outline of Twain's expectation for the series:

> Mr. Ford's letters will be written in all good faith and honesty, and I
> shall not mar them. I shall merely have a good deal to say. I trust that
> the discriminating reader will always be able to discover where Ford
> leaves off and I begin though I don't really intend that he shall be able
> to do that. As Mr. F. jogs along, I mean to write paragraph for paragraph
> with him, and I shall set down all that I know about the countries he
> visits, together with a good deal that neither I nor anybody else knows
> about them.

Close readers of the letters will find it obvious that the final two letters in the series were written by Ford and that Twain probably in-
serted them into the series without any revision. The style of description common in Twain's letters is noticeably absent, as is his
characteristic humor. The descriptions and place names for the last
letter from Japan lack Twain's customary attention to detail in
spelling as well.

With the Haiti sketch as a notable exception, the rest of Twain's
contributions to this series consist of Western material. Letter one describes Mono Lake in detail, designating it as the Dead Sea of California. In one sense, Twain was perhaps merely marking time, waiting
for Ford's letters to arrive. Yet Twain had a finely tuned sensibility for
catching his readers' interests, and he capitalized on his Eastern readers' curiosity about all things Western. Details from the sketches paint
a realistic picture of the California climate and effectively contrast
East and West in terms of worldview and lifestyle, including dress,
customs, and beliefs. These sketches do not present the romanticized,
exaggerated dime-novel versions current at the time of publication; already it is possible to see Twain exploding traditional Western mythol-
ogy, a distinguishing feature of his later novel, *Roughing It,* in his objective method of presentation and obvious lack of purple prose.

Nearly all the material used in the "Around the World" letters was
recycled into the later novel, *Roughing It,* often in revised form. The
descriptions of the pioneers shift perspective to fit the novel's narration, as do the descriptions of climate and some of the individuals
mentioned in the letters. The story of the Whiteman Cement Mine
that occurs in letter four is expanded and retold in *Roughing It,* as is

the description of pocket mining from letter five. The tale of Baker's Cat in letter five, a set piece of the dialect-narrated tall tale, resurfaces in the novel with little or no revision. The Silver Land Nabobs of letter six become expanded into more detailed individual characters, but the kernel of the idea occurs first in the *Express*.

The relatively brief discussion of Chinamen in letter seven is expanded for the novel as well. This same letter contains short descriptions of three famous desperadoes, Sam Brown, Jack Williams, and Joseph A. (Jack) Slade. Twain briefly makes note of the number of men each has killed and places them within the Wild West construct then prevalent among his Eastern readers. In the final draft of *Roughing It*, however, both Brown and Williams have disappeared, and Slade, the last and least of the *Express* examples, has become the prime example of the breed. Twain expanded to two-and-a-half chapters in the novel what in the newspaper had occurred as a squib. The novel provides a more complete description of Slade's life and death as illustrative of the entire assemblage of desperadoes in general, but the objectivity of the *Express* sketch seems noticeably absent. Twain relates the story from Thomas Dimmesdale's book, *The Vigilantes of Montana; being a Reliable Account of the Capture, Trial, and Execution of Henry Plummer's Notorious Road Agent Band* (1866), retaining the original romantic exaggeration but deflating that language in Slade's final death scene.

Letter number eight, the last of the series actually written by Twain, departs from Nevada territory and takes as its setting instead the Sandwich Islands, where the Twain persona recurs, this time as a reporter dining with a cannibal. The sketch exaggerates commonly held misconceptions about islanders' cannibalistic practices and foreshadows the final section of *Roughing It*, set in that same locale. It affords Twain the opportunity to satirize missionaries, to take a sideways slap at Frenchmen, and again to reiterate the power inherent in journalism. The king invites Twain to write about the island in order to negate the bad press it has received and to set "the record straight."

The remainder of the *Express* sketches are not so easily categorized, but they often reflect Twain's commentary on local, regional, or national events. He writes a glowing theatrical review of *A Midsummer Night's Dream* as performed at the Selwyn Theater (renamed the Globe in 1872), a burlesque tale of having his fortune told, and a detailed description of chromo-photography. On February 25, 1870, he published an editorial eulogy for Anson Burlingame, best known for his trade-treaty negotiations while he served as ambassador to China. Twain had met Burlingame during his stay in the Sandwich Islands, and Burlingame had been instrumental in gaining Twain access to survivors of the *Hornet* disaster in 1867. Twain's story was the first reportage of this event, a circumstance that contributed to his growing fame as a Western reporter. Burlingame is also credited with advising the author to cultivate an Eastern audience: "What you need now is the refinement of association. Refine yourself and your work. Never affiliate with inferiors; always climb."[16] Clearly the young reporter appreciated and took Burlingame's advice. While searching for an editorial post in 1869, he was most particular about the paper to which he would associate his name, as his letters to Livy and her parents illustrate.

Although during his later years, especially in the 1890s, Twain published essays on political topics, such essays are rudimentary or altogether absent in the *Express,* at least under the Twain byline. He stated in the "Salutatory" that he intended to steer clear of political writing: "I shall not often meddle in politics, because we have a political editor who is already excellent, and needs only to serve a term in the penitentiary in order to be perfect." For the most part the author remained true to his word. He champions George William Curtis in "The Ticket—An Explanation" but uses this short sketch as an opportunity to lampoon political editors who, although ignorant of the persons or issues involved, pretend political wisdom and endorse the party ticket without properly checking the credentials of nominees.

Twain offers a more sustained treatment of elections in general in "Running for Governor." In the essay, Twain decides to run for the office of governor of New York—naively believing that since his opponents are crooked politicians, he will be doing a service for the state. As the naive narrator, he demonstrates feigned surprise at the smear tactics of his opponents. The rhetorical style is again a burlesque; the Twain name is besmirched beyond his mother's recognition by the end of the sketch, and "Mark Twain" removes his name from the ballot in disgust. He endorses Curtis because he knows and respects the man and his stand on issues of importance, and Twain obviously believes that these should be the reasons for any political endorsement by a journalist. It is obvious in "Running for Governor" that Twain the erstwhile candidate is not forced out of the campaign because of his stand on important political issues of the day. He departs, instead, because his opponents prefer to mount an ad hominem campaign against him rather than to debate social or political issues.

"Dogberry in Washington" argues that the postal regulations for mailing manuscripts make it impossible for authors to take advantage of the purportedly lower rates for manuscripts. Twain's argument is language-based; the wording of the statute ensures that actual manuscripts do not qualify for the special rate. This topic of expenses would have been an issue near and dear to Twain, who mailed many of his submissions to the *Express* while he was on the road lecturing. These apparently did not qualify for the cheaper postal rate.

In "Curious Dream" Twain takes on a local issue. The sketch is framed as a dream, in which the narrator sees a parade of skeletons in varying stages of decomposition packing up their coffins and moving out to protest the graveyard's dilapidated condition. Through his conversation with one such migrant, Twain castigates the friends and family of the deceased for not maintaining the condition of fences, landscaping, and monuments. Although this and the two previous sketches might be of local or regional significance, Twain's theme in each touches on universal human issues. "Curious Dream" is an attempt to shame the community into renovating a cemetery that has become an eyesore through unconscionable neglect. The story also mocks an American tendency to disrespect the past.

In March 1870, approximately four months after Twain assumed his editorial duties at the *Express* and one month after his marriage to Olivia Langdon, he agreed to edit a "Memoranda" column for the *Galaxy*. In 1870 and 1871, the *Galaxy* was one of America's leading magazines, national in scope and catering to a more literate audience. Its editors, William C. and Francis P. Church, dedicated themselves to obtaining the best talent available. Their success can be measured in the acquisition not only of Twain's regular column but also of other authors' articles, poetry, or short fiction during the magazine's lifetime. During its twelve-year publication history, Henry James contributed twelve stories. Additional contributors of fiction included Rebecca Harding Davis, John William DeForest, Rose Terry Cooke, John Esten Cooke, and Constance Fenimore Woolson. Gideon Welles, Civil War Secretary of the Navy, contributed nineteen articles on various aspects of the war, General George A. Custer published two articles on army service in the West, and John Burroughs wrote critical articles in praise of Walt Whitman, which later led to the publication of some of his poems in the magazine. Although the editors were known to make changes to manuscripts without consulting the author, they did not exert any consistent, rigid control over their contributors. In April 1871, when Twain made his last contribution to the *Galaxy,* circulation was 22,136 copies.[17]

At a time when the standard pay rate for magazines was one dollar per page (the rate for the *Atlantic* in 1871), Twain told Francis P. Church in his March 11, 1870, letter: "If I can have entire ownership and disposal of what I write for the *Galaxy,* I will edit your humorous department for two thousand dollars ($2,000) a year—and I give you my word that I can start out tomorrow or any day I choose and make that money in two weeks, lecturing." Twain's first "Memoranda" contribution appeared in the May 1870 issue. He was given a free hand in determining his contributions to his "Department" for his $2,000 annual salary. He was required to produce ten pages of copy per month, and the *Galaxy* publishers reserved the right to publish the material in book form at the end of the year. The books would sell for $1.50 and Twain would receive a royalty of twenty cents per book. His salary was two-and-a-half times what the magazine usually paid its contributors.[18]

Twain had more important reasons for contributing to the *Galaxy* than monetary ones, however. His earliest journalistic efforts and his subsequent changes of employment illustrate his desire to reach an ever-wider audience. He might well have been content to remain writing for the *Virginia City Territorial Enterprise* and Joe Goodman since after the first few weeks Goodman allowed Twain to choose his own subject matter, "employing Clemens as a spinner of yarns and fancy sketches rather than a purveyor of pure, unvarnished truth."[19] As a reporter, Twain could be as accurate as any other gatherer of facts, but he found these tasks routine and boring. When the news day was slow, he was known to embellish the truth in order to fill space. Goodman apparently recognized where Twain's strengths as a writer lay and allowed him the license to practice them.

That license was revoked by the *San Francisco Daily Morning Call,* however, when Twain joined the staff in 1864. His *Enterprise* articles had been widely reprinted in Western periodicals, and Twain's Western reputation was well-established in 1863 when Artemus Ward (Charles F. Browne) lectured in Virginia City and its environs. He advised Twain to widen his reading audience; in a letter to his mother and sister in December 1863, Twain writes that Ward told him to "leave sage-brush obscurity, & journey to New York with him." Although Twain did not depart immediately for New York, he did decide to move to San Francisco, where his writing could reach a larger and more refined audience. The *Call*, however, hired him on as the local items reporter, a drudgery Twain came to hate within the first two weeks of employment. In addition to the long hours and routine assignments, several of Twain's articles were squelched before publication. The *Call* prided itself on being "the washerwoman's paper" and consequently was unreceptive to articles critical of the San Francisco police department or the unfair treatment of Chinamen. Twain took the Sandwich Islands assignment largely to escape the daily grind of local items.

Each employment change Twain made up to his editorship at the *Buffalo Express* shows an attempt to reach a wider and more aesthetically astute reading public; therefore, his decision to write for the *Galaxy*, one of the most popular and refined of the Eastern magazines, is not surprising. As Twain indicated in his March 22 and 24, 1870, letter to Mary Fairbanks, he was looking for an outlet for more creative efforts, his more "fine-spun" works. He also mentions in the same letter his qualms about writing for a daily, stating that those writers who do so "write themselves out" before long.

Twain's contributions to the "Memoranda" show little or no literary difference from the sketches he wrote exclusively for the *Express*. Bruce McElderry observes that few of the columns Twain submitted to the *Galaxy* consist of material dredged up from his journalistic past, with the exception of "Johnny Skae's Item" and "A Couple of Sad Experiences," in which he introduces the "Petrified Man" and "Bloody Massacre" sketches as burlesques and denounces the ignorance of the reading public who believed these sketches. However, eighteen sketches that appear in the "Memoranda" did double duty in the *Express*. In virtually all the cases that Twain published sketches simultaneously in both the *Express* and the *Galaxy*, it appears that he wrote the sketches particularly for the *Galaxy* but had no reservations about also printing them in his own newspaper. Even those sketches that technically appeared first in the *Express* were not really published "before" their appearance in the *Galaxy*, which, like magazines then and now, was published at least one week to ten days before the beginning of the month on the cover. Twain seems to have had no hand in any changes that occurred in the *Express* versions of the sketches except directing that they be reprinted. A collation of these sketches show numerous incidental changes and corruptions of the *Galaxy* text, but these do not seem to be authoritative. Consequently, we have decided in these cases to use the *Galaxy* versions as the copy-texts. Annotations in the text that follows indicate the order of appearance for all the items duplicated in the *Galaxy* and the *Express*.

Twain's personal and public obligations between May 1870 and April 1871 may account for the simultaneous publications of his sketches in the *Express* and the *Galaxy*. His editorship of the "Memoranda" column coincided almost exactly with the illnesses and deaths at home. In addition, he was working on other projects: he had promised completion of the manuscript that would eventually become *Roughing It* by January 1871; he was compiling *Sketches, New and Old;* and Riley had gone to the South African diamond mines with the intention of sending back data that might lead to the publication of yet another project. Even as energetic a writer as Twain could sometimes be could not do justice to such a monumental list of projects during the best of times. Given the turmoil of Twain's family life, the completion of all these projects on schedule became an absolute impossibility. Letters to Orion at the time indicate that his writing on *Roughing It* had come to a standstill, as had his work on the sketch book. While Twain may have fully intended the *Galaxy* column to contain his more "literary" material, both his circumstances and the time constraints dictated dual submissions to fulfill obligations. While Twain contributed four sketches to the *Express* in April 1870, in the nine subsequent months ending in January 1871 the number of sketches written exclusively for the *Express* drop off precipitously. Forty-one items by him, both signed and unsigned, have been identified in the *Express* for this period, but these include occasional editorials, obituaries, anonymous letters to the editor, as well as the sketches reprinted from the *Galaxy*. Of these forty-one, only about ten technically qualify as "original sketches," and more than half of these sketches appeared in April and May.[20] Recycling his own material for use in more than one place was something that would become commonplace for Mark Twain.

While one of the values of the *Buffalo Express* sketches, including those reprinted in the *Galaxy,* certainly lies in the fact that they represent the culmination of Twain's work as a journalist, they compare favorably with Twain's best humor, showing flashes of the brilliant author that would emerge. By March 1871, he was ready to end an almost twenty-year love-hate relationship with journalism and to begin a career as a novelist. The *Express* sketches that deal specifically with journalism as a theme show a progressive frustration with the newspaper as a creative outlet for writing. Ironically, the medium through which Twain first gained fame grew to be too constricting a mode for self-expression. Early in March 1871, the author complained in an unpublished letter to Orion: "Haven't I risked cheapening myself sufficiently by a year's periodical dancing before the public?"[21] By 1871, Twain had gained enough confidence in his ability to "earn his living by his pen" in earnest. The proceeds from *Innocents Abroad* were sufficiently lucrative to encourage his break from journalism and to allow him to concentrate his efforts on novels and lecturing thereafter.

While uneven, Twain's *Express* material is also noteworthy for his efficient use of previous work. Twain mined his newspaper files, notebooks, and memories for many of his sketches. "Curious Relic for Sale" presents a recycled sketch from unused work on *Innocents Abroad*. Kernels of ideas presented in the "Around the World" series stem from his Western experiences or notebook entries. The tale of "Baker's Cat" and "The Facts in the Great Land Slide Case" are prime examples of such material. Twain later compiled and revised these sketches, as well as much of the other Western material, when he was assembling *Roughing It*. "Dining with a Cannibal" foreshadows the eventual end of that novel. The best of the *Express* sketches were reprinted in *Sketches New and Old* (1875). "The Story of the Good Little Boy Who Did Not Prosper" and its companion piece, "The Bad Little Boy Who Did Not Come to Grief," both published in the *Galaxy* and the *Express*, foreshadow his characterizations of Tom Sawyer and Huck Finn in the later novels. Each of these sketches presents in early form the ideas that Twain later incorporated into larger, more sustained works.

Twain's humor for the *Express* rarely incorporated political satire. "Running for Governor" accentuates general issues of corruption in government, exploiting the theme merely for its value in creating or sustaining humor. The same is true for "A Mysterious Visit." Both sketches rely upon effects immediate to the narrator for the reader's amusement. "The Facts in the Case of George Fisher, Deceased," however, contains few elements of humor, with the possible exception of the hyperbole involved in the actual sum paid by congress and the continuous exaggeration of assets. It presages Twain's later anti-imperialist essays of the 1890s and early twentieth century, such as "My First Lie and How I Got Out of It" (1899), "To the Person Sitting in Darkness" (1901), "The Czar's Soliloquy" (1905), and "King Leopold's Soliloquy, A Defense of His Congo Rule" (1905).

Both "A Reminiscence of the Back Settlements" and "Baker's Cat" demonstrate the author's increasing skill in vernacular dialect. His back-country funeral director anticipates later characters such as Huck Finn and Hank Morgan, where Twain's powers of dialect evolved to their highest potential. Dick Baker, who tells the fantastic tale of his cat, Tom Quartz, shows a clear understanding of the use of Western dialect, which reaches its apex in Scotty Briggs in *Roughing It*. These early attempts at written dialect improve upon Twain's earlier, awkward attempts but do not reach the well-rounded and sustained later characterizations represented by Huck Finn or Hank Morgan.

Additionally, even in these early sketches, readers can sense Twain's underlying concern with and opposition to the Rationalist belief that a reasonably intelligent man can indeed recognize truth from falsehood and fact from fiction. Sketches such as "At the President's Reception," "The Facts in the Great Land Slide Case," "The Legend of the Capitoline Venus," and the other burlesques and hoaxes demonstrate and explore, in a general way, imperfections in human reasoning and a tendency toward participation in one's own deception by the world and its events because of a desire for the exotic or the sensational in one's own life. Irrational beliefs or desires interfere with man's ability to read accurately and to interpret the world around him. This complex issue is later dealt with in the king/duke sections of *Adventures of Huckleberry Finn* and even later in the Dawson's Landing townspeople's reactions to the Italian twins, but the seeds of this idea occur as early as the sketches from 1869 and 1870. Desire for riches, power, or sophistication often interfere with Twain's narrators' abilities to maintain realistic perceptions of themselves or their world (for example, in "A Big Thing" and "At the President's Reception").

These sketches command attention for Twain's changes in rhetorical style and narration, which would stand him in good stead in his new career as a novelist. The earliest sketches are easily recognizable as the work of "The Wild Humorist of the Pacific Slope." Even some of the last sketches reflect this style: his hallmarks are the bumbling, ignorant, or backwoods narrator as the butt of the jokes, his slapstick humor, and the (humorously) violent end to the stories. These motifs reflect the influence of humorists such as Artemus Ward, John Phoenix, George Washington Harris, and other well-known humorists of the mid-nineteenth century. The tall tale and the burlesque are their specialty, and Twain accepts them as his own, though he modifies them to his own terms.

These *Express* sketches often serve as narrative experiments in which Twain varies the position and the characteristics of the narrator to conform with the effect he wishes to create. The deadpan delivery of the narrator taken from Southwestern humor remains, but the Twain persona is alternately the bumpkin and the sophisticate. The settled and financially well-off Twain of "A Mysterious Visit," who considers himself to be a sophisticated man of the world, ultimately fools himself by his boasting and by his misperception of the Internal Revenue Department representative and his motives for visiting. Other sketches such as "A Big Thing" and "Browsing Around: Back from Yur-rup" attempt to shed light on how ordinary citizens can easily misinterpret seemingly factual information to their detriment and how the noveau riche can completely misconceive European sophistication.

Twain pioneers by adopting some unusual characters to tell his tales, an additional foreshadowing of the many narrators he would later create in his late works. He employs a ghost, a skeleton, and a "Wild Man" in three of the sketches. The story dictates the narration instead of the narrator imposing his presence upon the tale. Thus, narrational flexibility becomes a hallmark in Twain's writing, a condition that he comments on in his autobiography. When discussing the composition of *Joan of Arc,* Twain says:

> There is only one right form for a story and if you fail to find that form the story will not tell itself. You may try a dozen wrong forms but in each case you will not get very far before you discover that you have not found the right one—then that story will always stop and decline to go any further.[22]

The body of work that begins with his *Buffalo Express* editorship demonstrates that Twain had many stories to tell and that there were many ways to tell them. His narrational shifts illustrate his dedication to telling the story as it was meant to be told; such shifts required him to become an expert regarding the effects that they could create and then to find the correct one for each successive story. Twain the editor found or created many narrators, the perfect characters to tell his stories, and Twain the novelist profited from this editorial apprenticeship. Often rivaling his most accomplished work, Twain's *Buffalo Express* articles and sketches reveal the promise of an inimitable talent.

NOTES

1. Louis Budd's article, "Mark Twain as a Cultural Icon," reprinted in *The Cambridge Companion to Mark Twain* (New York: Cambridge University Press, 1995), details the appropriation of Twain's visual image or his characters, as does Bruce Michelson's introductory chapter to *Mark Twain on the Loose* (Amherst: University of Massachusetts Press, 1995).

2. Jeffrey Steinbrink, in *Getting to Be Mark Twain* (Berkeley: University of California Press, 1991), discusses the various negotiations in great detail, offering supporting evidence from Twain's correspondence from this time period.

3. John Harrison Mills, "Reminiscences." Unpublished manuscript, excerpted in Albert Bigelow Paine, *Mark Twain: A Biography* (New York and London: Harper and Brothers, 1912): 1: 388.

4. Earl D. Berry, "Mark Twain as a Newspaper Man," *Illustrated Buffalo Express,* 11 November 1917, 40.

5. *Mark Twain's Letters,* vol. 3, 1869, ed. Victor Fischer et al. (Berkeley and Los Angeles: University of California Press, 1992), 359–60, nn. 1, 2.

6. For detailed discussions of Twain's contributions to the *Express,* see Martin B. Fried, "Mark Twain in Buffalo," *Niagara Frontier* 5 (Winter 1959): 89–110; and Joseph B. McCullough, "A Listing of Mark Twain's Contributions to the Buffalo *Express,* 1869–1871," *American Literary Realism* 5 (Winter 1972): 61–70. Paul Baender, "Mark Twain and the Byron Scandal," *American Literature* 30 (January 1959): 467–85, argues convincingly for Twain authorship of the Byron/Stowe editorials. For indispensable evidence of Twain authorship of several unsigned pieces found in his correspondence, consult *Mark Twain's Letters,* vol. 3, and *Mark Twain's Letters,* vol. 4, 1870–1871, ed. Victor Fischer et al. (Berkeley and Los Angeles: University of California Press, 1995). Less reliable is Henry Duskis's *Forgotten Writings of Mark Twain* (New York: Philosophical Library, 1963), since many of Duskis's attributions have been disproved and others remain purely speculative.

7. For a full discussion of the Slocum/Byng sketches, see Joseph B. McCullough, "Mark Twain and the Hy Slocum-Carl Byng Controversy," *American Literature* 43 (March 1971): 42–59.

8. Bernard DeVoto, *Mark Twain in Eruption* (New York and London: Harper and Brothers, 1940), 251.

9. *Native American Humor,* 2d ed. (San Francisco: Chandler Publishing Co., 1960), 147.

10. *Galaxy,* "Memoranda," "A Couple of Sad Experiences," June 1870.

11. *Getting to Be Mark Twain,* 101–6.

12. Bruce Michelson discusses these sketches and the Franco-Prussian War in detail in *Mark Twain on the Loose,* 39–42.

13. Steinbrink, *Getting to Be Mark Twain,* discusses both sketches on pp. 96–99.

14. Steinbrink, *Getting to Be Mark Twain,* 98.

15. Bruce McElderry quotes the actual *Saturday Review* article in full in *Contributions to the Galaxy by Mark Twain* (Gainesville, Fla.: Scholars' Facsimiles and Reprints, 1961).

16. Quoted in Justin Kaplan, *Mr. Clemens and Mark Twain* (New York: Simon and Schuster, 1966), 81.

17. For this and other detailed information on Twain's publication in the *Galaxy,* we have relied upon Bruce McElderry's excellent study *Contributions to the Galaxy by Mark Twain.*

18. McElderry, *Contributions to the Galaxy by Mark Twain,* xii.

19. Nigey Lennon, *The Sagebrush Bohemian* (New York: Paragon, 1990), 26.

20. *Mark Twain's Letters,* 4: 101, n. 5.

21. Quoted in Martin Fried, "Mark Twain in Buffalo," 109.

22. Charles Neider, ed., *The Autobiography of Mark Twain* (New York: Harpers & Brothers, 1917, 1959), 266–67.

Mark Twain

at the *Buffalo Express*

PART I

Settling in to Editorial Duties

August 1869 – October 1869

"Salutatory"

Being a stranger, it would be immodest and unbecoming in me to suddenly and violently assume the associate editorship of the *Buffalo Express* without a single explanatory word of comfort or encouragement to the unoffending patrons of the paper, who are about to be exposed to constant attacks of my wisdom and learning. But this explanatory word shall be as brief as possible. I only wish to assure parties having a friendly interest in the prosperity of the journal, that I am not going to hurt the paper deliberately and intentionally at any time. I am not going to introduce any startling reforms, or in any way attempt to make trouble. I am simply going to do my plain, unpretending duty, when I cannot get out of it; I shall work diligently and honestly and faithfully at all times and upon all occasions, when privation and want shall compel me to do it; in writing, I shall always confine myself strictly to the truth, except when it is attended with inconvenience; I shall witheringly rebuke all forms of crime and misconduct, except when committed by the party inhabiting my own vest; I shall not make use of slang or vulgarity upon any occasion or under any circumstances, and shall never use profanity except in discussing house-rent and taxes. Indeed, upon second thought, I will not even use it then, for it is unchristian, inelegant and degrading—though to speak truly I do not see how house-rent and taxes are going to be discussed worth a cent without it. I shall not often meddle with politics, because we have a political editor who is already excellent, and only needs to serve a term in the penitentiary in order to be perfect. I shall not write any poetry, unless I conceive a spite against the subscribers.

Such is my platform. I do not see any earthly use in it, but custom is law, and custom must be obeyed, no matter how much violence it may do to one's feelings. And this custom which I am slavishly following now, is surely one of the least necessary that ever came into vogue. In private life a man does not go and trumpet his crime before he commits it, but your new editor is such an important personage that he feels called upon to write a "Salutatory" at once, and he puts into it all that he knows, and all that he don't know, and some things he thinks he knows but isn't certain of. And he parades his list of wonders which he is going to perform; of reforms which he is going to introduce, and public evils which he is going to exterminate; and public blessings which he is going to create; and public nuisances which he is going to abate. He spreads this all out with oppressive solemnity over a column and a half of large print, and feels that the country is saved. His satisfaction over it is something enormous. He then settles down to his miracles and inflicts profound platitudes and impenetrable wisdom upon a helpless public as long as they can stand it, and then they send him off Consul to some savage island in the Pacific in the vague hope that the cannibals will like him well enough to eat him. And with an inhumanity which is but a fitting climax to his career of persecution, instead of packing his trunk at once he lingers to inflict upon his benefactors a "Valedictory." If there is anything more uncalled for than a "Salutatory," it is one of those tearful, blubbering, long-winded "Valedictories"—wherein a man who has been annoying the public for ten years cannot take leave of them without sitting down to cry a column and a half. Still, it is the custom to write Valedictories, and custom should be respected. In my secret heart I admire my predecessor for declining to print a Valedictory, though in public I say and shall continue to say sternly, it is custom and he ought to have printed one. People never read them any more than they do the "Salutatories," but nevertheless he ought to have honored the old fossil—he ought to have printed a Valedictory. I said as much to him, and he replied:

"I have resigned my place—I have departed this life—I am journalistically dead, at present, ain't I?"

"Yes."

"Well, wouldn't you consider it disgraceful in a corpse to sit up and comment on the funeral?"

I record it here, and preserve it from oblivion, as the briefest and best "Valedictory" that has yet come under my notice.—*Mark Twain*

P.S.—I am grateful for the kindly way in which the press of the land have taken notice of my irruption into regular journalistic life, telegraphically or editorially, and am happy in this place to express the feeling.

Removal of the Capital

For a good many years there has been occasioned talk at the West about the removal of the national capital from Washington to some point more near the center of the Union; but as each ambitious city in the West (where every settlement is a metropolis in expectancy) coveted the dignity for itself, and all were rivals of one another in the matter, the proposition has never been until now, brought to any thing like a serious point of discussion.[1] The recent magnanimity, however, of a prominent journal in Chicago, which loftily waives the claims of that pre-eminent city and calls for the transportation of the general government, bag, baggage, and buildings, to St. Louis, has inflamed the hopes of the citizens of the town and set a serious movement on foot among them to agitate the question of removal. But the one newspaper in Chicago which, either sensationally or by way of a joke on the innocent St. Louisans, threw its vote for the election of St. Louis as the future capital, does not cast the vote of Chicago, all the rest of the inhabitants whereof are ready to take arms in resentment of the bare suggestion of a possibility that the seat of government could be shifted westward without gravitating Chicagoward by an irresistible attraction. At the same time Cincinnati is roused to vehement opposition, and all the lesser hamlets aspiring to the splendid prize are clamorously in the field. On the whole, therefore, we conclude that the question of the removal of the national capital westward may be safely left, as heretofore, to be negatively settled by the jealous rivalry of contending Western cities.

If there existed any good and sufficient reasons for the costly change, we of the Middle and Eastern states might interfere and settle the determination of a new site by our disinterested suffrages. But there are no such reasons. That of geography is only a pretense. Railroads and the telegraph have totally upset natural geography. Trigonometrical principles no longer apply in laying out the organization of a nation, either politically or commercially. It makes no difference, so far as concerns public interests, or the efficiency or the convenience of the working government, whether it is located in a corner, or on the border or at the center of the continent which it governs. From Washington it operates as effectively in California and Oregon as if its headquarters were on the Mississippi or with Brigham Young at Salt Lake.

The only convenience, so far as we can see, that is to be served by a removal westward, is that of the Congressmen who might be saved a day or two of railroad travel going to and coming from their session. Yet we have never heard a Western Representative complain of the distance for which he had to draw mileage. At all events, the nation is not likely to feel called upon to expend one or two hundred millions of dollars in providing new quarters for the government, merely to accommodate these gentlemen, so long as it is not found difficult to prevail upon them to serve their constituents at Washington.

One reason urged in favor of the change of capital we admit is a substantial one—viz: the ill-climate of Washington. But about the same climate, hot in summer and sloppy in winter, is to be found all along the line of middle latitude, which the advocates of removal are bound to follow. St. Louis, in respect, offers no improvement worth mentioning. To be placed in a really agreeable climate, bracing in winter and breezy in summer, our legislators and administrators would have to be brought North, to the region of the Lakes—Buffalo for example; and that, in fact, is the only sensible change that could be proposed. If our Western friends will insist on agitating the question of removal we may feel called upon to press it. *[Unsigned]*

August 18, 1869

T Lady Byron—Mrs. Stowe's Revelations

he revelation made by Mrs. Stowe in her *Atlantic* article,[2] of the mysterious and much-speculated-upon cause which drove Lady Byron from her husband, is one so terrible that it will be productive of an immense sensation in the world. She states that Lady Byron communicated to her, some four years before her death, but when she was in immediate apprehension of dying, the fact that Byron had become the father of a child by an incestuous *liaison* with his own sister, and that it was Byron's consciousness that his wife had discovered this crime which drove him so near to madness, and inspired him with the intense hatred of her which he manifested ever afterwards.

That some hideous secret of this character was disclosed by Lady Byron to a few friends who had her confidence has long been known. Her counsel, the celebrated Dr. Lushington,[3] was one of those to whom she imparted it, and although his lips were sealed concerning the nature of the revelation, he did not scruple to allude to it as having filled him with horror, and as having justified to his mind, entirely, the step which Lady Byron took, in separating from her husband without any explained cause.

The partisans of Lord Byron in the discussion of this dark and mysterious domestic rupture, have always made much of the refusal of Lady Byron to state her grievances, and have accused her with bitter severity of having surrounded the case with mystery in order to excite sinister suspicions and conjectures, by which Byron was injured more than he could have been by any charge that she had to bring against him. But the disclosure now made leaves no room to question the motive of the silence which she preserved.

We know, at last, what it was that drove Lady Byron, in horror, from her husband. It will still be debated, however, whether he was actually guilty of the monstrous crime of which he stands accused. The most incredulous will find it hard to throw doubt upon the testimony of Lady Byron, either by impeaching her sincerity or the trustworthiness of her judgment as to the certainty of the evidence by which she was convinced of the horrible fact; yet it seems almost incredible that any such damning infamy should have blackened the life of so conspicuous a man as Lord Byron, and still have been kept wholly concealed within the domestic circle. The case as it now stands will certainly excite more controversy than ever.

Mrs. Stowe's narrative throws no light upon the question as to how Lady Byron discovered her husband's crime, though it seems to be left for inference that confession was made to her by the sister, who died in her arms. The offspring of his guilt is also said to have died under her charge, after living four years. *[Unsigned]*

August 19, 1869

Inspired Humor

The New York *World* is not generally regarded as a humorous paper, but once in a while the arid solemnity with which it projects a comical idea into the body of one of its heaviest editorials would make Artemus Ward[4] turn in his grave.[5] For example, observe this, in Tuesday's leader: "The Democracy of New York this year must elect a Democratic Legislature, *an honest and incorruptible Democratic*

Legislature; an able and experienced Democratic Legislature." And again: "The Democratic party has for its task to completely redeem the State and the nation from Republican corruption, extravagance, and misrule." The humor of those two sentences rises to sublimity. And the manner of their expression has all that seemingly dense unconsciousness about it which is the soul of all true humor. Two better things than those remarks have not been said this year, even in Mr. Schuyler's[6] "Personal" column. The bare idea of an incorruptible Democratic New York Legislature is a burst of humor so grand, so enormous in its proportions, so supernatural in its conception, and withal so solemn and awe-imposing, that the provincial mind contemplates it with humbled posture and reverent head uncovered, feeling that the ground is holy and that the Presence that speaks is the dread and mighty Momus his very self.

The other joke, of loading down the astounded Democracy with such a task as the redeeming anything or anybody from corruption, extravagance and misrule, is fully as colossal as its brother. There is a volcanic magnificence about these two jests that fascinates while it terrifies the beholder. The pair should be placed on record together among the precious archives of the nation, and sent down to posterity as the most stupendous achievement which the world of humor gave birth to in the eventful nineteenth century. But with notes attached, explaining that this severely virtuous Democracy is the Democracy whose devotees plunged the nation into a monstrous civil war; burned colored orphan asylums; conducted the Andersonville prison; respected Andrew Johnson; removed Mr. Lincoln in an abrupt and peculiarly Democratic way; instituted the Ku-Klux-Klan; ran for Vice President the melancholy fragment which whisky had left of what was once Francis P. Blair;[7] sapped the public Treasury under Johnson by all the devices known to fraud; voted early and always for repudiation; and whose party's crowning work is its government of New York city; a party whose religion is to war against all moral and material progress, and who never were known to divert to the erection of a school house moneys that would suffice to build a distillery. The explanatory notes should go with the jokes, by all means. *[Unsigned]*

The "Monopoly" Speaks

It is held that there are two sides to every question.[8] Evidently the exciting coal question is no exception to the rule. It is absolutely necessary to the clear understanding of any matter that both sides should be heard—not in a war of fierce assertion and denial, but through candid statements from both parties, made up simply of the *facts* which each is able to present. From these an intelligent reader can easily sift the truth, and in no other way can he arrive at it. Up to the present time we have heard only the people's side of the coal question, though there could be no doubt that the coal men had a side also, which might be looked for whenever a lull in the storm and the cooling of passion should render it likely that a fair and respectful hearing would be granted to its expression. None of us can help being run away with by our feelings, occasionally, but sooner or later we give our judgment sway again, and are prepared to listen and analyze.

To-day we print an exhaustive article on the coal question, from the N.Y. *Evening Post,* whose correspondent seems to understand his subject, and whose remarks are entitled to weight, since they appear in a paper which has an established reputation for seeking for and presenting to its readers the truth, notwithstanding it does it sometimes at the temporary expense of popularity. This article will show that the present high prices of coal are owing to causes which could not be prevented, rather than to criminal combinations among coal monopolists.

We also print, in our local columns, under the head of "The Coal Question," a card from Mr. Slee,[9] the authorized business agent and general salesman of the group of companies known as the "Anthracite Coal Association," and who is the highest officer in their employ in Buffalo. This association which he represents is composed of the Delaware, Lackawanna and Western R.R. Co., the Pittston and Elmira Coal Co., and Mr. J. Langdon, and through his (Mr. Slee's) hands passes the business of the Association for all its extensive western ramifications and for Buffalo. His statement is authoritative; and being well known in commercial circles here as a gentleman of unimpeachable character, it can be relied on as true in all respects.

All the sides and phases of this coal question are worthy of calm and cool consideration. It is not well to jump to conclusions. The best way to go about the much wished-for consummation of a reduction in the price of coal, is to become thoroughly posted upon the coal question in all its bearings as it now stands. We always invite failure when we act upon deficient knowledge. Simply knowing how to turn a throttle valve does not make a man competent to run a steam engine safely. *[Unsigned]*

August 21, 1869

A Day at Niagara. Concerning the Falls. The Tamed Hackman

Niagara Falls is one of the finest structures in the known world.[10] I have been visiting this favorite watering place recently, for the first time, and was well pleased. A gentleman who was with me said it was customary to be disappointed in the Falls, but that subsequent visits were sure to set that all right. He said it was so with him. He said that the first time he went the hack fares were so much higher than the Falls that the Falls appeared insignificant. But that is all regulated now. The hackmen have been tamed, and numbered, and placarded, and blackguarded, and brought into subjection to the law, and dosed with Moral Principle till they are as meek as missionaries. They are divided into two clans, now, the Regulars and the Privateers, and they employ their idle time in warning the public against each other. The Regulars are under the hotel banners, and do the legitimate at two dollars an hour, and the Privateers prowl darkly on neutral ground and pick off stragglers at half price. But there are no more outrages and extortions. That sort of thing cured itself. It made the Falls unpopular by getting into the newspapers, and whenever a public evil achieves that sort of a success for itself, its days are numbered. It became apparent that either the Falls had to be discontinued or the hackmen had to subside. They could not dam the Falls, and so they damned the hackmen. One can be comfortable and happy there now.

SIGNS AND SYMBOLS

I drank up most of the American Fall before I learned that the waters were not considered medicinal. Why are people left in ignorance in that way? I might have gone on and ruined a fine property merely for the want of a little trifling information. And yet the sources of information at Niagara Falls are not meagre. You are sometimes in doubt there about what you ought to do, but you are seldom in doubt about what you must *not* do. No—the signs keep you posted. If an infant can read, that infant is measurably safe at Niagara Falls. In your room at the hotel you will find your course marked out for you in the most convenient way by means of placards on the wall, like these:

"Pull the bell-rope gently, but don't jerk."

"Bolt your door."

"Don't scrape matches on the wall."

"Turn off your gas when you retire."

"Tie up your dog."

"If you place your boots outside the door they will be blacked—but the house will not be responsible for their return." [This is a confusing and tanglesome proposition—because it moves you to deliberate long and painfully as to whether it will really be any object to you to have your boots blacked unless they *are* returned.]

"Give your key to the omnibus driver if you forget and carry it off with you."

Outside the hotel, wherever you wander, you are intelligently assisted by the signs. You cannot come to grief as long as you are in your right mind. But the difficulty is to *stay* in your right mind with so much instruction to keep track of. For instance:

"Keep off the grass."

"Don't climb the trees."

"Hands off the vegetables."

"Do not hitch your horse to the shrubbery."

"Visit the Cave of the Winds."

"Have your portrait taken in your carriage."

"Forty per cent. in gold levied on all pea-nuts or other Indian Curiosities purchased in Canada."

"Photographs of the Falls taken here."

"Visitors will please notify the Superintendent of any neglect on the part of employees to charge for commodities or services." [No inattention of this kind observed.]

"Don't throw stones down—they may hit people below."

"The proprietors will not be responsible for parties who jump over the Falls." [More shirking of responsibility—it appears to be the prevailing thing here.]

I always had a high regard for the Signers of the Declaration of Independence, but now they do not really seem to amount to much alongside the signers of Niagara Falls. To tell the plain truth, the multitude of signs annoyed me. It was because I noticed at last that they always happened to prohibit exactly the very thing I was just wanting to do. I desired to roll on the grass: the sign prohibited it. I wished to climb a tree: the sign prohibited it. I longed to smoke: a sign forbade it. And I was just in the act of throwing a stone over to astonish and pulverize such parties as might be picknicking below, when a sign I have just mentioned forbade that. Even that poor satisfaction was denied me, (and I a friendless orphan.)—There was no recourse, now, but to seek consolation in the flowing bowl. I drew my flask from my pocket, but it was all in vain. A sign confronted me which said:

"No drinking allowed on these premises."

On that spot I might have perished of thirst, but for the saving words of an honored maxim that flitted through my memory at the critical moment.—"All signs fail in a dry time." Common law takes precedence of the statutes. I was saved.

THE NOBLE RED MAN

The Noble Red Man has always been a darling of mine. I love to read about him in tales and legends and romances. I love to read of his inspired sagacity; and his love of the wild free life of mountain and forest; and his grand truthfulness, his hatred of treachery, and his general nobility of character; and his stately metaphorical manner of speech; and his chivalrous love for his dusky maiden; and the picturesque pomp of his dress and accoutrement. Especially the picturesque pomp of his dress and accoutrement. When I found the shops at Niagara Falls full of dainty Indian beadwork, and stunning moccasins, and equally stunning toy figures representing human beings who carried their weapons in holes bored through their arms and bodies, and had feet shaped like a pie, I was filled with emotion. I knew that now, at last, I was going to come face to face with the Noble Red Man. A lady clerk in a shop told me, indeed, that all her grand array of curiosities were made by the Indians, and that there were plenty about the Falls, and that they were friendly and it would not be dangerous to speak to them. And sure enough, as I approached the bridge leading over to Luna Island, I came upon a noble old Son of the Forest sitting under a tree, diligently at work on a bead reticule. He wore a slouch hat and brogans, and had a short black pipe in his mouth. Thus does the baneful contact with our effeminate civilization dilute the picturesque pomp which is so natural to the Indian when far removed from us in his native haunts. I addressed the relic as follows:

"Is the Wawhoo-Wang-Wang of the Wack-a-Whack happy? Does the great Speckled Thunder sigh for the war-path, or is his heart contented with dreaming of his dusky maiden, the Pride of the Forest? Does the mighty sachem yearn to drink the blood of his enemies, or is he satisfied to make bead reticules for the papooses of the pale face? Speak, sublime relic of by-gone grandeur—venerable ruin, speak!"

The relic said:

"An is it mesilf, Dinnis Hooligan, that ye'd be takin for a bloody Injin, ye drawlin' lantern-jawed, spider-legged divil! By the piper that played before Moses, I'll ate ye!"

I went away from there.

Bye and bye, in the neighborhood of the Terrapin Tower, I came upon a gentle daughter of the aborigines, in fringed and beaded buckskin moccasins and leggins, seated on a bench with her pretty wares about her. She had just carved out a wooden chief that had a strong family resemblance to a clothes pin, and was now boring a hole through his abdomen to put his bow through. I hesitated a moment and then addressed her:

"Is the heart of the forest maiden heavy? Is the Laughing-Tadpole lonely? Does she mourn over the extinguished council-fires of her race and the vanished glory of her ancestors? Or does her sad spirit wander afar toward the hunting grounds whither her brave Gobbler-of-the-Lightnings is gone? Why is my daughter silent? Has she aught against the pale-face stranger?"

The maiden said:

"Faix, an is it Biddy Malone ye dare to be callin' names! Lave this or I'll shy your lean carcass over the catharact, ye sniveling blagyard!"

I adjourned from there, also. "Confound these Indians," I said, "they told me they were tame—but, if appearances should go for anything, I should say they were all on the war-path."I made one more attempt to fraternise with them, and only one. I came upon a camp of them gathered in the shade of a great tree, making wampum and moccasins, and addressed them in the language of friendship:

"Noble Red Men, Braves, Grand Sachems, War-Chiefs, Squaws and High-you-Muck-a-Mucks, the pale face from the land of the setting sun greets you! You, Beneficent Polecat—you, Devourer-of-the-Mountains—you, Roaring-Thundergust—you, Bullyboye-with-a-Glass-Eye—the pale face from beyond the great waters greets you all! War and pestilence have thinned your ranks and destroyed your once proud nation. Poker, and seven-up, and a vain modern expense for soap, unknown to your glorious ancestors, have depleted your purses. Appropriating in your simplicity the property of others has gotten you into trouble. Misrepresenting facts, in your sinless innocence, has damaged your reputation with the soulless usurper. Trading for forty-rod whisky to enable you to get drunk and happy and tomahawk your families has played the everlasting mischief with the picturesque pomp of your dress, and here you are, in the broad light of the nineteenth century, gotten up like the ragtag and bobtail of the purlieus of New York! For shame! Remember your ancestors! Recall their mighty deeds! Remember Uncas![11]—and Red Jacket![12]—and Hole-in-the-Day![13]—and Horace Greeley![14] Emulate their achievements! Unfurl yourselves under my banner, noble savages, illustrious guttersnipes—"

"Down wid him!"

"Scoop the blagyard!"

"Hang him!"

"Burn him!"

"Dhrownd him!"

It was the quickest operation that ever was. I simply saw a sudden flash in the air of clubs, brickbats, fists, bead baskets, and moccasins— a single flash, and they all appeared to hit me at once, and no two of them in the same place. In the next instant the entire tribe was upon me. They tore all the clothes off me, they broke my arms and legs, they gave me a thump that dented the top of my head till it would hold coffee like a saucer; and to crown their disgraceful proceedings and add insult to injury, they threw me over the Horseshoe Fall and I got wet.

About ninety or a hundred feet from the top, the remains of my vest caught on a projecting rock and I was almost drowned before I could get loose. I finally fell, and brought up in a world of white foam at the foot of the Fall, whose celled and bubbly masses towered up several inches above my head. Of course I got into the eddy. I sailed round and round in it forty-four times—chasing a chip and gaining on it—each round trip a half a mile—reaching for the same bush on the bank forty-four times, and just exactly missing it by a hair's-breadth every time. At last a man walked down and sat down close to that bush, and put a pipe in his mouth, and lit a match, and followed me with one eye and kept the other on the match while he sheltered it in his hands from the wind. Presently a puff of wind blew it out. The next time I swept around he said:

"Got a match?"

"Yes—in my other vest. Help me out, please."

"Not for Joe."

When I came around again I said:

"Excuse the seemingly impertinent curiosity of a drowning man, but will you explain this singular conduct of yours?"

"With pleasure. I am the Coroner. Don't hurry on my account. I can wait for you. But I wish I had a match."

I said: "Take my place and I'll go and get you one."

He declined. This lack of confidence on his part created a coolness between us, and from that time forward I avoided him. It was my idea, in case anything happened to me, to so time the occurrence as to throw my custom into the hands of the opposition coroner over on the American side. At last a policeman came along and arrested me for disturbing the peace by yelling at people on the shore for help. The Judge fined me, but I had the advantage of him. My money was with my pantaloons, and my pantaloons were with the Indians.

Thus I escaped. I am now lying in a very critical condition. At least I am lying, anyway—critical or not critical.

I am hurt all over, but I cannot tell the full extent yet, because the doctor is not done taking the inventory. He will make out my manifest this evening. However, thus far he thinks only six of my wounds are fatal. I don't mind the others.

Upon regaining my right mind, I said:

"It is an awfully savage tribe of Indians that do the bead work and moccasins for Niagara Falls, doctor. Where are they from?"

"Limerick, my son."

I shall not be able to finish my remarks about Niagara Falls until I get better.—*Mark Twain*

Uncriminal Victims

If the proposed International Convention for the purpose of applying the humanities to prison discipline throughout the world ever meets—and it promises fairly enough at the present moment to do it—there is one item which it ought to take hold of and never let go till a reform in it is achieved. It is the imprisoning in noisome dungeons of men who are accused of no crime, but whose ruinous misfortune it has been to see other men break the law—innocent poor wretches whose ability to protect society, by bearing witness against criminals, procures imprisonment and suffering for themselves, instead of honor and compensation. We have seen the entire crew of a great clipper ship, young boys and all, kept in close confinement in a hideous jail for two months, simply that they might be on hand and ready to testify concerning a murder of which the chief mate was accused. And these people, guiltless of any wrong, came into court at last, listless, hollow-eyed, and tottering with weakness and disease, their spirits sapped of the zest of life and their untutored hearts filled with a hatred of a civilization that inflicts such devilish hardships in the interest of "justice." Many a witness thus restrained of his liberty has lost his health permanently, and some their lives, in consequence of the sufferings they had to undergo. The reason why the newspapers and pulpits and rostrums are not rampant with indignation against this system, is that it is only necessary to apply it to persons in the humblest walks of life, and therefore it is not brought vividly to the notice of those ranks of society that are able to reform evils. But suppose such a telegram as this should flash abroad over the land in all the newspapers:

> "Commodore Vanderbilt,[15] being a witness in the great criminal case of *The People agt. William Brown,* was imprisoned in the county jail two months ago, in accordance with law and custom, to await the sitting of the court. This long confinement in a dark and filthy cell, with its accompaniments of poisoned air, badly cooked food, etc., has resulted in the permanent impairing of the witness' health. His rags are alive with vermin, his body covered with malignant sores, and his mind half crazed by a blank inactivity to which it had never before been accustomed."

This would bring the injustice of the thing to the appreciation of the public in a striking manner, and a needed reform would quickly ensue. A trial should be made of it at once. All men would see at a glance that since the Commodore had not committed any crime, it could be only fair that his quarters should be made as clean and comfortable as possible and as much liberty and exercise allowed him as security against his escape would permit. In this country we have a pleasant fiction that we are all equal—that we are all Vanderbilts, or all common sailors, just as you choose—and therefore it is just that when we restrain a sailor witness of his liberty, we should look to it that he suffers as little from it as we would allow the Commodore to suffer. A Chicago paper records a remark of a prisoner in one of her loathsome dungeons which sounds touchingly enough, coming out of the darkness through the bars of such a purgatory:

> "I'se a witness. They put me in prison to keep me till a trial comes on; but they lets me walk about this floor through the day, and they don't lock the door on me when it comes night, but I'se a prisoner just as much as if I'd stole sumthin'."

Unquestionably the great international prison convention would do a worthy thing if it brought this system into such prominent notice as to compel the adoption of clean, airy and comfortable prisons for witness-captives throughout the world. *[Unsigned]*

August 24, 1869

The Byron Scandal

Mrs. Stowe's revelation of the horrible secret confided to her some years ago by Lady Byron is meeting with extensive condemnation and severe criticism. We are surprised at the generally angry tone in which it is discussed, failing to see much fairness or cool judgment exhibited anywhere in the strictures of those who make haste to resent the damning imputation cast upon Lord Byron's memory. To some, who cherish an ancient political grudge against the author of "Uncle Tom's Cabin" there seems to be a sufficient reason for savagely denouncing the story in the fact that it comes from Mrs. Stowe, whom they improve the occasion to abuse. In the minds of many more, a merely sentimental tenderness—the lingering remains of that fervid poetical and romantic passion which used to be kindled to burning in the susceptible hearts of young men and women by Byron's verse—is so painfully vexed by this terrible accusation brought against the poet that it flashes out a fierce retort without waiting for reason or consideration.

That there should be so much of this weak sentiment still left among the bad influences of Byron's poetry, to resist the exercise of a candid and just judgment concerning his life and character, is not a little surprising. Why should there be any eagerness to discredit and resent the revelation, which comes from the grave of Byron's wife? It may not be true; but the probabilities are, ten to one, that it is. Looked at coolly and critically, there is no denying that the reasons for believing it very greatly outweigh the reasons for doubting it. In what the world knows of Lord Byron, there is nothing to render the story intrinsically improbable. He was a bad man; as bad perhaps, as a man with a great intellect, a passionate animal nature, intense egotism and selfishness and little or no moral principle to restrain or govern either of these, could be. If it is possible for any human being to be guilty of licentiousness so unnatural and monstrous as that charged in Lady Byron's disclosure to Mrs. Stowe, why was it not possible in the case of this man, whose licentious depravity we know! If there is incredibility anywhere, it is in the supposition that any man could commit the crime in question. But it has been committed time and again. History furnishes examples enough, to say nothing of the current experience of society, and it is quite as possible that Byron may have added one to the horrid examples of unnatural vice in history as it is undoubted that other men of noted name and distinguished position did so before him.

The fact that he was a brilliant poet does not argue that he possessed a nature too refined for this foulness or depravity. The alliance of a poetical imagination and a subtle intellect with an animal constitution grossly sensual has been no uncommon thing, and Byron furnished as conspicuous an instance of it as the world ever had for its study. The beautiful and the bestial are at struggle with each other all through his writings, and the bestial so often mastered his pen that we cannot with reason refuse to believe, on good evidence, that it may have mastered the man even to the extent of this abhorrent crime.

So much for the intrinsic probability or improbability of the story of Lady Byron. And now as to the credibility of the testimony on which it rests. That Lady Byron was a woman, not only of remarkable loveliness, both in person and disposition, but of remarkable mental gifts, is a fact so established by the witnessing of all who ever knew her that it is certainly more difficult not to believe her statement in a case like this than to believe it. The evidence as to her sweetness of temper, her charitableness and her womanliness, are all against the supposition that she would wantonly invent or madly take up such a hideous tale against her husband, and with the reckless malice of a fiend disseminate it to blast his name. The evidence as to her fine intelligence is likewise all against the supposition that she could have been persuaded of its truth without sufficing proof. So far, therefore, as concerns the testimony on which her story rests, the probability is most decidedly in its favor; while in the story there is no such intrinsic improbability as makes it impossible of belief. We can more reasonably believe that Lord Byron was in one act of his vicious life a licentious beast, than we can believe that Lady Byron either malignantly lied, or recklessly, at the end of forty years' concealment, permitted the revelation of so monstrous a thing without knowing it to be true.

As for Mrs. Stowe's part in this disclosure, the only reasonable thing that can be said in criticism of her published narrative is that it is not satisfactorily nor skilfully written. Receiving the facts as she did, in the manner she did, from Lady Byron, it was her duty to make them public, especially since the publication of the memoir of Byron's most notorious mistress with its impudent slander of his wife. But she ought to have presented them, and must yet give them, more fully and satisfactorily. *[Unsigned]*

August 25, 1869

[A Fine Old Man]

John Wagner, the oldest man in Buffalo—104 years—recently walked a mile and a half in two weeks.[16] He is as cheerful and bright as any of these other old men that charge around so in the newspapers, and is in every way as remarkable. Last November he walked five blocks in a rain storm without any shelter but an umbrella, and cast his vote for Grant, remarking that he had voted for forty-seven Presidents—which was a lie. His "second crop of rich brown hair" arrived from New York yesterday, and he has a new set of teeth coming—from Philadelphia. He is to be married next week to a girl 102 years old, who still takes in washing. They have been engaged 89 years, but their parents persistently refused their consent until three days ago. John Wagner is two years older than the Rhode Island veteran, and yet has never tasted a drop of liquor in his life, unless you count whisky. *[Unsigned]*

August 26, 1869

Only a Nigger

A dispatch from Memphis mentions that, of two negroes lately sentenced to death for murder in that vicinity, one named Woods has just confessed to having ravished a young lady during the war, for which deed another negro was hung at the time by an avenging mob, the evidence that doomed the guiltless wretch being a hat which Woods now relates that he stole from its owner and left behind, for the purpose of misleading.[17] Ah, well! Too bad, to be sure! A little blunder in the administration of justice by Southern mob-law; but nothing to speak of. Only "a nigger" killed by mistake—that is all. Of course, every high toned gentleman whose chivalric impulses were so unfortunately misled in this affair, by the cunning of the miscreant Woods, is as sorry about it as a high toned gentleman can be expected to be sorry about the unlucky fate of "a nigger." But mistakes will happen, even in the conduct of the best regulated and most high toned mobs, and surely there is no good reason why Southern gentlemen should worry themselves with useless regrets, so long as only an innocent "nigger" is hanged, or roasted or knouted to death, now and then. What if the blunder of lynching the wrong man does happen once in four or five cases! Is that any fair argument against the cultivation and indulgence of those fine chivalric passions and that noble Southern spirit which will not brook the slow and cold formalities of regular law, when outraged white womanhood appeals for vengeance? Perish the thought so unworthy of a Southern soul! Leave it to the sentimentalism and humanitarianism of a cold-blooded Yankee civilization! What are the lives of a few "niggers" in comparison with the preservation of the impetuous instincts of a proud and fiery race? Keep ready the halter, therefore, oh chivalry of Memphis! Keep the lash knotted; keep the brand and the faggots in waiting, for prompt work with the next "nigger" who may be suspected of any damnable crime! Wreak a swift vengeance upon him, for the satisfaction of the noble impulses that animate knightly hearts, and then leave time and accident to discover, if they will, whether he was guilty or no. *[Unsigned]*

English Festivities.
And Minor Matters. Fishing

But seriously, (for it is well to be serious occasionally), Niagara Falls is a most enjoyable place of resort. The hotels are excellent and the prices not at all exorbitant. The opportunities for fishing are not surpassed in the country. In fact they are not even equalled elsewhere. Because in other localities certain places in the streams are much better than others, but at Niagara one place is just as good as another, for the reason that the fish do not bite anywhere, and so there is no use in your walking five miles to fish when you can depend on being just as unsuccessful nearer home. The advantages of this state of things have never heretofore been properly placed before the public.

GUIDES, PHOTOGRAPHERS AND SUCH

The weather is cool in Summer, and the walks and drives are all pleasant and none of them fatiguing. When you start out to "do" the Falls you first drive down about a mile and pay a small sum for the privilege of looking down from a precipice into the narrowest part of the Niagara river. A railway "cut" through a hill would be as comely if it had the angry river tumbling and foaming through its bottom. You can descend a staircase here, a hundred and fifty feet down, and stand at the edge of the water. After you have done it, you will wonder why you did it, but it will then be too late. The guide will explain to you, in his blood-curdling way, how he saw the little steamer, Maid of the Mist, descend the fearful rapids—how first one paddle-box was out of sight behind the raging billows, and then the other, and at what point it was that her smokestack toppled overboard, and where her planking began to break and part asunder, and how she did finally live through the trip, after accomplishing the incredible feat of traveling seventeen miles in six minutes, or six miles in seventeen minutes, I have really forgotten which. But it was very extraordinary, anyhow. It is worth the price of admission to hear the guide tell the story nine times in succession to different parties, and never miss a word or alter a sentence or a gesture.

Then you drive over the Suspension bridge and divide your misery between the chances of smashing down two hundred feet into the river below, and the chances of having the railway train overhead smashing down on to you. Either possibility is discomforting, taken by itself—but mixed together they amount in the aggregate to positive unhappiness. On the Canada side you drive along the chasm between long ranks of photographers standing guard behind their cameras, ready to make an ostentatious frontispiece of you and your decaying ambulance and your solemn crate with a hide on it which you are expected to regard in the light of a horse, and a diminished and unimportant background of sublime Niagara—and a great many people *have* the ineffable effrontery or the native depravity to aid and abet this sort of crime. Any day, in the hands of these photographers you may see stately pictures of papa, and mamma, and Johnny, and Bub, and Sis, or a couple of country cousins, all smiling hideously, and all disposed in studied and uncomfortable attitudes in their carriage, and all looming up in their grand and awe-inspiring imbecility before the snubbed and diminished presentment of that majestic presence whose ministering spirits are the rainbows, whose voice is the thunder, whose awful front is veiled in clouds—who was monarch here dead and forgotten ages before this hack-full of small reptiles was deemed temporarily necessary to fill a crack in the world's unnoted myriads, and will still be monarch here ages and decades of ages after they shall have gathered themselves to their blood relations the other worms and been mingled with the unremembering dust. There is no actual harm in making Niagara a background whereon to display one's marvelous insignificance in a good strong light, but it requires a sort of superhuman self-complacency to enable one to do it.

Further along they show you where that adventurous ass, Blondin,[18] crossed the Niagara river, with his wheelbarrow on a tightrope, but the satisfaction of it is marred by the reflection that he did not break his neck.

A DISMAL EXPERIENCE

When you have examined the stupendous Horse Shoe Fall till you are satisfied you cannot improve on it, you return to America by the new suspension bridge, and follow up the bank to where they exhibit

the Cave of the Winds. Here I followed instructions and divested myself of all my clothing and put on a water-proof jacket and overalls.
This costume is picturesque, but not beautiful. A guide similarly
dressed led the way down a fight of winding stairs which wound and
wound, and still kept on winding long after the thing ceased to be a
novelty, and then terminated long before it had begun to be a pleasure. We were then well down under the precipice, but still considerably above the level of the river. We now began to creep along flimsy
bridges of a single plank, our persons shielded from perdition by a
crazy wooden railing, to which I clung with both hands—not because I
was afraid, but because I wanted to. Presently the descent became
steeper and the bridge flimsier, and sprays from the American Fall began to rain down on us in fast-increasing sheets that soon became
blinding, and after that our progress was mostly in the nature of groping. Now a furious wind began to rush out from behind the waterfall,
which seemed determined to sweep us from the bridge and scatter us
on the rocks and among the torrents below. I remarked that I wanted
to go home. But it was too late. We were almost under the monstrous
wall of water thundering down from above, and speech was vain in
the midst of such a pitiless crash of sound. In another moment the
guide disappeared behind the grand deluge, and, bewildered by the
thunder, driven helplessly by the wind, and smitten by the arrowy
tempest of rain, I followed. All was darkness. Such a mad storming,
roaring and bellowing of warring wind and water never crazed my
ears before. I bent my head and seemed to receive the Atlantic on my
back. The world seemed going to destruction. I could not see anything,
the flood poured down so savagely. I raised my head, with open
mouth, and the most of the American cataract went down my throat.
If I had sprung a leak now, I had been lost. And at this moment I discovered that the bridge had ceased, and we must trust for a foot-hold
to the slippery and precipitous rocks. I never was so scared before and
survived it. But we got through at last, and emerged into the open
day where we could stand in front of the laced and frothy and
seething world of descending water and look at it. When I saw how
much of it there was, and how fearfully in earnest it was, I was sorry I
had gone behind it.

I said to the guide:

"Son, did you know what kind of an infernal place this was before
you brought me down here?"

"Yes."

This was sufficient. He had known all the horror of the place, and yet he brought me there. I regarded it as deliberate arson. I then destroyed him.

ENGLISH FESTIVITIES

I managed to find my way back alone to the place from whence I had started on this foolish enterprise, and then hurried over to Canada to avoid having to pay for the guide. At the principal hotel I fell in with the Major of the Forty-Second Fusileers and a dozen other hearty and hospitable Englishmen, and they invited me to join them in celebrating the Queen's[19] birth-day. I said I would be delighted to do it. I said I liked all the Englishmen I had ever happened to be acquainted with, and that I, like all my countrymen, admired and honored the Queen. But I said there was one insuperable drawback—I never drank anything strong upon any occasion whatever, and I did not see how I was going to do proper and ample justice to anybody's birth-day with the thin and ungenerous beverages I was accustomed to. The Major scratched his head and thought over the matter at considerable length; but there seemed to be no way of mastering the difficulty, and he was too much of a gentleman to suggest even a temporary abandonment of my principles. But by-and-bye he said:

"I have it. Drink soda water. As long as you never do drink anything more nutritious there isn't any impropriety in it."

And so it was settled. We met in a large parlor handsomely decorated with flags and evergreens, and seated ourselves at a board well laden with creature comforts, both solid and liquid. The toasts were happy and the speeches were good, and we kept it up until long after midnight. I never enjoyed myself more in my life. I drank thirty-eight bottles of soda-water. But do you know that that is not a reliable article for a steady drink? It is too gassy. When I got up in the morning I was full of gas and as tight as a balloon. I hadn't an article of clothing that I could wear except my umbrella.

After breakfast I found the Major making grand preparations again. I asked what it was for, and he said this was the Prince of Wales's[20] birth-day. It had to be celebrated that evening. We celebrated it. Much against my expectations, we had another splendid time. We kept it up till some time after midnight again. I was tired of soda, and so I changed off for lemonade. I drank several quarts. You may consider lemonade better for a steady drink than soda-water, but it isn't so. In the morning it had soured on my stomach. Biting anything was out of the question—it was equivalent to lock-jaw. I was beginning to feel worn and sad, too.

Shortly after luncheon I found the Major in the midst of some more preparations. He said this was the Princess Alice's[21] birth-day. I concealed my grief.

"Who is the Princess Alice?" I asked.

"Daughter of her Majesty the Queen," the Major said.

I succumbed. That night we celebrated the Princess Alice's birth-day. We kept it up as late as usual, and really I enjoyed it a good deal. But I could not stand lemonade. I drank a couple of kegs of ice water. In the morning I had tooth-ache, and cramps, and chilblains, and my teeth were on edge from the lemonade, and I was still pretty gassy. I found the inexorable Major at it again.

"Who is this for?" I asked.

"His Royal Highness, the Duke of Edinburgh,"[22] he said.

"Son of the Queen?"

"Yes."

"And this is his birth-day—you have'nt made any mistake?"

"No—the celebration comes off tonight."

I bowed before the new calamity. We celebrated the day. I drank part of a barrel of cider. Among the first objects that met my weary and jaundiced eye the next day was the Major, at his interminable preparations again. My heart was broken and I wept.

"Whom do we mourn this time?" I said.

"The Princess Beatrice,[23] daughter of the Queen."

"Here, now," I said, "It is time to begin to enquire into this thing. How long is the Queen's family likely to hold out? Who comes next on the list?

"Their Royal Highnesses Anne, Mary, Elizabeth, Gertrude, Augusta, William, Simon, Ferdinand, Irene, Sophia, Susannah, Socrates, Samson—"[24]

"Hold! There is a limit to human endurance. I am only mortal. What man dare do, I dare—but he who can celebrate this family in detail, and live to tell of it is less or more than a man. If you have to go through this every year, it is a mercy I was born in America, for I haven't constitution enough to be an Englishman. I shall have to withdraw from this enterprise. I am out of drinks. Out of drinks, and thirteen more to celebrate. Out of drinks, and only just on the outskirts of the family yet, as you may say. I am sorry enough to have to withdraw, but it is plain enough that it has to be done. I am full of gas and my teeth are loose, and I am wrenched with cramps, and afflicted with scurvy, and toothache, measles, mumps, and lock-jaw, and the cider last night has given me the cholera. Gentlemen, I mean well, but really I am not in a condition to celebrate the other thirteen. Give us a rest."

[I find, now, that it was all a dream. One avoids much dissipation by being asleep.]—*Mark Twain*

September 1, 1869

The Prodigal Son Returns

One hundred and sixty California pioneers have signified their intention of joining the proposed excursion East.[25] Invitations from Omaha, Chicago, Pittsburgh, Philadelphia and New York to entertain them, have been accepted. These gentlemen belong to an organization called the "Association of California Pioneers." The main qualification for membership is a residence in California in the "early days"—that is, before 1852. A man whose residence began after that time is not eligible — or was not, originally. The membership was very large, once, but death is thinning it faster and faster every year. They always follow a deceased brother to the grave in grand procession, and bury him with imposing ceremony. President Grant, Gen. Sherman, Gen. Sheridan, and many others among our distinguished men who sojourned on the Pacific coast twenty years ago, are honorary members of the Society, and are proud of it. Among those gray-haired and care-worn members who are shortly coming on this visit, will be dozens of men who saw "America" last when they were in the flush vigor of young manhood; when their step was quick and their eyes undimmed; when the future was a splendid prophecy and they yearned to go forth and seize upon its promises; when their spirits were proud and high and their hearts the home of dauntless courage; when all before them was an enchanted realm, whose curtaining mists should melt away and disclose palaces, temples and treasure houses, a faultless landscape and a cloudless sky. They have explored the mysteries that promised so much, and found disappointment. The romance of life has changed to hard reality long ago. Their dreams have been dissipated, their hopes have withered, and they are ready to retrace their steps now, and walk gravely and soberly over the ground that saw them in a different mood in those gallant days of their young crusade. What will home look like to these wanderers of twenty years? In the strong young men and women of to-day, how will they recognize the whimpering babies of 1849? How many times will they ask for remembered friends and be pointed to the churchyard? How vaguely remembered they will be themselves! How changed, how new and strange everything will seem, and how disappointed their old hearts will be! Their own dogs will bite them, if any remain still alive. These Pioneers are coming on a sorrowful pleasure-jaunt, the saddest pilgrimage they ever made.

The cities do well to feast them. They deserve well at the hands of their countrymen. They have built up a stately young empire out there under the sunset, and have not reaped full measure of benefit for themselves—for although the early pioneers made and lost fortunes every six months, the most of them ended by losing one fortune too many. *[Unsigned]*

September 4, 1869

The Byron Scandal

The Hartford *Post* closes an article in relation to Mrs. Stowe's article on Lord Byron in the September *Atlantic* with the following statement:[26]

"To this it is proper that we should add one or two statements that, so far as we know, have not appeared in print. When the advance sheets or the *Atlantic* paper were sent to Mr. MacMillan, the London publisher, he read them and promptly decided to print them in his magazine. The story was not unknown in England. And we may further remark that considering his position in English society, and his own interests, he would not have been likely to have published the paper if he had not had reason to think it well founded. This, of course, is only inferred, for even English publishers are not always above an inclination to sensational publications."

But another statement is of more consequence. We have heard that a Chancery suit is now pending in the English Court which will throw light upon the alleged offspring of the alleged incestuous intercourse of Lord Byron and Augusta. If this shall turn out to be true, it will be the most important piece of evidence yet offered, and we shall look for its confirmation or disavowal with profound interest. *[Unsigned]*

The Byron Question

The appearance in print of the solicitors of Lady Byron's family,[27] with a communication condemning Mrs. Stowe's revelations, will impart a new impulse to the discussion of the Byron scandal, which has begun to drag a little. Mrs. Stowe must expect to find herself assailed with more virulent Byronic enthusiasm than ever. And yet, judging from what we learn of their communication by cable, the solicitors of Lady Byron's family inferentially confirm the truth of her story—so much so, indeed, as to leave no doubt whatever that they and the family for whom they speak know, or believe, the essential matter of these revelations to be a fact not susceptible of denial. They pronounce it to be "not a complete or authentic statement," and say that it "does not involve any direct evidence"—which is unquestionably the exact reverse of a contradiction. The necessary inference is, that it does not tell the whole story of Byron's crime in authentic detail, as it might be told, but that, so far as it does reveal, there is no denying the truth of it.

And really this is all that the world is concerned to know. Authentic details in a case of so revolting a nature are only hungered for by the prurient gossips and scandal mongers of society. But the question whether Lord Byron, so long the idol and poetical demi-god of a decent age, was or was not the most unspeakably infamous of wretches, is a question which all men and women who respect literature may feel a reasonable and just interest in having satisfactorily determined. What is more if Lord Byron was that beastly animal, whose lusts knew no commonly human restraint, the world, which has set his image in its pantheon, is entitled to know the fact; has suffered a gross imposition in the concealment and might with justice curse that person who had power to make the revelation and yet kept it hid.

These solicitors protest against Mrs. Stowe's disclosure as a "gross breach of trust." We prefer to believe that Mrs. Stowe is her own best judge of the obligations involved in what passed, in privacy and confidence, between her and Lady Byron. We decline to believe that she has violated aught that was honorable in the matter, as between herself and Byron's wife, while, assuming that she was honorably at liberty to make this disclosure public, in the exercise of her own discretion and judgment, there is no question that it was her duty to set it before the world. The public has its rights, in the treatment of such a hideous fact, along side of the consideration of which all talk of poets' memories and the sanctity of graves, family feelings and the scandal of persons, is pulling sentiment and frivolous rant. *[Unsigned]*

September 4, 1869

Journalism in Tennessee

The editor of the *Memphis Avalanche*[28] swoops thus mildly down upon a correspondent who posted him as a Radical:[29] "While he was writing the first word, the middle word, dotting his i's, crossing his t's, and punching his period, he knew he was concocting a sentence that was saturated with infamy and reeking with falsehood." — *Exchange.*[30]

I was told by the physician that a Southern climate would improve my health, and so I went down to Tennessee and got a berth on the *Morning Glory and Johnson County War-Whoop,* as associate editor. When I went on duty I found the chief editor sitting tilted back in a three-legged chair with his feet on a pine table. There was another pine table in the room, and another afflicted chair, and both were half buried under newspapers and scraps and sheets of manuscript. There was a wooden box of sand, sprinkled with cigar stubs and "old soldiers,"[31] and a stove with a door hanging by its upper hinge. The chief editor had a long-tailed black cloth frock coat on, and white linen pants. His boots were small and neatly blacked. He wore a ruffled shirt, a large seal ring, a standing collar of obsolete pattern and a checkered neckerchief with the ends hanging down. Date of costume, about 1848. He was smoking a cigar and trying to think of a word. And in trying to think of a word, and in pawing his hair for it, he had rumpled his locks a good deal. He was scowling fearfully, and I judged that he was concocting a particularly knotty editorial. He told me to take the exchanges and skim through them and write up the "Spirit of the Tennessee Press," condensing into the article all of their contents that seemed of interest.

I wrote as follows:

"SPIRIT OF THE TENNESSEE PRESS

"The editors of the *Semi-Weekly Earthquake* evidently labor under a misapprehension with regard to the Ballyhack railroad. It is not the object of the company to leave Buzzardville off to one side. On the contrary they consider it one of the most important points along the line, and consequently can have no desire to slight it. The gentlemen of the *Earthquake* will of course take pleasure in making the correction.

"John W. Blossom, Esq., the able editor of the Higginsville *Thunderbolt and Battle Cry of Freedom,* arrived in the city yesterday. He is stopping at the Van Buren House.

"We observe that our contemporary of the Mud Springs *Morning Howl* has fallen into the error of supposing that the election of Van Werter is not an established fact, but he will have discovered his mistake before this reminder reaches him, no doubt. He was doubtless misled by incomplete election returns.

"It is pleasant to note that the city of Blathersville is endeavoring to contract with some New York gentlemen to pave its well nigh impassable streets with the Nicholson pavement.[32] But it is difficult to accomplish a desire like this since Memphis got some New Yorkers to do a like service for her and then declined to pay for it. However the *Daily Hurrah* still urges the measure with ability, and seems confident of ultimate success.

"We are pained to learn that Col. Bascom, chief editor of the *Dying Shriek for Liberty,* fell in the street a few evenings since and broke his leg. He has lately been suffering with debility, caused by over-work and anxiety on account of sickness in his family, and it is supposed that he fainted from the exertion of walking too much in the sun."

I passed my manuscript over to the chief editor for acceptance, alteration or destruction. He glanced at it and his face clouded. He ran his eye down the pages, and his countenance grew portentous. It was easy to see that something was wrong. Presently he sprang up and said:

"Thunder and lightning! Do you suppose I am going to speak of those cattle that way? Do you suppose my subscribers are going to stand such gruel as that? Give me the pen!"

I never saw a pen scrape and scratch its way so viciously, or plough through another man's verbs and adjectives so relentlessly. While he was in the midst of his work somebody shot at him through the open window and marred the symmetry of his ear.

"Ah," said he, "that is that scoundrel Smith, of the *Moral Volcano* — he was due yesterday." And he snatched a navy revolver from his belt and fired. Smith dropped, shot in the thigh. The shot spoiled Smith's aim, who was just taking a second chance, and he crippled a stranger. It was me. Merely a finger shot off.

Then the chief editor went on with his erasures and interlineations. Just as he finished them a hand-grenade came down the stove pipe, and the explosion shivered the stove into a thousand fragments. However, it did no further damage, except that a vagrant piece knocked a couple of my teeth out.

"That stove is utterly ruined," said the chief editor.

I said I believed it was.

"Well, no matter—don't want it this kind of weather. I know the man that did it. I'll get him. Now *here* is the way this stuff ought to be written."

I took the manuscript. It was scarred with erasures and interlineations till its mother wouldn't have known it, if it had had one. It now read as follows:

"SPIRIT OF THE TENNESSEE PRESS

"The inveterate liars of the *Semi-Weekly Earthquake* are evidently endeavoring to palm off upon a noble and chivalrous people another of their vile and brutal falsehoods with regard to that most glorious conception of the nineteenth century, the Ballyhack railroad. The idea that Buzzardville was to be left off at one side originated in their own fulsome brains—or rather in the settlings which *they* regard as brains. They had better swallow this lie, and not stop to chew it, either, if they want to save their abandoned, reptile carcasses the cowhiding they so richly deserve.

"That ass, Blossom of the Higginsville *Thunderbolt and Battle-Cry of Freedom,* is down here again, bumming his board at the Van Buren.

"We observe that the besotted blackguard of the Mud Springs *Morning Howl* is giving out, with his usual propensity for lying, that Van Werter is not elected. The heaven-born mission of journalism is to disseminate truth—to eradicate error—to educate, refine and elevate the tone of public morals and manners, and make all men more gentle, more virtuous, more charitable, and in all ways better, and holier and happier—and yet this black-hearted villain, this hell-spawned miscreant, prostitutes his great office persistently to the dissemination of falsehood, calumny, vituperation and degrading vulgarity. His paper is notoriously unfit to take into the people's homes, and ought to be banished to the gambling hells and brothels where the mass of reeking pollution which does duty as its editor, lives and moves, and has his being.

"Blathersville wants a Nicholson pavement—it wants a jail and a poor-house more. The idea of a pavement in a one-horse town with two gin-mills and a blacksmith shop in it, and that mustard-plaster of a newspaper, the *Daily Hurrah!* Better borrow of Memphis, where the article is cheap. The crawling insect, Buckner, who edits the *Hurrah*, is braying about this pavement business with his customary loud-mouthed imbecility, and imagining that he is talking sense. Such foul, mephitic scum as this verminous Buckner, are a disgrace to journalism.

"That degraded ruffian, Bascom, of the *Dying Shriek for Liberty,* fell down and broke his leg yesterday—pity it wasn't his neck. He says it was 'debility caused by overwork and anxiety!' It was debility caused by trying to lug six gallons of forty-rod whiskey[33] around town when his hide is only gauged for four, and anxiety about where he was going to bum another six. He 'fainted from the exertion of walking too much in the sun!' And well he might say that—but if he would walk *straight* he would get just as far and not have to walk half as much. For years the pure air of this town has been rendered perilous by the deadly breath of this perambulating pestilence, this pulpy bloat, this steaming, animated tank of mendacity, gin and profanity, this Bascom! Perish all such from out the sacred and majestic mission of journalism!"

"Now *that* is the way to write—peppery and to the point. Mush-and-milk journalism gives me the fan-tods."

About this time a brick came through the window with a splintering crash, and gave me considerable of a jolt in the middle of the back. I moved out of range—I began to feel in the way. The chief said:

"That was the Colonel, likely. I've been expecting him for two days. He will be up, now, right away."

He was correct. The "Colonel" appeared in the door a moment afterward, with a dragoon revolver in his hand. He said:

"Sir, have I the honor of addressing the white-livered poltroon who edits this mangy sheet?"

"You have—be seated, Sir—be careful of the chair, one of the legs is gone. I believe I have the pleasure of addressing the blatant, black-hearted scoundrel, Col. Blatherskite Tecumseh?"

"The same. I have a little account to settle with you. If you are at leisure, we will begin."

"I have an article on the 'Encouraging Progress of Moral and Intellectual Development in America' to finish, but there is no hurry. Begin."

Both pistols rang out their fierce clamor at the same instant. The chief lost a lock of hair, and the Colonel's bullet ended its career in the fleshy part of my thigh. The Colonel's left shoulder was clipped a little. They fired again. Both missed their men this time, but I got my share, a shot in the arm. At the third fire both gentlemen were wounded slightly, and I had a knuckle chipped. I then said I believed I would go out and take a walk, as this was a private matter and I had a delicacy about participating in it further. But both gentlemen begged me to keep my seat and assured me that I was not in the way. I had thought differently, up to this time.

They then talked about the elections and the crops a while, and I fell to tieing up my wounds. But presently they opened fire again with animation, and every shot took effect—but it is proper to remark that five out of the six fell to my share. The sixth one mortally wounded the Colonel, who remarked, with fine humor, that he would have to say good morning, now, as he had business up town. He then inquired the way to the undertaker's and left. The chief turned to me and said:

"I am expecting company to dinner and shall have to get ready. It will be a *favor* to me if you will read proof and attend to the customers."

I winced a little at the idea of attending to the customers, but I was too bewildered by the fusillade that was still ringing in my ears to think of anything to say. He continued:

"Jones will be here at 3. Cowhide him. Gillespie will call earlier, perhaps—throw him out of the window. Ferguson will be along about 4—kill him. That is all for to-day, I believe. If you have any odd time, you may write a blistering article on the police—give the Chief Inspector rats. The cowhides are under the table; weapons in the drawer—ammunition there in the corner—lint and bandages up there in the pigeon-holes. In case of accident, go to Lancet, the surgeon, down stairs. He advertises—we take it out in trade."

He was gone. I shuddered. At the end of the next three hours I had been through perils so awful that all peace of mind and all cheerfulness had gone from me. Gillespie had called, and thrown *me* out of the window. Jones arrived promptly, and when I got ready to do the cowhiding, he took the job off my hands. In an encounter with a stranger, not in the bill of fare, I had lost my scalp. Another stranger, by the name of Thompson, left me a mere wreck and ruin of chaotic rags. And at last, at bay in the corner, and beset by an infuriated mob of editors, blacklegs, politicians and desperadoes, who raved and swore and flourished their weapons about my head till the air shimmered with glancing flashes of steel, I was in the act of resigning my berth on the paper when the chief arrived, and with him a rabble of charmed and enthusiastic friends. Then ensued a scene of riot and carnage such as no human pen, or steel one either, could describe. People were shot, probed, dismembered, blown up, thrown out of the window. There was a brief tornado of murky blasphemy, with a confused and frantic war-dance glimmering through it, and then all was over. In five minutes there was silence, and the gory chief and I sat alone and surveyed the sanguinary ruin that strewed the floor around us. He said:

"You'll like this place when you get used to it." I said:

"I'll have to get you to excuse me. I think maybe I might write to suit you, after a while, as soon as I had had some practice and learned the language—I am confident I could. But to speak the plain truth, that sort of energy of expression has its inconveniences, and a man is liable to interruption. You see that, yourself. Vigorous writing is calculated to elevate the public, no doubt, but then I do not like to attract so much attention as it calls forth. I can't write with comfort when I am interrupted so much as I have been to-day. I like this berth well enough, but I don't like to be left here to wait on the customers. The experiences are novel, I grant you, and entertaining, too, after a fashion, but they are not judiciously distributed. A gentleman shoots at you, through the window, and cripples *me;* a bomb-shell comes down the stove-pipe for your gratification, and sends the stove door down *my* throat; a friend drops in to swap compliments with you, and freckles *me* with bullet holes till my skin won't hold my principles; you go to dinner, and Jones comes with his cowhide, Gillespie throws me out of the window, Thompson tears all my clothes off, and an entire stranger takes my scalp with the easy freedom of an old acquaintance; and in less than five minutes all the blackguards in the country arrive in their war paint and proceed to scare the rest of me to death with their tomahawks. Take it all together, I never have had such a spirited time in all my life as I have had to-day. No. I like you, and I like your calm, unruffled way of explaining things to the customers, but you see I am not used to it. The Southern heart is too impulsive — Southern hospitality is too lavish with the stranger. The paragraphs which I have written to-day, and into whose cold sentences your masterly hand has infused the fervent spirit of Tennesseean journalism, will wake up another nest of hornets. All that mob of editors will come—and they will come hungry, too, and want somebody for break-

fast. I shall have to bid you adieu. I decline to be present at these festivities. I came South for my health—I will go back on the same errand, and suddenly. Tennessee journalism is too stirring for me." After
which, we parted, with mutual regret, and I took apartments at the
hospital.—*Mark Twain*

September 7, 1869

More Byron Scandal

Mrs. Stowe's brother, Rev. Thomas K. Beecher,[34] of Elmira, who
furnishes a column of miscellany every Friday for the *Advertiser,* offers a timely word of wisdom to a popular correspondent of the Elmira
Review, a weekly literary journal, the occasion being the correspondent's published views concerning the Byron scandal. What Mr.
Beecher says to "Ishmael"[35] will apply equally well to many another
writer in the country who has deemed the flinging of inelegant personalities at Mrs. Stowe legitimate "argument," where materials for
refuting her testimony were not to be had:

A FEW WORDS TO ISHMAEL

Mrs. Stowe has erred in judgment, so we think, in re-opening the
Byron scandal. But does such an error justify such words as these?

"The aching desire that some people have for notoriety, to be talked
about, even to be cursed rather than not to be noticed at all, can be
the only possible excuse that I can imagine for this woman to lug into
view family secrets in which the world can find nothing but the nasti-
est interest. The result she *pretends* to aim at, is to clear up the life
and character of Lady Byron, and to tell to mankind the other side of
a story, neither view of which should ever have been known outside of
a criminal court."—*Saturday Eve. Review*

When Ishmael has lived a few more years and attained the great
fame which his talent promises to win for him, he will then be able to
understand that Mrs. Stowe may possibly obey other and higher motives than desire for notoriety. Meanwhile, he will permit us to say
that it is not graceful in him, nor will it prove advantageous to his
reputation in the long run, to assail the motives or challenge the sincerity of one who is, as yet, so much his senior in age and superior in

literary and christian reputation as Mrs. Stowe. Such words as the following are in bad taste:

"Mrs. Harriet Beecher Stowe, she who set the world a-sniveling over an imaginary Eva and an impossible darky."

It is a pity that a man should write such coarse words of discourtesy, who is able to conceive and express shortly after, such excellent wisdom as is found in the following apothegms:

"The common understanding is incapable of choosing correctly—it must be led." True, very true. "The right way must be pointed out and followers will come in plenty." True again. Followers will come, too, if the wrong way be pointed out. "That man stands best in the respect of the world who says what he thinks under all circumstances." Not quite. The world would respect Ishmael a little more if he would hide some of his thoughts, and we can name four or five men in this city who would be more respected if they concealed their obscenity and blasphemy, which they cannot help thinking, mayhap. But Ishmael writes well. *[Unsigned]*

September 9, 1869

G Butler on the Byron Scandal

en. B.F. Butler[36] is out, in the Boston *Journal,* with a long and elaborate *legal* argument against Mrs. Stowe's "True Story." Coming from so shrewd a lawyer, it could not be otherwise than searching and ingenious. He presents no new matter, but simply attempts to show that Mrs. Stowe's evidence, viewed from a lawyer's standpoint, is insufficient to convict. He places Mrs. Stowe in the witness box and cross-questions her. The "True Story" has been subjected to all the other tests known to literature, and in them all, sentiment, charity toward the dead, personal abuse of the author of the "Story," and other outside helps, have been brought to bear to make out each writer's case—and now comes the final one, the purely *legal* test, with its chilly, matter-of-fact analysis of tender episodes, its pitiless dissection of pathetic tradition, its bland indifference to poetry and sentiment, and its unfeeling subpoenaing of romantic conjecture and gushing theory to come into court and be sworn. It is delicious to note with what serene satisfaction, judicial gravity and toothsome relish, this old lawyer-surgeon sits down to his work with the "True Story's" stark body before him and a mind all made up to flay it, carve it and scrape the skeleton. The legal view was the only one left untried, and surely it ought to close the examination.

The General opens with the observation that "nowhere with more precision than in the courts of justice have rules been established by which the truth of any narration of fact can be investigated." And therefore since those same rules are about alike in all countries, it is fair to presume that they are the best tests which can be applied to any statement. Voltaire says that the "balancing of probabilities is the science of the judges." The General then states what two or three of the judicial rules are, and proposes to apply them to the investigation of Mrs. Stowe's and Lady Byron's evidence. The rules are:

First: Evidence proving a very improbable position must be accurate, credible and conclusive, in as great degree as is the improbability of the fact to be established. To illustrate: Facts that are usual and of ordinary and daily occurrence, such as giving notice of the dishonor of a bill of exchange to an indorser or drawer, are sufficiently proved by the slightest presumptive evidence. But grave or solemn facts, or those involving abnormal conditions, either of mind or conduct, require the highest degree of proof to establish them. Specially is this the case when the party asserting the fact has in any way deprived the person denying it of any evidence in his favor, or there exists any motive, personal or pecuniary, for falsification or mistake.

Secondly: Such has been found to be the temptations arising out of the domestic relations to pervert and distort oral communications, that courts do not allow husbands and wives to give the private conversations between themselves as evidence of the facts therein asserted as against each other. And this is a rule of almost inflexible public policy.

Again, it has usually been held in the courts that a chain of circumstances where each link can of itself be fully ascertained and understood, may be more conclusive presumptive evidence of the fact to which it leads than the memory or relation of fact by any single witness, however otherwise credible. In other words, that it is more consonant with human experience to find error or perversity in the conscience, or mistake in the memory of man, than in the reliance which may be placed upon a chain of presumptive proof.

Then the General says:

"A cursory examination of Mrs. Stowe's article shows that it contravenes all of these as well as every other rule of evidence. It is the

story of the wife—admittedly justly aggrieved by the gross misconduct of the husband in other respects—consisting largely of conversations with the husband, narrated more than fifty years after the
events, and retold thirteen years after the telling of the tale, of a most
improbable and almost incredible fact of horrible outrage upon herself
and society, affecting deeply the rights and feelings of other and innocent persons; unsupported by any other evidence; told confessedly for
her own self-vindication, while confessing that the wife had caused
the memoirs of her husband, wherein his side of the story had been
told, to be destroyed more than a quarter of a century previously; and
herself had waited until every mouth had been closed in death who
could, as living witnesses, controvert the statement.

"Contradicted, it will be seen, by every other circumstance of the
lives of the persons—Lord Byron and his sister—to be affected by it,
the "True Story of Lady Byron's Life," as related by Mrs. Stowe, illus-
trates more forcibly the reason and good sense of the rules of evidence, than any case that may ever be tried in a court of justice, and
is equally suggestive as to the danger of taking the story of the
wrongs of domestic life solely from the lips of one of the parties."

The General then makes this threat at Lady Byron's "motive" for
making her disclosure to Mrs. Stowe—a motive which he considers
puerile:

"How could Lady Byron or her advisers believe that the interest of
the masses of the people of England in the cheap edition of Lord Byron's poems would be diminished by the publication of the fact by his
wife that he had been guilty of incest with his only sister and that the
wife had assented to that intimacy by living with him during quite
their whole married life until she was driven away? Nor is it explained how it was supposed that this disclosure was to go hand in
hand with the cheap edition to the people of England. Was it to be put
up by the publishers as an advertisement to that cheap edition?"

Next, the General remarks that five years after Byron's separation
from his wife Lord B. wrote to a friend to send him, along with some
other books, a Bible, and remarks casually, that he has one, but as it
was his sister's last gift to him, he wishes to use it carefully. And the
General desires to know if an incestuous sister would be likely to
make such a book her latest gift to the partner of her guilt?

And next the General observes that with the "memorandum with
dates affixed" before her, given her by Lady Byron, Mrs. Stowe *twice*
refers to the marriage having existed *two* years, when all men know it

was only *one*. And he scouts the idea that Lady B.'s memory could have ever grown defective on this point, for the sting of one of Byron's epigrams was bound to rankle there and keep her recollections clear while she lived—to wit:

TO PENELOPE

This day, of all our days, has done
The worse for me and you:
'Tis just six years since we were *one*
And *five* since we were *two*.

In this connection the General says it is a legal maxim that a mistake or a mis-statement in one particular of the evidence, casts doubt upon the whole of it.

The General doubts that Byron ever said, in the carriage, that Lady B. would find she had "married a devil." He says it was not possible for this remark, (or one similar to it,) to become public at that time (as it did,) except through the lady's maid, who was the third party in the carriage and not a friend to Byron. The General thinks her evidence would not answer in the courts.

Mrs. Stowe avers that the incestuous intercourse had had a year's existence when Byron's marriage took place. Yet, the General remarks, Byron took his new wife to visit his sister and her husband for a matter of 17 days—and he don't think *that* was a likely thing for a man to do under such circumstances.

The General says Byron's sister was 31 years of age, the mother of children and the honored and respected occupant of an exalted place in society—and therefore the General considers that these facts weigh strongly against the plausibility of the charge of incest brought against her.

The General notes the fact that Lady Byron did not hesitate to expose other people less guilty than she believed her sister-in-law to be—for she discovered letters proving an improper intimacy between Lord Byron and a married lady, and she promptly forwarded these to the injured husband. The General inquires why she spared her sister-in-law?

Next the General throws cold water on Augusta's "child of sin," and wishes to know if it would not have been more natural for Augusta to lump it with her other children and let her husband stand for its father, than to put herself and her brother into Lady Byron's power by

giving the child into Lady B.'s keeping and disclosing the dreadful secret of its parentage? And, above all, he wishes to know why Mrs.
Stowe does not speak out plainly and state whether she means to say
that the "child of sin" was Augusta's or not? Finally, the General
wishes to know if it could be possible that Byron should write letters
demanding reasons for his wife's desertion "when he had driven her
away for a deadly guilty reason which he know too well of?"

The General closes as follows:

"That correspondence Byron desired to have published, and put it
into the hands of his publishers for that purpose after his death. That
correspondence Lady Byron caused to be destroyed, so far as he was
concerned. She had, it is to be presumed, on her part at least, his letters to her at the time of her consultation with Mrs. Stowe. Did she
show those letters to Mrs. Stowe? They would have been the most
valuable "memoranda with the dates affixed," to throw light upon this
question. Do those letters exist now in the hands of her executor or
friends? If so, it is due to the memory of her child's father, it is due to
literature—nay, to religion and to the world—that those letters
should be published and the truth made known. If the correspondence
is of a character like that stated by Lord Byron, it is entirely and totally incompatible with this late statement of his wife. True, it is said
that she stated to Dr. Lushington, her lawyer, that which surprised
and shocked him; and he says that after that statement he could not
have advised a coming together of the parties. But it must be remembered that her mother had gone down to consult Dr. Lushington on
the theory of insanity, one which Lushington found, upon personal examination, to be false. Then, Lady Byron says, she herself went and
made a statement, which, Dr. Lushington said, convinced him that
they could not live in harmony any more, and he would have nothing
to do with trying to effect it. Was that statement incest? Lady Byron
nowhere says that it was. Copies of the letters which she took from
Byron's desk, showing his intrigue with a married woman, would
have been sufficient to convince Dr. Lushington that the parties had
better separate, one would think. But without the necessity of believing that, she accused, to him, a noble lady of incest. Lady Byron further says in her statement that she had never communicated to her
parents the facts upon which she grounded the separation. Miss Martineau[37] is made to say by Mrs. Stowe the same thing in behalf of
Lady Byron. May we not inquire why a secret so deadly that the wife
kept it from her father and mother during all the years of her life,

was a proper one to be disclosed to a lawyer only, or to the world through the columns of an American magazine?"

Upon review of the whole matter, in the light of all the evidence of contemporary facts, of the suppression of the documentary evidence by the wife, of the extraordinary manner in which this story is given to the public, is it not more consonant with human reason to conclude that the story of Lord Byron, if we have it correctly detailed to us, was a delusion or mistake, that this horrible crime in two persons has been committed, and remained unrevealed, except to a select few until this day? We may admit that Lady Byron herself believed this story. We may admit, without scruple, that Mrs. Stowe believes it; but Lady Byron may have believed upon very insufficient evidence, Mrs Stowe evidently has taken her belief for the proof of the fact without the slightest examination of the grounds of that statement. But it may be asked, what motive could Lady Byron have for putting forward this story? Mrs. Stowe, in apologizing for her, feels that there is a necessity for some explanation for the manner in which, and the causes for which, Lady Byron separated from her husband. The world has felt that, up to to-day, accusing him of the ordinary infidelities of a husband would not be sufficient. She took him with those; she lived with him with those; she invited him to her bed, and caused her mother to indorse the invitation, after learning them all. In the language of the law, she condoned all these. May she not have felt that no other excuse was left her except the one now so unfortunately, and we may hope without an unkind thought toward her—so untruthfully put forward? But we are not required to find motives; we are dealing only with the facts—and the evidence to sustain them.

We have curtailed the General a good deal, but have presented the vital points of his argument. We wish all sides to have a hearing in this Byron matter, and therefore to Tilton, Count Johannes, R. Shelton Mackenzie,[38] and a dizzy list of smaller disputants we have added the legal analysis and the judicial opinion of General Ben Butler, merely remarking that the courts acquit most of the men that everybody knows ought to be hanged, and therefore even legal modes of investigation can hardly be received as infallible. By the tone of the English press it would seem that the General has tried this case too late to save his clients there, at least. *[Unsigned]*

The Last Words of Great Men

Marshal Neil's last words were: *"L'armee francaise!"*
(The French army.) —Exchange.[39]

What a sad thing it is to see a man close a grand career with a plagiarism in his mouth.[40] Napoleon's last words were, *"Téte d'armée."* (Head of the Army.) Neither of those remarks amounts to anything as "last words," and reflect little credit upon the utterers. A distinguished man should be as particular about his last words as he is about his last breath. He should write them out on a slip of paper and take the judgment of his friends on them. He should never leave such a thing to the last hour of his life, and trust to an intellectual spurt at the last moment to enable him to say something smart with his latest gasp and launch into eternity with grandeur. No—a man is apt to be too much fagged and exhausted, both in body and mind, at such a time, to be reliable; and may be the very thing he wants to say, he cannot think of to save him; and besides, there are his weeping friends bothering around; and worse than all, as likely as not he may have to deliver his last gasp when he is not expecting to. A man cannot always expect to think of a natty thing to say under such circumstances, and so it is pure egotistic ostentation to put it off. There is hardly a case on record where a man came to his last moment unprepared and said a good thing—hardly a case where a man trusted to that last moment and did not make a solemn botch of it and go out of the world feeling absurd.

Now there was Daniel Webster.[41] Nobody could tell *him* anything. *He* was not afraid. *He* could do something neat when the time came. And how did it turn out? Why, his will had to be fixed over; and then all his relations came; and first one thing and then another interfered, till at last he only had a chance to say "I still live,"[42] and up he went. Of course, he didn't still live, because he died—and so he might as well have kept his last words to himself as to have gone and made such a failure of it as that. A week before that, fifteen minutes of calm reflection would have enabled that man to contrive some last words that would have been a credit to himself and a comfort to his family for generations to come.

And there was John Quincy Adams.[43] Relying on his splendid abilities and his coolness in emergencies, *he* trusted to a happy hit at the last moment to carry him through, and what was the result? Death smote him in the House of Representatives, and he observed, casually, "This is the last of earth." The last of earth! Why the "last of earth," when there was so much more left? If he had said it was the last rose of summer, or the last run of shad, it would have had just as much point to it. What he meant to say, was, "Adam was the first and Adams is the last of earth," but he put it off a trifle too long, and so he had to go with that unmeaning observation on his lips.

And there we have Napoleon.[44] *"Tete d'armee."* That don't mean anything. Taken by itself, "Head of the army" is no more important than "Head of the police." And yet that was a man who could have said a good thing if he had barred out the doctor and studied over it a while. And this Marshal Neil, with half a century at his disposal, could not dash off anything better, in his last moments, than a poor plagiarism of another man's last words which were not worth plagiarizing in the first place. "The French army!" Perfectly irrelevant—perfectly flat—utterly pointless. But if he had closed one eye significantly and said, "The sub- scriber has made it *lively* for the French army," and then thrown a little of the comic into his last gasp, it would have been a thing to remember with satisfaction all the rest of his life. I do wish our great men would quit saying these flat things just at the moment they die. Let us have their next-to-their-last words for a while, and see if we cannot patch up something from them that will be a little more satisfactory. The public does not wish to be outraged in this way all the time.

But when we come to call to mind the last words of parties who took the trouble to make proper preparation for the occasion, we im- mediately notice a happy difference in the result.

There was Chesterfield. Lord Chesterfield had labored all his life to build up the most shining reputation for affability and elegance of speech and manners the world has ever seen. And could you suppose he failed to appreciate the efficiency of characteristic "last words" in the matter of seizing the successfully driven nail of such a reputation and clinching it on the other side for ever? Not he. He prepared him- self. He kept his eye on the clock and his finger on his pulse. He awaited his chance. And at last, when he knew his time was come, he pretended to think a new visitor had entered, and so, with the rattle in his throat emphasized for dramatic effect, he said to the servant, "Shin around John, and get the gentleman a chair." And then he died, amid thunders of applause.

Next we have Benjamin Franklin.[45] Franklin the author of Poor Richard's quaint sayings; Franklin the immortal axiom-builder, who used to sit up nights reducing the rankest old threadbare platitudes to crisp and snappy maxims that had a nice, varnished, original look in their new regimentals; who said, "Virtue is its own reward;" who said, "Procrastination is the thief of time;" who said, "Time and tide wait for no man," and "Necessity is the mother of invention;" good old Franklin, the Josh Billings[46] of the eighteenth century—though sooth to say, the latter transcends him in proverbial originality as much as he falls short of him in correctness of orthography. What sort of tactics did Franklin pursue? He pondered over his last words for as much as two weeks, and then when the time came he said "None but the brave deserve the fair,"[47] and died happy. He could not have said a sweeter thing if he had lived till he was an idiot.

Byron[48] made a poor business of it, and could not think of anything to say, at the last moment, but "Augusta—sister—Lady Byron—tell Harriet Beecher Stowe"—etc., etc.—but Shakespeare was ready and said, "England expects every man to do his duty!"[49] and went off with splendid eclat.

And there are other instances of sagacious preparation for a felicitous closing remark. For instance:

Joan of Arc[50] said—"Tramp, tramp, tramp, the boys are marching."[51]

Alexander the Great[52] said—"Another of, of those Santa Cruz punches, if you please."

The Empress Josephine[53] said—"Not for Jo——" and could get no further.

Cleopatra[54] said—"The Old Guard dies, but never surrenders!"[55]

Sir Walter Raleigh[56] said—"Executioner, can I take your whetstone a moment, please?"

John Smith said—"Alas, I am the last of my race!"[57]

Queen Elizabeth[58] said—"Oh, I would give my kingdom for one moment more—I have forgotten my last words."

And Red Jacket, the noblest Indian brave that ever wielded tomahawk in defence of a friendless and persecuted race, expired with these touching words upon his lips: *"Wawkawampanoosuc, winnebagowallawallasagamoresaskatchewan."* There was not a dry eye in the wigwam.

Let not this lesson be lost upon our public men. Let them take a healthy moment for preparation, and contrive some last words that shall be neat and to the point. Let Louis Napoleon[59] say:

"I am content to follow my uncle, still—I do not desire to improve on his last words. Put me down for 'tete d'armee.'"

And Garret Davis:[60] "Let me recite the unabridged dictionary."

And H.G.:[61] "I desire now, to say a few words on political economy."

And Mr. Bergh:[62] "Only take part of me at a time if the load will be fatiguing to the hearse-horses."

And Andrew Johnson:[63] "I have been an alderman, member of Congress, Governor, Senator, Pres—adieu, you know the rest."

And Seward:[64] "Alas!—ka."

And Grant:[65] "O."

All of which is respectfully submitted, with the most honorable intentions.—*Mark Twain*

P.S.—I am obliged to leave out the illustrations, this time. The artist finds it impossible to make pictures of people's last words.

September 11, 1869

Personal

This is to inform lyceums that, after recently withdrawing from the lecture field for next Winter, I have entered it again (until Jan. 10), because I was not able to cancel all my appointments, it being too late, now, to find lecturers to fill them.[66] This is also to request that invitations for me be addressed to Mr. James Redpath,[67] 20 Bromfield street, Boston, my lecture agent (instead of to me as heretofore), and thus some delay and inconvenience will be avoided.—*Mark Twain*, Office *Buffalo Express*, Sept. 9, 1869

September 11, 1869

"Mr. and Mrs. Byron"
Figaro Overhears a Conversation
on the International Topic

The other day, Mr. Editor, while I was in my room endeavoring to write out an elaborate and exhaustive essay on "Woman in her various

degrees of Fermentation," I gradually became aware that a brisk conversation was being carried on in the room adjoining mine, which is
used by my landlady, Mrs. Peasely, as a sort of undress parlor to receive irrepressible callers in.[68] I listened and learned by her voice that
the visitor was another boarding-house keeper of E — — street, whom,
for convenience, I will call Miss Grace De Griddle, a maiden lady of
mature years and infantile intellect. Applying my ear to a defective
part of the partition, I overheard the following interesting colloquy:

"No," said Miss De Griddle, "I don't think it becomes her at all. She
ought to have it cut with points and trimmed all around with star
spangled buglers; but did you notice, my dear Mrs. P., that her husband wears that old-fashioned percussion cap yet?"

"You don't say so!" ejaculated Mrs. P.; "then they can't be getting
along so well as we had feared."

"No, indeed," replied Miss De G., "they never can get along and give
such board as they do—spring chickens and sweet potatoes twice a
week; why the bare idea is suggestive of ultimate bankruptcy and
starvation! But, by the way, my dear Peasely, my main errand over
was to see if you wouldn't swap some of your last week's pork stew for
some of my baked beans of week before last; they are real nice, but
somehow my boarders don't seem to take to them, and I want to give
them something new."

"Certainly," said Mrs. P., "I'll trade and be glad to; the boarders are
getting impatient with the stew, and I remember hearing Mr. Mellowhead remark only this morning that he would like some real old fashioned baked beans, and I think yours have been baked long enough to
be sufficiently old-fashioned by this time. I'll send over a wash tub full
of the stew immediately after dark."

"O, thanks," said Miss De G., warmly, and "O, my dear Peasely, I
wanted to ask you what it means this "Byron's Candle" they're talking
about so much—now if it's any better than kerosene I'm going to use
it, for kerosene does smell so it makes my nose look like ex-President
Johnson's."

"Ah!" said Mrs. P., "your fleeting forty-five years of innocence and
inexperience illy qualify you to comprehend the nature of the Byron
scandal. It is something, my dear, smelling infinitely worse than
kerosene. It is something," said Mrs. P., waxing eloquent, "which
reaches on high and plucks a beauteous form from the highest niche
of fame's proud summit. Which blackens o'er a name long gleaming
there in bright and glorious concupiscence. Which digs down deep into

the portals of the tomb, and drags the eternal sleeper forth to stamp upon his clay the name of "Fiend," and this, all this, is the work of Harriet Beecher Stowe."

"The work of Harriet Beecher's toe!" exclaimed Miss De Griddle in innocent surprise, "what a remarkably powerful toe Harriet Beecher must have."

"There you are at fault again," said Mrs. P——; "I said nothing about Harriet Beecher's vulgar toe. I said *Harriet Beecher* Stowe— Stowe—to stow away, to eat like a boarder from the country. Mrs. Stowe," continued Mrs. P——, "is an authoress; she wrote 'Uncle Tom's Cabin,'" the Emancipation Proclamation, the Dred Scott Decision, and I believe several other colored works. But now that the wretched negro is snatched from the fatherly care of his owner and compelled to live by his own exertions, she has abandoned him to his fate, be it ever so cruel. Be he racked upon a seat in Congress or tortured with red-hot newspaper articles; be he persecuted by politicians, or bored by auguries of utter amalgamation, it is alike a matter of indifference to her now; she has got an engagement. Did you ever hear of Byron?"

"Byron," said Miss De G., thoughtfully, "Mr. Byron, where does he board? I can't call him to mind; but O, Mrs. P., you've made me so nervous telling about the poor niggers being racked, tortured, burnt with red hot things and bored with augers, that I can't think of nothing; Byron—O, I remember, he used to board with me and sleep in the room over the woodshed."

"Pshaw! How stupid," said Mrs. P——, in disgust, "You're thinking of Brown, no doubt—I mean Byron, the greatest poet of modern times."

"O, I see," said Miss De G. "He wrote verses. How nice."

"Yes," said Mrs. P., "he did write verse, but he's dead now; and Mrs. Stowe has been telling a terrible story which was told her by Mrs. Byron, while she was sick with the bilious fever, but entirely out of her head, as there wasn't a word of truth in it, as I know to a certainty, for my Aunt used to wash for Count Johannes,[69] and had the whole story direct from his chamber-maid, who of course knew all about it.

"The facts are something like this. When Byron was a child his mother threw a flat iron at Byron *pere,* which falling on the foot of the unfledged songster, mashed the nail so completely off his second toe that it never grew again.[70] This unhappy accident seemed to affect all his after life, for as he grew up his mind became painfully sensitive to the charms of all the neighboring females and he was in great misery.

"Shortly after this he fell extensively in love, and proposed energetically by return mail to a large circle of fair friends. He was not universally accepted but soon after became the unhappy victim of a Miss Milldam (I believe).[71] They lived happily together for twenty-five minutes, and it was during these delicious moments that the gifted poet wrote those wonderful lines:

> Your nose is red,
> I feel quite blue,
> I've got the [acne]
> And so have you.[72]

"But genius was not properly appreciated by Mrs. Byron, nor Miss Milldam could not see why the writing of Childe Harold[73] should make her husband so savage and morose as of course it must do, or why Sardinaplus[74] or any other man should keep him from her side all night, thus widening their differences and lengthening their gas bill.

"She also took to accusing him of the deficiency in his boot, which was so harrowing to his feelings that he sat down and wrote "Harrow-on-the-Hill." She also became jealous of an aged and very respectable sister of Mr. Byron's, of whom she claimed he had written thus:

> O, dearly I love you my sister Augusta,
> So soft and so gentle, not sullen and crusty;
> Twixt us here shall e're be so constant and true an
> Affection like that between Haidee and Juan;
> That the world shall look off from the page of my glory,
> To the *Atlantic Monthly* for that other story.

"O, my, how nice," said Miss De G.; "how I should like to have some one make poetry about me."

"Byron," said Mrs. P., without deigning to notice her companion's remark, "soon became estranged from his wife and obtained a position on General Halleck's staff, and was very efficient at the siege of Corinth, of which he gives an interesting account in his works. After this he became a voluntary exile and a wanderer upon the earth, varying the monotony of his life with many *affaire d'amour*, which means love affairs, and thus continued till he came to Missolonghi in Greece."[75]

"Well," interrupted Miss De Griddle, "I hope he married Miss Long-eye and settled down to"—just at this point a girl burst into the room and breathlessly gasped out, "Oh, Miss De Griddle, come home right off. Mr. Spongegrub, the man that owes you ten dollars for board, is packing up his clothes and signing to all the expressmen out of the window, and we all think he's going to run away." "If that's the case," said Miss De G.,"I must hurry home and form an attachment for the fellow's trunk," and she went.

There's no telling how long the erudite Mrs. P. would have went on but for this interruption; her narrative seemed as lucid as any of them, though.

The public has now heard both sides, but unfortunately only one end of the Byron story.

I trust the other will come along sometime during the next century.

Yours, eavesdropsically, *Figaro*

[Not signed as Mark Twain]

September 13, 1869

The Gates Ajar

The book notices of the *Overland Monthly*,[76] of San Francisco, have achieved a celebrity which is great in America and still greater in England, as models of piquancy, critical analysis and felicitous English. As most people have read "Gates Ajar,"[77] the *Overland's* remarks upon that book will be of interest. After reviewing "Men, Women and Ghosts,"[78] it says:

A separate consideration of *The Gates Ajar*, by the same author, is suggested rather by a distinctiveness of subject than by any distinctiveness of style; and, perhaps, by the fact that it is a later book. It is certainly a more mature and elaborate performance. While it preserves all the characteristic faults and virtues of *Men, Women and Ghosts*, it is much more powerful in effect; and so long as there are death and bereavement in this world, and the necessity for books of consolation, it will have a permanent, intrinsic value. The question of the heterodoxy or orthodoxy of its consolations will, we fear, have very little to do with its specific value as a consoler. Wounded hearts that find balm and healing in it, will not greatly care if it is not endorsed by the Faculty. There will, of course, be those, equally sincere, who always find a good deal of heroism of self-sacrifice—not a bad thing for wounded hearts, by the way—in being told that their natural longings and affections are sinful, as there are constitutions that are still only moved by calomel and ipecac. It is not very long ago that water was carefully kept from fever patients. We may deplore the theory that in-flicted this needless suffering, but we can not but respect the consci-entious invalid, who, with water within his reach, resisted the temp-tation. By which we mean simply to claim, in advance, for those who can not find consolation in Miss Phelps' "reconstructed" heaven, an equal sympathy with those who can.

In regard to heaven, we probably *know* a little of it as Miss Phelps does; and shall not commit the folly of opposing speculation with spec-ulation. The person who first takes the trouble to define the indefin-able always has the advantage. That heaven, however, is an abode of felicity, incompatible with our earthly conditions, is the general, vague belief of mankind. What constitutes the felicity, of course, differs with the taste and education; but the point of incompatibility has been generally, though vaguely admitted. Here, however, Miss Phelps takes a square issue. Perhaps it would not be entirely fair to her to say that she believes heaven to be a place where little boys find balloons that they lose on earth, or where good girls, like "Miss Clotildy," are per-mitted to have a piano—for these she uses as illustrations; but it would be no less unfair for us to look upon the Deacon's idea that heaven was a place to play upon a golden harp, (with which instru-ment, in a mundane sphere, he was unfamiliar,) as the general belief of more orthodox folk. Indeed, Miss Phelps is probably as unreliable in defining the belief of other people as she is of her own. We are most of us a good deal better or worse than our creeds; and the few of us that do get into heaven will probably get there by reason of something which we may never be able to state with theological accuracy.

It is, perhaps, this very defect in logic which makes *The Gates Ajar* a consolation to bereaved humanity. Reason grates harshly on the suffering sense; logic can not "make Death other than Death;" but the flow of tender womanly sympathy, and the instinctive analysis of sorrow which is so peculiarly feminine, soothe where the clearest statement of an after-life fails. And if Miss Phelps has, with womanly tact, worked up some half-truths into pleasantly delusive perspec-tive, who shall blame her? If the weeping wife be consoled with the thought that her departed husband awaits her in heaven, to renew the vows and conjugal devotion which were theirs on earth, why should we suggest to her that this fact would make a second mar-riage unpleasant? Women have, ere this, sincerely mourned a first husband, and as sincerely loved and wedded a second.

In the narrative on which those speculations are strung, Miss Phelps exhibits a characteristic disregard for human life; burning up one woman whose husband holds opposite views, and killing her own friend and consoler by cancer for the sake of her corroborative testimony, *in extremis*. The victims are artistically, and even pathetically put out of the way—the description of "Aunt Winnifred's" death being very touching, and not greatly overdone—but we cannot help thinking that there is something as grimly puritanical in this sort of "lesson" as in any of the harsh doctrines she opposes. Yet we must repeat, that the book is wholesome for its feminine sympathy, and for its recognition of that Abiding Love whose gates are ever ajar. *[Unsigned]*

September 18, 1869

The "Wild Man"

"Interviewed"

There has been so much talk about the mysterious "wild man" out there in the West for some time, that I finally felt that it was my duty to go out and "interview" him. There was something peculiarly and touchingly romantic about the creature and his strange actions, according to the newspaper reports. He was represented as being hairy, long-armed, and of great strength and stature; ugly and cumbrous; avoiding men, but appearing suddenly and unexpectedly to women and children; going armed with a club, but never molesting any creature, except sheep or other prey; fond of eating and drinking, and not particular about the quality, quantity or character of the beverages and edibles; living in the woods like a wild beast; seeming oppressed and melancholy, but never angry; moaning, and sometimes howling, but never uttering articulate sounds. Such was "Old Shep" as the papers painted him. I felt that the story of his life must be a sad one—a story of suffering, disappointment, exile—a story of man's inhumanity to man in some shape or other—and I longed to persuade the secret from him.

. . .

"Since you say you are a member of the press," said the wild man, "I am willing to tell you all you wish to know. Bye and bye you will comprehend why it is that I am so ready to unbosom myself to a newspaper man when I have so studiously avoided conversation with other people. I will now unfold my strange story. I was born with the world we live upon, almost. I am the son of Cain."

"What!"

"I was present when the flood was announced."

"Which!"

"I am the father of the Wandering Jew."

"Sir!"

I moved out of reach of his club, and went on taking notes, but keeping a wary eye on him the while. He smiled a melancholy smile, and resumed:

"When I glance back over the dreary waste of ages, I see many a glimmering land mark that is familiar to my memory. And oh, the leagues I have traveled! the things I have seen! the events I have helped to emphasize! I was at the assassination of Caesar. I marched upon Mecca with Mahomet. I was in the Crusades, and stood with Godfrey when he planted the banner of the cross upon the battlements of Jerusalem. I—"

"One moment, please—have you given these items to any other journal? Can I—"

"Silence! I was in the Pinta's shrouds with Columbus when America burst upon his vision. I saw Charles I[79] beheaded. I was in London when the Gunpowder Plot[80] was discovered. I was present at the trial of Warren Hastings.[81] I was on American soil when Lexington was fought—when the Declaration was promulgated—when Cornwallis[82] surrendered—when Washington died. I entered Paris with Napoleon after Elba. I was present when you mounted your guns and manned your fleets for your war of 1812—when the South fired upon Sumpter—when Richmond fell—when the President's life was taken. In all the ages, I have helped to celebrate the triumphs of genius, the achievements of arms, the havoc of storm, fire, pestilence and famine."

"Your career has been a stirring one. Might I ask how you came to locate in these dull Kansas woods, when you have been so accustomed to excitement during what I may term such a protracted period, not to put too fine a point upon it?"

"Listen. Once I was the honored servitor of the noble and the illustrious" (here he heaved a sigh and passed his hairy hand across his eyes), "but in these degenerate days I am become the slave of quack doctors and newspapers. I am driven from pillar to post and hurried up and down; sometimes with stencil-plate and paste brush to defile the fences with cabalistic legends, and sometimes in grotesque and extravagant character for the behest of some driving journal. I attended to that Ocean Bank robbery[83] some weeks ago, when I was hardly rested from finishing up the pow-wow about the completion of the Pacific Railroad; immediately I was spirited off to do an atrocious murder for the New York papers; next to attend the wedding of a patriarchal millionaire; next to raise a hurrah about the great boat race; and then, just when I had begun to hope that my old bones were to have a rest, I am bundled off to this howling wilderness to strip, and jibber, and be ugly and hairy, and pull down fences, and waylay sheep, and scare women and children, and waltz around with a club and play 'Wild Man' generally—and all to gratify the whim of a bedlam of crazy newspaper scribblers? From one end of this continent to the other, I am described as a gorilla, with a sort of human seeming about me—and all to gratify this quill-driving scum of the earth!"

"Poor old carpet-bagger!"

"I have been served infamously, often, in modern and semi-modern times. I have been compelled by base men to create fraudulent history and personate all sorts of impossible humbugs. I wrote those crazy Junius letters;[84] I moped in a French dungeon for fifteen years, and wore a ridiculous Iron Mask;[85] I poked around your Northern forests, among your vagabond Indians, a solemn French idiot, personating the ghost of a dead Dauphin, that the gaping world might wonder if we had 'a Bourbon among us;' I have played sea-serpent off Nahant,[86] and Woolly-Horse and What-is-It for the museum; I have 'interviewed' politicians for the *Sun*, worked all manner of miracles for the *Herald*, ciphered up election returns for the *World*, and thundered Political Economy through the *Tribune*. I have done all the extravagant things that the wildest invention could contrive, and done them well, and *this* is my reward—playing Wild Man in Kansas without a shirt!"

"Mysterious being, a light dawns vaguely upon me—it grows apace—what—what is your name?"

"SENSATION!"

"Hence, horrible shape!"

It spoke again:

"Oh, pitiless fate, my destiny hounds me once more. I am called. I go. Alas, is there no rest for me?"

In a moment the Wild Man's features began to soften and refine, and his form to resume a more human grace and symmetry. His club changed to a spade, and he shouldered it and started away, sighing profoundly and shedding tears.

"Whither, poor shade?"

"TO DIG UP THE BYRON FAMILY!"

Such was the response that floated back upon the wind as the sad spirit shook its ringlets to the breeze, flourished its shovel aloft, and disappeared beyond the brow of the hill.

All of which is in strict accordance with the facts.

[L.S] Attest: *Mark Twain*

September 25, 1869

Rev. H. W. Beecher
His Private Habits

The great preacher never sleeps with his clothes on.[87] Once, when remonstrated with upon the singularity of his conduct in this respect and the pernicious effect the example might possibly have upon the younger members of his congregation, he replied with the frank and open candor that has always characterized him, that he would give worlds to be able to rid himself of the custom—and added that the anguish he had suffered in trying to break himself of the habit had made him old before he was ninety. Mr. Beecher never wears his hat at dinner. He does not consider it healthy. It does not immediately break down one's constitution, but is slow and sure. He knows one case where a man persisted in the habit in spite of the tears and entreaties of his friends, until it was too late, and he reaped the due reward of his rashness—for it carried him off at last, at the age of a hundred and six. Had that man listened to reason, he might have lived to be a comfort to his parents and a solace to their declining years.

Mr. Beecher never swears. In all his life a profane expression has never passed his lips. But if he were to take it into his head to try it once, he would make even that disgusting habit seem beautiful—he would handle it as it was never handled before, and if there was a wholesome moral lesson hidden away in it anywhere, he would ferret it out and use it with tremendous effect. Panoplied with his grand endowments—his judgment, his discriminating taste, his felicity of expression, his graceful fancy—if Mr. Beecher had a mind to swear, he would throw into it an amount of poetry, and pathos, and splendid imagery, and moving earnestness, and resistless energy, topped off and climaxed with a gorgeous pyrotechnic conflagration of filagree and fancy swearing, that would astonish and delight the hearer and forever after quiver through his bewildered memory an exquisite confusion of rainbows and music, and thunder and lightning. A man of a high order of intellect and appreciation could sit and listen to Mr. Beecher swear for a week without getting tired.

Mr. Beecher is very regular in his habits. He always goes to bed promptly between nine and three o'clock, and never upon any account allows himself to vary from this rule. He is just as particular about getting up, which he does the next day, generally. He considers that to this discipline, and to this alone, he is indebted for the rugged health he has enjoyed ever since he adopted it.

Mr. Beecher does not go around and get advertisements for the *"Plymouth Pulpit."* If he does it, it is without his knowledge or consent. If such a report has been started, it is an absolute duty to refute it in this article. However, no such report has yet been heard of, and therefore it is not necessary to do more than refute it in a purely general way at this time. Mr. Beecher *could* augment the bulk of the pamphlet to which his sermons are attached if he chose to go around and solicit advertising, but he would not dream of doing such a thing. He has no time for such recreation. He has to preach, and he has to make the dedication speeches for all sorts of things, and he is obliged to make a few remarks on nearly all distinguished occasions, because very often Mr. Greeley is busy and cannot come. And besides, he has to carry on his farm.

Mr. Beecher's farm consists of thirty-six acres, and is carried on on strict scientific principles. He never puts in any part of a crop without consulting his book. He plows and reaps and digs and sows according to the best authorities—and the authorities cost more than the other farming implements do. As soon as the library is complete, the farm will begin to be a profitable investment. But book farming has its drawbacks. Upon one occasion, when it seemed morally certain that the hay ought to be cut, the hay book could not be found—and before it was found it was too late and the hay was all spoiled. Mr. Beecher raises some of the finest crops of wheat in the country, but the unfavorable difference between the cost of producing it and its market value after it is produced has interfered considerably with its success as a commercial enterprise. His special weakness is hogs, however. He considers hogs the best game a farm produces. He buys the original pig for a dollar and a half and feeds him forty dollars' worth of corn, and then sells him for about nine dollars. This is the only crop he ever makes any money on. He loses on the corn, but he makes seven dollars and a half on the hog. He does not mind this, because he never expects to make anything on corn, anyway. And any way it turns out, he has the excitement of raising the hog any how, whether he gets the worth of him or not. His strawberries would be a comfortable success if the robins would eat turnips, but they won't, and hence the difficulty.

One of Mr. Beecher's most harassing difficulties in his farming operations comes of the close resemblance of different sorts of seeds and plants to each other. Two years ago, his far-sightedness warned him that there was going to be a great scarcity of water melons, and therefore he put in a crop of twenty-seven acres of that fruit. But when they came up they turned out to be pumpkins, and a dead loss was the consequence. Sometimes a portion of his crop goes into the ground most promising sweet potatoes, and comes up the infernalest carrots—though I never have heard him express it just in that way. When he bought his farm, he found one egg in every hen's nest on the place. He said that here was just the reason why so many farmers failed—they scattered their forces too much—concentration was the idea. So he gathered those eggs together and put them all under one experienced old hen. That hen roosted over that contract night and day for eleven weeks, under the anxious personal supervision of Mr. Beecher himself, but she could not "phase" those eggs. Why? Because they were those infamous porcelain things which are used by ingenious and fraudulent farmers as "nest eggs." But perhaps Mr. Beecher's most disastrous experience was the time he tried to raise an immense crop of dried apples. He planted fifteen hundred dollars worth, but never a one of them sprouted. He has never been able to understand, to this day, what was the matter with those apples.

Mr. Beecher's farm is not a triumph. It would be easier on him if he worked it on shares with some one; but he cannot find any body who is willing to stand half the expense, and not many that are able. Still, persistence in any cause is bound to succeed. He was a very inferior farmer when he first began, but a prolonged and unflinching assault upon his agricultural difficulties has had its effect at last, and he is now fast rising from affluence to poverty.

I shall not say anything about Mr. Beecher's sermons. They breathe the truest and purest spirit of religion; they are models of pulpit oratory, and they are proofs that the subject which is the nearest to the interests of mankind can be put to nobler uses than the chloroforming of congregations. Mr. Beecher has done more than any other man, perhaps, to inspire religion with the progressive spirit of the nineteenth century, and make it keep step with the march of intellectual achievement and the generous growth of men's charities and liberal impulses. It is such men as Beecher that persuade religious communities to progress to something better than witch-burning when the spirit of the time progresses from ex-wagons to stage-coaches, and bye and bye to steamboats; and who persuade such communities to progress beyond the endorsing of slavery with their Bibles when the spirit of the time progresses to the subordination of the steamboat to the railroad and the discarding of pony-expresses for the telegraph. He has done as much as any man to keep the people from reading their Bibles by the interpretations of the eighteenth century while they were living far along in the nineteenth. His name will live. His deeds will honor his memory. He has set his mark upon his epoch, and years hence, when the people turn over the bales and bundles of this generation's ideas, they will find "H. W. B." stenciled on a good many of them.—*Mark Twain*

September 30, 1869

The Ticket—Explanation

Under the proper head will be found the telegram from the State Convention announcing the nominations. As the political editor of this paper, Mr. Larned,[88] is absent, attending that Convention; and as I do not know much about politics, and am not sitting up nights to learn; and as I am new to the Atlantic seaboard and its political leaders, and consequently am not able to make oath that I am perfectly posted concerning the history, services, morals, politics and virtues of any of these nominees except GEORGE WILLIAM CURTIS,[89] I shall discreetly hold my peace.

I am satisfied that these nominations are all right and sound, and that they are the only ones that can bring peace to our distracted country, (the only political phrase I am perfectly familiar with and competent to hurl at the public with fearless confidence—the other editor is full of them,) but being merely satisfied isn't safe enough. I always like to *know*, before I shout. But I go for Mr. Curtis with all my strength!

Being certain of him, I hereby shout all I know how. But the others may be a split ticket, or a scratched ticket, or whatever you call it.

I will let it alone for the present. It will keep. The other young man will be back to-morrow, and *he* will shout for it, split or no split—rest assured of that. He will prance into this political ring with his toma-hawk and his war-whoop, and then you will hear a crash and see the scalps fly. He has none of my diffidence. He knows all about these nominees—and if he don't, he will let on to, in such a natural way as to deceive the most critical. He knows everything—he knows more than Webster's Unabridged and the American Encyclopedia—but whether he knows anything about a subject or not he is perfectly will-ing to discuss it. When he gets back, he will tell you all about these candidates, as serenely as if he had been acquainted with them a hundred years—though, speaking confidentially, I doubt if he ever heard of any of them till to-day. I am right well satisfied it is a good, sound, sensible ticket, and a ticket to win—but wait till *he* comes.

In the meantime, I go for GEORGE WILLIAM CURTIS, and take the chances.—*Mark Twain*

October 1, 1869

Engineer Griffin

We have received, and publish to-day, Judge Barrett's severe speech in full to the most remarkable jury of these latter days—that Pike County jury.[90] We printed an extract from it a day or two ago. When Alfred the Great devised and left behind him the most endur-ing remembrancer of his reign, the Trial by Jury, it is likely that the possibility of a Pike County Pennsylvania jury did not occur to him.

We do not yet know what the testimony was that was given before these twelve apostles of perjury, and yet we are able to state without diffidence that they acquitted a man who had been clearly proven guilty before their faces—for his guilt was so manifest *that the pris-oner's own counsel deserted his cause.* With the public sympathy all in favor of a client, we have yet to hear of a lawyer who deserted such a client while he believed in his heart there was a shred of evidence in his favor that was not utterly frivolous. It is not the lawyer nature.

There was no room in this case for romance, sentiment, poetical justice. It was a plain case of duty, with its lines rigidly marked—no margin left for predilections or preferences. If any of us saw a man stand up uncovered, with his hand on the Bible, and take a solemn oath that he would climb over a fence, and then saw him at once proceed to crawl under it, we would marvel to hear any one try to excuse such a deliberate perjury. This is precisely what the Pike county jury did. They stood up in Court and called God to witness that they would find in accordance with the evidence: the evidence proved the prisoner guilty—they acquitted him.

When sentinels go to sleep on guard they are shot. A sentimental Pike county jury would acquit them and a Pike county auditory would applaud the act. The sentinel is shot, not in a spirit of revenge, but because *the law requires it,* because the due protection of the army renders it necessary, and because sleeping becomes criminal when the sleeper has human lives in trust. The Pike county jury were not authorized to *pardon* a guilty man—the peculiar nature of their oaths took that privilege from them. It then remained with the Governor only.

"Pike county" is a name that once meant little or nothing, but it bids fair to acquire a descriptive and peculiar significance yet. Parties from the wilds of Indiana and portions of Ohio who still make annual excursions down the Ohio in "broad horns," peddling pumpkins and hoop-poles, which they raise to a certain dignity by calling them "fruit and furniture," are always spoken of by river men as "Pike county" people. Most of the first overland emigrants to California were from the backwoods of Missouri, and endowed with an ignorance whose density was something marvelous. They were said to hail from "Pike county." At this day, on the whole Pacific coast, "Pike county" refers to any individual, from anywhere, who is dull and ignorant. Pike county, Pennsylvania, comes forward, now, in the persons of her asinine jury, to sustain the ancient grandeur of the name. For a year or two, at least, we shall hear verdicts spoken of as being "worthy of a Pike county jury"—and we shall all know what it means. It is time that "Pike county" were put in the dictionary, as being short for ignorance, stupidity, perjury. *[Unsigned]*

October 2, 1869

The Latest Novelty
Mental Photographs

I have received from the publishers, Leypoldt & Holt, New York, a neatly printed page of questions, with blanks for answers, and I am requested to fill those blanks. These questions are so arranged as to ferret out the most secret points of a man's nature without his ever noticing what the idea is until the thing is done and his "character" gone forever. A number of these sheets are bound together and called a Mental Photograph Album. Nothing could induce me to fill those blanks but the asseveration of these gentlemen that it will benefit my race by enabling young people to see what I am and giving them an opportunity to become like somebody else. This candor overcomes my scruples. I have but little character, but what I have I am willing to part with for the public good. I would have been a better man if I had had a chance, but things have always been against me. I never had any parents, hardly—only just a father and mother—and so I have had to struggle along the best way I could. I do not boast of this character, further than that I built it up by myself, at odd hours, during the last thirty years, and without other educational aid than I was able to pick up in the ordinary schools and colleges. I have filled the blanks as follows:

WHAT IS YOUR FAVORITE

Color?—Any thing but dun.
Flower?—The night-blooming Sirius.*
Tree?—Any that bears forbidden fruit.
Object in Nature?—A dumb belle.
Hour in the Day?—The leisure hour.
Season of the Year?—The lecture season.
Perfume?—Cent. per cent.
Gem?—The Jack of Diamonds, when it is trump.
Style of Beauty?—The Subscriber's.
Names, Male and Female?—*M'aimez* (Maimie) for a
     female, and Tacus and Marius, for males.
Painters?—Sign-painters.
Musicians?—Harper & Bros.

Piece of Sculpture?—The Greek Slave, with his hod.

Poet?—Robert Browning, when he has a lucid interval.

Poetess?—Timothy Titcomb.

Prose Author?—Noah Webster, LL.D.

Characters in Romance?—The Byron Family.

In History?—Jack, the Giant Killer.

Book to take up for an hour?—Vanderbilt's pocket-book.

What book (not religious) would you part with last?—
The one I might happen to be reading on a railroad during the disaster season.

What epoch would you choose to have lived in?—
Before the present Erie—it was far safer.

Where would you like to live?—In the moon, because there
is no water there.

Favorite Amusement?—Hunting the "tiger" or some kindred game.

Favorite Occupation?—"Like dew on the gowan—lying."

What trait of Character do you most admire in man?—
The noblest form of cannibalism—love for his fellow man.

In Woman?—Love for *her* fellow man.

What trait do you most detest in each?—That "trait" which
you put "or" to to describe its possessor.

If not yourself, who would you rather be?—The Wandering
Jew, with a nice annuity.

What is your idea of Happiness?—Finding the buttons all on.

Your idea of Misery?—Breaking an egg in your pocket.

What is your *bete noire?*—[What is my which?]

What is your Dream?—Nightmare, as a general thing.

What do you most dread?—Exposure.

What do you believe to be your Distinguishing Characteristic?—
Hunger.

What is the Sublimest Passion of which human nature is
capable?—Loving your sweetheart's enemies.

What are the Sweetest Words in the world?—"Not guilty."

What are the Saddest?—"Dust unto dust."

What is your Aim in Life?—To endeavor to be absent when
my time comes.

What is your Motto?—Be virtuous and you will be eccentric.

But, jesting aside, the Mental Photograph Album is a novel and ingenious idea. If one will take the trouble to write answers to those

questions, seriously and conscientiously, he will discover, when he is done, that he has made a record whereby a stranger may gather a pretty fair estimate of his real nature and the peculiar bent of his character. A well-filled Album of this kind ought to make an entertaining "book to take up for an hour."—*Mark Twain*

* I grant you this is a little obscure—but in explaining to the unfortunate that Sirius is the dog-star and blooms only at night, I am afforded an opportunity to air my erudition. [It is only lately acquired.]

PART II

Lighting Out for the Lecture Circuit

October 1869 – January 1870

Around the World
Letter No. 1

New York, October 10

[I am just starting out on a pleasure trip around the globe, *by proxy.*[91] That is to say, Professor D. R. Ford, of Elmira College, is now making the journey for me, and will write the newspaper account of his (our) trip. No, not that exactly—but he will travel and write letters, and I shall stay at home and add a dozen pages to each of his letters. One of us will furnish the fancy and the jokes, and the other will furnish the facts. I am equal to either department, although statistics are my best hold. I am perfectly satisfied now. I have long had a desire to travel clear around the world in one grand, comprehensive picnic excursion, but the fatigue and vexation of it formed one drawback, and the expense another. The necessary thing was to get somebody to divide those discomforts with, and so make them bearable. This is now accomplished. I stay at home and stand the fatigue, and the Professor travels and stands the expense. While my Double is roaming about the Great Plains, and Nevada and California, my half of the letters will be at a disadvantage, because I shall be hampered by an intimate personal knowledge of those localities; but when he gets into Japan, and China, and India, I can soar with a gorgeous freedom because I don't know any thing about those lands.

[Professor Ford is a scholarly man; a man whose attainments cover a vast field of knowledge. His knowledge is singularly accurate, too; what he knows he is *certain* of, and likewise what he knows he has a happy faculty of communicating to others. He is a man of high social standing and unspotted character. He is a warm personal friend of mine—which is to his discredit, perhaps, but would you have a man perfect? He is a minister of the Gospel, and a *live* one—a man whose religion broadens and adorns his nature; not a religion that dates a man back into the last century and saps his charity and makes him a bigot. Mr. Ford's letters will be written in all good faith and honesty, and I shall not mar them. I shall merely have *a good deal to say.* I trust that the discriminating reader will always be able to discover where Ford leaves off and I begin though I don't really intend he *shall* be able to do that. As Mr. F. jogs along, I mean to write paragraph for paragraph with him, and I shall set down all that I know about the countries he visits, together with a good deal that neither I nor anybody else knows about them.

[Mr. Ford had reached Salt Lake City a few days ago, and by this time is prowling among the silver mines of Nevada. His letters are on their way hither, no doubt, but in the meantime I will begin the journey unassisted, with a sketch or so of my own about The Dead Sea of California, and some other curious features of that country. The Professor will sail for Japan in the steamer America, which leaves San Francisco on the 4th of November. A twenty-five or thirty day sea voyage, doubled, makes a long interregnum, and so his Japanese letters will not begin to arrive before January. However, I can run this duplicate correspondence by myself till then. With the reader's permission I will now begin—and what I say about Mono Lake may be accepted as strictly true. I shall tell no lies about it.]—*Mark Twain*

The Dead Sea

Mono Lake[92] or the Dead Sea of California, is one of her most extraordinary curiosities, but being situated in a very out-of-the-way corner of the country, and away up among the eternal snows of the Sierras, it is little known and very seldom visited. A mining excitement carried me there once, and I spent several months in its vicinity. It lies in a lifeless, treeless, hideous desert, 8000 feet above the level of the sea, and is guarded by mountains 2000 feet higher, whose summits are hidden always in the clouds. This solemn, silent, sailless sea—this lonely tenant of the loneliest spot on earth—is little graced with the picturesque. It is an unpretending expanse of greyish water, about a hundred miles in circumference, with two islands in its centre, mere upheavals of rent, and scorched and blistered lava, snowed over with grey banks and drifts of pumice stone and ashes, the winding sheet of the dead volcano, whose vast crater the lake has seized upon and occupied.

The lake is 200 feet deep, and its sluggish waters are so strong with alkali that if you only dip the most hopelessly soiled garment into them once or twice, and wring it out, it will be found as clean as if it had been through your ablest washerwoman's hands. While we camped there our laundry work was easy. We tied the week's washing astern of our boat, and sailed a quarter of a mile, and the job was complete, all to the wringing out. If we threw the water on our heads and gave them a rub or so, the white lather would pile up three inches high. This water is not good for bruised places and abrasions of the skin. We had a valuable dog. He had raw places on him. He had more raw places on him than sound ones. He was the rawest dog I almost ever saw. He jumped overboard one day to get away from the flies. But it was bad judgment. In his condition, it would have been just as comfortable to jump into the fire. The alkali water nipped him in all the raw places simultaneously, and he struck out for the shore with considerable interest. He yelped and barked and howled as he went—and by the time he got to the shore there was no bark to him—for he had barked the bark all out of his inside, and the alkali water had cleaned the bark all off his outside, and he probably wished he had never embarked in any such enterprise. He ran round and round in a circle, and pawed the earth and clawed the air, and threw double summersets, sometimes backwards and sometimes forwards, in the most frantic and extraordinary manner. He was not a demonstrative dog, as a general thing, but rather of a grave and serious turn of mind, and I never saw him take so much interest in any thing before. He finally struck out over the mountains, at a gait which we estimated at about 250 miles an hour, and he is going yet. This was about five years ago. We look for what is left of him along here every day.

A white man cannot drink the water of Mono Lake, for it is nearly pure lye. It is said that the Indians in the vicinity drink it sometimes, though. It is not improbable, for they are among the purest liars I ever saw. [There will be no additional charge for this joke, except to parties requiring an explanation of it. This joke has received high commendation from some of the ablest minds of the age. Horace Greeley remarked to a friend of mine that if he were ever to make a joke like that, he would not desire to live any longer.]

There are no fish in Mono Lake—no frogs, no snakes, no pollywogs— nothing, in fact, that goes to make life desirable. Millions of wild ducks and sea gulls swim about the surface, but no living thing exists *under* the surface, except a white feathery sort of worm, one-half an inch long, which looks like a bit of white thread frayed out at the sides. If you dip up a gallon of water, you will get about fifteen thousand of these. They give to the water a sort of grayish-white appearance. Then there is a fly, which looks something like our house fly. These settle on the beach to eat the worms that wash ashore—and any time, you can see there a belt of flies an inch deep and six feet wide, and this belt extends clear around the lake—a belt of flies one hundred miles long. If you throw a stone among them, they swarm up so thick that they look dense, like a

cloud. You can hold them under water as long as you please—they don't
mind it—they are only proud of it. When you let them go, they pop up
to the surface as dry as a patent office report, and walk off as unconcernedly as if they had been educated especially with a view to afford-
ing instructive entertainment to man in that particular way. Providence leaves nothing to go by chance. All things have their uses and
their part and proper place in Nature's economy. The ducks and gulls
eat the flies, the flies eat the worms—the Indians eat the flies—the
wild oats eat the Indians—the white folks eat the wild oats when the
crops fail—and thus all things are lovely.

Mono Lake is 150 miles in a straight line from the ocean—and between it and the ocean are one or two ranges of mountains—yet thousands of sea-gulls go there every season to lay their eggs and rear
their young. One would as soon expect to find sea-gulls in Tennessee.
And in this connection let us observe another instance of Nature's wisdom. The islands in the lake being merely huge masses of lava, coated
over with ashes and pumice stone, and utterly innocent of vegetation
or anything that would burn; and the sea-gulls' eggs being entirely
useless to any body unless they be cooked, Nature has provided an unfailing spring of boiling water on the largest island, and you can put
your eggs in there, and in four minutes you can boil them as hard as
any statement I have made during the past fifteen years. Within ten
feet of the boiling spring is a spring of pure cold water, sweet and
wholesome. So, in that island you get your board and washing free of
charge—and if nature had gone further and furnished a nice American
hotel clerk who was crusty and disobliging, and didn't know any thing
about the time tables, or the railroad routes—or—any thing—and was
proud of it—I would not wish for a more desirable boarding house.

Half a dozen little mountain brooks flow into Mono Lake, but not a
stream of any kind flows out of it. It neither rises nor falls, apparently, and what it does with its surplus water is a dark and bloody
mystery. All the rivers of Nevada sink into the earth mysteriously after they have run 100 miles or so—none of them flow to the sea, as is
the fashion of rivers in all other lands.

There are only two seasons in the region round about Mono Lake—
and these are, the breaking up of one Winter and the beginning of the
next. More than once I have seen a perfectly blistering morning open
up with the thermometer at ninety degrees at eight o'clock, and seen
the snow fall fourteen inches deep and that same identical thermometer go down to forty-four degrees under shelter, before 9 o'clock at

night. Under favorable circumstances it snows at least once in every single month in the year in the little town of Mono.[93] So uncertain is the climate in Summer that a lady who goes out visiting cannot hope to be prepared for all emergencies unless she takes her fan under one arm and her snow shoes under the other. When they have a Fourth of July procession it generally snows on them, and they do say that as a general thing when a man calls for a brandy toddy there, the bar keeper chops it off with a hatchet and wraps it up in a paper, like maple sugar. And it is further reported that the old soakers haven't any teeth—wore them out eating gin cocktails and brandy punches. I don't endorse that statement—I simply give it for what it is worth— and it is worth—well, I should say, millions, to any man who can believe it without straining himself. But I do endorse the snow on the Fourth of July—because I know that to be true.

[To Be Continued]

October 19, 1869

Mark Twain
His Greetings to the
California Pioneers of 1849

The California Pioneers of 1849, who are now on a grand railway excursion to the East, were entertained at a Delmonico banquet in New York Wednesday evening. Among the letters received and read upon the occasion was the following characteristic epistle sent by Mark Twain:

Elmira, October 11, 1869

To the California Pioneers.

Gentlemen: Circumstances render it out of my power to take advantage of the invitation extended to me through Mr. Simonton, and be present at your dinner in New York.[94] I regret this very much, for there are several among you whom I would have a right to join hands with on the score of old friendship, and I suppose I would have a sublime general right to shake hands with the rest of you on the score of kinship in Californian ups and downs in search of fortune. If I were to tell some of my experiences, you would recognize Californian blood in me, I fancy. The old, old story would sound familiar, no doubt. I have the

usual stock of reminiscences. For instance: I went to Esmeralda[95] early.
I purchased largely in the "Wide West,"[96] the "Winnemucca,"[97] and
other fine claims, and was very wealthy. I fared sumptuously on bread
when flour was $200 a barrel, and had beans every Sunday when none
but blooded aristocrats could afford such grandeur. But I finished by
feeding batteries in a quartz mill at $15 a week, and wishing I was a
battery myself and had some body to feed *me*. My claims in Esmeralda
are there yet. I suppose I could be persuaded to sell. I went to the Humboldt District[98] when it was new. I became largely interested in the
"Alba Nueva,"[99] and other claims with gorgeous names, and was rich
again—in prospect. I owned a vast mining property there. I would not
have sold out for less than $400,000, at that time—but I will now. Fi-
nally I walked home—some 200 miles—partly for exercise and partly
because stage fares were expensive. Next I entered upon an affluent career in Virginia City, and by a judicious investment of labor and the
capital of friends, became the owner of about all the worthless wildcat
mines there were in that part of the country. Assessments did the business for me there. There were 117 assessments to one dividend, and the
proportion of income to outlay was a little against me. My financial
thermometer went down to thirty-two degrees Farenheit [sic], and the
subscriber was frozen out. I took up extension on the main lead—
extensions that reached to British America in one direction and to the
Isthmus of Panama in the other—and I verily believe I would have
been a rich man if I had ever found those infernal extensions. But I did-
n't. I ran tunnels till I tapped the Arctic Ocean, and I sunk shafts till I
broke through the roof of perdition, but those extensions turned up
missing every time. I am willing to sell all that property, and throw in
the improvements. Perhaps you remember the celebrated "North Orphir?"[100] I bought that mine. It was very rich in pure silver. You could
take it out in lumps as big as a filbert. But when it was discovered that
those lumps were melted half-dollars, and hardly melted at that, a
painful case of "saltin" was apparent, and the undersigned adjourned to
the poorhouse again. I paid assessments on "Hale & Norcross"[101] till
they sold me out, and I had to take in washing for a living—and the
next month that infamous stock went up to $7000 a foot. I own millions
and millions of feet of affluent silver leads in Nevada—in fact I own the
entire undercrust of that country, nearly, and if Congress would move
that State off my property so that I could get at it, I would be wealthy
yet. But no, there she squats—and here am I. Failing health persuades
me to sell. If you know of any one desiring a permanent investment, I

can furnish him one that will have the virtue of being eternal.

I have been through the California mill, with all its "dips, spurs, and angles, variations and sinuosities." I have worked there at all the different trades and professions known to the catalogue. I have been every thing, from a newspaper editor down to cowcatcher on a locomotive, and I am encouraged to believe that if there had been a few more occupations to experiment on, I might have made a dazzling success at last, and found out what mysterious design Providence had in view in creating me.

But you perceive that although I am not a pioneer, I have had a sufficiently variegated time of it to enable me to talk pioneer like a native, and feel like a Forty-Niner. Therefore, I cordially welcome you to your old remembered homes and your long-deserted firesides, and close this screed with the sincere hope that your visit here will be a happy one, and unembittered by the sorrowful surprises that absence and lapse of years are wont to prepare for wanderers; surprises which come in the form of old friends missed from their places; silence where familiar voices should be; the young grown old; change and decay every where; home a delusion and a disappointment; strangers at the hearth-stone; sorrow where gladness was; tears for laughter; the melancholy pomp of death where the grace of life had been!

With all good wishes for the Returned Prodigals, and regrets that I cannot partake of a small piece of the fatted calf (rare and no gravy), I am, yours cordially, *Mark Twain*

October 23, 1869

The Legend of the Capitoline Venus

CHAPTER I

[*Scene—An Artist's Studio in Rome.*][102]

"Oh, George, I *do* love you!"

"Bless your dear heart, Mary, I know that—*why* is your father so obdurate!"

"George, he means well, but art is folly to him—he only understands groceries. He thinks you would starve me."

"Confound his wisdom—it savors of inspiration. Why am not I a money making, bowelless grocer, instead of a divinely gifted sculptor with nothing to eat?"

"Do not despond, Georgy, dear—all his prejudices will fade away as soon as you shall have acquired fifty thousand dol—"

"Fifty thousand demons! Child I am in arrears for my board!"

CHAPTER II

[*Scene—A Dwelling in Rome.*]

"My dear sir, it is useless to talk. I haven't any thing against you, but I can't let my daughter marry a hash of love, art and starvation—I believe you have nothing else to offer."

"Sir, I am poor, I grant you. But is fame nothing? The Hon. Bellamy Foodle, of Arkansas, says that my new statue of America is a clever piece of sculpture, and he is satisfied that my name will one day be famous."

"Bosh! What does that Arkansas ass know about it? Fame's nothing—the market price of your marble scare-crow is the thing to look at. Took you six months to chisel it, and you can't sell it for a hundred dollars. No, sir! Show me fifty thousand dollars and you can have my daughter—otherwise she marries young Simper. You have just six months to raise the money in. Good morning, sir."

"Alas! Woe is me!"

CHAPTER III

[*Scene—The Studio.*]

"Oh, John, friend of my boyhood, I am the unhappiest of men."

"You're an ass!"

"I have nothing left to love but my poor statue—and see, even she has no sympathy for me in her cold marble countenance—so beautiful and so heartless!"

"You're a fool!"

"Oh, John!"

"Oh, fudge! Didn't you say you had six months to raise the money in?"

"Don't deride my agony, John. If I had six centuries what good would it do? How could it help a poor wretch without name, capital or friends!"

"Idiot! Coward! Baby! Six months to raise the money in—and five will do!"

"Are you insane?"

"Six months—an abundance. Leave it to me. I'll raise it."

"What do you mean, John? How on earth can you raise such a monstrous sum for *me*?"

"*Will* you let that be *my* business and not meddle? Will you leave the thing in my hands? Will you swear to submit to whatever I do? Will you pledge me to find no fault with my actions?"

"I am dizzy—bewildered—but I swear."

John took up a hammer and deliberately smashed the nose of America! He made another pass and two of her fingers fell to the floor—another, and part of an ear came away—another, and a row of toes were mangled and dismembered—another, and the left leg, from the knee down, lay a fragmentary ruin!

John put on his hat and departed.

George gazed speechless upon the battered and grotesque nightmare before him for the space of thirty seconds, and then wilted to the floor and went into convulsions.

John returned presently with a carriage, got the broken-hearted artist and the broken-legged statue aboard, and drove off, whistling low and tranquilly. He left the artist at his lodgings, and drove off and disappeared down the *Via Quirinalis* with the statue.

CHAPTER IV

[*Scene—The Studio.*]

"The six months will be up at two o'clock to-day! Oh, agony! My life is blighted. I would that I were dead. I had no supper yesterday. I have had no breakfast to-day. I dare not enter an eating-house. And hungry?—don't mention it! My bootmaker duns me to death—my tailor duns me—my landlord haunts me. I am miserable! I haven't seen John since that awful day. *She* smiles on me tenderly when we meet in the great thoroughfares, but her old flint of a father makes her look in the other direction in short order. Now who is knocking at that door? Who is come to prosecute me? That malignant villain the bootmaker, I'll warrant. *Come in!*"

"Ah, happiness attend your highness—Heaven be propitious to your grace! I have brought my lord's new boots—ah, say nothing about the pay, there is no hurry, none in the world. Shall be proud if my noble lord will continue to honor me with his custom—ah, adieu!"

"Brought the boots himself! Don't want his pay! Taken his leave with a bow and a scrape fit to honor majesty withal! Desires a continuance of my custom! Is the world coming to an end? Of all the—*come in!*"

"Pardon signor, but I have brought your new suit—"

"*Come in.*"

"A thousand pardons for this intrusion, your worship! But I have prepared the beautiful suite of rooms below for you—this wretched den is but ill suited to—"

"*Come in!*"

"I have called to say that your credit at our bank sometime since unfortunately interrupted, is entirely and most satisfactorily restored, and we shall be most happy if you will draw upon us for say—"

"*Come in!*"

"My noble boy, she is yours! She'll be here in a moment! Take her—marry her—love her—be happy!—God bless you both! Hip, hip, hur—"

"*Come in!*"

"Oh, George, my own darling, we are saved!"

"Oh, Mary, my own darling, we *are* saved—but I'll swear I don't know why!"

CHAPTER V

[*Scene—A Roman Cafe.*]

One of a group of American gentlemen reads and translates from the weekly edition of *Il Slangwhanger di Roma* as follows:

"WONDERFUL DISCOVERY!—Some six months ago Signor John Smitthe, an American gentleman now some years a resident of Rome, purchased for a trifle a small piece of ground in the Campagna, just beyond the tomb of the Scipio family, from the owner, a bankrupt relative of the Princess Borghese. Mr. Smitthe afterward went to the Minister of the Public Records and had the piece of ground transferred to a poor American artist named George Arnold, explaining that he did it as payment and satisfaction for pecuniary damage accidentally done by him long since upon property belonging to Signor Arnold, and further observed that he would make additional satisfaction by improving the ground for Signor A., at his own charge and cost. Four weeks ago, while making some necessary excavations upon the property Signor Smitthe unearthed the most remarkable ancient statue that has ever been added to the opulent art treasures of Rome. It was an exquisite figure of a woman, and though sadly stained by the soil and the mould of ages, no eye could look unmoved upon its ravishing beauty. The nose, the left leg from the knee down, an ear and also the toes of the right foot and two fingers of one of the hands were gone, but otherwise the noble figure was in a remarkable state of preservation. The government at once took military possession of the statue, and appointed a commission of art critics, antiquaries and cardinal princes of the church to assess its value and determine the remuneration that must go to the owner of the ground in which it was found. The whole affair was kept a profound secret until last night. In the meantime the commission sat with closed doors, and deliberated. Last night they decided unanimously that the statue is a Venus, and the work of some unknown but sublimely gifted artist of the third century before Christ. They consider it the most faultless work of art the world has any knowledge of.

"At midnight they held a final conference and decided that the Venus was worth the enormous sum of *ten million francs!* In accordance with Roman law and Roman usage, the government being half owner in all works of art found in the Campagna, the State has naught to do but pay five million francs to Mr. Arnold and take permanent possession of the beautiful statue. This morning the Venus will be removed to the Capitol, there to remain, and at noon the commission will wait upon Signor Arnold with His Holiness the Pope's order upon the Treasury for the princely sum of five million francs in gold."

Chorus of Voices. — "Luck! It's no name for it!"

Another Voice. — "Gentlemen, I propose that we immediately form an American joint stock company for the purchase of lands and excavation of statues, here, with proper connections in Wall street to bull and bear the stock."

All. — "Agreed."

CHAPTER VI

[Scene — The Roman Capitol.]

"Dearest Mary, this is the most celebrated statue in the world. This is the renowned 'Capitoline Venus' you've heard so much about. Here she is with her little blemishes 'restored' (that is patched) by the most noted Roman artists — and the mere fact that they did the humble patching of so noble a creation will make their names illustrious while the world stands. How strange it seems — this place! The day before I last stood here, ten happy years ago, I wasn't a millionaire — bless your soul, I hadn't a cent. And yet I had a good deal to do with making Rome mistress of this grandest work of ancient art the world contains."

"The worshipped, the illustrious Capitoline Venus — how much she is valued at! Ten millions of francs!"

"Yes — *now* she is."

"And oh, Georgy, how divinely beautiful she is!"

"Ah, yes—but nothing to what she was before that blessed John Smith broke her leg and battered her nose. Ingenious Smith!—gifted Smith—noble Smith! Author of all our bliss! Hark! Do you know what that wheeze means? Mary, that brat has got the whooping cough. Will you *never* learn to take care of the children!"

THE END

The Capitoline Venus is still in the Capitol at Rome, and is still the most charming and most illustrious work of ancient art the World can boast of. But if ever it shall be your fortune to stand before it and go into the customary ecstasies over it, don't permit this true and secret history of its origin to mar your bliss—and when you read about gigantic Petrified Men being dug up near Syracuse[103] in the State of New York, keep your own counsel,—and if the Barnum that buried them there offers to sell to you at an enormous sum, don't you buy. Send him to the Pope!—*Mark Twain*

October 30, 1869

Around the World
Letter No. 2

[These letters are written jointly by Prof. D.R. Ford and Mark Twain. The Professor is now about to sail from San Francisco to Japan, and of course could not run back to visit Hayti. Yet it was manifest that Hayti ought to be visited at once, and a very peculiar state of things existing there illustrated in such a manner as to give the American public a better appreciation of it than they could gather from mere frozen facts and figures in the New York papers. Therefore the undersigned has attended to it.]

Adventures in Hayti

TROPICAL ASPECTS

AT SEA, OFF PORT-AU-PRINCE, OCTOBER 5—As I stepped ashore at the above-named place to-day, I was assailed by a swarm of darkies of all ages and all degrees of hilarity and raggedness.[104] But it was a peaceful assault. They only wanted to carry my valise to the hotel.

In the midst of the clamor I felt the valise passing from me. I was helpless. I simply followed it, making no complaint. It was on the head of a bright little darkey who depended solely on his personal comeliness for attractiveness—he had nothing on but a shirt. And the length of time that had elapsed since that shirt was at the laundry was longer than the shirt itself, I should judge.

We wound in and out among narrow streets bordered by small houses scantily furnished, and generally with pigs, cats and parrots and naked colored children littering the dilapidated little front porches; a monkey or two making trouble with all these parties in turn; a glimpse through the open door of an insignificant stock of wares of sale—such as oranges, pine-apples, coconuts, bread, sausages, cigars, brooms, herrings, cheap prints of saints carrying their bleeding hearts outside their shirt-bossoms—and tending the grocery, a stout wench in parti-colored turban, calico dress, wide open at the breast, cigartie in mouth, no shoes, no stockings. Occasionally we passed genteel houses, entirely surrounded by verandahs, and these verandahs close-shut-tered to keep out the heat. In the yards attached to these houses were tall, thick-bodied cocoa-palms, with foliage like a bunch of swamp-flags exaggerated—the cocoa peculiar to the West Indies. And of course in these yards was a world of flowering tropical plants—curious, gorgeous, outlandish-looking things that had the air of being glaringly out of place with no greenhouse glass arranged around them.

ODORS OF WAR

It was the hottest part of the day, and so there were not many peo-ple stirring. We met two companies of soldiers on their way to embark for the northern coast where the *Quaker City*[105] is bombarding Fort Picolet. *The Quaker City!* It seems strange to speak of her as being en-gaged in such work—the very ship in which a hundred of us pilgrims make a famous pic-nic excursion half round the world about two years ago. But she seems a good warrior. She just riddled one of Sal-nove's war vessels in a sea-fight two or three days ago.

A NEAT SPECULATION

The third citizen I met, addressed me in Spanish, and said he was going down to Bejar to post himself on a hill and observe the battle which must come off there in a day or two, between the insurgents and the government troops, and he would take it as a very great favor if I would sell him the field-glass that was suspended from my shoulder.

I said I did not care particularly to part with it, but still—what would he give? He said:

"I am willing to pay forty thousand dollars."

"What!"

"Forty thousand dollars."

"My friend, are you insane?"

He took a package out of a sort of knapsack which was slung about him, and deliberately counted out forty new and handsome one-thousand dollar Haytian greenbacks. We exchanged. I felt small and mean, thus to take advantage of a lunatic, but then—what would you have done? I then resumed my journey, with an unusually sneaking expression in my countenance.

EXTORTION

Arrived at my hotel, I asked the small colored boy what I owed him for carrying my valise.

"Nine hund'd dollahs, sah."

I fainted.

When I came to, a number of people were about me applying restoratives and doing what else they could to help me. That soulless colored boy was standing there, cold, serene.

I said:

"How much did you say, boy?"

"Nine hund'd dollahs, sah—reg'lar price, sah."

I appealed to the bystanders for protection. An old gentleman of noble countenance and commanding presence said the boy was right—he was charging only the usual rate. I looked at the other faces. They all mutely endorsed the venerable conspirator's statement.

I sadly handed the boy a thousand dollar bill. He walked off.

I was stupefied with amazement. "Gentlemen," I said, "what does this mean? There's a hundred dollars change coming to me."

"True," they old party said, "but it is not the custom to regard a trifle like that."

Stunned and dizzy, I hurried to my room and threw myself on the bed, almost satisfied that I had lost my reason. I applied tests. I repeated the multiplication table without making a mistake. It was plain that my comprehension of numbers was unimpaired. I repeated "The Boy Stood on the Burning Deck," without a blunder. It was plain that my memory was sound. I read one of Mrs. Browning's poems and clearly understood the sense of it. It was plain that my intellectual faculties were in a condition of even unusual vigor. Then what in the world was the matter? Had I not suddenly developed a monomania— a craziness about money, only?

A FELLOW SUFFERER

Somebody knocked. Then the door opened and a poor, sad-looking American woman of about thirty-five years, entered. I seated her with alacrity, and with interest, too, for I was glad enough to have a kind, troubled face to look into, and gather from it sympathy for my own sorrow. She said:

"Sir, I am a stranger to you, but grief makes me bold. My husband died two months ago, and left me in this strange land with little money and not a friend in all the island. My oldest son was soon kidnapped and carried away to fight in the war. Our little property was ten miles from here, and I was living there at the time. My youngest child was lying sick of a fever. These sorrows were not enough. A week ago the insurgents came at night and burned my house to the ground. My sick child I saved—my other children saved themselves. But my escape was narrow. A soldier cut me with his sabre—you can see the stitched gash if you will look while I part my hair on the back of my head—just there—do you see it? And this dress—do you observe the scorched place at the bottom? The fire was that close behind me. Think how sadly I am situated. I would give the world to get home again to America, if only to die. Can you not help me? *Will* you not help me? A friendly schooner captain will give me a free passage, but my creditors will not let me go till they are paid. Oh, I do not mean that all my creditors are so hard with me—no, the trifles I owe to most of them they have freely canceled on their books. But the butcher and the grocer still hold out. They will not let me go. I beseech you sir, help me in this great extremity. I would not go to any but an American—and it has cost me tears to come to you. But I want to go *so* much, and these bills are but a trifle—you cannot miss so small a sum—and if—"

"Say no more, Madam! Say no more. You shall go home. I'll pay this villain grocer and this bloody butcher. Pack your trunk."

"Heaven bless you, sir."

With that she fell upon my neck, poor creature, and gave way to her tears. I was moved myself, and finding all efforts to keep back my own tears fruitless, I yielded and wept. At the end of five minutes I said:

"Cheer up Madam, cheer up! All's well now. I'll set this thing right in a jiffy. What's the amount?"

"I am not certain,—my poor head has been sadly tortured of late— but I think that sixty thousand dollars will—"

I jumped through the second-story window, sash and all.

A PRINCELY BILL

I wandered round the town for three hours, as crazy as a loon—perfectly desperate. It was plain enough to me, now, that I had gone mad on the subject of money. How I had ever come to do such a thing was a mystery, for I had always been a sort of a spendthrift, a man who had never worshipped gold or greenbacks to any alarming extent. But I was reluctant to accept the situation, anyhow, and so I said to myself that by this time Charley must have bought all the things we wanted and got the bills to the hotel. I would go and pay them. I would see if this dismal hallucination was still in force. When I arrived, I told the landlord to make out his own bill and add the tradesmen's bills to it, and give it me as quickly as possible. Then I sat down to wait, a smothering volcano of impatience and anxiety—for if my mind was not straight by this time, I dreaded that my madness might increase, under my distress, and drive me to commit some fearful crime. I shuddered, presently, when I thought I felt a desire creeping through me to spring upon a decrepit old man near me and throttle him. I moved away and turned my back—and then I covertly threw my pocket knife out of the window. Now the bill came. I read thus—I translate:

Mark Twain to Kingston House Dr.
  To room rent (2 percent) $3600
   " removing baggage to room 900
               4500
  To tradesmen's bill as follows:
   6 bunches bananas 2700
   12 pine apples 2000
   10 dozen oranges 900

```
5 boxes cigars  . . . . . . . . . . . . . .98,000
2 baskets claret . . . . . . . . . . . . .22,000
2  "  champagne . . . . . . . . . . . . .88,000
7 dozen lemons . . . . . . . . . . . . . . .800
1 pair boots  . . . . . . . . . . . . . . .21,000
1 dozen socks . . . . . . . . . . . . . .13,500
2 dozen handkerchief  . . . . . . . .43,000
```

Rec'd payment $295,400

Two hundred and ninety-five thousand four hundred dollars! I read this bill over deliberately six or seven times, and never said a word. Then I said I would step out and get a breath of fresh air.

. . .

I got it—the breath of fresh air. I walked gently around the corner, whistling unconcernedly. And then I glanced back, and seeing nobody watching me, I sauntered toward the American packet ship, at the rate of about eleven or twelve miles and hour. I picked Charley up on the way. We hid between decks a couple of hours, till the vessel was out of sight of land. We were safe. So was the valise, and the cigars and things—the landlord had them. I trust he has them yet. We have parted to meet no more. I have seen enough of Hayti. I never did take much interest in Hayti, anyhow.—*Mark Twain*

P.S.—I understand it all now. I have been talking with the captain. It is very simple, when one comprehends it. The fact is, the war has been raging so long that Haytian credit is about dead, and the treasury sapped pretty dry. Therefore one dollar in gold will buy eighteen hundred to two thousand dollars' worth of Haytian greenbacks, according to the tenor of the current war news. I wish I had my valise back.

It is a darling country to live in, that Hayti. Board two hundred and eleven thousand dollars a month in the best hotels, and ice cream three hundred dollars a saucer.

The Paraguay Puzzle

Is Lopez[106] a gentleman or a devil—an exalted patriot or a gory re-production in modern history of the worst of Roman despots? How are we to conclude? We look on this picture and then we look on that, as we have the Paraguayan Dictator delineated to us by two successive American Ministers, and we stand in bewilderment between them. First came back Minister Washburne,[107] with a terrible story to recite, which made the American blood run cold with horror, and then hot with rage; a story of outrage and insolence toward the government which he represented, as well as of monstrous and merciless malignity in the domestic rule of the beleaguered Dictator. Next followed the two rescued victims, Bliss and Masterman, whom Washburne in his es-cape had been forced to leave behind in the clutches of the tyrant, and whose narrative gave more than confirmation to the Ambassador's tale. But with them came puzzling contradictions from Admiral Davis, the commander of our squadron in South American waters, and now, at last, we have Minister McMahon[108] back with a flat denial of all that Washburne, Bliss and Masterman have represented. If we are to believe General McMahon, the redoubtable Lopez, so far from being a monster of the hideous mien hitherto portrayed, is really a gentleman of the first water in point of benign amiability and courtesy—the idol of his devoted subjects—the master spirit of a heroic contest—the ad-miring friend of the United States, from whom he and his patriotic cause merit the most cordial sympathy.

Now what does this mean? What is the secret at the bottom of so broad a contradiction? Upon whom is the lying in the case to be fa-thered, and what does the lying signify? Has Lopez suborned and re-tained McMahon, or is it the fact, as Lopez charged, that Minister Washburne and his two attaches were in the pay of the allied enemies of Paraguay, and parties to a conspiracy against the Dictator? Some-thing there is, certainly, in this Paraguayan business that has a stench of rottenness disgraceful to American diplomacy, and it de-mands to be hunted out.

Judging upon general principles, as between the two accounts of Lopez and his government, that of Minister McMahon seems to us the most improbable. Lopez comes of a bad school of rulers. We all know the merciless, iron-handed rigor of the Dictatorship established by the famous Dr. Francia. It stands in history almost alone and unparalleled—the perfect model of unmixed and unmitigated absolutism. It left hardly the vestige of an independent spirit in the people of the country. Politically speaking, according to all accounts, it made them a nation of children, helpless for themselves, and more resembling the Chinese in submissive incapability than any other known people outside of the Asiatic races. The absolute power which Francia founded, Lopez undoubtedly wields to-day, and the state of things represented by Minister Washburne is far more in keeping with the circumstances of the nation and with the character of its government than is that which we have delineated in roseate colors by his successor, General McMahon.

Of Mr. Bliss, who is one of the witnesses against Lopez, something is known in this region of country, and he certainly has the confidence of those best acquainted with him. As we learn of him, he is one of the last among men to be suspected of intrigue and conspiracy, being a mildly impassioned student, devoted to the pursuits of science, which led him into Paraguay. In the New York *Herald,* of Saturday, we find a long letter from Mr. Bliss, in which Minister McMahon is boldly arraigned upon the charge of having been bribed to complicity with the misdeeds of Lopez. Mr. Bliss writes:

> The truth is, that General McMahon is the apologist of Lopez for money. I proceed to give the proof. At the capture of the positions of Lopez in Valentinas in December last, the carriage of the Dictator fell into the hands of the allies. Among the trophies were an array of documents from the archives of Lopez himself, whose publication has silenced in South America all apologists for the barbarian. There were the records of the daily executions and deaths by torture, which in six months had swept from existence the very flower of Paraguay. Six hundred prominent natives and foreigners had their fate briefly recorded in that register of judicial assassinations.
>
> But the damning fact for General McMahon is this. In the carriage of Lopez were taken documents bearing his own seal and signature which give the key to the conduct of General McMahon. In one of these Lopez executes a deed of gift of his entire property, amounting to hundreds of thousands of dollars, to his notorious mistress, Madame Eliza Lynch, and constitutes General Martin T. McMahon trustee of all this property. Here we have the milk in the coconut. General McMahon is the pecuniary cats-paw of Lopez, bribed by him with untold sums to save from

threatened capture all his personal property as stated by Mr. Washburne, consisted of the confiscated specie of the victims of Lopez.

This document was published at the time in the newspapers all over South America and Europe, and, I think, in this country. I held my peace, hoping it might prove a forgery, but every subsequent occurrence has demonstrated its genuineness. The fact that General McMahon immediately constituted himself guardian of the mistress and of the bastard children of Lopez throws a strong confirmatory light upon these facts. General McMahon has never contradicted the authenticity of that letter, and for all the damning inference which must be drawn from it I doubt whether he will now dare to do so. He may do as he chooses— deny the charge or pass it unnoticed—but the truth will out, and the complicity of General McMahon with the bandit and outlaw Lopez will be fully proved by testimony mountain high.

These are explicit charges, and the government cannot allow them to go uninvestigated. Indeed, an investigation, we believe, is in progress, and let us hope that it will result in some more satisfactory conclusion than we usually get from such official judgments so that the actual truth of this rotten Paraguay business may be positively known. *[Unsigned]*

November 10, 1869

A Good Letter

Mark Twain's Idea of It

The most useful and interesting letters we get here from home are from children seven or eight years old.[109] This is a petrified truth. Happily they have got nothing else to talk about but home, and neighbors and family—things their betters think unworthy of transmission thousands of miles. They write simply and naturally and without strain for effect. They tell all they know, and then stop. They seldom deal in abstractions or homilies. Consequently their epistles are brief; but, treating as they do of familiar scenes and persons, always entertaining. Now, therefore, if you would learn the art of letter-writing, let a child teach you. I have preserved a letter from a little girl eight years of age—preserved it as a curiosity, because it was the only letter I ever got from the States that had any information in it. It ran thus:

St. Louis, 1865

"Uncle Mark, if you was here I could tell you about Moses in the bulrushes again, I know it better now. Mr. Sowberry has got his leg broke off a horse. He was riding it on Sunday. Margaret, that's the Maid, Margaret has taken all the spittoons, and slop buckets and old jugs out of your room, because she says she don't think you are coming back any more, you have been gone too long. Sissy McElroy's mother has got another little baby. She has them all the time. It has got little blue eyes, like Mr. Swimley that boards there and looks just like him. I have got a new doll, but Johnny Anderson pulled one of the legs out. Miss Dusenberry was here yesterday; I gave her your picture, but she didn't want it. My cat has got more kittens—oh! you can't think—twice as many as Lottie Belden's. And there's one, such a sweet little buff one with a short tail, and I named it for you.

All of them's got names now—General Grant, and Halleck,[110] and Moses, and Margaret, and Dueteronomy, and Captain Semmes, and Exodus, and Leviticus, and Horace Greeley—all named but one, and I am saving it because the one I named for you's been sick all the time since, and I reckon it'll die. [It appears to be mighty rough on the short-tailed kitten for naming it for me. I wonder how the reserved victim will stand it.] Uncle Mark, I do believe Hattie Caldwell likes you, and I know she thinks you are pretty, because I heard her say nothing could hurt your good looks—nothing at all—she said, even if you were to have the small pox ever so bad, you would be just as good looking as you were before. And ma says she's ever so smart. [Very.] So no more this time, because General Grant and Moses are fighting.

Annie[111]

This child treads on my toes in every other sentence with perfect looseness, but in the simplicity of her time of life she doesn't know it.

I consider that a model letter—an eminently readable and entertaining letter, and, as said before, it contains more matter of interest and real information than any letter ever received from the East. I had rather hear about cats at home and their truly remarkable names, than listen to a lot of stuff about people I am not acquainted with, or read "The Evil Effects of the Intoxicating Bowl,"[112] illustrated on the back with the picture of a rugged scalawag pelting away right and left in the midst of his family circle with a junk bottle.—*Mark Twain*

Hanging to Slow Music

The coarse and bungling brutalities that used to be very commonly incident to the execution of criminals had much effect in creating a sentiment opposed to capital punishment.[113] But latterly the hanging business has been undergoing a kind of refinement that is equally disgusting, and even more calculated to raise the question whether civilization cannot dispense with the gallows and sustain no moral or social detriment from the loss. Within the last two or three years the performance of the hangman has in some manner taken on the character of a sort of ceremony of canonization. The most ecstatic exhibitions of piety that we get now-a-days are from the elevation of the Sheriff's trap-door, in a momentary glimpse of some transformed ruffian exhorting with the noose at his neck—and the more blood he has washed from his murderous fingers the more touching saintliness of aspect he is made to put on. As a stage for the performance of hysterical religious melo-dramas, we have been sick enough of the gallows for some time to vote with Bovee and Greeley on the capital punishment question; but the new feature introduced day before yesterday up in New Hampshire, of turning the pious criminal off to an accompaniment of slow music, caps the climax of disgust: "A choir of ladies, by his request, sang one of his favorite hymns, commencing 'My latest sun is sinking fast, my race is nearly run.'" So says our accounts of the edifying scene, received yesterday morning by telegraph. The brute in this case had chopped an old man and an old woman to death with an axe in order to steal their little wealth of $500, and of course he arrived at the rope's end in an eminent state of saintliness—so much so that nothing short of a choir of ladies, to sing his favorite hymn, could justly sentimentalize the occasion of his strangulation. Pah! We are either hanging too many saints or playing too awful farces. That is plain. *[Unsigned]*

November 13, 1869

Around the World
Letter No. 3

[These letters are written jointly by Professor D. R. Ford and Mark Twain. The former does the actual traveling, and such facts as escape his notice are supplied by the latter, who remains at home.]

California—Continued

MORE CLIMATE

There are other kinds of climate in California—several kinds—and some of them very agreeable. The climate of San Francisco is mild and singularly equable.[114] The thermometer stands at about seventy degrees the year round. It hardly changes at all. You sleep under one or two light blankets Summer and Winter, and never use a mosquito bar. Nobody ever wears Summer clothing. You wear black broadcloth—if you've got it—in August and January, just the same. It is no colder, and no warmer, in the one month than the other. You don't use overcoats and you don't use fans. It is just as pleasant a climate as could be contrived, and is the most unvarying in the whole world. The wind blows there a good deal in the Summer months, but then you can go over to Oakland, if you want to—three or four miles away—it don't blow there. It has only snowed twice in San Francisco in nineteen years, and then it only remained on the ground long enough to astonish the children, and set them to wondering what the feathery stuff was.

During eight months of the year, straight along, the skies are bright and cloudless and never a drop of rain falls. But when the other four months come along, the most righteous thing you can do will be to go and steal an umbrella. Because you'll need it. Not just one day, but one hundred and twenty days in unvarying succession. When you want to go visiting, or attend church, or the theatre, you never look up at the clouds to see whether it is likely to rain or not—you look at the almanac. If it is winter, it will rain—there is little use in bothering about that—and if it is summer, it *won't* rain, and you can not help it. You never see a lightning-rod, because it never thunders and it never lightens. And after you have listened for six or eight weeks, every night, to the dismal monotony of these quiet rains, you will wish in your heart the thunder *would* leap and crash and roar along those drowsy skies once, and make everything alive—you will wish the prisoned lightnings *would* cleave the dull firmament asunder and light it with the red splendors of hell for *one* little instant. You would give any *thing* to hear the old familiar thunder again and see the lightning strike somebody. And along in the Summer, when you have suffered about four months of lustrous, pitiless sunshine, you are ready to go down on your knees and beg for rain—hail— snow—thunder and lightning—anything to break the monotony— you'll take an earthquake, if you can't do any better. And the chances are that you'll get it, too.

Sandy Fertility

San Francisco is built on sand hills, but they are prolific sand hills. They yield a generous vegetation. All your rare flowers, which people in "the States" rear with such patient care in parlor flower pots and green houses, flourish luxuriantly in the open air there all the year round. Calla lilies, all sorts of geraniums, passion flowers, moss roses—I don't know the names of a tenth part of them. I only know that while New Yorkers are burdened with banks and drifts of snow, Californians are burdened with banks and drifts of flowers, if they only keep their hands off and let them grow. And I have heard that we have here that rarest and most curious of all flowers, the beautiful *Espiritu Santo,* as the Spaniards call it—or flower of the Holy Spirit— though I never have seen it anywhere but in Central America—down on the Isthmus. In its cup is the daintiest little fac-simile of a dove, as pure and white as snow. The Spaniards have a superstitious reverence for it. The blossom has been conveyed to the States, submerged in ether; and the bulb has been taken thither also, but every attempt to make it bloom after it arrived, has failed.

Climate Resumed

I have spoken of the endless Winter of Mono, California, and the eternal Spring of San Francisco. Now if we travel a hundred miles in a straight line, we come to the eternal Summer of Sacramento. One never sees Summer clothing or mosquitoes in San Francisco—but they can be found in Sacramento. Not always and unvaryingly, but about 143 months out of twelve years, perhaps. Flowers bloom there, always, you can easily believe—people suffer and sweat, and swear, morning, noon and night, and wear out their dearest energies fanning themselves. It gets pretty hot there, but if you go down to Fort Yuma you will find it hotter. Fort Yuma is probably the hottest place on earth. The thermometer stays at 120 in the shade there all the time— except when it relents and—goes higher. It is a U.S. military post, and its occupants get so used to the terrific heat that they are bound to suffer without it. There is a tradition (attributed to John Phoenix)[115] that a very, very wicked soldier died there, once, and of course he went straight to the hottest corner of perdition, ——, and the next day he telegraphed back for his blankets. There is no doubt about the truth of this statement—there *can* be no doubt about it—for I have seen the place where that soldier used to board. With a French lady by the name of O'Flannigan, and she lives there yet. Sacramento is fiery Summer always, and you can gather roses, and eat strawberries and ice-cream, and wear white linen clothes, and pant and perspire at eight or nine o'clock in the morning, and take the cars, and at noon put on your furs and your skates and go skimming over frozen Donner Lake, seven thousand feet above the valley, among snow banks fifteen feet deep, and in the shadow of grand mountain peaks that lift their frosty crags ten thousand feet above the level of the sea. There is a transition for you! Where will you find another like it in the Western hemisphere? And I have swept around snow-walled curves of the Pacific Railroad in that vicinity, 6000 feet above the sea, and looked down as the birds do, upon the everlasting summer of the Sacramento Valley, with its green fields, its feathery foliage, its silver streams, all slumbering in the mellow haze of its enchanted atmosphere, and all infinitely softened and spiritualized by distance—a rich, dreamy, exquisite glimpse of fairy land, made all the more charming and striking that it was caught through a forbidding gateway of ice and snow and savage crags and precipices.

DESOLATION

It was in this Sac Valley that a deal of the most lucrative of the early gold mining was done, and you may still see, in places, its grassy slopes and levels torn and guttered and disfigured by the avaricious spoilers of fifteen and twenty years ago. You may see such disfigurements far and wide over California—and in some such places, where only meadows and forests are visible—not a living creature, not a house, no stick or stone or remnant of a ruin, and not a sound, not even a whisper to disturb the Sabbath stillness—you will find it hard to believe that there stood at one time a wildly, fiercely-flourishing little city, of two thousand or three thousand souls, with its newspaper, fire company, brass band, volunteer militia, bank, hotels, noisy Fourth of July processions and speeches, gambling hells crammed with tobacco smoke, profanity, and rough-bearded men of all nations and colors, with tables heaped with glittering gold dust sufficient for the revenues of a German principality—streets crowded and rife with business—town lots worth $400 a front foot—labor, laughter, music, dancing, swearing, fighting, shooting, stabbing—a bloody inquest and a man for breakfast every morning—*every thing* that goes to make life happy and desirable—all the appointments and appurtenances of a thriving and prosperous and promising young city,—and *now* nothing is left but a lifeless, homeless solitude. The men are gone, the houses have vanished, even the *name* of the place is forgotten. In no other land do towns so absolutely die and disappear, as in the old mining regions of California.

THE CRUSADING HOST

It was a driving, vigorous restless population in those days. It was a *curious* population in those days. It was the *only* population of the kind that the world has ever seen gathered together, and it is not likely that the world will ever see its like again. For, mark you, it was an assemblage of 200,000 *young* men—not simpering, dainty, kid-gloved weaklings, but stalwart, muscular, dauntless young braves, brimful of push and energy, and royally endowed with every attribute that goes to make up a peerless and magnificent manhood—the very pick and choice of the world's glorious ones. No women, no children, no gray and stooping veterans,—none but erect, bright-eyed, quick-moving, strong-handed young giants—the strangest population, the finest population, the most gallant host that ever trooped down the startled solitudes of an unpeopled land. And where are they now? Scattered to the ends of the earth—or prematurely aged and decrepit—or shot or stabbed in street affrays—or dead of disappointed hopes and broken hearts—all gone, or nearly all—victims devoted upon the altar of the golden calf—the noblest holocaust that ever wafted its sacrificial incense heavenward. California has much to answer for in this destruction of the flower of the world's young chivalry.

It was a splendid population—for all the slow, sleepy, sluggish-brained sloths staid at home—you never find that sort of people among pioneers—you can not build pioneers out of that sort of material. It was that population that gave to California a name for getting up astounding enterprises and rushing them through with a magnificent dash and daring, and a princely recklessness of cost or consequences, which she bears unto this day—and when she projects a new astonisher, the grave world smiles and admires as usual, and says, "well, that is California all over."—*Mark Twain*

November 20, 1869

Civilized Brutality

A Western exchange, commenting upon the recent trapeze accident in St. Louis, where a young girl, perilling her life for the amusement of a theatre full of men and women spectators, lost her balance while swinging in mid air upon one foot and fell twenty-five feet to the floor, curiously enough remarks that "the parent who would trade in this manner upon the life of his daughter ought to have been tied up by the audience and publicly lashed." Now, really, that would have been a sublime exhibition of impudence on the part of the audience. By what right, pray, could the spectators in such a case lash the parent? Were they not parties to the inhuman "trade"? Were not they the purchasers of what the girl's father sold? Was it not because he found them eager buyers that he put the life of his daughter into the market and made brutal merchandise of it? And what moral superiority has the buyer over the seller in transactions of that kind?

The reckless peril in which this unhappy girl nightly placed her person and her life was the fulfillment of a tacit but well understood bargain between herself, or those who controlled her, and the people who nightly formed the audience assembled to witness her performance. They paid her for sporting with death, and the deadly sport was their amusement. They hired her to afford them the brutal gratification of the excitement of the feeling that they might possibly witness just that catastrophe which did occur. Let the fact be plainly acknowledged. It was that ghastly possibility which made the relish of the entertainment. Without its barbaric spice who would have been attracted? Take away the peril from "M'lle Zagrina's" performance,

leaving it every other feature, of graceful posturing, of supple movement and of admirable dexterity—what favor would it have found,
and with whom? Lower the trapeze upon which she swung and lithely
balanced herself, down to an elevation of five feet only from the floor,
instead of twenty-five, and where would she find spectators to pay for
the exhibition of her graceful feats? Secure by any means the *safety* of
the girl in life and limb, and what theatre could profitably engage
her? We say again, it is the deadliness of the performer's peril in all
these exhibitions that brings men and women to see them. It is because a tremerous nerve, or a miss or a slip of the hand or foot is
death or mutilation to the reckless actor in the scene, that the scene
gathers its eager spectators. The risk of the wretched subject of their
applause is what they enjoy, and *all* that they enjoy. Unacknowledged
to themselves, perhaps, a savage and barbarous thirst for the excitement of the possible horror of death is in their hearts—a thirst which
differs by how much from that which carried Roman dames and
maids and Senators and the Roman rabble to the amphitheatre sixteen centuries ago, when gladiators fought and Christian martyrs
were torn by wild beasts?

The fact is, our civilization is scarcely more than a thin coating of
varnish over barbarism. If we scratch the skin of the average modern
citizen of Christian America, or England, or Germany, of France, we
find a man underneath who very much resembles, after all, the old
Roman of Caesar's day, or the Goth who marched out of the Northern
forests to conquer Rome. He has the ancient barbarous instinct strong
within him yet, and his sixteen or eighteen centuries of culture have
only served to refine its original coarseness. From the gladiatorial
arena to the tournament field—from the tournament to the bull fight
and the bear garden—from thence to the prize ring and from the
prize ring to the exhibitions of the trapeze and the Blondin tight
rope—are but the gradations of a refinement in taste that leaves the
essential inhumanity of the feeling which they have successively grat-
ified actually untouched. The soul of the primitive savage, lurking yet
in the breast of the sleek gentleman and the dainty lady of our civilization to-day, demands these grim antics with death for the flavor of
their entertainments. While the merciless demand is made, its
wretched purveyors will be always ready—even as the gladiators for
a Roman spectacle were never wanting. Can we do nothing better
than to lash *them? [Unsigned]*

Browsing Around

NOTABLE THEATRICAL EVENT

BOSTON, NOV., 1869—Boston has resurrected "Midsummer Night's Dream," and done it after a more splendid fashion than has ever been attempted with a Shakesperian [sic] play in America before.[116] In consequence, Selwyn's theatre is likely to be crowded for many a coming night. Some of the scenery in this new wonder is marvelous.[117] In one part of the play the curtain rises upon a spectacle some thing like this: In the foreground a lake as smooth and as glossy as a mirror; about its borders a luxurious growth of tropical plants; in the center a very small island, with one or two stately trees on it, whose roots are hidden among blossoming plants—and both the trees and the plants are faithfully mirrored in the lake; beyond, are two or three similar islands, one behind another, and each glassing itself in the water—the outlines of the trees and reflections growing fainter and fainter in the receding distance; in the far background the lake narrows to a winding river, which is soon lost among towering mountains. All this in a rich, dreamy sort of twilight. Presently a mellow radiance begins to suffuse the sky behind the mountains; it grows, brightens, and a silver edge of the moon peeps above a distant crag; in a few moments the entire moon appears, casts an amber glory over trees, islands, lake and river—drifts behind a cloud—appears again—is lost behind a crag, but marks its course with a silver edge as it moves along—then comes out full in the heavens again, and straightway its wrinkled and glittering reflection comes shimmering across the water, just as you have seen a catspaw of wind mark its approach on a river. It is enchantingly beautiful. Nature herself could not spirit away a twilight more deftly and replace it with the tender lustre of the moon more happily. Presently this scene becomes a panorama. The islands go drifting away out of sight, the lake grows broader and broader, till its burnished surface stretches away into an enchanted distance; and now its perfect naturalness is made still more noticeable, as curves and shreds of seaweed and other trifles floating on its surface drift into the quivering track of the moon and instantly are lit up with a bright sheen—and then drift out again and take the dull hue they had before. Directly, right in the foreground, a small island glides into view with a venerable ruin on it—five or six grim, monstrous pillars, with massive capstones, and about their bases the fallen entablatures, wreathed with ivy. Imagine the picture of the glittering sea round about this lonely old temple on its patch of island, and the yellow disk of the moon appearing and disappearing as it shows between the black columns one moment, gilding their flutings, and hides behind an intervening one the next. The temple glides away, and we lose it and regret it. But shortly the placid sea begins to assume a chilly look, and in another moment a vast iceberg, undermined with huge arches, comes into view—then a brilliant group of such. An arch of blinding light (the aurora borealis) falls upon the scene, and whatsoever wanders into it—flitting fairies, swimming water-sprites, swans, domed and pinnacled icebergs—are glorified for that moment, as if the lightnings clothed them. The clouds in the sky are filled with all manner of fantastic little devils and such things, and presently among the clouds appears a great, round, dimly defined disk, with two female figures in it, royally attired, but with such a soft, exquisite film about them that they seem unreal, intangible, spiritualized—an illusion, a dream, a vision, almost a part of the cloudy surroundings.

But I forebear. I am so taken with this thing that I shall be betrayed into "gushing" presently, if I do not desist. Mark you, I am not setting up for a theatrical critic. Nothing of the kind. I innocently think this whole spectacle is the finest thing I ever saw. Adepts in theatrical criticism may see faults that I wot not of. Let them. They are the sufferers, not I. I suppose if I were a doctor I would see consumption where ignorant people only saw and admired a blush on a handsome face; and I might see a death warrant in what another man took for a beautiful complexion; and I suppose that in cases where the ignorant were charmed with what seemed a romantic languor, I would say, "Blue mass is what she wants—the young woman's liver is out of order." I do not wish to be a theatrical critic, or a doctor. For when I see such a thing as this "Midsummer Night's Dream," I wish to "gush;" and when I see female beauty I wish to "gush" again and continue to gush. I will take the enjoyment for my share, I am content that the critics and the doctors may take all the liver complaint there may be in the scenery and the women.

A Fair Career Closed

The late railway accident in California cut off a young man who was a shining example of how generous Fortune can be, and how fickle. I refer to the Hon. Alexander W. Baldwin,[118] United States District

Judge for the District of Nevada. He was a fortunate and distinguished son of a distinguished father, (Hon. Joseph G. Baldwin, once a Supreme Judge of California, and the author of a formerly exceedingly popular book, "The Flush Times of Alabama and Mississippi.") At about the age of twenty-seven, young Baldwin was a member of the law firm of Stewart,[119] (now United States Senator) Kirkpatrick, & Baldwin, of Virginia City, Nevada. It was then that I knew him first. It was said that at one time, in those days, (it was in the heyday of the silver excitement,) the earnings of the firm reached two hundred thousand dollars in three months. The firm achieved such a reputation for winning cases, that for a long time a case was considered already won when they consented to take hold of it. Bye-and-bye Mr. Stewart was made a Senator, and before Baldwin had more than compassed his thirtieth year he was raised to the great eminence of an United States District Judge, an appointment which is made for life—and if I remember rightly it carried with it also the possibility of young Baldwin's being called to sit temporarily upon the Supreme Bench of the United States during the absence or illness of Judge Field. At any rate, few youths, starting from nothing, find themselves wealthy and firmly anchored in a grand and permanent position at thirty, as was the case with this one. Young Baldwin married a young lady of excellent family and rare personal attractions and accomplishments. They provided themselves a luxurious home. They had servants, horses, books, pictures, money without stint, friends, power, high distinction—what else could they want? Fortune did all that for them. Was it not a brave outpouring of dazzling favors?

But Fortune was always fickle, always will be. A telegram flashes across the continent, and topples all this grandeur to the earth—makes a gilded mockery of all this luxury—turns the joy to sorrow, the contentment to tears, hangs crepe upon every reminiscence of this brilliant young life! A mangled corpse, a widow in her weeds, a vague, awful blank—these are what the telegram suggests.

> Death is nothing, when it releases some wretch who has been cuffed and harried and hunted by hard fortune all his friendless life, but it is grisly and hideous, when it chills a glad heart and dethrones an exultant spirit.

GETTING MY FORTUNE TOLD

I had heard so much about the celebrated fortune teller, Madame ———, (I decline to advertise for her in this paragraph) that I went to see her yesterday. She has a dark complexion naturally, and this effect is heightened by artificial aids which cost her nothing. She wears curls, very black ones, and I had an impression that she gave their native attractiveness a lift with rancid butter. She wears a reddish check handkerchief, cast loosely around her neck, and it was plain that her other one is slow getting back from the wash. I presume she takes snuff. At any rate, something resembling it had lodged among the hairs sprouting from a picturesque mole on her upper lip. I know she likes garlic—I knew that as soon as she sighed. She looked at me searchingly for nearly a minute, with her black eyes, and then said:

"It is enough. Come!"

She started down a very dark and dismal corridor, I stepping close after her. Presently she stopped and said that as the way was crooked and so dark, perhaps she had better get a light. But it seemed ungallant to allow a woman to put herself to so much trouble for me, and so I said:

"It is not worth while, madam. If you will heave another sigh, I think I can follow it."

So we got along all right. Arrived at her official and mysterious den, she asked me to tell her the date of my birth, the exact hour of that occurrence, and the color of my grandmother's hair. I answered as accurately as I could. Then she said:

"Young man, summon your fortitude—do not tremble. I am about to reveal the past."

"Information concerning the future would be, in a general way, more—"

"Silence! You have had much trouble, some joy, some good fortune, some bad. Your great grandfather was hanged."

"That is a l——"

"Silence! Hanged, sir. But it was not his fault. He could not help it."

"I am glad you do him justice."

"Ah—grieve, rather, that the jury did. He was hanged. His star crosses yours in the fourth division, fifth sphere. Consequently, you will be hanged also."

"In view of this cheerful—"

"I *must* have silence. Yours was not, in the beginning, a criminal nature, but circumstances changed it. At the age of nine you stole sugar. At the age of fifteen you stole money. At twenty you stole horses. At twenty-five you committed arson. At thirty, hardened in crime, you became an editor. Since then your descent has been rapid. You are now a public lecturer. Worse things are in store for you. You will be sent to Congress. Next to the penitentiary. Finally, happiness will come again—all will be well—you will be hanged."

I was now in tears. It seemed hard enough to go to Congress. But to be hanged—this was too sad, too dreadful. The woman seemed surprised at my grief. I told her the thoughts that were in my mind. Then she comforted me—this blessed woman reconciled me, made me contented, even happy.

"Why, man," she said, "hold up your head—*you* have nothing to grieve about. Listen. You will live in New Hampshire. In your sharp need and distress the Brown family will succor you—such of them as Pike the assassin left alive.[120] They will be benefactors to you. When you shall have grown fat upon their bounty, and are grateful and happy, you will desire to make some modest return for these things, and so you will go to the house some night and brain the whole family with an axe. You will borrow funds from the deceased, and disburse them in riotous living among the rowdies and courtezans of Boston. Then you will be arrested, tried, condemned to be hanged, thrown into prison. Now is your happy day. You will be converted—you will be converted just as soon as every effort to compass pardon, commutation or reprieve has failed—and then! Why, then, every morning and every afternoon, the best and purest young ladies of the village will assemble in your cell and sing hymns. This will show that assassination is respectable. Then you will write a touching letter, in which you will forgive all those recent Browns. This will excite the public admiration. No public can withstand magnanimity. Next, they will take you to the scaffold, with great eclat, at the head of an imposing procession composed of clergymen, officials, citizens generally, and young ladies walking pensively two and two, and bearing bouquets and immortelles. You will mount the scaffold, and while the great concourse stand uncovered in your presence, you will read your sappy little speech which the minister has written for you. And then, in the midst of a grand and impressive silence, they will swing you into per——, Paradise, my son. There will not be a dry eye on the ground. You will be a hero! Not a rough there but will envy you. Not a rough there but will resolve to emulate you.

And next, a great procession will follow you to the tomb—will weep over your remains—the young ladies will sing again the hymns made dear by sweet associations connected with the jail, and as a last tribute of affection, respect, and appreciation of your many sterling qualities, they will walk two and two around your bier and strew wreaths

of flowers on it. And lo, you are canonized! Think of it, son—ingrate,
assassin, robber of the dead, drunken brawler among thieves and har-
lots in the slums of Boston one month, and the pet of the pure and innocent daughters of the land the next! Fool!—so noble a fortune and
yet you sit here grieving!"

"No, Madame," I said, "you do me wrong, you do indeed. I am perfectly satisfied. I did not know before that my great grandfather was
hanged, but it is of no consequence. He has probably ceased to
bother about it by this time—and I have not commenced, yet. I confess, madam, that I do something in the way of editing, and lecturing, but the other crimes you mention have escaped my memory. Yet
I must have committed them—you would not deceive an orphan. But
let the past be, as it was, and let the future be as it may—these are
nothing. I have only cared for one thing. I have always felt that I
should be hanged some day, and some how the thought has annoyed
me considerably—but if you can only assure me that I shall be
hanged in New Hampshire—"

"Not a shadow of a doubt!"

"Bless you, my noble benefactress!—excuse this embrace—you
have removed a great load from my breast. To be hanged in New
Hampshire, is happiness—it leaves an honored name behind a man,
and introduces him at once into the best New Hampshire society in
the other world."

I then took leave of the fortune-teller. But seriously, is it well to glo-
rify a murderous villain on the scaffold, as Pike was glorified in New
Hampshire a few days ago? Is it well to turn the penalty for a bloody
crime into a reward? Is it just to do it? Is it safe?

LECTURING

I find it a pleasant business in New England. The railway trips are
short, an so they are never fatiguing. And then one has the Saturday
nights for holidays. I am to remain here all the season. I have taken
no engagements outside of New England, except in New York, Brooklyn, Washington, Philadelphia, and half a dozen places on my road
home to Buffalo.—*Mark Twain*

December 3, 1869

The Richardson Murder

The tragedy enacted a few days ago in the office of the New York *Tribune,* and which became complete yesterday morning by the death of its victim, Albert D. Richardson, has furnished a rare theme to certain journalists who are always found ready to pounce upon such opportunities for a display of the exceeding delicacy of their moral sensibilities.[121] Perhaps we are wrong, but we cannot help distrusting the genuineness of the morality which sermonizes with so much indignant severity upon the relations that existed between Mr. Richardson and the lady who, just before the death of the murdered man, became his wife. It is possible that Mr. Richardson deserved the condemnation which these ready moralists have so eagerly heaped upon him; but whether he did or did not depends upon the circumstances under which he and Mrs. McFarland became affianced to each other. If he wrought in any way the alienation of her affections from her former husband—if he intruded himself between those two, and brought about the separation which placed him in possession of the woman—then we say amen to any strictures upon his conduct that may be pronounced in the name of society and its moral laws. But that is a question of fact which remains undetermined to public knowledge. It is the question of verity between the murderer and the murdered man. Assuming that the story of what had passed, as told by Mr. Richardson and his friends, is the true story, it is no honest morality that feels the bitter offense pretended in some of the eloquent homilies we have been reading upon the subject. A drunken, vagabond, abusive husband *may* drive the purest wife to seek separation from him, so long as law is found any where to accord it to her; an upright and honorable man *may* find himself drawn to such a woman, in that worse than widowed state, first by sympathy and then by love, and feel that both he and she are justified in taking advantage of the laws which give her divorce and make her free to become his wife. The laws that render such a case possible may be, as they no doubt are, lamentably wrong; but who dare say that in a like situation he or she would refuse to contemplate them or refuse to invoke them? Dare they who so piously cast their stones at the murdered Richardson make oath that they would not love, and would not seek to win, and would not wed a woman under such circumstances as those out of which his relations with Mrs. McFarland grew—assuming that he has told them truly? We doubt. We distrust their homilies. We don't believe that the real laxities in society are improved at all by such false refinements in moralizing. *[Unsigned]*

December 4, 1869

Browsing Around

"BACK FROM YURRUP"

BOSTON, NOVEMBER, 1869—Have you ever seen a family of fools just back from Europe—or Yurrup, as they pronounce it? They never talk *to* you, of course, being strangers, but they talk to each other and *at* you till you are pretty nearly distracted with their clatter; till you are sick of their ocean experiences; their mispronounced foreign names; their dukes and emperors; their trivial adventures; their pointless reminiscences; till you are sick of their imbecile faces and their relentless clack, and wish it had pleased Providence to leave the clapper out of their empty skulls.

I traveled with such a family one eternal day, from New York to Boston, last week. They had spent just a year in "Yurrup," and were returning home to Boston. Papa said little, and looked bored—he had simply been down to New York to receive and cart home his cargo of traveled imbecility. Sister Angeline, aged 23, sister Augusta, aged 25, and brother Charles, aged 33, did the conversational drivel, and mama purred and admired, and threw in some help when occasion offered, in the way of remembering some French barber's—I should say some French Count's—name, when they pretended to have forgotten it. They occupied the choice seats in the parlor of the drawing-room car, and for twelve hours I sat opposite to them—was their *vis-a-vis*, they would have said, in their charming French way.

Augusta—"Plague that nahsty (nasty) steamer! I've the headache yet, she rolled so the fifth day out."

Angeline—"And well you may. *I* never saw such a nahsty old tub. I never want to go in the *Ville de Paris* again. Why *didn't* we go over to London and come in the *Scotia?*"

Aug—"Because we were fools!"

[I fervently endorsed that sentiment.]

Ange—"Gustie, what made Count Caskowhisky drive off looking so blue, that last Thursday of Pairy? (Paris, she meant.) Ah, own up, now!"

Aug—"Now, Angie, how you talk! I *told* the nahsty creature I would not receive his attentions any longer. And the old duke his father kept boring me about him and his two million francs a year till I sent *him* off with a flea in his ear."

Chorus.—"Ke-he-he!! Ha-ha-ha!"

Charles—[Pulling a small silken cloak to pieces.] "Angie, where'd you get this cheap thing?"

Ange—"You, Cholly, let that alone! Cheap! Well, how could I help it? There we were, tied up in Switzerland—just down from Mon Blong (Mont Blanc, doubtless)—couldn't buy anything in those nahsty shops so far away from Pairy. I had to put up with that slimpsy forty-dollar rag—but bless you, I couldn't go naked!"

Chorus.—"Ke-he-he!"

Aug—"Guess who I was thinking of? Those ignorant persons we saw first in Rome and afterwards in Venice—those—"

Ange—"Oh, ha-ha-ha! He-he-he! It *was* so funny! Papa, one of them called the Santa della Spiggiola the Santa della Spizziola! Ha-ho-ha! And she thought it was Canova[122] that did Michael Angelo's Moses! Only *think* of it!—Canova a sculptor and the Moses a picture! I thought I should die! I guess I let them see by the way I laughed, that they'd made fools of themselves, because they blushed and sneaked off."

[Papa laughed faintly, but not with the easy grace of a man who was certain he knew what he was laughing about.]

Aug.—"Why Cholly,! Where did you get those nahsty Beaumarchais[123] gloves? Well, I *wouldn't*, if I were you!"

Mamma—[With uplifted hands.] "Beaumarchais, my son!"

Ange—"Beaumarchais! Why how can you! Nobody in Pairy wears those nahsty things but the commonest people."

Charles—"They *are* a rum lot, but then Tom Blennerhasset gave 'em to me—he wanted to do something or other to curry favor, I s'pose."

Ange—"Tom Blennerhasset!"

Aug—"Tom Blennerhasset!"

Mamma—"Tom Blennerhasset! And have you been associating with *him!*"

Papa—[suddenly interested.] "Heavens, what has the son of an honored and honorable old friend been doing?"

Chorus.—"Doing! Why, his father has endorsed himself bankrupt for friends—that's what the matter!"

Ange—"Oh, mon Dieu, j'ai faim! Avez-vous quelque chose de bon, en votre poche, mon cher frere? Excuse me for speaking French, for, to tell the truth, I haven't spoken English for so long that it comes dreadful awkward. Wish we were back in Yurrup—c'est votre desire aussi, n'est-ce pas, mes cheres?"

And from that moment they lapsed into barbarous French and kept it up for an hour—hesitating, gasping for words, stumbling head over heels through adverbs and participles, floundering among adjectives, working miracles of villainous pronunciation—and neither one of them ever by any chance understanding what another was driving at.

By that time, some new comers had entered the car, and so they lapsed into English again and fell to holding everything American up to scorn and contumely in order that they might thus let those new comers know they were just home from "Yurrup." They kept up this little game all the way to Boston—and if ever I can learn when their funeral is to take place, I shall lay aside every other pleasure and attend it. To use their pet and best beloved phrase, they were a "nahsty" family of American snobs, and there ought to be a law against allowing such to go to Europe and misrepresent the nation. It will take these insects five years, now, to get done turning up their noses at every thing American and making damaging comparisons between their own country and "Yurrup." Let us pity their waiting friends in Boston in their affliction.

COMPLICATED PICTURE MAKING

I have been looking at Mr. Prang's[124] great chromo establishment. It ought to be called the Temple of Patience. No American need ever hope to become a successful chromo artist. Only a German patience and evenness of temperament can endure such pains-taking tediousness. One month of it would turn an American's hair gray, two months would make him bald, three would strike him blind, four would drive him crazy, and five would kill him. Would you like to try?

You have often seen Prang's chromo of a little boy asleep in a chair, and a cat surreptitiously helping herself to a pudding in his lap—a pleasant little picture that grows on you and holds you with its naturalness. It is all simplicity—there is nothing gaudy about it—and yet each of those small pictures goes through a lithographic printing-press nineteen separate and distinct times! First, a sheet of fine transparent ising-glass is laid on the original painting, and on this the artist etches in delicate outline the prominent features of the picture, just as children copy engravings by the help of the window glass. The etching is in lithographic ink, and is easily transferred to the smooth surface of a block of lithographic stone by a heavy pressure. Proofs are printed from it for the use of the chromo artist. On one stone he draws the groundwork surrounding the boy and the cat, and this is printed in a faint pinkish tint. On another stone he draws the boy's legs, arms, and part of the cat. These are printed in a sort of mild leaden color. On another stone he draws again all that was drawn before, and adds a string hanging from the wall, which is to support a broom. This is printed in brown, for instance. He draws portions of the boy on three or four more stones, and adds the broom, the pot and the ball, leaving blank spots for the pudding, for the gloss on the hair, and the sheen where the light falls on the child's knee. When all these stones are printed on a sheet, one on top of another and all of different colors, you begin to discern a vague, shadowy resemblance to a sleeping boy—ghostly, spiritual, dreamy, uncertain. Some printed proofs show nothing but two or three splotches of red scattered seemingly at random on the broad white surface. In subsequent proofs they appear in their proper places, and become a red division of the boy's ball, the cat's tongue, and so on. Thus, patch upon patch, and smirch upon smirch of color, the boy and his cat are drawn and redrawn, printed and reprinted for nineteen times, on a sheet of paper, till at last the chaos of arms and legs, tails and paws, tints and splotches, are harmoniously blended together, and the finished picture is before you. And then at a distance of six feet it is a nice judge that can tell it from the original oil painting.

Chromos are printed from sixteen to twenty-six times, usually, according to the elaboration that may be necessary. The finest, and certainly the most elaborate chromo yet issued in this country is Mr. Prang's latest—the "Pompeian Mother"—a picture of an elegantly dressed lady of that damaged city, sitting in her chamber with her child standing by her side. It required *forty-two* separate printings to complete this dainty picture, and of course the artist had to draw it on forty-two different stones. He remarked that he was much interested in it till he had drawn it about twenty-seven times, but towards the last he began to get tired of it—he began to hanker after something fresh. He says he can blindfold himself, now, and get drunk on nineteen different kinds of liquor, and go deaf and dumb and crazy, and stand on his head, with one arm in a sling and the other tied behind him, and draw that picture straight through and never miss a line. I do not believe it. The circumstances would be against him.

After the picture had been printed in colors forty-two times, the same artist had to draw it entire, once more, on stone, and *engrave* it, and then cut lines across it and up and down, and every way, to represent the threads of the coarse canvass of an oil painting and the places where the colors in an oil painting stand out from the surface. The finished picture is laid on this stone and run through a steam press that comes down it with the weight of a couple of continents, and there is your picture with a surface as rough and raspy as any oil picture in the kingdom. The artist's four tedious months of slaving over the same old tiresome picture is at an end—for a coat of varnish is all that is needed now to make the Pompeian Mother ready for the picture stores. Four months' ceaseless work repeating the same picture—am I not right in saying that no American need ever hope to succeed as a chromo artist? Solomon could not have said a wiser thing, I do not care how much he strained himself.

JOSH BILLINGS

Joshua is still lecturing hereabouts in the New England towns. Lately he took a contract to deliver eight lectures in various cities, for the benefit of a young colored man, a protégé of the gentleman who contracted for the lectures. Billings says this is a benevolent object, the idea being to raise means to give the young colored fellow an education, and if the thing proves a success he thinks of delivering a course of lectures in his own behoof and devoting the proceeds to acquiring a knowledge of how to spell in a little more elegant and hostile manner.

His last literary venture, the "Farmer's Allminax," is a pleasant conceit and happily executed. It exhibits a marvelous facility in the handling of the signs of the zodiac and in the construction of poetry suited to any latitude and to all climatic and geographical diversities and peculiarities. The pamphlet is selling handsomely and profitably. Let me offer an extract or two of Josh's pungent but fearfully and wonderfully spelled philosophy:

"A nu milk Cow is stepmother tu every man's baby.

"Whenever I kan find a real hansum woman engaged in the wimmin's rights bizziness, then I am going tew take mi hat under mi arm and jine the procession.

"Piety is like beans, it seems to do the best on a poor sile.

"Most men go through life az rivers go to the sea, bi following the lay ov the ground.

"How many people there iz whose souls hang in them like the pith in a goose-quill."

In his "Hints to Boarding House Keepers," Billings says:

"Be kerful how yu soks yure makrel; too mutch sokeing takes the wear out ov them."

But the book only costs a quarter—for further particulars, buy it.
—*Mark Twain*

December 4, 1869

The Law of Divorce

A communication published in another column[125] presents a Roman Catholic's view of the Richardson-McFarland affair. Without desiring to engage in any controversy with the writer, we have two or three questions to suggest by way of reply to his remarks.

Does the state of domestic morality in those countries where the absolute Roman Catholic law of indissoluble marriage prevails (in France, Spain, or Italy, for example) compare favorably with that found in any American community—even in those where the facilitation of divorce has been carried to the worst lengths by loose legislations?

Is it not likely that circumstances, such as those under which Mrs. McFarland and Mr. Richardson became attached to each other, would have produced in one of those countries where the Roman Catholic law of wedlock prevails, something worse than this scandal of a divorce and an *ante-mortem* marriage rite performed by a Christian minister?

Is there not, between the iron law of Roman Catholicism at one extreme, and the lax legislation of Indiana and Connecticut at the other, a just medium of moral policy relative to the matrimonial bond which tends to the best social state? *[Unsigned]*

Around the World
Letter No. 4

[These letters are written jointly by Professor D.R. Ford and Mark Twain. The former does the actual traveling, and such facts as escape his notice are supplied by the latter, who remains at home.]

California—Continued

THE "EARLY DAYS"

But they were rough in those times! They fairly reveled in gold, whisky, fights and fandangoes, and were unspeakably happy. The honest miner raked a hundred to a thousand dollars out of his claim a day, and what with the gambling dues and the other entertainments, he hadn't a cent the next morning, if he had any sort of luck. They cooked their own bacon and beans, sewed on their own buttons, washed their own shirts—blue woolen ones—and if a man wanted a fight on his hands without any annoying delay, all he had to do was to appear in public in a white shirt or a stove-pipe hat, and he would be accommodated. For those people hated aristocrats. They had a particular and malignant animosity toward what they called a "biled shirt."

In his sketch entitled "The Luck of Roaring Camp," Mr. Bret Harte[126] has deftly pictured the roughness and lawlessness of a California mining camp of the early days, and also its large-hearted charity and compassion—for these traits are found in all true pioneers. Roaring Camp becomes blessed by the presence of a wandering, sickly woman and her little child—rare and coveted treasures among rude men who still yearned in secret for the mothers and sisters and children they loved and cherished in other days. This wanderer—the only woman in Roaring Camp—died, and the honest miners took charge of the orphan little one in a body. They washed it and dressed it and fed it—getting its garments on wrong end first as often as any other way, and pinning the garments *to* the child occasionally and wondering why the baby wasn't comfortable—and the food these inexperienced nurses lovingly concocted for it was often rather beyond its capabilities, since it was neither an alligator nor an ostrich.

But they meant well, and the baby thrived in spite of the perilous kindnesses of the miners. But it was manifest that *all* could not nurse the baby at once, and so they passed a law that the best behaved man should have it for one day, and the man with the cleanest shirt the next day, and the man whose cabin was in the neatest order the next, and so on. And the result was, that a handsome cradle was bought, and carted from cabin to cabin, according to who won the privilege of nursing that day—and the handsome cradle made such a contrast to the unhandsome furniture, that gradually the unhandsome furniture disappeared and gave way for a neater sort—and then ambitious male nurses got to washing up and putting on clean garments every day, and some of them twice a day—and rough, boisterous characters became gentle and soft-spoken, since only the well-behaved could nurse the baby. And, in fine, the lawless Roaring Camp became insensibly transformed into a neat well-dressed, orderly and law-abiding community, the wonder and admiration of all the mining world. All this, through the dumb teaching, the humanizing influence, the uninspired ministering of a little child.

THE SEX ON EXHIBITION

In those days men would flock in crowds to catch a glimpse of that rare and blessed spectacle, a woman! Old inhabitants tell how, in a certain camp, the news went abroad early in the morning that a woman was come! They had seen a calico dress hanging out of a wagon down at the camping ground—sign of emigrants from over the great plains. Everybody went down there, and a shout went up when an actual, bona fide dress was discovered fluttering in the wind! The male emigrant was visible. The miners said:

"Fetch her out!"

He said: "It is my wife, gentlemen—she is sick—we have been robbed of money, provisions, everything, by the Indians—we want to rest."

"Fetch her out! We've got to see her!"

That was the only reply.

He "fetched her out," and they swung their hats and sent up three rousing cheers and a tiger; and they crowded around and gazed at her, and touched her dress, and listened to her voice with the look of men who listened to a *memory* rather than a present reality—and then they collected twenty-five hundred dollars in gold and gave it to the man, and swung their hats again and gave three more cheers, and went home satisfied.

EXORBITANT RATES

A year or two ago I dined in San Francisco with the family of a pioneer, and talked with his daughter, a young lady whose first experience in San Francisco was an adventure, though she herself did not remember it, as she was only two or three years old at the time. Her father said that, after landing from the ship, they were walking up the street, a servant leading the party with the little girl in her arms. And presently a huge miner, bearded, belted, spurred, and bristling with deadly weapons—just down from a long mining campaign in the mountains, evidently barred the way, stopped the servant, and stood gazing, with a face all alive with gratification and astonishment. Then he said, reverently:

"Well, if it ain't a child!" And then he snatched a little leather sack out of his pocket and said to the servant:

"There's a hundred and fifty dollars in dust, there, and I'll give it to you to let me kiss the child!"

That anecdote is *true*.

But see how things change. Sitting at that dinner table, listening to that anecdote, if I had offered double the money for the privilege of kissing the same child, I would have been refused. Seventeen added years had far more than doubled the price.

TOUCHING SPECTACLE

And while upon this subject I will remark that once in Star City, in the Humboldt Mountains, I took my place in a sort of long, post-office single-file of miners, to patiently await my chance to peep through a crack in a cabin and get a sight of the splendid new sensation—a genuine, live Woman! And at the end of three-quarters of an hour my turn came, and I put my eye to the crack, and there she was, with one arm akimbo, and tossing flap-jacks in a frying pan with the other. And she was 165 years old, and hadn't a tooth in her head. However, she was a woman and therefore we were glad to see her and to make her welcome.

THE FAMOUS "CEMENT" MINE

It was somewhere in the neighborhood of Mono Lake that the wonderful Whiteman cement mine[127] was supposed to lie. Every now and then it would be reported that this mysterious Mr. W. had passed stealthily through Esmeralda at dead of night, and then we would have a wild excitement—because he must be steering for his secret mine, and now was the time to follow him. In less than three hours after daylight all the horses and mules and donkeys in the vicinity would be bought, hired or stolen, and half the community would be off for the mountains, following in the wake of Whiteman. But W. would drift about through the mountain gorges for days together, in a purposeless sort of way, until the provisions of the miners ran out, and they would have to go back home. I have known it reported at eleven at night, in a large mining camp, that W. had just passed through, and in two hours, the streets, so quiet before, would be swarming with men and animals. Every individual would be trying to be very secret, but yet venturing to whisper to just one neighbor that W. had passed through. And long before daylight—this in the dead of Winter—the stampede would be complete and the camp deserted, and the whole population gone chasing after W. I ought to know, because I was one of those fools myself.

But it was enough to make a fool of nearly any body. The tradition was that in the early immigration, twenty years ago, three young Germans, brothers, who had survived an Indian massacre on the Plains, wandered on foot through the deserts, avoiding all trails and roads, and simply holding a westerly direction and hoping to find California before they starved or died of fatigue. And in a gorge in the mountains they sat down to rest one day, when one of them noticed a curious vein of cement running along the ground, shot full of lumps of shining yellow metal. They saw that it was gold, and that here was a fortune to be acquired in a single day. The vein was about as wide as a curb stone, and fully two-thirds of it was pure gold. Every pound of the wonderful cement was worth well-nigh $200. Each of the brothers loaded himself with about twenty-five pounds of it, and then they covered up all traces of the vein, made a rude drawing of the locality and the principal landmarks in the vicinity, and started westward again. But troubles thickened about them. In their wanderings one brother fell and broke his leg, and the others were obliged to go on and leave him to die in the wilderness. Another, worn out and starving, gave up by and bye, and lay down to die, but after two or three weeks of incredible hardships, the third reached the settlements of California exhausted, sick, and his mind deranged by his sufferings. He had thrown away all his cement but a few fragments, but these were sufficient to set everybody wild with excitement. However, he had had enough of the cement country, and nothing could induce him to lead a

party thither. He was entirely content to work on a farm for wages. But he gave W. his map, and described the cement region as well as he could, and thus transferred the curse to that gentleman—for when I had my accidental glimpse of Mr. W. in '62, he had been hunting for the lost mine, in hunger and thirst, poverty and sickness, for twelve or thirteen years. Some people believed he had found it, but most people believed he hadn't. I saw a piece of cement as large as my fist which was said to have been given to W. by the young German, and it was of rather a seductive nature. Lumps of virgin gold were as thick in it as raisins in a slice of fruit cake. The privilege of working such a mine about one week would be sufficient for a man of reasonable desires.
—*Mark Twain*

December 18, 1869

Around the World
Letter No. 5

[These letters are written jointly by Professor D.R. Ford and Mark Twain. The former does the actual traveling, and such facts as escape his notice are supplied by the latter, who remains at home.]

California—Continued

"POCKET" MINING

In one little corner of California is found a species of mining which is seldom or never mentioned in print. It is called "pocket-mining" and I am not aware that any of it is done outside of that little corner. The gold is not evenly distributed through the surface dirt, as in ordinary placer mines, but is collected in little spots, and they are very wide apart and exceedingly hard to find, but when you do find one you reap a rich and sudden harvest. There are not now more than 20 pocket miners in that entire little region. I think I know every one of them personally. I have known one of them to hunt patiently about the hillsides every day for 8 months without finding gold enough to make a snuff-box—his grocery bill running up relentlessly all the time—and then I have seen him find a pocket and take out of it a thousand dollars in two dips of his shovel. I have seen him take out $3000 in two hours, and go and pay up every cent of his indebtedness, then enter on a dazzling spree that finished the last of his treasure before the night was gone. And the next day he bought his groceries on credit as usual, and shouldered his pan and shovel and went off to the hills hunting pockets again happy and content. This is perhaps the most fascinating of all the different kinds of mining, and furnishes a very handsome percentage of victims to the lunatic asylum. Honest toil and moderate gains in shops and on farms have their virtues and their advantages. When a man consents to seek for sudden riches he does it at his peril. [No charge.]

Pocket hunting is an ingenious process. You take a spadeful of earth from the hill-side and put it in a large tin pan and dissolve and wash it gradually away till nothing is left but a teaspoonful of fine sediment. Whatever gold was in that earth has remained, because, being the heaviest, it has sought the bottom. Among the sediment you will find half a dozen shining particles no larger than pin-heads. You are delighted. You move off to one side and wash another pan. If you find gold again, you move to one side further, and wash a third pan. If you find *no* gold this time, you are delighted again, because you know you are on the right scent. You lay an imaginary plan, shaped like a fan, with its handle up the hill—for just where the end of the handle is, you argue that the rich deposit lies hidden, whose vagrant grains of gold have escaped and been washed down the hill, spreading farther and farther apart as they wandered. And so you proceed up the hill, washing the earth and narrowing your lines every time the absence of gold in the pan shows that you are outside the spread of the fan; and at last 20 yards up the hill your lines have converged to a point—a single foot from that point you cannot find any gold. Your breath comes short and quick, you are feverish with excitement; the dinner-bell may ring its clapper off, you pay no attention; friends may die, weddings transpire, houses burn down, they are nothing to you; you sweat and dig and delve with a frantic interest—and all at once you strike it! Up comes a spade full of earth and quartz that is all lovely with soiled lumps and leaves and sprays of gold. Sometimes that one spadeful is all—$500. Sometimes the nest contains $10,000, and it takes you three or four days to get it all out. The pocket-miners tell of one nest that yielded $60,000 and two men exhausted it in two weeks, and then sold the ground for $10,000 to a party who never got $300 out of it afterward.

The hogs are good pocket hunters. All the summer they root around the bushes, and turn up a thousand little piles of dirt, and then the miners long for the rains; for the rains beat upon these little piles and wash them down and expose the gold, possibly right over a pocket. Two pockets were found in this way by the same man in one day. One had $5,000 in it and the other $8,000. That man could appreciate it, for he hadn't had a cent for about a year.

In Tuolumus lived two miners who used to go to the neighboring village in the afternoon and return every night with household supplies. Part of the distance they traversed a trail, and nearly always sat down to rest on a great boulder that lay beside the path. In the course of thirteen years they had worn that boulder tolerably smooth, sitting on it. By and by two vagrant Mexicans came along and occupied the seat. They began to amuse themselves by chipping off flakes from the boulder with a sledge-hammer. They examined one of these flakes and found it rich with gold. That boulder paid them $800 afterward. But the aggravating circumstance was that these "Greasers" knew that there must be more gold where that boulder came from, and so they went panning up the hill and found what was probably the richest pocket that region has yet produced. It took three months to exhaust it, and it yielded $120,000. The two American miners who used to sit on the boulder are poor yet, and they take turn about in getting up early in the morning to curse those Mexicans—and when it comes down to pure ornamental cursing, the native American miner is gifted above the sons of men.

I have dwelt at some length upon this matter of pocket mining, because it is a subject that is seldom referred to in print, and therefore I judged that it would have for the reader that interest which naturally attaches to a novelty.

Baker's Cat

Speaking of sagacity it reminds me of Dick Baker, pocket miner of Deadhorse Gulch.[128] Whenever he was out of luck and a little downhearted, he would fall to mourning over the loss of a wonderful cat he used to own (for where women and children are not, men of kindly impulses take up with pets, for they must love something.) And he always spoke of the strange sagacity of that cat with the air of a man who believed in his secret heart that there was something human about it—may be even supernatural.

I heard him talking about this animal once. He said, "Gentlemen, I used to have a cat here, by the name of Tom Quartz, which you'd a took an interest in I reckon—most any body would. I had him here 8 year—and he was the remarkablest cat *I* ever see. He was a large gray one of the Tom specie, and he had more hard, nat'ral sense than any man in this camp—and a *power* of dignity—he wouldn't a let the Gov'ner of California be familiar with him. He never ketched a rat in his life—'peared to be above it. He never cared for nothing but mining. He knowed more about mining, that cat did, than any man *I* ever see. You couldn't tell *him* nothing about placer diggings—and as for pocket mining, why he was just born for it. He would dig out after me and Jim when we went over the hills prospecting, and he would trot along behind us for as much as five mile, if we went so far. And he had the best judgment about mining ground—why you never see anything like it. When we went to work, he'd scatter a glance around, and if he didn't think much of the indications, he would give a look as much as to say, 'Well, I'll have to get you to excuse *me*,' and without another word he'd hyste his nose into the air and shove for home. But if the ground suited him, he would lay low and keep dark till the first pan was washed and then he would sidle up and take a look, and if there was about six or seven grains of gold *he* was satisfied—he didn't want no better prospect'n that—and then he would lay down on our coats and snore like a steamboat till we'd struck the pocket, and then get up and superintend.

"Well, bye and bye, up comes this quartz excitement. Every body was into it—every body was picking and blasting instead of shoveling dirt on the hill side—every body was putting down a shaft instead of scraping the surface. Nothing would do Jim, but *we* must tackle the ledges, too, and so we did. We commenced putting down a shaft, and Tom Quartz he begin to wonder what in the Dickens it was all about. *He* hadn't ever seen any mining like that before, and he was all upset, as you may say—he couldn't come to a right understanding of it no way—it was too many for *him*. He was down on it, too, you bet you—he was down on it powerful—and always appeared to consider it the cussedest foolishness out. But that cat, you know, he was *always* agin new fangled arrangements—somehow he never could abide 'em. You know how it is with old habits. But by and by Tom Quartz begin to git sort of reconciled a little, though he never *could* altogether understand that eternal sinking of a shaft and never panning out any thing. At last he got to coming down in the shaft, hisself, to try to cipher it out. And when he'd get the blues, and feel kind o' scruffy, aggravated and disgusted—knowing as he did, that the bills was running up all the time and we warn't making a cent—he would curl up on a gunny sack in the corner and go to sleep. Well, one day when the shaft was down about 8 foot, the rock got so hard that we had to put in a blast—the first blasting we'd ever done since Tom Quartz was born. And then we lit the fuse and clumb out and got off about 50 yards—and forgot and left Tom Quartz sound asleep on the gunny sack. In about a minute we seen a puff of smoke bust up out of the hole, and then everything let go with an awful crash, and about four million tons of rocks and dirt and smoke and splinters shot up about a mile and a half into the air, and by George, right in the midst of it was old Tom Quartz going end over end, and a snorting and a sneezing, and a clawing and a reaching for things like all possessed. But it warn't no use, you know, it warn't no use. And that was the last we see of *him* for about two minutes and a half, and then all of a sudden it begin to rain rocks and rubbage, and directly he come down ker-whop about ten foot off from where we stood. Well, I reckon he was p'raps the orneriest looking beast you ever see. One ear was sot back on his neck, and his tail was stove up, and his eye-winkers was swinged off, and he was all blacked up with powder and smoke and all sloppy with mud and slush from one end to the other. Well sir, it warn't no use to try to apologize—we couldn't say a word. He took a sort of a disgusted look at hisself, and then he looked at us—and it was just exactly as if he had said— "Gents, May be *you* think it's smart to take advantage of a cat that 'ain't had no experience of quartz mining, but *I* think *different*"—and then he turned on his heel and marched off home without ever saying another word.

"That was jest his style. And may be you won't believe it, but after that you never see a cat so prejudiced agin quartz mining as what he was. And by and bye when he *did* get to going down in the shaft agin, you'd a been astonished at his sagacity. The minute we'd touch off a blast and the fuse'd begin to sizzle, he'd give a look as much as to say: 'Well, I'll have to get you to excuse *me*,' and it was surprising, the way he'd shin out of that hole and go for a tree.

"Sagacity? It ain't no name for it. 'Twas *inspiration*!"

I said, "Well, Mr. Baker, his prejudice against quartz mining *was* remarkable, considering how he came by it. Couldn't you ever cure him of it?"

"*Cure him*! NO. When Tom Quartz was sot once, he was *always* sot—and you might a blowed him up as much as 3 million times and you'd never a broke him of his cussed prejudice agin quartz mining."

The affection and the pride that lit up Baker's face when he delivered this tribute to the firmness of his humble friend of other days will always be a vivid memory with me. —*Mark Twain*

December 25, 1869

Ye Cuban Patriot
A Calm Inspection of Him

Just at this time our souls are wrenched with sympathy for the Cuban "patriot,"[129] and with hatred for his inhuman oppressor. Our journals are filled with the struggles, the sufferings and the noble deeds of this patriot, and nothing on earth can get our attention for a moment unless it has some thing to do with him. The tears that are shed over his misfortunes every day would float a navy; the daily ink that is lavished upon the limning of his virtues would float another one, and a month of the prayers that are offered for his lifting up, if concentrated upon the world's dead, might precipitate the final resurrection. We are bound up, heart and soul, in our Cuban "patriot." We live but for him, we should die if he were taken from us. Daily we cry, "Holy, holy, holy, and perfect and beautiful is Heaven's beloved, the sublime Cuban 'patriot!'"

And how grand a character he is! How gallant, how lofty, how magnanimous! His career, from the moment his heart is first stirred with patriotic emotions, till that heart ceases to beat, is a chivalrous romance. He begins by shouting "Down with the Spaniard!" in the streets of Havana. Then he and a hundred of his fellows are captured by a handful of soldiers and thrown into prison. Here they take the oath to the government, hire out to it as spies upon other patriots, and finish by denouncing a hundred of their personal friends to the government at so much a head. Those parties are duly shot, garoted, or hanged in the public plaza, or otherwise made away with according to the peculiar taste of the commandant in the matter of executions.

Next, the patriot escapes to the country and resumes patriotism once more. A few hundreds of them band together, and then we hear of gallant deeds! They pounce upon deserted plantations and burn up the sugar crop and the negro quarter—and forthwith our great journals shriek the tidings of "Another Grand Patriot Victory!"

Then the government troops capture half the knightly gang and shut them up in a barn and burn them alive. And instantly our great journals, and our Congressmen, and ourselves, rage about the brutal inhumanity of Spain—and with all our hearts we hate those Spaniards for burning up those pure patriots, and we know we are sincere, too, notwithstanding we cannot somehow help feeling rather glad they did it.

Pretty soon the great journals tell us, in thundering display lines, how the patriot warrior Don Aguilar Jesus Maria Jose y John the Baptist Bustamente made a brilliant dash upon the great plantation of Senor Madre de Dios el Calderon Gewhillikins de Valladolid and burned up the whole concern, considering it best on the whole to do this, inasmuch as Senor Valladolid's political opinions were exactly of the universal Cuban pattern and could never by any possibility be depended upon to remain in one shape two hours at a time unless the holder of the same were asleep or dead. And further, the papers tell us how the patriot Bustamente and his six hundred followers next marched Valladolid and his family down the road some thirteen miles, on foot, and with ropes around their necks for convenience of steering them, and then, while the helpless parents and children knelt and pleaded piteously for life, boldly carved them to pieces with bowie knives. And all America shouts, "Hurrah for gallant Cuba!—down with her hated oppressor!" And fiercely we besiege Congress to "recognize" the struggling patriots and reward their single-hearted virtue with our appreciative protection.

Right away we hear that the Spanish troops and Bustamente's army have met and fought a tremendous battle. We gloat over the particulars. We thrill from head to heel as we read how that the battle raged furiously from eight in the morning till six in the evening, resulting in the complete destruction of eleven barns, two plantations, three saw-mills, one hospital and its patients, and the total rout of the enemy, with a loss of sixteen wounded, and also one killed by being run over by a wagon. But we grieve sore to hear that the patriot Bustamente was taken prisoner by the brutal Spanish horde, and our hearts sink, and suffer and break when we hear that his captors lassoed him and dragged him three miles to the military prison at the heels of a galloping horse, and then decided that it was just as cheap to confine what was left of him in a coffin. And how we do abuse the uncivilised sort of warfare those Spaniards wage!

But soon we rejoice once more, when we hear that the unconquerable patriots, from a safe hiding place in the hills, have sent out emissaries and fomented a conspiracy among the slaves which has resulted in a gentle midnight massacre, by the blacks, of a couple of dozen slumbering families of white people, accompanying the deed with the usual Cuban impartiality as to whether the families were "patriots" or friends of the government.

And while we are still rejoicing over this victory, we learn how that the patriot instigators of it, being close pressed, laid down their arms, took the oath to serve Spain, and then for a consideration informed on and helped to capture all those slaves and furnish each of them with twelve hundred trifling lashes on the bare back with ox whips, in the course of which entertainment some of the slaves died—and the rest followed suit the next day. But oh, they died in a glorious cause. They died to free their country from the oppressor. It is sweet to die for one's native land. Those poor humble blacks will live in history, for nearly a year.

In his self-sacrificing struggles for his country's freedom, the Cuban patriot makes valorous use of every method and every contrivance that can aid the good cause. Murder, theft, burglary, arson, assassination, rape, poison, treachery, mendacity, fratricide, matricide, homicide, parricide, and all sides but suicide, are instruments in his hands for the salvation of his native land—and the same are instruments in the hands of the "oppressor" for the damnation of the same. Both parties, patriots and government servants alike, stand ready at any moment, apparently, to sell out body, soul and boots, politics, religion and principles, to anybody that will buy—and they seem equally ready to give the same away for nothing whenever their lives stand in peril. Both sides massacre their prisoners; both sides are as proud of burning a deserted plantation or conquering, capturing, scalping and skinning a crippled blind idiot, as any civilised army would be of taking a fortified city; both sides make a grand school-boy pow-wow over it every time they fight all day long and kill a couple of sick women and disable a jackass; both sides lie, and brag, and betray, and rob, and destroy; a happy majority of both sides are fantastic in costume, grotesque in manner, half civilised, unwashed, ignorant, bigoted, selfish, base, cruel, brutal, swaggering, plantation-burning semi-devils, and it is devoutly to be hoped that an all-wise Providence will permit them to go on eating each other up until there isn't enough left of the last ragamuffin of the lot to hold an inquest on. Amen.

Now there you have a sober, quiet opinion of the idolized Cuban "patriot" and his cause, and one which is impartial and full of charity. I have read about the Cuban "patriot" and the Cuban "oppressor," and the ghastly atrocities which they are pleased to call "warfare," till I seem almost to have got enough. Everybody knows that the Cuban "oppressor" is a very devil incarnate, and if thoroughly impartial newspaper accounts of the doings in Cuba were furnished us everybody would see that the Cuban "patriot" is another devil incarnate just exactly like him. They are of the same breed, the same color, they speak the same language and dishonor the same religion, and verily their instincts are precisely and unvaryingly the same. I do not love the Cuban patriot or the Cuban oppressor either, and I never want to see our government "recognize" anything of theirs but their respective corpses. If the *Buffalo Express* thinks differently, let it say it in its editorials, but not over the signature of yours, with emotion.—*Mark Twain*

Boston, December, 1869

December 29, 1869

An Indignant Rebuke

At the session of the Board of Trade of this city yesterday morning, the following resolutions were offered by Mr. N. C. Simons in relation to the infamous article of the Albany *Argus* on the death of Edwin M. Stanton,[130] which was quoted in the editorial columns of the *Express* yesterday morning:

> Whereas, The Albany *Argus* of December 25th instant,[131] contains an article in relation to the death of Hon. Edwin M. Stanton, which we cannot but look upon as outraging the finer feelings of humanity by insulting the memory of the dead ere the grace had closed over his lifeless clay, therefore, be it
> *Resolved,* That we hereby express our earnest indignation against so flagrant an outrage upon the decencies of journalism; and be it further
> *Resolved,* That the trustees of this board be requested to discontinue the subscription of this board to the Albany *Argus,* and to expunge it from its files.

After the article referred to and the resolutions had been read by the Secretary it was moved by Mr. Simons and seconded by Mr.

William Stimpson that the resolutions be adopted.

A motion to lay the resolutions on the table was made and lost by a decided majority. The question recurring on the adoption of the resolutions, a spirited debate ensued. Several gentlemen were urgently in favor of their immediate adoption, while others were in favor of quietly dropping the *Argus* from the list without formal action, lest it should establish a mischievous precedent for introducing political matters into the action of a body so entirely commercial in its character as the Board of Trade. With a few unimportant exceptions, every one speaking to the question, without regard to political affinities, united in denouncing the article as an outrage which placed the *Argus* outside the pale of decent journalism. At length an influential member of the Board took the floor, and after expressing his detestation of the flagrant indecency which pervaded the article in question, urged that inasmuch as it was dictated by political hatred, any hasty formal action in the Board might be used as a precedent in introducing political considerations into the future action of the Board. He therefore implored that the subject might rest for one day. His remarks produced a visible effect, but as the motion to lay on the table had already been voted down, a member offered, as the easiest solution of the matter, a motion to adjourn, which was put and carried.

The refusal to lay the resolutions on the table, and the subsequent adjournment of the Board pending the question of adoption, are as significant and nearly as decisive as final action would have been. A rebuke of this kind, from a body representing to as large an extent as does the Board of Trade the wealth and intelligence of our city, is one which should have an effect in reforming such infamous indecencies of political journalism. *[Unsigned]*

December 30, 1869

The Hyenas

Among the hyenas howling around the grave of Edwin M. Stanton, the brute that was let loose by the Albany *Argus* seemed likely to enjoy the distinction of being so much the most devilish creature in the pack that the rest would fall back in mute admiration and wonder. He finds a rival, however, in Memphis, belonging to the *Avalanche* newspaper of that place, which has always been able to boast of the superiority of its kennel. The hideous and horrid cry that breaks from the latter we scarcely dare convey to the ears of our readers, and yet it is best that they should hear it:

A bad man has gone to his long account. A villain has shuffled off this mortal coil.[132] A despot has kicked the bucket. There was great rejoicing in Pandemonium yesterday. Since that eventful day when Adam and Eve manufactured clothes out of fig leaves, there has been many large gatherings in hell and on earth. But the cavalcade that turned out in the infernal regions to greet E. M. Stanton, who died yesterday, was, in all probability, the largest that ever paid tribute to a congenial spirit. Stevens[133] had been awarded the premium for being the biggest sinner in all purgatory, and he is no doubt now jealous of Stanton, who he knows will put in for the medal, with a good prospect of winning it. That mawkish sentimentality which would throw the mantle of oblivion over the misdeeds of dead rascals can not be observed in chronicling the death of E. M. Stanton. The most exquisite tortures served Stanton enjoyment. The tyranny of Tiberius was forgotten in his enormities. He reveled for several years in tormenting all over whom he had power; but when he offended heaven and earth by hanging an innocent woman like a dog, God visited him with His righteous anger, and since the consummation of this atrocious deed Stanton's physical system commenced decaying and breaking up; and without a single tie on earth, destitute of all belief in the Christian religion, he died, and a little soul steeped in sin went to the devil.

Commenting upon this fearful outbreak of rebel malignity, the Cincinnati *Gazette* remarks: "For real, downright, simon-pure devilishness, both in expression and sentiment, it is unequaled by any thing we remember to have seen since the close of the war. It is only paralleled by some of the effusions that used to be found in the same sheet during the rebellion, or by the writings of that gentle editor under whom Mark Twain served during his alleged sojourn in Tennessee."

Connected with this subject we must express our surprise at the tone taken by the *Courier* yesterday in alluding to the resolutions which were brought before the Board of Trade, denunciatory of the infamous article of the Albany *Argus* upon Mr. Stanton's death. We did look for some expression from the *Courier* in condemnation of the blasphemous and satanic spirit of that article. Its own remarks upon the death of the great War Secretary, though unjust, were decent and of human temper. It might have honored itself by protesting against the horrid ferocity of political hatred with which the *Argus* pursued a great man to his grave. Instead of which it tacitly approves and defends the shameful article by attacking the gentleman who proposed a condemnatory resolution in the Board of Trade. The *Courier*, by this course, assumes its share of responsibility for such a devilish spirit in the Democratic party, and its share of the disgrace. *[Unsigned]*

January 1, 1870

An Awful—Terrible Medieval Romance

CHAPTER I

The Secret Revealed

It was night.[134] Silence reigned in the grand old feudal castle of Klugenstein. The year 1222 was drawing to a close. Far away up in the tallest of the castle's towers a single light glimmered. A secret council was being held there. The stern old lord of Klugenstein sat in a chair of state meditating. Presently he said, with a tender accent:

"My Daughter!"

A young man of noble presence, clad from head to heel in knightly mail, answered:

"Speak, father!"

"My daughter, the time is come for the revealing of the mystery that hath puzzled all your young life. Know, then, that it had its birth in the matters which I shall now unfold. My brother Ulrich is the great Duke of Brandenburgh. Our father, on his deathbed, decreed that if no son were born to Ulrich, the succession should pass to my house, provided a son were born to me. And further, in case no son were born to either, but only daughters, then the succession should pass to Ulrich's daughter, if she proved stainless; if she did not my daughter should succeed, if she retained a blameless name. And so I, and my old wife here, prayed fervently for the good boon of a son, but the prayer was in vain. You were born to us. I was in despair. I saw the mighty prize slipping from my grasp, the splendid dream vanishing away. And I had been so hopeful! Five years had Ulrich lived in wedlock, and yet his wife had borne no heir of either sex.

"'But hold,' I said, 'all is not lost.' A saving scheme had shot athwart my brain. You were born at midnight. Only the leech, the nurse, and six waiting women knew your sex. I hanged them every one before an hour had sped. Next morning all the barony went mad with rejoicing over the proclamation that a son was born to Klugenstein, and heir to mighty Brandenburgh! And well the secret has been kept. Your mother's own sister nursed your infancy, and from that time forward we feared nothing.

"When you were ten years old, a daughter was born to Ulrich. We grieved, but hoped for good results from measles, or physicians, or other natural enemies of infancy, but were always disappointed. She lived, she throve—Heaven's malison upon her! But it is nothing. We are safe. For, Ha-ha! have we not a son? And is not our son the future Duke? Our well-beloved Conrad is it not so?—for, woman of eight and twenty years as you are, my child, none other name than that hath ever fallen to *you!*

"Now it hath come to pass that age hath laid its hand upon my brother, and he waxes feeble. The cares of State do tax him sore. Therefore he wills that you shall come to him and be already Duke in act though not yet in name. Your servitors are ready—you journey forth to-night.

"Now listen well. Remember every word I say. There is a law as old as Germany that if any woman sit for a single instant in the great ducal chair before she hath been absolutely crowned in presence of the people, she shall die! So heed my words. Pretend humility. Pronounce your judgments from the Premier's chair, which stands at the foot of the throne. Do this until you are crowned and safe. It is not likely that your sex will ever be discovered, but still it is the part of wisdom to make all things as safe as may be in this treacherous earthly life."

"Oh, my father, is it for this my life hath been a lie! Was it that I might cheat my unoffending cousin of her rights? Spare me, father, spare your child!"

"What huzzy! Is this my reward for the august fortune my brain has wrought for you? By the bones of my father, this puling sentiment of thine but ill accords with my humor. Betake thee to the Duke! instantly! And beware how thou meddlest with my purpose!"

Let this suffice, of the conversation. It is enough for us to know that the prayers, the entreaties and the tears of the gentle-natured girl availed nothing. They nor any thing could move the stout old lord of Klugenstein. And so, at last, with a heavy heart, the daughter saw the castle gates close behind her and found herself riding away in the darkness surrounded by a knightly array of armed vassals and a brave following of servants.

The old baron sat silent for many minutes after his daughter's departure, and then he turned to his sad wife and said:

"Dame, our matters seem speeding fairly. It is full three months since I sent the shrewd and handsome Count Detzin on his devilish mission to my brother's daughter Constance. If he fail, we are not wholly safe — but if he do succeed, no power can bar our girl from being Duchess e'en though ill fortune should decree she never should be Duke!"

"My heart is full of bodings, yet all may still be well."

"Tush, woman! Leave the owls to croak. To bed with ye, and dream of Brandenburgh and grandeur!"

CHAPTER II

Festivity and Tears

Six days after the occurrences related in the above chapter, the brilliant capital of the Duchy of Brandenburgh was resplendent with military pageantry, and noisy with the rejoicings of loyal multitudes, for Conrad, the young heir to the crown, was come. The old Duke's heart was full of happiness, for Conrad's handsome person and graceful bearing had won his love at once. The great halls of the palace were thronged with nobles who welcomed Conrad bravely, and so bright and happy did all things seem, that he felt his fears and sorrows passing away and giving place to comforting contentment.

But in a remote apartment of the palace, a scene of a different nature was transpiring. By a window stood the Duke's only child, the Lady Constance. Her eyes were red and swollen, and full of tears. She was alone. Presently she fell to weeping anew, and said aloud:

"The villain Detzin is gone—has fled the dukedom! I could not believe it at first, but alas it is too true. And I loved him so. I dared to love him though I knew the Duke my father would never let me wed him. I loved him—but now I hate him! With all my soul I hate him! Oh, what is to become of me! I am lost, lost, lost! I shall go mad!"

CHAPTER III

The Plot Thickens

A few months drifted by. All men published the praises of the young Conrad's government and extolled the wisdom of his judgments, the mercifulness of his sentences and the modesty with which he bore himself in his great office. The old Duke soon gave every thing into his hands, and sat apart and listened with proud satisfaction while his heir delivered the decrees of the crown from the seat of the Premier. It seemed plain to him that one so loved and praised and honored of all men as Conrad was could not be otherwise than happy. But strangely enough, he was not. For he saw with dismay that the Princess Constance had begun to love him! The love of the rest of the world was happy fortune for him, but this was freighted with danger. And he saw, moreover, that the delighted Duke had discovered his daughter's passion likewise, and was already dreaming of a marriage. Every day somewhat of the deep sadness that had been in the princess's face faded away; every day hope and animation beamed brighter from her eye; and bye and bye even vagrant smiles visited the face that had been so troubled.

Conrad was appalled. He bitterly cursed himself for having yielded to the instinct that had made him seek the companionship of one of his own sex when he was new and a stranger in the palace—when he was sorrowful and yearned for a sympathy such as only women can give or feel. He now began to avoid his cousin. But this only made matters worse, for naturally enough, the more he avoided her the more she cast herself in his way. He marveled at this at first; and next it startled him. The girl haunted him; she hunted him; she happened upon him at all times and in all places, in the night as well as in the day. She seemed singularly anxious. There was surely a mystery somewhere.

This could not go on forever. All the world was talking about it. The Duke was beginning to look perplexed. Poor Conrad was becoming a very ghost through dread and dire distress. One day as he was emerging from a private ante-room attached to the picture gallery, Constance confronted him, and seizing both his hands in hers, exclaimed:

"Oh, why do you avoid me? What have I done—what have I said, to lose your kind opinion of me—for surely I had it once? Conrad, do not despise me, but pity a tortured heart! I cannot, cannot hold the words unspoken longer lest they kill me—I love you Conrad! There, despise me if you must, but they *would* be uttered!"

Conrad was speechless. Constance hesitated a moment, and then, misinterpreting his silence, a wild gladness flamed in her eyes, and she flung her arms about his neck and said:

"You relent! you relent! You *can* love me—you *will* love me! Oh, say you will, my own, my worshipped Conrad!"

Conrad groaned aloud. A sickly pallor overspread his countenance, and he trembled like an aspen. Presently, in desperation he thrust the poor girl from him and cried:

"You know not what you ask! It is forever and ever impossible!" And then he fled like a criminal and left the princess stupefied with amazement. A minute afterward she was crying and sobbing there, and Conrad was crying and sobbing in his chamber. Both were in despair. Both saw ruin staring them in the face.

Bye and bye Constance rose slowly to her feet and moved away, saying:

"To think that he was despising my love at the very moment that I thought it was melting his cruel heart! I hate him! He spurned me; did this man—he spurned me from him like a dog!"

CHAPTER IV

The Awful Revelation

Time passed on. A settled sadness rested once more upon the countenance of the good Duke's daughter. She and Conrad were seen together no more now. The Duke grieved at this. But as the weeks wore away, Conrad's color came back to his cheeks and his old-time vivacity to his eye, and he administered the government with a clear and steadily ripening wisdom.

Presently a strange whisper began to be heard about the palace. It grew louder, it spread farther. The gossips of the city got hold of it. It swept the Dukedom! And this is what the whisper said:

"The Lady Constance hath given birth to a child!"

When the Lord of Klugenstein heard it, he swung his plumed helmet thrice around his head and shouted:

"Long live Duke Conrad!—for lo, his crown is sure, from this day forward! Detzin has done his errand well, and the good scoundrel shall be rewarded!"

And he spread the tidings far and wide, and for eight and forty hours no soul in all the barony but did dance and sing, carouse and illuminate, to celebrate the great event, and all at proud and happy old Klugenstein's expense.

CHAPTER V

The Frightful Catastrophe

The trial was at hand. All the great lords and barons of Brandenburgh were assembled in the Hall of Justice in the ducal palace. No space was left unoccupied where there was room for a spectator to stand or sit. Conrad, clad in purple and ermine, sat in the Premier's chair, and on either side sat the great judges of the realm. The old Duke had sternly commanded that the trial of his daughter should proceed, without favor, and then had taken to his bed broken hearted. His days were numbered. Poor Conrad had begged, as for his life, that he might be spared the misery of sitting in judgment upon his cousin's crime, but it did not avail.

The saddest heart in all that great assemblage was in Conrad's breast.

The gladdest was in his father's. For unknown to his daughter, "Conrad," the old Baron Klugenstein was come, and was among the crowd of nobles, triumphant in the swelling fortunes of his house.

After the heralds had made due proclamation and other preliminaries had followed, the venerable Lord Chief Justice said:

"Prisoner, stand forth!"

The unhappy princess rose and stood unveiled before the vast multitude. The Lord Chief Justice continued:

"Most noble lady, before the great judges of this realm it hath been charged and proven that out of holy wedlock your grace hath given birth unto a child, and by our ancient law the penalty is death, excepting in one sole contingency, whereof his grace the acting Duke, our good Lord Conrad, will advertise you in his solemn sentence now—wherefore, give heed."

Conrad stretched forth the reluctant sceptre and in the self-same moment the womanly heart beneath his robe yearned pityingly toward the doomed prisoner and the tears came into his eyes. He opened his lips to speak, but the Lord Chief Justice said quickly:

"Not there, your Grace, not there! It is not lawful to pronounce judgment upon any of the ducal line save from the ducal throne!"

A shudder went to the heart of poor Conrad, and a tremor shook the iron frame of his old father likewise. Conrad had not been crowned—dared he profane the throne? He hesitated and turned pale with fear. But it must be done. Wondering eyes were already upon him. They would be suspicious eyes if he hesitated longer. He ascended the throne. Presently he stretched forth the sceptre again, and said:

"Prisoner, in the name of our sovereign lord Ulrich, Duke of Brandenburgh, I proceed to the solemn duty that hath devolved upon me. Give heed to my words. By the ancient law of the land, except you produce the partner of your guilt and deliver him up to the executioner you must surely die. Embrace this opportunity—save yourself while yet you may. Name the father of your child!"

A solemn hush fell upon the great court—a silence so profound that men could hear their own hearts beat. Then the princess slowly turned, with eyes gleaming with hate, and pointing her finger straight at Conrad, said:

"Thou art the man!"

An appalling conviction of his helpless, hopeless peril struck a chill to Conrad's heart like the chill of death itself. What power on earth could save him? To disprove the charge, he must reveal that he was a woman; and for an uncrowned woman to sit in the ducal chair was death! At one and the same moment, he and his grim old father swooned and fell to the ground.

[The remainder of this thrilling and eventful story will NOT be found in the *Weekly Buffalo Express,* notwithstanding the fact that the paper can be had of all thoroughly respectable newsdealers, at the low price of one dollar and a half a year.

The truth is, I have got my hero (or heroine) into such a particularly close place that I do not see how I am ever going to get him (or her) out of it again—and therefore I will wash my hands of the whole business and leave that person to get out the best way that offers—or else stay there. I thought it was going to be easy enough to straighten out that little difficulty, but it looks different, now.

If *Harper's Weekly* or the New York *Tribune* desire to copy these initial chapters into the reading columns of their valuable journals, just as they do the opening chapters of *Ledger* and *New York Weekly* novels, they are at liberty to do so at the usual rates, provided they "trust."]—*Mark Twain*

January 6, 1870

Mrs. Stowe's Vindication

The full detail which Mrs. Stowe now gives of the disclosures made to her by Lady Byron, relative to the hideous crime of Lord Byron, completely crushes all the theories, suppositions and ingenious cobweb arguments that have been contrived for the purpose of discrediting her first statement.[135] The straits to which those who hate the author of "Uncle Tom's Cabin" and admire the bestial poet are driven may be seen in the impudently dishonest dodging to which the New York *World* resorts. It says in editorial comments upon the narrative from Mrs. Stowe's book, printed elsewhere in its own columns:

Even the testimony of Lady Byron on the question of incest (and this is Mrs. Stowe's strongest card) is anything but conclusive. She (Lady Byron) states that one evening after her marriage, she, Lord Byron, and Mrs. Leigh were together, when her husband indulged in such familiarity with his sister that she (Lady Byron) left the room, and thenceforth suspected her husband of committing incest. What such testimony would be worth in court no intelligent reader need by told.

The fact that Lady Byron proceeded in the same connection to say that she afterwards held conversations with Lord Byron on the subject *"in which he boldly avowed the connection as having existed in time past, and as one that was to continue in time to come, and implied that she must submit to it"*—he (Byron) denying the peculiar sinfulness of the connection, and saying that he "longed for the stimulus of a new kind of vice"—is coolly ignored by the *World*. Indeed there is no facing it, by those who are determined not to acknowledge the overwhelming weight of probability in favor of the truthfulness of Lady Byron's testimony, as against mere hypothetically constructed arguments. *[Unsigned]*

January 8, 1870

Around the World
Letter No. 6

[These letters are written jointly by Professor D.R. Ford and Mark Twain. The former does the actual traveling, and such facts as escape his notice are supplied by the latter, who remains at home.]

"Early Days" in Nevada
SILVER LAND NABOBS

One of the curious features of Pacific Coast life is the startling uncertainty that marks a man's career in the mines. He may spring from poverty to wealth so suddenly as to turn his hair white and then after a while he may become poor again so suddenly as to make all that white hair fall off and leave his head as clean as a billiard ball. The great Nevada silver excitement of '58–'59 was prolific in this sort of vicissitudes.

Two brothers, teamsters, did some hauling for a man in Virginia City, and had to take a small segregated portion of a silver mine in lieu of $300 cash. They gave an outsider a third to open the mine, and they went on teaming. But not long. Ten months afterward the mine was out of debt and paying each owner $8000 to $10,000 a month—say $100,000 a year. They had that handsome income for just about two years—and they dressed in the loudest kind of costumes and wore mighty diamonds, and played poker for amusement, these men who had seldom had $20 at one time in all their lives before. One of them is tending bar for wages, now, and the other is serving his country as Commander-in-Chief of a street car in San Francisco at $75 a month. He was very glad to get that employment, too.

One of the earliest nabobs that Nevada was delivered of wore $6000 worth diamonds in his bosom, and swore he was unhappy because he couldn't spend his money as fast as he made it. But let us learn from him that persistent effort is bound to achieve success at last. Within a year's time his happiness was secure; for he hadn't a cent to spend.

Another Nevada nabob boasted an income that often reached $16,000 a month; and he used to love to tell how he had worked in the very mine that yielded it, for $5 a day, when he first came to the country. Three years afterward he attained to the far more exceeding grandeur of working in it again, at *four* dollars a day.

The silver and sage-brush State has knowledge of another of these pets of fortune—lifted from actual poverty to affluence almost in a single night—who was able to offer $100,000 for a position of high official distinction, shortly afterward, and did offer it—and a little over a year ago a friend saw him shoveling snow on the Pacific Railroad for a living, away up on the summit of the Sierras, some 7,000 feet above the level of comfort and the sea. The friend remarked that it must be pretty hard work, though, as the snow was twenty-five feet deep, it promised to be a steady job, at least. Yes, he said, he didn't mind it *now*, though a month or so ago when it was sixty-two feet deep and still a snowing, he wasn't so much attached to it. Such is life.

Then there was John Smith. That wasn't his name, but we will call him that. He was a good, honest, kind-hearted fellow, born and reared in the lower ranks of life, and miraculously ignorant. He drove a team, and the team belonged to another man. By and bye he married an excellent woman, who owned a small ranch—a ranch that paid them a comfortable living, for although it yielded but little hay, what little it did yield was worth from $250 to $500 in gold per ton in the market. Presently Smith traded a few acres of the ranch for a small undeveloped silver mine in Gold Hill.[136] He opened the mine and built a little unpretending ten-stamp mill. Eighteen months afterward he quit raising hay, for his mining income had reached a most comfortable figure. Some people said it was $30,000 a month, and others said it was $60,000. Smith was very rich any how. He built a house out in the desert—right in the most forbidding and otherwise howling desert—and it was currently reported that that house cost him a quarter of a million. Possibly that was exaggerated somewhat, though it certainly was a fine house and a costly one. The bed steads cost $400 or $500 apiece.

And then the Smiths went to Europe and traveled. And when they came back Smith was never tired of telling about the fine hogs he had seen in England, and the gorgeous sheep he had seen in Spain, and the fine cattle he had noticed in the vicinity of Rome. He was full of the wonder of the old world, and advised every body to travel. He said a man never imagined what surprising things there were in the world till he had traveled.

One day, on board ship, the passengers made up a pool of $500, which was to be the property of the man who should come nearest to guessing the run of the vessel for the next twenty-four hours. Next day, toward noon, the figures were all in the purser's hands in sealed envelopes. Smith was serene and happy, for he had been bribing the engineer. But another party won the prize! Smith said:

"Here, that won't do! He guessed two miles wider of the mark than I did."

The purser said, "Mr. Smith, you missed it further than any man on board. We traveled two hundred and eight miles yesterday."

"Well sir," said Smith, "that's just where I've got you, for I guessed two hundred and nine. If you'll look at my figgers again you'll find a 2 and two naughts, which stands for 200, don't it?—and after em you'll find a 9 (2009), which stands for two hundred and nine. I reckon I'll take that money, if you please."

Well, Smith is dead. And when he died he wasn't worth a cent. The lesson of all this is, that one must *learn how* to do everything he does—one must have experience in being rich before he can *remain* rich. The history of California will prove this to your entire satisfaction. Sudden wealth is an awful misfortune to the average run of men. It is wasting breath to instruct the reader after this fashion, though, for no man was ever convinced of it yet till he had tried it himself—and I am around now hunting for a man who is afraid to try it. I haven't had any luck so far.

All the early pioneers of California acquired more or less wealth, but an enormous majority of them have not got any now. Those that have, got it slowly and by patient toil.

The reader has heard of the great Gould & Curry silver mine of Nevada. I believe its shares are still quoted in the stock sales in the New York papers. The claim comprised 1200 feet, if I remember rightly, or may be it was 800 and I think it all belonged originally to two men whose name it bears. Mr. Curry owned two-thirds of it—and he said that he sold it out for twenty-five hundred dollars in cash, and an old plug horse that ate up his market value in hay and barley in 17 days by the watch. And he said that Gould sold out for a pair of second-hand government blankets and a bottle of whiskey that killed nine men in three hours, and that an unoffending stranger that smelt the cork was disabled for life. Four years afterward the mine thus disposed of was worth on the San Francisco market seven million six hundred thousand dollars in gold coin.

In the early days a poverty-stricken Mexican who lived in a canon right back of Virginia City, had a stream of water as large as a man's wrist trickling from the hillside on his premises. The Ophir Company segregated 100 ft. of their mine and swapped it to him for the stream of water. The 100 ft. proved to be the richest part of the entire mine; four years after the swap, its market value (including its mill), was $1,500,000. I was down in it about that time, 600 ft. under the ground, and about half of it caved in over my head—and yet, valuable as that property was, I would have given the entire mine to have been out of that. I do not wish to brag—but I can be liberal if you take me right.

An individual who owned 20 feet in the Ophir mine before its great riches were revealed to men, traded it for a horse, and a very sorry looking brute he was too. A year or so afterward, when Ophir stock went up to $3000 a foot, this man, who hadn't a cent, used to say he was the most startling example of magnificence and misery the world had ever seen—because he was able to ride a 60,000-dollar horse and yet had to ride him bareback because he couldn't scare up cash enough to buy a saddle. He said if fortune were to give him another 60,000-dollar horse it would ruin him.

The shiftless people I have been talking about have settled sedimentally down to their proper place on the bottom, but the solid mining prosperity of California and Nevada continues—the two together producing some $40,000,000 annually in gold and silver. White Pine is giving birth to the usual number of suddenly created nabobs, but three years hence nearly every one of them will be scratching for wages again. Petroleum bred a few of these butterflies for the eastern market. They don't live long in Nevada. I was worth half a million dollars myself, once, for ten days[137]—and now I am prowling around the lecture field and the field of journalism, instructing the public for a subsistence. I was just as happy as the other butterflies, and no wiser—except that I am sincerely glad that my supernatural stupidity lost me my great windfall before it had a chance to make a more inspired ass of me than I was before. I am satisfied that I do not know enough to be wealthy and live to survive it. I had two partners in this brilliant stroke of fortune. The sensible one is still worth a hundred thousand dollars or so—he never lost his wits—but the other one (and by far the best and worthiest of our trio), can't pay his board.

I was personally acquainted with the several nabobs mentioned in this letter, and so for old acquaintance sake, I have swapped their occupations and experiences around in such a way as to keep the Pacific public from recognizing these once notorious men. I have no desire to drag them out of their retirement and make them uncomfortable by exhibiting them without mask or disguise—I merely wish to use their fortunes and misfortunes for a moment for the adornment of this newspaper article.—*Mark Twain*

January 15, 1870

A Ghost Story
By the Witness

I took a large room, far up Broadway, in a huge old building whose upper stories had been wholly unoccupied for years, until I came. The place had long been given up to dust and cobwebs, to solitude and silence. I seemed groping among the tombs and invading the privacy of the dead, that first night I climbed up to my quarters. For the first time in my life a superstitious dread came over me; and as I turned a dark angle of the stairway and an invisible cobweb swung its lazy woof in my face and clung there, I shuddered as one who had encountered a phantom.

I was glad enough when I reached my room and locked out the mould and the darkness. A cheery fire was burning in the grate, and I sat down before it with a comforting sense of relief. For two hours I sat there, thinking of bygone times; recalling old scenes, and summoning half-forgotten faces out of the mists of the past; listening, in fancy, to voices that long ago grew silent for all time, and to once familiar songs that nobody sings now. And as my reverie softened down to a sadder and sadder pathos, the shrieking of the winds outside softened to a wail, the angry beating of the rain against the panes diminished to a tranquil patter, and one by one the noises in the street subsided, until the hurrying footsteps of the last belated straggler died away in the distance and left no sound behind.

The fire had burned low. A sense of loneliness crept over me. I arose and undressed, moving on tip-toe about the room, doing stealthily what I had to do, as if I were environed by sleeping enemies whose slumbers it would be fatal to break. I covered up in bed, and lay listening to the rain and wind and the faint creaking of distant shutters, till they lulled me to sleep.

I slept profoundly, but how long I do not know. All at once I found myself awake, and filled with a shuddering expectancy. All was still. All but my own heart—I could hear it beat. Presently the bed clothes began to slip away slowly toward the foot of the bed, as if some one were pulling them! I could not stir; I could not speak. Still the blankets slipped deliberately away, till my breast was uncovered. Then with a great effort I seized them and drew them over my head. I waited, listened, waited. Once more that steady pull began, and once more I lay torpid a century of dragging seconds till my breast was naked again. At last I roused my energies and snatched the covers back to their place and held them with a strong grip. I waited. By and bye I felt a faint tug, and took a fresh grip. The tug strengthened to a steady strain—it grew stronger and stronger. My hold parted, and for the third time the blankets slid away. I groaned. An answering groan came from the foot of the bed! Beaded drops of sweat stood upon my forehead. I was more dead than alive. Presently I heard a heavy footstep in my room—the step of an elephant, it seemed to me—it was not like any thing human. But it was moving *from* me—there was relief in that. I heard it approach the door—pass out without moving bolt or lock—and wander away among the dismal corridors, straining the floors and joists till they creaked again as it passed—and then silence reigned once more.

When my excitement had calmed, I said to myself, "This is a dream—simply a hideous dream." And so I lay thinking it over until I convinced myself that it *was* a dream, and then a comforting laugh relaxed my lips and I was happy again. I got up and struck a light; and when I found that the locks and bolts were just as I had left them, another soothing laugh welled in my heart and rippled from my lips. I took my pipe and lit it, and was just sitting down before the fire, when—down went the pipe out of my nerveless fingers, the blood forsook my cheeks, and my placid breathing was cut short with a gasp! In the ashes on the hearth, side by side with my own bare foot print, was another, so vast that in comparison mine was but a tiny infant's! Then I had *had* a visitor, and the elephant tread was explained.

I put out the light and returned to bed palsied with fear. I lay a long time, peering into the darkness and listening. Then I heard a grating noise overhead, like the dragging of a heavy body across the floor; then the throwing down of the body, and the shaking of my windows in response to the concussion. In distant parts of the building I heard the muffled slamming of doors. I heard, at intervals, stealthy footsteps creeping in and out among the corridors, and up and down the stairs. Sometimes these noises approached my door, hesitated, and went away again. I heard the clanking of chains faintly, in remote passages, and listened while the clanking grew nearer—while it wearily climbed the stairways, marking each move by the loose surplus of chain that fell with an accented rattle upon each succeeding step as the goblin that bore it advanced. I heard muttered sentences; half-uttered screams that seemed smothered violently; and the swish of invisible garments, the rush of invisible wings. Then I became conscious that my chamber was invaded—that I was not alone. I heard sighs and breathings about my bed, and mysterious whisperings. Three little spheres of soft phosphorescent light appeared on the ceiling directly over my head, clung and glowed there a moment, and then dropped—two of them upon my face and one upon the pillow. They spattered, liquidly, and felt warm. Intuition told me they had turned to gouts of blood as they fell—I needed no light to satisfy myself of that. Then I saw pallid faces, dimly luminous, and white uplifted hands, floating bodiless in the air—floating a moment and then disappearing. The whispering ceased and the voices and the sounds, and a solemn stillness followed. I waited and listened. I felt that I must have light, or die. I was weak with fear. I slowly raised myself toward a sitting posture, and my face came in contact with a clammy hand! All strength went from me, apparently, and I fell back like a stricken invalid. Then I heard the rustle of a garment—it seemed to pass to the door and go out.

When everything was still once more, I crept out of bed, sick and feeble, and lit the gas with a hand that trembled as if it were aged with a hundred years. The light brought some little cheer to my spirits. I sat down and fell into a dreamy contemplation of that great footprint in the ashes. By and bye its outlines began to waver and grow dim. I glanced up and the broad gas-flame was slowly wilting away. In the same moment I heard that elephantine tread again. I noted its approach, nearer and nearer, along the musty halls, and dimmer and dimmer the light waned. The tread reached my very door and paused—the light had dwindled to a sickly blue, and all things about me lay in a spectral twilight. The door did not open, and yet I felt a faint gust of air fan my cheek, and presently was conscious of a huge, cloudy presence before me. I watched it with fascinated eyes. A pale glow stole over the Thing; gradually its cloudy folds took shape—an arm appeared, then legs, then a body, and last a great sad face looked out of the vapor. Stripped of its filmy housings, naked, muscular and comely, the majestic Cardiff Giant loomed above me!

All my misery vanished—for a child might know that no harm could come with that benignant countenance. My cheerful spirits returned at once, and in sympathy with them the gas flamed up brightly again. Never a lonely outcast was so glad to welcome company as I was to greet the friendly giant. I said:

"Why, is it nobody but you? Do you know, I have been scared to death for the last two or three hours? I am most honestly glad to see you. I wish I had a chair——. Here, here don't try to sit down in that thing!"

But it was too late. He was in it before I could stop him, and down he went—I never saw a chair shivered so in my life.

"Stop, stop, you'll ruin ev——"

Too late again. There was another crash, and another chair was resolved into its original elements.

"Confound it, haven't you got any judgment at all! Do you want to ruin all the furniture on the place? Here, here, you petrified fool——"

But it was no use. Before I could arrest him he had sat down on the bed, and it was a melancholy ruin.

"Now what sort of a way is that to do? First you come lumbering about the place bringing a legion of vagabond goblins along with you to worry me to death, and then when I overlook an indelicacy of costume which would not be tolerated anywhere by cultivated people except in a respectable theatre, and not even there if the nudity were of *your* sex, you repay me by wrecking all the furniture you can find to sit down on. And why will you? You damage yourself as much as you do me. You have broken off the end of your spinal column, and littered up the floor with chips off your hams till the place looks like a marble-yard. You ought to be ashamed of yourself—you are big enough to know better."

"Well, I will not break any more furniture. But what am I to do? I have not had a chance to sit down for a century." And the tears came into his eyes.

"Poor devil," I said, "I should not have been so harsh with you. And you are an orphan, too, no doubt. But sit down on the floor here—nothing else can stand your weight—and besides, we cannot be sociable with you away up there above me; I want you down where I can perch on this high counting-house stool and gossip with you face to face."

So he sat down on the floor, and lit a pipe which I gave him, threw one of my red blankets over his shoulders, inverted my sitz-bath on his head, helmet fashion, and made himself picturesque and comfortable. Then he crossed his ancles, while I renewed the fire, and exposed the flat honey-combed bottoms of his prodigious feet to the grateful warmth.

"What is the matter with the bottom of your feet and the back of your legs, that they are gouged up so?"

"Infernal chilblains—I caught them clear up to the back of my head, roosting out there in Newell's farm. But I love the place; I love it as one loves his old home. There is no peace for me like the peace I feel when I am there."

We talked along for half an hour, and then I noticed that he looked tired, and spoke of it.

"Tired!" he said. "Well I should think so. And now I will tell you all about it, since you have treated me so well. I am the spirit of the Petrified Man that lies across the street there in the Museum. I am the ghost of the Cardiff Giant. I can have no rest, no peace, till they have given that poor body burial again. What was the most natural thing for me to do, to make men satisfy this wish? Terrify them into it!— haunt the place where the body lay! So I haunted the museum night after night. I even got other spirits to help me. But it did no good, for nobody ever came to the museum at midnight. Then it occurred to me to come over the way and haunt this place a little. I felt that if I ever got a hearing I must succeed, for I had the most efficient company that perdition could furnish. Night after night we have shivered around through these mildewed halls, dragging chains, groaning, whispering, tramping up and down stairs, till to tell you the truth I am almost worn out. But when I saw a light in your room to-night I roused my energies again and went at it with a deal of the old freshness. But I am tired out—entirely fagged out. Give me, I beseech you, give me some hope!"

I lit off my perch in a burst of excitement, and exclaimed:

"This transcends every thing!—every thing that ever did occur! Why you poor blundering old fossil, you have had all your trouble for nothing—you have been haunting a *plaster cast* of yourself—the real Cardiff Giant is in Albany! Confound it, don't you know your own remains?"

I never saw such an eloquent look of shame, of pitiable humiliation, overspread a countenance before.

The Petrified Man rose slowly to his feet and said:

"Honestly, *is* that true?"

"As true as I am sitting here."

He took the pipe from his mouth and laid it on the mantel, then stood irresolute a moment, (unconsciously, from old habit, thrusting his hands where his pantaloons pockets should have been, and meditatively dropping his chin on his breast) and finally said:

"Well—I *never* felt so absurd before. The Petrified Man has sold every body else, and now the infamous fraud has ended by selling its own ghost! My son, if there is any charity left in your heart for a poor friendless phantom like me, don't let this get out! Think how *you* would feel if you had made such an ass of yourself."

I heard his stately tramp die away, step by step down the stairs and out into the deserted street, and felt sorry that he was gone, poor fellow—and sorrier still that he carried off my red blanket and my bath-tub.—*Mark Twain*

New York, January

Around the World
Letter No. 7

[These letters are written jointly by Professor D.R. Ford and Mark Twain. The former does the actual traveling, and such facts as escape his notice are supplied by the latter, who remains at home.]

Pacific Coast—Concluded

CHINAMEN

One of California's curiosities the people in the States will some day become familiar with through the Pacific Railroad. I mean the Chinamen. California contains 70,000 of them, and every ship brings more. There is a Chinese quarter in every city and village in California and Nevada, for Boards of Aldermen will not allow them to live all around town just wherever they choose to locate. This is not a hardship, for they prefer to herd together.

Peculiarities and Superstitions

They are a people who fondly stick to their ancient customs. They dress in the quaint costumes their ancestors wore 500 years ago. They build temples, gaudy with gilding and hideous with staring idols, and there they worship after the fashion of their fathers. A strict record is kept by their chiefs of the name and residence of every Chinaman, and when he dies his body is sent back to China for burial—for they can never get to their Heaven unless they start from China. And besides, Chinamen worship their ancestors, and they all want their share of worship after they are done with this world. Even when the Chinese government sells a shipload of degraded and criminal coolies to a Cuban or Sandwich Island planter, it is strictly stipulated that the body of every one of them must be sent back to China after death.

The Chinamen being smart, shrewd people, take to some few of our commercial customs and virtues, but somehow we can't make great headway in the matter of civilizing them. We can teach them to gamble a little, but somehow we can't make them get drunk. It is discouraging—because you can't regenerate a being that won't get drunk.

The Chinaman is the most frugal, industrious and thrifty of all creatures. No matter how slender are the wages you pay him he will manage to lay up money. And Chinamen are the most gifted gardeners in the world. Give one of them a sandbank that would not support a lizard, and he will make it yield generous crops of vegetables. The Chinaman wastes *nothing*. Every thing has a value in his eyes. He gathers up all the cast-away rags and bones and bits of glass, and makes marketable articles of them. And he picks up all the old fruit cans you throw away and melts them up to get the tin and solder. When a white man discards a gold placer as no longer worth anything, the patient Chinaman, always satisfied with small profits, and never in a hurry to get rich, takes possession and works it contentedly for years.

The Chinaman makes a good cook, a good washerwoman, a good chambermaid, a good gardener, a good banker's clerk, a good miner, a good railroad laborer, a good *anything* you choose to put him at—for these people are all educated, they are all good accountants, they are very quiet and peaceable, they never disturb themselves about politics; they are so tractable, quick, smart, and naturally handy and ingenious, that you can teach them anything; they have no jealousies; they never lose a moment, never require watching to keep them at work; they are gifted with a world of patience, endurance and contentment. They are the best laboring class America has ever seen—and they do not care a cent who is President. They are miserably abused by the laws of California, but that sort of thing will cease, some day. It was found just about impossible to build the California end of the Pacific Railroad with white men at $3 per day and take care of all the broils and fights and strikes; but they put on Chinamen at a dollar a day and "find" themselves, and *they* built it without fights or strikes or anything, and saved the bulk of their wages, too. You will have these long-tailed toilers among you in "the States" some day, but you will find them right easy to get along with—and you will like them, too, because they will stand a heap of abuse. You will find them ever so convenient, because when you get mad you can snatch a club and go out and take satisfaction out of a Chinaman. The native American Negro is getting so insolent, now, that the patriot from Ireland cannot take a little recreation out of him without getting into trouble. So the Chinaman will afford a needed relief.

Modest Villainy

As evidence that Chinamen are satisfied with small gains, I will re-mark that they drill five holes into the edge of gold coins—drill clear through from edge to edge—and save the gold thus bored out and fill up the hole with some sort of metallic composition that does not spoil the ring of the coin. Their counterfeiters put nine parts good metal and only one part base metal in their bogus coins—and so it is very lucra-tive in the long run and the next thing to impossible to detect the cheat. It is only greedy bungling *Christian* counterfeiters that blunder into trouble, by trying to swindle their fellow creatures too heavily.

DESPERADOES

Another curious feature about California life was the breed of des-peradoes she reared and fostered on her soil and afterward distrib-uted over adjacent Territories through her Vigilance Committees when she had had enough of their exploits.[138] These men went armed to the teeth with monstrous revolvers, and preyed upon each other. Their slightest misunderstandings were settled on the spot by the bullet; but they very rarely molested peaceable citizens. They robbed and gambled and killed people for three or four years, and then "died with their boots on," as they phrased it; that is, they were killed themselves—almost invariably—and they never expected any other fate, and were very seldom disappointed.

Sam Brown

Sam Brown,[139] of Nevada, killed sixteen men in his time, and was journeying toward Esmeralda to kill a seventeenth, who had stopped the breath of a friend of his, when a party of law-abiding citizens way-laid him and slaughtered him with shot guns. Mourners were exceed-ing scarce at his funeral. It is said that Sam Brown called for a drink at the bar of the Slaughter House in Carson City one morning (a sa-loon so nicknamed because so many men had been killed in it) and in-vited a stranger up to drink with him. The stranger said he never drank and wished to be excused. By the custom of the country, that was a deadly insult, and so Brown very properly shot him down. He left him lying there and went away, warning everybody to let the body alone, because it was *his* meat, he said. And it is said, also, that he came back after awhile and made a coffin and buried the man himself—though I never could quite believe that without assistance.

Virginia City was full of desperadoes, and some of the pleasantest newspaper reporting I ever did was in those days, because I reported the inquests on the entire lot of them, nearly. We had a fresh one pretty much every morning. Toward the last it was melancholy to see how the material was running short. Those were halcyon days! I don't know what halcyon days are, but that is the proper expression to use in this connection, I believe.

Jack Williams

Jack Williams[140] was one of the luckiest of the Virginia City desperadoes. He killed a good many men. He was a kind-hearted man, and gave all his custom to a poor undertaker who was trying to get along. But by and bye some body poked a double barrelled shot gun through a crack while Williams was sitting at breakfast, and riddled him at such a rate that there was hardly enough of him left to hold an inquest on—and then the poor unfortunate undertaker's best friend was gone, and he had to take in his sign. Thus he was stricken in the midst of his prosperity and his happiness—for he was just on the point of getting married when Jack Williams was taken away from him, and of course he had to give it up then.

Cemeterial Curiosities

It is said that the first twenty-six graves in the cemetery at Virginia City were those of men who all died by the bullet.[141] And the first six in another of those towns contained the bodies of a desperado and five of his victims—and there in the bosom of his family, made dear to him by ties of blood, he calmly sleeps unto this day.

Mr. Slade

At the Rocky Ridge station in the Rocky Mountains, in the old days of overland stages and pony expresses, I had the gorgeous honor of breakfasting with Mr. Slade,[142] the Prince of all the desperadoes; who killed twenty-six men in his time; who used to cut off his victims' ears and send them as keepsakes to their relatives; and who bound one of his victims hand and foot and practiced on him with his revolver for hours together—a proceeding which seems almost inexcusable until we reflect that Rocky Ridge is away off in the dull solitudes of the mountains, and the poor desperadoes have hardly any amusements. Mr. Slade afterward went to Montana and began to thin out the population as usual—for he took a great interest in trimming the census and regulating the vote—but finally the Vigilance Committee captured him and hanged him, giving him just fifteen minutes to prepare himself in. The papers said he cried on the scaffold.

The Vigilance Committee is a wholesome regulator in the new countries, and bad characters have a lively dread of it. In Montana one of these gentlemen was placed on his mule and informed that he had precisely fifteen minutes to leave the country in. He said, "Gents, if this mule don't balk, five'll answer."

But that is sufficient about the desperadoes. I merely wished to make passing mention of them as a Californian production.—*Mark Twain*

January 29, 1870

Around the World
Letter No. 8

[These letters are written jointly by Professor D.R. Ford and Mark Twain. The former does the actual traveling, and such facts as escape his notice are supplied by the latter, who remains at home.][143]

Dining with a Cannibal

[The same being the King of Easter Island
in the Pacific Ocean.]

AT SEA, PACIFIC OCEAN, NOV. 20— "Just at this instant," continued the King, "she reached him, and he was saved!—for as the shark opened his great jaws she thrust her *Kaboosh* between them, noble girl! propped them wide apart, ran her arm down his throat, into his gullet, and recovered the gentleman's watch! Come here, child and show the foreigner the Shark's tooth-marks on your shoulder."

"I see, I see. It was an intrepid deed. It was noble to save the poor white man from so ghastly a death. And this is the girl that taught you to add bread-fruit to the *poi?*"[144]

"Yes, the same—the very same. To *four-finger* poi, you understand—
not to all sorts. I will show you—I will make you understand. In the
Sandwich Islands and the Marquessas, they make poi out of the taro-
root, only. *Then,* you know, they wouldn't dream of——. However, I
was going to tell you. The native takes the taro-root, which is much
like what you describe a turnip to be, and wraps it in plantain leaves,
and puts it in a hole in the ground which he has lined with hot stones,
don't you see?—covers it up, lets it roast. Takes it out, pounds it in a
great stone dish with a large stone pestle; adds water to this mush,
from time to time, to thin it. He sets it away (it is poi, now,) in large
calabashes.[145] It looks like so much flour paste. At meals all the family
and friends sit around the calabash on their haunches, just as you
and I are doing—except that the poor common *Kanakas*[146] are naked,
of course. Ah! no, my friend—because you see me, the great king, in
short collar and spectacles, you must not imagine that the common
subject must ape grandeur and put on clothes. They sit around the
calabash, and all eat from it with their hands. Each inserts his fingers
and stirs them briskly around till a portion of the pulpy mass adheres
to them—then tilts back his head, lets the suspended tail of pulp descend into his open mouth—then his fingers follow and he sucks the
remainder from them.* Now if the pulp be thick, you can use one finger; if it be thinner, you must use two, or three, or four fingers, accordingly. But, as I told you, it was this inspired girl that invented the
method of thickening four finger poi with bread-fruit—and also the
flavoring it with carcasses of the delicious bird which in your tongue
you term the grasshopper."

"Blessed girl!"

"Blessed girl indeed. But pardon me—you—you seem distressed."

"It is nothing. Poi, even in its native nastiness, is only mildly delicious to me—the addition to it of the wild game you mention——"

"Ah, say no more. I perceive. But try *this* dish. It is a fry of bananas
and plantains, with oranges sliced in it, and just a spoonful or so of
the delightful chirimoya added to give it tone. *I* conceived the idea of
adding the angleworms."

"It was inspiration."

"I so regard it. It is so considered by the great chiefs. To the common herd it is *tabu.*[147] That is to say, prohibited. Now as regards those
missionaries," continued the king, reflectively scratching his head
with the fork which I had presented him, and which he had already
learned to use a good deal, though not always in a strictly legitimate

way, "as regards those missionaries, I will say, that their landing here was unexpected, but I hastened to give them every protection. And I gave them full privilege to teach. They were the first whites that some of my people had seen, and of course these simple natives had a natural curiosity to experiment upon them![148] I could not reasonably deny them this little gratification, though I counseled them to practice as little cruelty upon the strangers as was compatible with a fair desire for information and the necessity of wholesome amusement. They removed Johnson's ears, and that was a thing which I regretted seriously until it was explained to me that a great chief's little sick child desired them to play with—and if you could have seen how much more contented and restful the poor young thing was after it acquired them, you would have felt how blessed a thing it is to contribute to the happiness of even a little child."

"It was the impulse of a generous heart—it was a spirit of liberality as rare as it is beautiful. And how did Johnson like it!"

"Oh, Johnson said it was the will of God. It was like Johnson to say that. But the missionaries were right well treated, on the whole. The natives tried various interesting experiments upon them, such as scorching them, and scalping them, and all that sort of thing, and I killed one of them myself, not in malice, but because I had a curious caprice to see how he would go with onions. He was a failure. Old and tough. Underdone, my *wahine*[149] said—a shade too venerable *I* said. Give em pungency and tenderness for a combination. Onions and infancy is *my* idea of comfort. But here comes a dish which you will like, my good *haole*—baked dog and yams—project your teeth in this direction and nip this slice from the contrivance which you call a fork. A man, if he be anything of an epicure, is bound to like this dish. It is, *par excellence,* the national dish—no *luau* is complete without it. A *luau* is a great feast, my friend,—that is what the word means. Do you know that the edible dog of this land is a perfectly proper and elegant beast for human consumption? It is even so. He is never, *never* allowed to touch meat. He is fed wholly on poi—a strictly vegetable diet. He is reared in the house—sleeps with his owner, male or female—rides horseback with them—travels in the boat with them—is their inseparable pet and companion. They love him tenderly in life, and in death they turn not away from him. They eat him. They stuff his body full of plantains, bananas, yams and other dainties, and cook him among hot stones buried in a hole in the ground. Not a breath of the aroma, not a drop of the combined juices, escapes. *You* people don't know how to cook. No, as I was saying, the Kanakas experimented a good deal on the missionaries, in the interest of science, and the experiments were generally fatal, though I urged them not to waste the missionaries, for we could not know when we would have another lot. But among those that survived was Williams, and it was *he* that sent home those damaging reports to your country, in which he spoke of the treatment of his brethren in a peevish, fault finding spirit, ill becoming to his sacred calling. I suppose your people believed every word of it, and just jumped to the conclusion that we were a bad, inhospitable race. Never explained about Johnson's ears, perhaps?— never told *why* I killed that other fellow?—confound me, it does seem to me that some people take pleasure in misrepresenting things, and bringing obloquy upon their fellow-creatures. Sometimes I feel as if I had rather be dead and at rest. The world seems so shameless in its judgments, and one's life is so embittered by the malicious criticisms of those whose hearts are not in sympathy with him."

"It *was* pitiful in that Williams, after all you had done for his party."

"I should say so! But never mind, let's be cheerful, anyway. How are you making out? Let me help you to a fried plantain. Take some more of the pup? No? Try some of the human being? By George, this fellow is done to a charm. You'll like him. He was a Frenchman—splendid chap—young and hale and hearty, beautiful to look upon. Do you prefer white meat or dark? Let me help you to some of the breast. Ah me, I have known this youngster for thirteen years—fished with him, swam with him, sailed with him, gave a couple of my sisters and four aunts to him. I loved him. He was always good. He is good now."

Taking up a fragment of his late brother-in-law, the king took a bite and then gazed long and pensively upon the remainder, till by-and-bye the muscles of his mouth began to twitch with emotion, and presently two or three great tears welled from his eyes and coursed down his cheeks. Then, in a choking voice, he murmured:

"Alas, they have fried him!"

I laid down the breast bone of the deceased and burst into tears also. Such is the sympathetic power of grief. It was nothing to me whether they fried him or boiled him; it was nothing to me how this poor foreigner was cooked; I was only eating him out of a vain curiosity, and not because I loved him, not because I respected him, not because I wished to curry favor with his relatives. Yet I wept.

"They have fried him!" said the King. "Alas, poor Gaultier. However, let us cheer up, let us be content. But I will have my cook for breakfast for this—and I will fry *him,* and see how he likes it. There is nothing like a sharp example, to teach a man, my friend. But don't be idle, sir—take some more of the fried Frenchman. I ought to be ashamed to offer you such a dish, but you see how I am situated. He ought to have been baked—this fellow ought. We always bake a Frenchman—we never think of frying him. But I wish you had known this fellow—so kind, so gentle, so loving, and you see yourself how tender he is. But that Williams business—I wish you would straighten that up for me when you go back to America. If your people could only know the facts in the case, they would not blame me. It is a little hard, after I have spent all those years in building up a good name, to have it all knocked in the head by this shabby adventurer. Now what he called a "hideous revel," and a "feast of devils," and all sorts of vile and wicked names, was nothing in the world, I give you my sacred honor, but a simple barbecue—seventeen old crippled natives, no account under the sun, just an expense to the community, and I fricasseed them to give a little treat to some visiting town chiefs, (Aldermen you call them in your country,) who were here for a day or two from Wonga Island. "Feast of devils," Indeed! Feast of dried-up skinny old rapscallions that the island is a thousand times better off without, and I am sure it was honorable in us to be hospitable to those strangers. Though between you and me it was an awful swindle on them— tough, oh, don't mention it!—more cholera morbus[150] and indigestion, and general suffering among those chiefs, *you* never saw the like of it in your life! Now Twain, you see how much truth there was in Williams' statements?—all that row about nothing. You can set this thing right in your country—you can do it easy—simply just explain the facts—and anything I can do for you, I'll do it—you can depend on *me.* Send me a copy of your Weekly. I can't read it, but a little literature can't hurt a man, anyhow. Caesar's ghost!"

"Oh Heaven! what is the matter, your gracious majesty?"

"Oh, misery, Oh murder, Oh desperation!"

"Oh *what* is it, your imperial majesty!—I beseech you!"

He had sprung to his feet, and his fixed eyes were staring wildly at the fried meat before him.

"Oh my brain reels! This hair a Frenchman's hair? There *must* be some mistake! A horrid suspicion bursts upon me! Ah, what is this I see?—this thing?—this accusing mark! *A strawberry on the left arm!*—it is, it is, my long-lost brother!"

Alas, it was even so. It was his long-lost brother—what was left of him. Poor, poor fellow, he was only fit to be shoveled into a basket and given to the poor, now. The king fell to the floor insensible. He grew worse and worse, and the next day his removal to the country was ordered. Many sympathising relatives and friends followed the palanquin and did what they could to alleviate the sufferings of their unhappy sovereign.

It turned out afterward that the sweetheart of the Frenchman had made a surreptitious exchange of marketing in the king's kitchen before daylight on that fatal day. She had bought the king's brother from a wandering tribe that belonged in the great wilderness at the other end of the island. She bought him purposely to make that exchange, though of course she did not know who he was. The girl and the Frenchman escaped from the island in a canoe that very night and were happily married. Or drowned, I don't know which. I would have liked to taste that Frenchman.

*NOTE.—This is the process really followed in all the South Pacific Islands.—*Mark Twain*

PART III

Back to Buffalo

February 1870–May 1870

Nasby's Lecture

We offer no apologies for declining to stab a fellow journalist in the back with that most pitiful of all weapons, a "synopsis" of his speech.[151] The meanest man which a sadly imperfect world has produced may have been the originator of many and many a microscopic villainy, but unless he also devised the shining littleness which is termed "synopsizing" an unoffending stranger's lecture, he lived in vain and his mission on earth was a failure. Suffice it then, that last night the apostle of Democracy held the interested attention of his audience during an hour and a half of sarcastic warfare upon the doctrines of the Anti-Women's Rights people. His points were put neatly and driven home with telling force. His humor was enjoyable; his logic was ingenious; his arguments were searching, and as these several qualities were inspired with their highest effectiveness by the convincing earnestness of Mr. Nasby's manner, there was no feature lacking to render this pleasing lecture and an effort of rare excellence. Nasby's former lecture, "Cussed be Canaan,"[152] was a distinguished success, and was warmly praised throughout the country. It is a pleasure to us to be able to say that his present lecture has met with just a similar reception. His former lecture had for its life principle a good and noble motive, viz.: the political and social as well as the legal recognition of the negro. The present lecture has also a generous motive, and as usual, to Nasby's credit be it said, his heart is in his work, where it always is, whether the work be popular or not. *[Unsigned]*

Anson Burlingame

On Wednesday, in St. Petersburg, Mr. Burlingame[153] died of a short illness. It is not easy to comprehend, at an instant's warning, the exceeding magnitude of the loss which mankind sustains in this death—the loss which all nations and all peoples sustain in it. For he had outgrown the narrow citizenship of a state, and become a citizen of the world; and his charity was large enough and his great heart warm enough to feel for all its races and to labor for them. He was a true man, a brave man, an earnest man, a liberal man, a just man, a generous man, in all his ways and by all his instincts a noble man; he was a man of education and culture, a finished conversationalist, a ready, able and graceful speaker, a man of great brain, a broad and deep and weighty thinker. He was a great man—a very, very great man. He was imperially endowed by nature; he was faithfully befriended by circumstances, and he wrought gallantly always, in whatever station he found himself.

He was a large, handsome man, with such a face as children instinctively trust in, and homeless and friendless creatures appeal to without fear. He was courteous at all times and to all people, and he had the rare and willing faculty of being always *interested* in whatever a man had to say—a faculty which he possessed simply because nothing was trivial to him which any man or woman or child had at heart. When others said harsh things about even unconscionable and intrusive bores after they had retired from his presence, Mr. Burlingame often said a generous word in their favor, but never an unkind one.

A chivalrous generosity was his most marked characteristic—a large charity, a noble kindliness that could not comprehend narrowness or meanness. It is this that shows out in his fervent abolitionism, manifested at a time when it was neither very creditable nor very safe to hold such a creed; it was this that prompted him to hurl his famous Brooks-and-Sumner speech in the face of an astonished and insulted South at a time when all the North was smarting under the sneers and taunts and material ruffianisms of admired and applauded Southerners. It was this that made him so warmly espouse the cause of Italian liberty—an espousal so pointed and so vigorous as to attract the attention of Austria, which empire afterward refused to receive him when he was appointed Austrian Envoy by Mr. Lincoln. It was this trait which prompted him to punish Americans in China when they imposed upon the Chinese. It was this trait which moved him, in framing treaties, to frame them in the broad interest of the world, instead of selfishly seeking to acquire advantages for his own country alone and at the expense of the other party to the treaty, as had always before been the recognized "diplomacy." It was this trait which was and is the soul of the crowning achievements of his career, the treaties with America and England in behalf of China. In every labor of this man's life there was present a good and noble motive; and in nothing that he ever did or said was there any thing small or base. In real greatness, ability, grandeur of character, and achievement, he stood head and shoulders above all the Americans of to-day, save one or two.

Without any noise, or any show, or any flourish, Mr. Burlingame did a score of things of shining mark during his official residence in China. They were hardly heard of away here in America, but he was not working for applause. When he first went to China, he found that with all their kingly powers, American envoys were still not of much consequence in the eyes of their country-men of either civil or official position. But he was a man who was always "posted." He knew all about the state of things he would find in China before he ever sailed from America. And so he took care to demand and receive additional powers before he turned his back upon Washington. When the customary consular irregularities placidly continued and he notified those officials that such irregularities must instantly cease, and they inquired with insolent flippancy what the consequence might be in case they didn't, he answered blandly that he would *dismiss* them from the highest to the lowest! [He had quietly come around with absolute authority over their official lives.] The consular irregularities ceased. A far healthier condition of American commercial interests ensued there.

To punish a foreigner in China was an unheard-of thing. There was no way of accomplishing it. Each Embassy had its own private district or grounds, forced from the imperial government, and into that sacred district Chinese law officers could not intrude. All foreigners guilty of offences against Chinamen were tried by their own countrymen in these holy places, and as no Chinese testimony was admitted, the culprit almost always went free. One of the very first things Mr. Burlingame did was to make a Chinaman's oath as good as a foreigner's; and in his ministerial court, through Chinese and American testimony combined, he very shortly convicted a noted American ruffian of murdering a Chinaman. And now a community accustomed to light sentences were naturally startled, when, under Mr. Burlingame's hand, and bearing the broad seal of the American Embassy, came an order to take him out and hang him!

Mr. Burlingame broke up the "extra-territorial" privileges, as they were called, as far as our country was concerned, and made justice as free to all and as untrammeled in the metes and bounds of its jurisdiction, in China, as ever it was in any land.

Mr. Burlingame was the leading spirit in the comparative policy. He got the Imperial College established. He procured permission for an American to open the coal mines of China. Through his efforts China was the first country to close her ports against the war vessels of the Southern Confederacy; and Prince Kung's order, in this matter, was singularly energetic, comprehensive and in earnest. The ports were closed then, and never opened to a Southern war-ship afterward.

Mr. Burlingame "construed" the treaties existing between China and the other nations. For many years the ablest diplomatists had vainly tried to come to a satisfactory understanding of certain obscure clauses of these treaties, and more than once powder had been burned in consequence of failures to come to such understandings. But the clear and comprehensive intellect of the American Envoy reduced the wordy tangle of diplomatic phrases to a plain and honest handful of paragraphs, and these were unanimously and thankfully accepted by the other foreign envoys, and officially declared by them to be a thorough and satisfactory elucidation of all the uncertain clauses in the treaties.

Mr. Burlingame did a mighty work, and made official intercourse with China lucid, simple and systematic, thenceforth for all time, when he persuaded that government to adopt and accept the code of international law by which the civilized nations of the earth are guided and controlled.

It is not possible to specify all the acts by which Mr. Burlingame made himself largely useful to the world during his official residence in China. At least it would not be possible to do it without making this sketch too lengthy and pretentious for a newspaper article.

Mr. Burlingame's short history—for he was only forty-seven—reads like a fairy tale. Its successes, its surprises, its happy situations, occur all along, and each new episode is always an improvement upon the one which went before it.

He begins life as an assistant in a surveying party away out on the Western frontier; then enters a branch of a Western college; then passes through Harvard with the honors; becomes a Boston lawyer and looks back complacently from his high perch upon the old days when he was a surveyor-nobody in the woods; becomes a State Senator, and makes laws; still advancing, goes to the Constitutional Convention and makes regulations wherewith to rule the makers of laws; enters Congress and smiles back upon the Legislature and the Boston lawyer, and from these standpoints smiles still back upon the country surveyor, recognizes that he is known to fame in Massachusetts; challenged Brooks and is known to the nation; next, with a long stride upward, he is clothed with ministerial dignity and journeys to the under side of the world to represent the youngest in the court of the oldest of the nations; and finally, after years go by, we see him moving serenely among the crowned heads of the old world, a magnate, with secretaries and under secretaries about him, a retinue of quaint, outlandish Orientals in his wake, and a long following of servants—and the world is aware that his salary is unbelievably enormous, not to say imperial, and likewise knows that he is invested with power to make treaties with all the chief nations of the earth; and that he bears the stately title of AMBASSADOR, and in his person represents the mysterious and awful grandeur of that vague Colossus, the Emperor of China, his mighty empire and his four hundred millions of subjects! Down what a dreamy vista his backward glance must stretch, now, to reach the insignificant surveyor in the Western woods!

He was a good man, and a very, very great man. America lost a son, and all the world a servant, when he died.—*Mark Twain*

February 28, 1870

The Blondes

By some unexplained law of human nature, the farther below insult a person is, the easier it is to insult him; the nearer he comes to being a beast, the more rigidly does he demand to be considered a gentleman; the lower he is sunk in character and position, the more delicately sensitive is he, and the quicker does he take fire at criticism.

Now who would suppose those Lydia Thompson Blondes[154] could be insulted?—or anybody connected with them, male or female? The idea seems grotesque, and yet those people are as dainty in their feelings, and are as easily wounded and as cruelly smitten by any little unkind allusion to their supernatural nastiness, as if they really had a reminiscence of decency still lingering in some out-of-the-way corner of their systems.

Seriously, would not you suppose that if you could do what Miss Lydia Thompson and Miss Pauline Markham do every day, that you could bear a good deal in the way of criticism? Do you know what it is they do? They come on stage naked, to all intents and purposes; padded; painted; powdered; oiled; enameled; and glorified with false hair. They are coarsely, vulgarly voluptuous. Their faces are in keeping with this character, and are very nearly expressionless save when lighted by a sort of vivacious imbecility which admirers of theirs term "intellectual sparkle." Their stage performance is entirely in keeping with their dress, personnel, etc. They dance dismal dances, assisted by a melancholy rabble of painted, tinselled, gamey old skeletons, who spin on one toe and display their relics beseechingly to dull pitlings who refuse to hunger for them and will not applaud. And they play pieces that are vapid and pointless; pitiable medleys of dramatised idiocy, a tiresome clack of rhymes, and a doleful procession of tasteless jokes made toothsome with obscenity. About one scene is generally enough to satisfy a person of only a mere ordinary groveling taste. For instance, that auction scene—wherein you may hear, in fifteen minutes, more abject silliness, and more bad rhymes, and aimless jokes, vulgarity, slang and obscenity, issue from female lips than ought to be distributed over the female utterances of fifteen years of all the sherowdies that be upon the stage—and where you may hear an audience delightedly applaud a velocipede song that is the very ecstacy of insipidity, and laugh exhaustingly over the contortions of two or three male blondes who are trying to burlesque some species of character or other, but are simply burlesquing human nature and degrading human dignity.

Now one would not suppose that mere human ingenuity, unassisted by supernatural help, could devise a remark or combination of remarks that would hew, or beat, or bore a blast through the sensibilities of this sort of people and produce an insult. And yet that thing has been done. A Chicago editor has accomplished this feat. He has insulted the Blondes, in a critical newspaper article. The Blondes have retaliated in the manner usual with that class of persons—by waylaying him boldly and without fear, with cowhides and revolvers—five of them! Two women and three men. [We mention the men simply to be statistically accurate; they were not dangerous; one of them, armed with a revolver, let the assaulted critic take a cowhide away from him, and the other two fearlessly pulled hair from behind. It is thought that if there had been nineteen or twenty more of such men there, the scribe would have been in a right close place.] We have no commiserations to offer him. The satisfaction of reflecting that he has succeeded in harpooning the sensibilities of the Blondes ("stabbing" their sensibilities would be a neater and prettier thing to say, but the figure would be too mild,) ought to afford him a degree of comfort sufficient to make him insensible to the physical pains the assault has left with him.

These Blondes we have been describing recently entertained the Common Council of the city of Cincinnati with a dinner. [Cincinnati, it will be remembered, is the city whose Common Council does not allow the Bible to be read in the common schools.] *[Unsigned]*

March 8, 1870

Personal

The paragraph now going the rounds of the press to the effect that I am going to withdraw from Buffalo and the *Buffalo Express* is entirely foundationless.[155] I am a permanency here. I am prospering well enough to please my friends and distress my enemies, and consequently am in a state of tranquil satisfaction. I will regard it as a favor if those journals that printed the item referred to will also mention this correction.

SAMUEL L. CLEMENS
"Mark Twain"
Buffalo, March 7

March 9, 1870

"More Wisdom"[156]

They that go down to the sea in ships, see the wonders of the deep;"[157] and they that buy coal mines in Pennsylvania and work them see wonders likewise.

They see the wonder of finding themselves suddenly stripped of their independence and converted into the servants of their own employees.

They learn to come and go, do and undo, bow and scrape, simper, smile, shuffle and smirk, at the behest of the "Miner's Union."[158]

They enjoy the wonder of seeing orderly men murdered and little or no notice taken of it by Pennsylvania law officers sworn to execute the statutes, but who prefer perjury to unpopularity, apparently.

They enjoy also the wonder of seeing a legislature lavish all its solicitude upon the miner, without seeming to reflect that his employer has a soul to save too.

They enjoy, finally, the spectacle of a legislature delivering into the hands of an irresponsible mob the actual control of property belonging wholly to their employers.

Such are some of the wonders these men see. The secret of it all lies in the fact that the members of the Miners' Union are a political power. They have votes, and therefore legislatures must not offend them nor petty officers see the small indiscretions which they commit with scalping knife and Derringer.[159]

But the latest wonder is a certain thing which has just become a law in Pennsylvania. It is, that every mine shall be under the control of three persons, whose prerogative it shall be to order alterations in the manner of opening or working it, and who shall also close up and stop work upon such mine when in their discretion it shall seem proper to do so. And who appoints these autocrats? The owners of the mine? No. *Their employees do it.*[160]

Nothing need now be deemed impossible to a Pennsylvania legislature.

And who is it into whose hands the legislature has given this high appointing power? Simply an irresponsible society of men who hold meetings, pass laws, and enforce them by the agencies of terrorism and blood. When a man goes to work in a colliery tabooed by the Miners' Union, they stick a notice on his door-post suggesting that he resign his situation with all convenient dispatch—and they emphasize this suggestion by printing at its top the sign of a coffin.

That these "coffin notices," as they are called, are not inspired by empty bravado, may be gathered from the following telegram, dated Shamokin, March 5, and signed by an old and respectable resident of that locality.:

"Luke Fidler colliery was going to work without the Union. The 'Mollie McGuires' of the Union men murdered the watchman. Three superintendents in one colliery in Shamokin have been murdered since the troubles in the coal mining districts began, and nothing done about it."[161]

Those are the sort of people who are to choose three absolute sovereigns to preside over each mine. These are the people for whose "protection" the Pennsylvania legislature is straining itself to provide. It seems an unnecessary courtesy while ammunition is so cheap.

After saying so much about it, do we suggest a remedy? A remedy for secret assassination; for blind and deaf and dumb officers of justice; for mob terrorism; for truckling legislatures? No; there is no remedy for these things. That is, no remedy that can be brought into instant use. There is one, but time is required for it. It applies itself, and is simply that remedy which comes to the relief of all disorder, viz: the teaching of reason and fair dealing to all parties concerned, through the convincing agencies of hardship, disaster and weariness of fighting each other.

However, should the Pennsylvania legislature take the only step now left it to take for the "protection" of those persecuted lambs, the miners, and make them absolute, joint and equal owners with the present nominal proprietors of the collieries, it is fair to presume that the millennium of peace and order in that Pandemonium[162] would be greatly hastened. Until then, let us continue, as is usual and proper, to wail for the poor oppressed and down-trodden miner, whose only solace, in this cold world, is putting up his little "coffin notice" on his neighbor's door and then helping to get him ready for the funeral. *[Unsigned]*

March 12, 1870

"A Big Thing"
The Richest Silver Mine in the World in Kentucky

[From the *Louisville Journal*]

A very respectable gentleman, a physician, who resides near this city, informs us that he discovered a silver mine of unparalleled richness in Grayson County,[163] in this State. He is the possessor of the secret of discovering the presence of buried and hidden metals and while prospecting and experimenting upon a tract of 4000 acres of land which he owns in that county, he discovered a deposit of nearly pure silver. He says that he has taken out a number of pieces of the ore, which, upon being assayed, were found to contain a larger per cent. of silver than any ore hitherto discovered. The mines are almost inexhaustible. White Pine is a mere pocket compared with this mine. The national debt could be paid from the product of the mine and scarcely be missed. The gentleman is very confident that he has got a big thing, and as soon as the roads get good in the Spring he will commence the work of developing the mine in earnest.

How familiar that old gushing, tiresome bosh is! If this "very respectable gentleman, a physician," had learned his trade in the silver regions of Nevada in the flush times of '63 and '4, he could not clatter off his little narrative with a happier glibness. In fact, he *must* have served his apprenticeship there; he must have done it, for his story is so marvelously like the old frantic Nevada style. If you will notice, he comes to this credulous editor in the same old mysterious way—no names mentioned, nor no precise locality or definite abiding place, but he looms vague and vast in the solemn garb of an awful "respectability,"—and away up on top of that, he piles the impressive grandeur of a Physician's Diploma. Oh, this fine old "respectable" dodge—how many trusting communities have I seen it bring to grief!

There you have Mystery and Respectability—two things that were never wanting in accounts of grand silver discoveries in Nevada. Next, it will be observed, this mysterious physician "is the possessor of the secret of discovering the presence of buried and hidden metals." How customary was this same remarkable gift in Nevada once! I have seen more than four hundred "gold-finders," first and last, but I never saw anybody that ever heard of one of them ever finding anything. So strange, so very strange it seems, and yet it is so true. Even at this distant day it is not without a pang that I recall how for four dreadful weeks I followed step by step in the track of a "Professor" with a hazel stick in his hand,—a "divining rod"—which was to turn and tilt down and point to the gold whenever we came to any. But we never came to any, I suppose. At least it never pointed but once and that was straight at the centre of a pile of granite boulders two hundred and fifty feet high. But I followed that man through chaparral, and sagebrush, and rocky canyons, and over barren, blasted deserts and dreary and hideous mountains, in hunger, thirst and wretchedness till both of us were nearly dead, and ought to have been entirely so if it be any object to administer rigid, uncompromising justice in this world. And now, after such a long, long time, how pleasant it is to "tree" one of those old-time "possessors of the secret," and hear him sing his same old tune. How softly, sweetly familiar the "whang" of it is! And to think how, only seven short years ago, I would have gazed, with an awe-stricken curiosity and a shuddering belief in his mysterious power, upon this Kentucky doctor and his "divining rod!" Ah, how times do change! The divining rod man, who long ago fell from his high estate in Nevada, and became a creature to be jeered at and hooted, turns up in far off Louisville, at this distant day, in all his pristine "respectability," and is endorsed by the *Journal*. Well, well, well, how I would delight to see once more that poor harmless old fraud, the man who "possesses the secret!"

Mystery, Respectability, and Secret and Peculiar Power. How the ancient Nevada ear-marks do stick out. He "discovered a deposit of nearly pure silver." That is just as it used to be, exactly. Inexperienced people imagine that gold and silver, in mining countries, lie scattered around in slugs and ingots on the surface of the ground, and simply have to be gathered up. Therefore, the speculator who has such a class in his eye (like a Kentucky population, for instance,) boldly declares his discovery of mines of "nearly pure silver!" It is a good card for the inexperienced—a most excellent card—but how serenely would an old miner give such a thing the go-by. Because he would say to himself that if the stuff really *were* nearly pure silver, that was a mine to be shunned as if it bore sulphurets of small pox or pyrites of cholera; because there were ninety-nine chances in favor of its being a mere "pocket" that would work out in a week and not pay for the time and trouble expended on it. It used to be profitable to find that kind of mines in Nevada, but now that the people have been educated by scorching experience, the speculator who would get them to bite with any sort of cheerfulness must bait his hook with a mine that yields only a paltry fifty ounces of silver to two thousand pounds of ore— that is to say, fifty dollars a ton. The ore of the surest and most lasting mines does not pay more. This Louisville mine which professes to yield "nearly pure" silver—say twenty thousand dollars a ton—is situated just right. It was a happy sagacity, a more than human wisdom, that located it in Kentucky instead of Nevada.

The Kentucky doctor has the good old fashion of "taking a number of pieces of the ore" (carefully selected from the mass for their particular and peculiar richness,) "for assay"—and upon that assay bases his declaration that his ore is nearly pure silver—which is just the same as saying a desperado's one virtue, courage, and proving by it that the mass of him goes twenty thousand dollars to the ton in pure virtue, and hence he is a saint. Just the same as assaying one raisin in a fruitcake, and thus proving that the cake is a solid mass of raisins.

"The mine inexhaustible!" This man was educated in Nevada. There can be no sort of question about it. And he is one of those good old-time wonder discoverers (an extinct race, there, now,) who really believes in his own marvel. I can see him as plainly, bending over the Louisville reporter's desk, talking low and excitedly, fishing out of his rusty overcoat pocket a fragment of white rock streaked with blue, and spasmodically smacking it against his tongue—then examining it closely and anxiously, maybe with a little eye-glass like a short ferule—giving it another lick and a still closer examination—then a feverish:

"There, there it is!—see it? right there at the end of my finger!" [showing a poor little speck of ore.] "Rich?—Oh, don't mention it! That's from the Christopher Columbus—there's ten thousand tons just like that in sight! This other piece is from the extension of the Columbus—and this is from the Poor Man's Hope—and this from the Last Chance—and this from the Black Avenger—and this is from the Home Ticket—and this from the Branch Mint—and this—"

And by this time, or a little later, the reporter's table is freighted with rocky fragments, and the miner's overcoat pockets are exhausted. But not his wind. Oh, no—that never gives out. He goes on to say— (how dear the old familiar brag is to me)—he goes on to say that:

"White Pine is a mere pocket compared with this mine!" [And the reporter infallibly gets infected with the miner's feverish extravagance and makes that same remark in his paper on his own personal responsibility. It will be observed by the extract we copy that the reporter has never seen either the mine or the assay.]

"THE NATIONAL DEBT COULD BE PAID FROM THE MINE AND SCARCELY BE MISSED!" Come to these arms, thou deathless, thou eternal, thou perennial household-word of the Speculating Imposter of the good old times! How many, many National Debts have I seen paid with this same sort of mines! And how many, many just such mines have I seen, which could pay that debt "without missing it"—mines that (in fancy) paid that debt, interest and all, and then died sighing plaintively for more National Debts to conquer. Died, and left their own debts unpaid and their stockholders paupers. Proceed, now, you Louisville benefactor. The national finances are safe once more. You have "got the world by the scruff of the neck"—(how *did* you manage to forget to say that?— how *could* you have forgotten it, and it such a blood relation of all your other talk? I never saw one of your kind before, that hadn't "the world by the scruff of the neck." This Kentucky doctor must have said that, and the reporter basely left it out.)

Next, we have some more time-honored Nevada cant about the mysterious physician being "very confident" (after all that absolute certainty, he dwindles down in the same old stupid Nevada way to being "very confident"—as if any man's being "very confident" was evidence of any thing,) that he has got a "big thing" (the same old popular slang of the canyons and gulches,) and:

"As soon as the roads get good this Spring—"

And so forth and so on—but in the meantime he is infallibly and un-

questionably willing to part with just a few shares—only a few to especial and particular friends, and merely as a personal favor—and if he
cannot get one price he will cheerfully take another. These bad roads
and wintry weather have sold many a "nearly pure" silver mine that
would have remained on the discoverer's hands if it had been possible
for people to visit and examine it. I never knew one of these marvelous
discoveries to be made in good weather. It is singular, but it is true.

"In the Spring" the doctor is going to "develop the mine in earnest."
Which is another unfortunate expression—for any novice knows that
a "nearly pure" silver vein requires no "development." Would one go
gravely to work to "develop" water in a river, or ice in the polar regions, or rocks in a New Hampshire "farm?" Are not such things in
such places already "developed?" And is not likewise the metal in a
mine that is "nearly pure" silver and "contains a larger per cent. of silver than any ore hitherto discovered?" I have seen two silver mines
whose ore yielded twenty thousand dollars a ton (they lasted forty-
eight hours), but they did not need any "developing."

Mystery, Respectability, "Possession of the Secret;" Incredible Richness; Ingenuity in Selecting Specimens for Assay; National Debt to be
Liquidated; the Customary Dwindling from the Imposing Grandeur of
Absolute Certainty to "The Gentleman is Very Confident;" and finally,
the resolve to "Develop"—"When the Roads are Better." Such is the inventory. Such is the old, old, threadbare formula of an empty, baseless,
bottomless "ASTOUNDING DISCOVERY" of the "early days" of each and
every new mining country that ever was opened up since the world began. There is not a trademark missing. In fact, a new one is added. For,
through all this old stale bait projects the point of a hook such as was
never used in the mining-fraud fisheries before, probably—this, the
quiet reference to those "4000 acres of land" which the doctor owns—
and I feel driven to borrow and wager enormous sums of money that
he will not care the value of a straw whether he ever "develops" a
shovelful of his marvelous mine or sells a foot of it, provided he suc-
ceeds in getting rid of those 4000 acres of his at a comfortable figure.

This mighty noise about a dazzling mining discovery is a familiar
old imposture, but this is surely the first time that ever it was used to
create a sale for *land*. In a mining country the people would let the
doctor have a certain little share of his mine and they would take the
rest—and it never would occur to them that it was necessary to buy
his land before they dug through it to get at their silver. Because,
when you have "taken up" a mine you have a legal right to dig for

it,—and if another man owns the farm that is on top of it, it is a very grave misfortune for him, because the only way he has of protecting that farm from destruction, is to move it.

Finally—and without meaning any impertinence or any offence—I wish to ask the Louisville reporter the old familiar question, so common among reporters in the mines: "How many 'feet' did the doctor give you?" ("Feet" are shares.) *We* always got "feet," in Nevada, for whooping about a Nearly-Pure-Silver-National-Debt-Liquidator in this gushing way.—*Mark Twain*

Buffalo, March 12

March 19, 1870

A Mysterious Visit

The first notice that was taken of me when I "settled down," recently, was by a gentleman who said he was an assessor, and connected with the U.S. Internal Revenue Department.[164] I said I had never heard of his branch of business before, but I was very glad to see him, all the same,—would he sit down? He sat down. I did not know anything particular to say, and yet I felt that people who have arrived at the dignity of keeping house must be conversational, must be easy and sociable in company. So in default of anything else to say, I asked him if he was opening his shop in our neighborhood.

He said he was. [I did not wish to appear ignorant, but I *had* hoped he would mention what he had for sale.]

I ventured to ask him "how was trade?" and he said "So-so."

I then said we would drop in, and if we liked his house as well as any other, we would give him our custom.

He said he thought we would like his establishment well enough to confine ourselves to it—said he never saw anybody who would go off and hunt up another man in his line after trading with him once.

That sounded pretty complacent, but barring that natural expression of villainy which we all have, the man looked honest enough.

I do not know how it came about, exactly, but gradually we appeared to melt down and run together, conversationally speaking, and then everything went along as comfortably as clockwork.

We talked, and talked, and talked—at least I did. And we laughed, and laughed, and laughed—at least he did. But all the time, I had my presence of mind about me—I had my native shrewdness turned on, "full head," as the engineers say. I was determined to find out all about his business, in spite of his obscure answers—and I was determined to have it out of him without his suspecting what I was at. I meant to trap him with a deep, deep ruse. I would tell him all about my own business, and he would naturally so warm to me during this seductive burst of confidence that he would forget himself and tell me about *his* affairs before he suspected what I was about. I thought to myself, My son, you little know what an old fox you are dealing with. I said:

"Now you never would guess what I made lecturing this winter and last spring?"

"No—don't believe I could, to save me. Let me see—let me see. About two thousand dollars maybe? But no—no, sir, I know you couldn't have made that much. Say seventeen hundred, maybe?"

"Ha-ha! I knew you couldn't. My lecturing receipts for last spring and this winter were fourteen thousand, seven hundred and fifty dollars—what do you think of that!"

"Why, it is amazing—perfectly amazing. I will make a note of it. And you say even this wasn't all?"

"All? Why bless you there was my income from the *Buffalo Express* for four months—about—well, what should you say to about eight thousand dollars, for instance?"

"Say! Why I should say I should like to see myself rolling in just such another ocean of affluence. Eight thousand! I'll make a note of it. Why, man!—and on top of all this I am to understand that you had still more income?"

"Ha-ha-ha! Why you're only in the suburbs of it, so to speak. There's my book, "The Innocents Abroad"—price $3.50 to $5.00, according to the binding. Listen to me. Look me in the eye. During the last four months and a half, saying nothing of sales before that—but just simply during the four months and a half ending March 15, 1870, we've sold ninety-five thousand copies[165] of that book! Ninety-five thousand! Think of it. Average four dollars a copy, say. It's nearly four hundred thousand dollars, my son. I get half!"[166]

"The suffering Moses! I'll set *that* down. Fourteen-seven-fifty—eight—two hundred. Total, say—well, upon my word, the grand total is about two hundred and thirteen or fourteen thousand dollars. *Is* that possible?"

"Possible! If there's any mistake it's the other way. Two hundred and fourteen thousand, cash, is my income for this year if *I* know how to cipher."

Then the gentleman got up to go. It came over me most uncomfortably that I had made my revelations for nothing, besides being flattered into stretching them considerably by the stranger's astonished exclamations. But no; at the last moment the gentleman handed me a large envelope and said it contained his advertisement; and that I would find out all about his business in it; and that he would be happy to have my custom—would in fact be proud to have the custom of a man of such prodigious income; and that he used to think there were several wealthy men in Buffalo, but when they come to trade with him he discovered that they barely had enough to live on; and that in truth it had been such a weary, weary age since he had seen a rich man face to face, and talked with him, and touched him with his hands, that he could hardly refrain from embracing me—in fact, would esteem it a great favor if I would *let* him embrace me.

This so pleased me that I did not try to resist, but allowed this simple hearted stranger to throw his arms about me and weep a few tranquilizing tears down the back of my neck. Then he went his way.

As soon as he was gone, I opened his advertisement. I studied it attentively for four minutes. I then called up the cook and said:

"Hold me while I faint. Let Maria turn the batter-cakes."

Bye and bye, when I came to, I went down to the rum mill on the corner and hired an artist by the week to sit up nights and curse that stranger, and give me a lift occasionally in the day time when I came to a hard place.

Ah, what a miscreant he was! His "advertisement" was nothing in the world but a wicked tax-return—a string of impertinent questions about my private affairs occupying the best part of four foolscap pages of fine print—questions, I may remark, gotten up with such marvelous ingenuity that the oldest man in the world couldn't understand what the most of them were driving at—questions, too, that were calculated to make a man report about four times his actual income to keep from swearing to a lie. I looked for a loophole, but there did not appear to be any. Inquiry No. 1 covered my case, as generously and as amply as an umbrella could cover an ant hill:

"What were your profits, in 1869, from any trade, business or vocation, wherever carried on?"

And that inquiry was backed up by thirteen others of an equally searching nature, the most modest of which required information as to whether I had committed any burglary, or highway robbery, or by any arson or other secret source of emolument, had acquired property which was not enumerated in my statement of income as set opposite to inquiry No. 1.[167]

It was plain that that stranger had enabled me to make an ass of myself. It was very, very plain, and I went out and hired another artist. By working on my vanity the stranger had seduced me into declaring an income of $214,000. By law, $1000 of this was exempt from income tax—the only relief I could see, and it was only a drop in the ocean. At the legal five per cent., I must pay over to the government the appalling sum of ten thousand six hundred and fifty dollars, income tax.

[I may remark, in this place, that I did not do it.]

I am acquainted with a very opulent man, whose house is a palace, whose table is regal, whose outlays are enormous, yet a man who has no income, as I have often noticed, by the revenue returns; and to him I went for advice, in my distress.[168] He took my dreadful exhibition of receipts, he put on his glasses, he took his pen, and presto!—I was a pauper! It was the neatest thing that ever was. He did it simply by deftly manipulating the bill of "DEDUCTIONS." He set down my "State, national and municipal taxes" at so much; my "losses by shipwreck, fire, etc.," at so much; my "losses on sales of real estate"—on "live stock sold"—on "payments for rent of homestead"—on "repairs, improvements, interest"—on "previously taxed salary as an officer of the United States army, navy, revenue service," and other things. He got astonishing "deductions" out of each and every one of these matters— each and every one of them. And when he was done he handed me the paper and I saw at a glance that during the year 1869 my income, in the way of profits, had been *one thousand two hundred and fifty dollars and forty cents.*

"Now," said he, "the thousand dollars is exempt by law. What you want to do is to go and swear this document in and pay tax on the two hundred and fifty dollars."

[While he was making this speech his little boy Willie lifted a two dollar greenback out of his vest pocket and vanished with it, and I would bet anything that if my stranger were to call on that little boy to-morrow he would make a false return of his income.]

"Do you," said I, "do you always work up the 'deductions' after this fashion in your own case, sir?"

"Well, I should say so! If it weren't for those eleven saving clauses under the head of 'Deductions' I should be beggared every year to support this hateful and wicked, this extortionate and tyrannical government."

This gentleman stands away up among the very best of the solid men of Buffalo—the men of moral weight, of commercial integrity, of unimpeachable social spotlessness—and so I bowed to his example. I went down to the revenue office, and under the accusing eyes of my old visitor I stood up and swore to lie after lie, fraud after fraud, villainy after villainy, till my immortal soul was coated inches and inches thick with perjury and my self-respect was gone forever and ever.

But what of it? It is nothing more than thousands of the highest, and richest, and proudest, and most respected, honored and courted men in America do every year. And so I don't care. I am not ashamed. I shall simply, for the present, talk little and wear fire-proof gloves, lest I fall into certain habits irrevocably.—*Mark Twain*

March 19, 1870

Literary Guide to *Williams & Packard's System of Penmanship*

It is a handsome volume, a graceful green bound thing, fit for the centre-table.[169] And in it appears to be concentrated all the information about penmanship that a man could need in the writing of any thing, from a receipt for a keg of mackerel up to an unabridged dictionary.

After the pupil has learned thoroughly the "correct position" of hand and pen, the book dashes at once and elaborately into the subject of Penmanship, and proceeds to teach him how to form each and every letter of the alphabet by arbitrary and inexorable rule. He cannot take this book and learn how to make its high-toned capital A and then go off and make the rest of the letters in a mere general way. No, B confronts him, and then C, and D, and all the rest. He is not done till he gets through. But when the pupil *has* gone through the pages devoted to instructions, he will have learned how to make every letter of the alphabet with an accuracy of form, an elegance of shape, and an exquisiteness of finish that touch upon the marvelous. He will then be able to see the benefit of the elaborate drilling and training he has been subjected to. We desire to remark, here, that merely idling along through this book, in order to review it, has so improved our handwriting that the present page looks not a whit like the first page of this review. It seems hardly possible, now, that we could have been the uncultivated person we were when we wrote that first page. The reader can himself see that this article has improved from the start.

The remaining fifty or seventy-five pages of the book are made up of fine copy-plates with all necessary instructions attached, printed on delicately tinted paper; and there are also beautiful flourishy penmanship birds that look like a conflagration; and naked Cupids sitting on rose buds learning patiently to write by the Williams & Packard System, and not apparently caring two cents about the thorns; and pictures of scrolls, and flowers, and all those kind of things that are so simple and easy to do with a pen, after you know how. The Williams & Packard is a system of penmanship which has made steady progress in the favor of the public during the past few years, until at last it has reached an eminence not heretofore accorded to any predecessor.

We are glad to be able to speak so warmly in commendation of this work, for it is published by "Dan Slote,"[170] (Slote, Woodman & Co., 119 and 121 William Street, New York,) our stateroom-mate in the "Quaker City" Excursion—whose portrait we have printed on page 288 of *The Innocents Abroad,*[171] and whom we have described on page 28 of the same book to be "an intelligent young gentleman, cheerful of spirit, unselfish, full of generous impulses, patient, considerate, and wonderfully good-natured." It is an enormous degree of excellence to claim for a mere human being, but Dan holds good to the character to this hour. To say we wish his publication success is to put it tamely, insipidly. We wish it a success that shall sweep the land like a hurricane and the ocean like a typhoon, and gather together the surplus greenbacks of all the peoples of the earth and bury his establishment under them a mile and a half deep. This, together with the further wish that Dan may live to enjoy this great prosperity just as long as he wants to. *[Unsigned]*

The Facts in the Great Land Slide Case

It was in the early days of Nevada Territory.[172] The mountains are very high and steep about Carson, Eagle and Washoe Valleys—very high and very steep, and so when the snow gets to melting off fast in the Spring and the warm surface-earth begins to moisten and soften, the disastrous land-slides commence. You do not know what a land-slide is, unless you have lived in that country and seen the whole side of a mountain taken off some fine morning and deposited down in the valley, leaving a vast, treeless, unsightly scar upon the mountain's front to keep the circumstance fresh in your memory all the years that you may go on living within seventy miles of that place.

General Buncombe[173] was shipped out to Nevada in the invoice of Territorial officers, to be United States Attorney. He considered himself a lawyer of parts, and he very much wanted an opportunity to manifest it—partly for the pure gratification of it and partly because his salary was Territorially meagre (which is a strong expression.) Now the older citizens of a new territory look upon the rest of the world with a calm, unmalignant contempt as long as it keeps out of the way—when it gets in the way they snub it. Sometimes this latter takes the shape of a practical joke.

One morning Dick Sides[174] rode furiously up to General Buncombe's door in Carson City and rushed into his presence without stopping to tie his horse. He seemed much excited. He told the General that he wanted him to defend a suit for him and would pay him five hundred dollars if he achieved a victory. And then, with violent gestures and a world of profanity, he poured out his griefs. He said it was pretty well known that for some years he had been farming (or ranching as the more customary term is,) in Washoe District, and making a successful thing of it, and furthermore it was known that his ranch was situated just in the edge of the valley, and that Tom Morgan[175] owned a ranch immediately above it on the mountain side. And now the trouble was that one of those hated and dreaded land-slides had come and slid Morgan's ranch, fences, cabins, cattle, barns and every thing down on top of *his* ranch and exactly covered up every single vestige of his property, to a depth of about six feet. Morgan was in possession and refused to vacate the premises—said he was occupying his own cabin and not interfering with any body else's—and said cabin was standing on the same dirt and same ranch it had always stood on, and would like to see any body make him vacate.

"And when I reminded him," said Sides, weeping, "that it was on top of my ranch and that he was trespassing, he had the infernal meanness to ask me why didn't I *stay* on my ranch and hold possession when I see him coming! Why didn't I *stay* on it, the blathering lunatic—and by George, when I heard that racket and looked up that hill it was just like the whole world was a ripping and a tearing down that mountain side—trees going end over end in the air, rocks as big as a house jumping about a thousand feet high and busting into ten million pieces, cattle literally turned inside out and a-coming head on with their tails hanging out between their teeth—Oh, splinters, and cord-wood, and thunder and lightning, and hail and snow, odds and ends of hay stacks and things, and dust—Oh, dust ain't no name for it—it was just clouds, solid clouds of dust!—and in the midst of all that wrack and destruction sot that cussed Morgan on his gate-post, a-wondering why I didn't stay and hold possession; likely! Umph! I just took one glimpse of that speckticle, General, and I lit out'n the country in three jumps exactly.

"But what grinds me is that that Morgan hangs on there and won't move off'n that ranch—says it's his'n and he's going to keep it—likes it better'n he did when it was higher up the hill. Mad! Well, I've been so mad for two days I couldn't find my way to town—been wandering around in the brush in a starving condition—got any thing here to drink, General? But I'm here *now,* and I'm a-going to law. You hear *me!*"

Never in all the world, perhaps, were a man's feelings so outraged as were the General's. He said he had never heard of such high-handed conduct in all his life as this Morgan's. And he said there was no use in going to law—Morgan had no shadow of right to remain where he was—nobody in the wide world would uphold him in it, and no lawyer would take his case and no judge listen to it. Sides said that right there was where he was mistaken—every body in town sustained Morgan; Hal Brayton,[176] a very smart lawyer, had taken his case; the courts being in vacation, it was to be tried before a referee, and ex-Governor Roop[177] had already been appointed to that office and would open his court in the largest parlor of the Ormbsy House[178] at 2 that afternoon.

The innocent General was amazed. He said he had suspected before that the people of that Territory were fools, and now he knew it. But he said rest easy, rest easy and collect the witnesses, for the victory

was just as certain as if the conflict were already over. Sides wiped
away his tears and left.

At 2 in the afternoon referee Roop's Court opened, and that re-
morseless old joker appeared throned among his sheriffs, his witnesses, and a "packed" jury, and wearing upon his face a fraudulent
solemnity so awe-inspiring that some of his fellow-conspirators had
misgivings that maybe he had not comprehended, after all, that this
was merely a joke. An unearthly stillness prevailed, for at the slightest noise the judge uttered sternly the command:

"Order in the Court!"

And the sheriffs promptly echoed it. Presently the General elbowed
his way through the crowd of spectators, with his arms full of law-
books, and on his ears fell an order from the judge which was the first
respectful recognition of his high official dignity that had ever saluted
them, and it saturated his whole system with pleasure:

"Way for the United States Attorney!"

The witnesses were called—legislators, high government officers,
ranch men, miners, Indians, Chinamen, negroes. Three-fourths of
them were called by the defendant Morgan, but no matter, their testimony invariably went in favor of the plaintiff Sides. Each new witness
only added new testimony to the absurdity of a man's claiming to own
another man's property because his farm had slid down on top of it.
Then the Morgan lawyers made their speeches, and seemed to make
singularly weak ones—they did really nothing to help the Morgan
cause. And now the General, with a great glow of triumph on his face,
got up and made a mighty effort; he pounded the table, he banged the
law-books, he shouted, and roared, and howled, he quoted from every
thing and every body, poetry, sarcasm, statistics, history, pathos, and
blasphemy, and wound up with a grand war-whoop for free speech,
freedom of the press, free schools, the Glorious Bird of America and
the principles of eternal justice! [Applause.]

When the General sat down, he did it with the comfortable conviction that if there were any thing in good strong testimony, a big
speech and believing and admiring countenances all around, Mr. Morgan's cake was dough. Ex-Governor Roop leant his head upon his
hand for some minutes, thinking profoundly, and the still audience
waited breathlessly for his decision. Then he got up and stood erect,
with bended head and thought again. Then he walked the floor with
long, deliberate strides, and his chin in his hand, and still the audience waited. At last he returned to his throne and seated himself. The

sheriffs commanded the attention of the Court. Judge Roop cleared his throat and said:

"Gentlemen, I feel the great responsibility that rests upon me this day. This is no ordinary case. On the contrary it is plain that it is the most solemn and awful that ever man was called upon to decide. Gentlemen, I have listened attentively to the evidence, and the weight of it, the overwhelming weight of it is in favor of the plaintiff Sides. I have listened also to the remarks of counsel, with high interest—and especially will I commend the masterly and irrefutable logic of the distinguished gentleman who represents the plaintiff. But gentlemen, let us beware how we allow human testimony, human ingenuity in argument and human ideas of equity to influence us to our undoing at a moment so solemn as this! Gentlemen, it ill becomes us, worms as we are, to meddle with the decrees of Heaven. It is plain to me that Heaven, in its inscrutable wisdom, has seen fit to move this defendant's ranch for a purpose. We are but creatures, and we must submit. If Heaven has chosen to favor the defendant Morgan in this marked and wonderful manner; and if Heaven, unsatisfied with the position of the Morgan ranch upon the mountain side, has chosen to remove it to a position more eligible and more advantageous for its owner, it ill becomes us, insects as we are, to question the legality of the act. No—Heaven created the ranches and it is Heaven's perogative to rearrange them, to experiment with them, to shift them around at its pleasure. It is for us to submit, without repining. I warn you that this thing which has happened is a thing with which the sacrilegious hands and brains and tongues of men must not meddle. Gentlemen, it is the verdict of this court that the plaintiff, Richard Sides, has been deprived of his ranch by the visitation of God! And from this decision there is no appeal."

Buncombe seized his cargo of law books and plunged out of the court room a raving madman, almost. He pronounced Roop to be a miraculous ass, a fool, an inspired idiot. In all good faith he returned at night and remonstrated with Roop upon his extravagant decision, and implored him to walk the floor and think for half an hour, and see if he could not figure out some sort of modification of the verdict. Roop yielded at last and got up to walk. He walked two hours and a half, and at last his face lit up happily and he told Buncombe it had occurred to him that the ranch underneath the new Morgan ranch still belonged to Sides, that his title to the ground itself was just as good as it had ever been, and therefore he was of the opinion that Sides had a right to dig it out from under there and—

The General never waited to hear the end of it. He was always an impatient and irascible man, that way. At the end of two weeks he got it through his understanding that he had been played upon with a joke.—*Mark Twain*

April 12, 1870

Mark Twain on Agriculture

The following letter refers to an arrangement under which our associate, Mark Twain, is to edit and conduct one of the departments in *The Galaxy*:[179]

Buffalo, April 2

Mr. F. P. Church, Editor of the Galaxy:

DEAR SIR: My own paper, the *Buffalo Express,* does not occupy my entire time, and therefore I accept your offer, and from the present time forward will edit and conduct a "Department of Agriculture" in *The Galaxy* Magazine. I thank you for leaving to me the selection of a department; and in choosing that of Agriculture I feel that my judgment has answered your highest expectations.

I have not made this choice at haphazard. After careful survey of the ground, I saw that the subject of agriculture had been wholly overlooked by the magazines of the day as a sensational topic, and that all that was necessary for us to do was to enter in and seize this rich opportunity. Fortune is secured to us. Nothing can prevent such a consummation. In this virgin soil I will insert a reaping-hook that shall blossom like the rose; upon this sailless desert I will launch a triumphal barge; in this deep mine of affluence will I plant a sturdy tree of prosperity whose fragrance shall slake the hunger of the naked, and whose sheltering branches shall stretch abroad until they wash the shores of the remotest lands of the earth.

(I never can touch the subject of Agriculture without getting excited. But you understand what I mean.) Under the head of "Memoranda" I shall take hold of this neglected topic, and by means of a series of farming and grazing articles of blood-curdling interest will proceed to lift the subject of Agriculture into the first rank of literary respectability.

Herewith please find my manuscript for your May number.—*Mark Twain*

P.S.—I have no practical knowledge of Agriculture, but that need
not interfere. You may have noticed that the less I know about a subject the more confidence I have, and the more new light I throw on it.

April 16, 1870

The New Crime
Legislation Needed

This country, during the last thirty or forty years, has produced
some of the most remarkable cases of insanity of which there is any
mention in history.[180] For instance, there was the Baldwin case, in
Ohio, twenty-two years ago. Baldwin, from his boyhood up, had been
of a vindictive, malignant, quarrelsome nature. He put a boy's eye out,
once, and never was heard upon any occasion, to utter a regret for it.
He did many such things. But at last he did something that was serious. He called at a house just after dark, one evening, knocked, and
when the occupant came to the door, shot him dead and then tried to
escape but was captured. Two days before, he had wantonly insulted a
helpless cripple, and the man he afterward took swift vengeance upon
with an assassin bullet, knocked him down. Such was the Baldwin
case. The trial was long and exciting; the community was fearfully
wrought up. Men said this spiteful, bad-hearted villain had caused
grief enough in his time, and now he should satisfy the law. But they
were mistaken. Baldwin was insane when he did the deed—they had
not thought of that. By the arguments of counsel it was shown that at
half-past ten in the morning on the day of the murder, Baldwin became insane, and remained so for eleven hours and a half exactly.
This just covered the case comfortably, and he was acquitted. Thus, if
an unthinking and excited community had been listened to instead of
the arguments of counsel, a poor, crazy creature would have been held
to a fearful responsibility for a mere freak of madness. Baldwin went
clear, and although his relatives and friends were naturally incensed
against the community for their injurious suspicions and remarks,
they said let it go for this time, and did not prosecute. The Baldwins
were very wealthy. This same Baldwin had momentary fits of insanity
twice afterward, and on both occasions killed people he had grudges
against. And on both these occasions the circumstances of the killing
were so aggravated, and the murders so seemingly heartless and

treacherous, that if Baldwin had not been insane he would have been hanged without the shadow of a doubt. As it was, it required all his political and family influence to get him clear in one of the cases, and cost him not less than $10,000 to get clear in the other. One of these men he had notoriously been threatening to kill for twelve years. The poor creature happened, by the merest piece of ill-fortune, to come along a dark alley at the very moment that Baldwin's insanity came upon him, and so he was shot in the back with a gun loaded with slugs. It was exceedingly fortunate for Baldwin that his insanity came on him just when it did.

Take the case of Lynch Hackett, of Pennsylvania. Twice, in public, he attacked a German butcher by the name of Bemis Feldner, with a cane, and both times Feldner whipped him with his fists. Hackett was a vain, wealthy, violent gentleman, who held his blood and family in high esteem and believed that a reverent respect was due his great riches. He brooded over the shame of his chastisement for two weeks, and then, in a momentary fit of insanity armed himself to the teeth, rode into town, waited a couple of hours until he saw Feldner coming down the street with his wife on his arm, and then, as the couple passed the doorway in which he had partially concealed himself, he drove a knife into Feldner's neck, killing him instantly. The widow caught the limp form and eased it to the earth. Both were drenched with blood. Hackett jocosely remarked to her that as a professional butcher's recent wife she could appreciate the artistic neatness of the job that left her in a condition to marry again, in case she wanted to. This remark, and another which he made to a friend, that his position in society made the killing of an obscure citizen simply an "eccentricity" instead of a crime, were shown to be evidences of insanity, and so Hackett escaped punishment. The jury were hardly inclined to accept these as proofs, at first, inasmuch as the prisoner had never been insane before the murder, and under the tranquilizing effect of the butchering had immediately regained his right mind—but when the defence came to show that a third cousin of Hackett's wife's stepfather was insane, and not only insane but had a nose the very counterpart of Hackett's, it was plain that insanity was hereditary in the family and Hackett had come by it by legitimate inheritance. Of course the jury then acquitted him. But it was a merciful providence that Mrs. H.'s people had been afflicted as shown, else Hackett would certainly have been hanged.

However, it is not possible to account all the marvelous cases of insanity that have come under the public notice in the last thirty or forty years. There was the Durgin case in New Jersey three years ago. The servant girl, Bridget Durgin, at dead of night invaded her mistress' bedroom and carved the lady literally to pieces with a knife. Then she dragged the body to the middle of the floor and beat and banged it with chairs and such things. Next she opened the feather beds and strewed the contents around, saturated everything with kerosene and set fire to the general wreck. She now took up the young child of the murdered woman in her blood-smearing hands, and walked off, through the snow, with no shoes on, to a neighbor's house a quarter of a mile off, and told a string of wild, incoherent stories about some men coming and setting fire to the house; and then she cried piteously, and without seeming to think there was anything suggestive about the blood upon her hands, her clothing and the baby, volunteered the remark that she was afraid those men had murdered her mistress! Afterward, by her own confession and other testimony, it was proved that the mistress had always been kind to the girl, consequently there was no revenge in the murder; and it was also shown that the girl took nothing away from the burning house, not even her own shoes, and consequently robbery was not the motive. Now the reader says, "Here comes that same old plea of insanity again." But the reader has deceived himself this time. No such plea was offered in her defence. The judge sentenced her, nobody persecuted the Governor with petitions for her pardon, and she was promptly hanged.

There was that youth in Pennsylvania, whose curious confession was published a year ago. It was simply a conglomeration of incoherent drivel from beginning to end—and so was his lengthy speech on the scaffold afterward. For a whole year he was haunted with a desire to disfigure a certain young woman so that no one would marry her. He did not love her himself, and did not want to marry her, but he did not want anybody else to do it. He would not go anywhere with her, and yet was opposed to anybody else's escorting her. Upon one occasion he declined to go to a wedding with her, and when she got other company, lay in wait for the couple by the road, intending to make them go back or kill the escort. After spending sleepless nights over his ruling desire for a full year, he at last attempted its execution— that is, attempted to disfigure the young woman. It was a success. It was permanent. In trying to shoot her cheek (as she sat at the supper table with her parents and brother and sisters) in such a manner as to mar its comeliness, one of his bullets wandered a little out of the course and she dropped dead. To the very last moment of his life he bewailed the ill luck that made her move her face just at the critical moment. And so he died apparently about half persuaded that somehow it was chiefly her own fault that she got killed. This idiot was hanged. The plea of insanity was not offered.

The recent case of Lady Mordaunt,[181] in England, had proved beyond cavil that the thing we call common prostitution in America is only insanity in Great Britain. Her husband wanted a divorce, but as her cheerful peculiarities were the offspring of lunacy and consequently she could not be held responsible for them, he had to take her to his bosom again. It is sad to think of a dozen or two of great English lords taking advantage of a poor crazy woman. In this country, if history be worth anything to judge by, the husband would have rented a graveyard and stocked it, and then brought the divorce suit afterward. In which case the jury would have brought *him* in insane, not his wife.

Insanity certainly is on the increase in the world, and crime is dying out. There are no longer any murders—none worth mentioning, at any rate. Formerly, if you killed a man, it was possible that you were insane—but now if you kill a man it is *evidence* that you are a lunatic. In these days, too, if a person of good family and high social standing steals any thing, they call it *kleptomania,* and send him to the lunatic asylum. If a person of high standing squanders his fortune in dissipation and closes his career with strychnine or a bullet, "Temporary Aberration" is what was the trouble with *him*. And finally, as before noted, the list is capped with a new and curious madness in the shape of wholesale adultery.

Is not this insanity plea becoming rather common? Is it not so common that the reader confidently expects to see it offered in every criminal case that comes before the courts? And is it not so cheap, and so common, and often so trivial, that the reader smiles in derision when the newspaper mentions it? And is it not curious to note how very often it wins acquittal for the prisoner? Lately it does not seem possible for a man to so conduct himself, before killing another man, as not to be manifestly insane. If he talks about the stars he is insane. If he appears nervous and uneasy an hour before the killing, he is insane. If he weeps over a great grief, his friends shake their heads and fear that he is "not right." If, an hour after the murder, he seems ill at ease, pre-occupied and excited, he is unquestionably insane.

Really, what we want now, is not laws against crime, but a law against *insanity*. There is where the true evil lies.

And the penalty attached should be imprisonment, not hanging. Then, it might be worth the trouble and expense of trying the Gen. Coleses, and the Gen. Sickleses and the McFarlands,[182] because juries might lock them up for brief terms, in deference to the majesty of the law; but it is not likely that any of us will ever live to see the murderer of a seducer hanged. Perhaps, if the truth were confessed, few of us *wish* to live that long.

Since I seemed to have wandered into the McFarland case without especially intending to do it, (for my original idea was merely to call attention to how many really crazy people are hanged these days, and how many that never were crazy a moment in their lives are acquitted of crime on the plea of insanity,) I will venture to suggest—simply as an opinion, and not as an assertion—that the main reason why we shall never succeed in hanging this mean, small villain, McFarland, is, that his real crime did not consist in killing Richardson, but in so conducting himself long before that, as to estrange his wife's affections from himself and drive her to the love and protection of another man. If they would quash this present suit and try him on that, we would get the unreluctant fangs of justice on him sure, if what one good man says against McFarland is worth as much as what another good man says in his favor. We might all consent that he was a criminal in his treatment of his wife at that time, but, somehow we hesitate to condemn him to the scaffold for this act of his whereby he inflicted a penalty for a wrong which, down in our secret hearts, we feel is beyond the ability of all law to punish amply and satisfactorily.

No, when a man abuses his wife as McFarland seems to have abused his, any jury would punish him severely, and do it with a relish. But when a man kills the seducer of his wife, a jury cannot be found that will condemn him to suffer for murder. Therefore, it is fair to consider that McFarland's real crime is not in court in New York, now, but is left out of the indictment.

If I seem to have wandered from my subject and thrown in some surplusage, what do I care? With these evidences of a wandering mind present to the reader, am I to be debarred from offering the customary plea of Insanity?—*Mark Twain*

April 23, 1870

The Story of the Good Little Boy
Who Did Not Prosper

[*Mark Twain in the* Galaxy.]

[The following has been written at the instance of several literary
friends, who thought that if the history of "The Bad Little Boy who did
not Come to Grief" (a moral sketch which I published five or six years
ago) was worthy of preservation several weeks in print, a fair and unprejudiced companion-piece to it would deserve a similar immortality.—
EDITOR MEMORANDA.][183]

Once there was a good little boy by the name of Jacob Blivens.
He always obeyed his parents, no matter how absurd and unreason-
able their demands were; and he always learned his book, and never
was he late at Sabbath school. He would not play hookey, even when
his sober judgment told him it was the most profitable thing he could
do. None of the other boys could ever make that boy out, he acted so
strangely. He wouldn't lie, no matter how convenient it was. He just
said it was wrong to lie, and that was sufficient for him. And he was
so honest that he was simply ridiculous. The curious ways that that
Jacob had surpassed every thing. He wouldn't play marbles on Sunday,
he wouldn't rob birds' nests, he wouldn't give hot pennies to organ-
grinders' monkeys; he didn't seem to take any interest in any kind of
rational amusement. So the other boys used to try to reason it out and
come to an understanding of him, but they couldn't arrive at any satisfactory conclusion; as I said before, they could only figure out a sort
of vague idea that he was "afflicted," and so they took him under their
protection, and never allowed any harm to come to him.

This good little boy read all the Sunday-school books; they were his
greatest delight. This was the whole secret of it. He believed in the
good little boys they put in the Sunday-school books; he had every
confidence in them. He longed to come across one of them alive, once;
but he never did. They all died before his time, maybe. Whenever he
read about a particularly good one, he turned over quickly to the end
to see what became of him, because he wanted to travel thousands of

miles and gaze on him; but it wasn't any use; that good little boy always died in the last chapter, and there was a picture of the funeral, with all his relations and the Sunday-school children standing around the grave in pantaloons that were too short, and bonnets that were too large, and everybody crying into handkerchiefs that had as much as a yard and a half of stuff in them. He was always headed off in this way. He never could see one of those good little boys, on account of his always dying in the last chapter.

Jacob had a noble ambition to be put in a Sunday-school book. He wanted to be put in, with pictures representing him gloriously declining to lie for his mother, and she weeping for joy about it; and pictures representing him standing on the doorstep giving a penny to a poor beggar-woman with six children, and telling her to spend it freely, but not to be extravagant, because extravagance is a sin; and pictures of him magnanimously refusing to tell on the bad boy who always lays wait for him around the corner, as he came from school, and welted him over the head with a lath, and chased him home, saying "Hi! hi!" as he proceeded. This was the ambition of young Jacob Blivens. He wished to be put into a Sunday-school book. It made him feel a little uncomfortable sometimes when he reflected that the good little boys always died. He loved to live, you know, and this was the most unpleasant feature about being a Sunday-school book boy. He knew it was not healthy to be good. He knew it was more fatal than consumption to be so supernaturally good as the boys in the books were; he knew that none of them had ever been able to stand it long, and it pained him to think that if they put him in a book he wouldn't ever see it, or even if they did get the book out before he died, it wouldn't be popular without any picture of his funeral in the back part of it. It couldn't be much of a Sunday-school book that couldn't tell about the advice he gave to the community when he was dying. So, at last, of course he had to make up his mind to do the best he could under the circumstances—to live right, and hang on as long as he could, and have his dying speech all ready when his time came.

But somehow, nothing ever went right with this good little boy; nothing ever turned out with him the way it turned out with the good little boys in the books. They always had a good time, and the bad boys had the broken legs; but in this case there was a screw loose somewhere, and it all happened just the other way. When he found Jim Blake stealing apples, and went under the tree to read to him about the bad little boy who fell out of a neighbor's apple tree, and broke his arm, Jim fell out of the tree too, but he fell on *him* and broke *his* arm, and Jim wasn't hurt at all. Jacob couldn't understand that. There wasn't anything in the books like it.

And once, when some bad boys pushed a blind man over in the mud, and Jacob ran to help him up and receive his blessing, the blind man did not give him any blessing at all, but whacked him over the head with his stick and said he would like to catch him shoving *him* again and then pretending to help him up. This was not in accordance with any of the books. Jacob looked them all over to see.

One thing that Jacob wanted to do was to find a lame dog that hadn't any place to stay, and was hungry and persecuted, and bring him home and pet him and have that dog's imperishable gratitude. And at last he found one, and was happy; and he brought him home and fed him, but when he was going to pet him the dog flew at him and tore all the clothes off him except those that were in front, and made a spectacle of him that was astonishing. He examined authorities, but he could not understand the matter. It was of the same breed of dogs that was in the books, but it acted very differently. Whatever this boy did, he got into trouble. The very things the boys in the books got rewarded for turned out to be about the most unprofitable things he could invest in.

Once when he was on his way to Sunday school he saw some bad boys starting off pleasuring in a sail-boat. He was filled with consternation, because he knew from his reading that boys who went sailing on Sunday invariably got drowned. So he ran out on a raft to warn them, but a log turned with him and slid him into the river. A man got him out pretty soon, and the doctor pumped the water out of him and gave him a fresh start with his bellows, but he caught cold and lay sick abed nine weeks. But the most unaccountable thing about it was that the bad boys in the boat had a good time all day, and then reached home alive and well, in the most surprising manner. Jacob Blivens said there was nothing like these things in the books. He was perfectly dumbfounded.

When he got well he was a little discouraged, but he resolved to keep on trying, anyhow. He knew that so far his experiences wouldn't do to go in a book, but he hadn't yet reached the allotted term of life for good little boys, and he hoped to be able to make a record yet, if he could hold on till his time was fully up. If every thing else failed, he had his dying speech to fall on.

He examined his authorities, and found that it was now time for him to go to sea as a cabin boy. He called on a ship captain and made his application, and when the captain asked for his recommendations he proudly drew out a tract and pointed to the words: "To Jacob Blivens, from his affectionate teacher." But the captain was a coarse, vulgar man, and he said, "Oh, that be blowed! *that* wasn't any proof that he knew how to wash dishes or handle a slush-bucket, and he guessed he didn't want him." This was altogether the most extraordinary thing that ever had happened to Jacob in all his life. A compliment from a teacher, on a tract, had never failed to move the tenderest emotions of ship captains and open the way to all offices of honor and profit in their gift—it never had in any book that ever *he* had read. He could hardly believe his senses.

This boy always had a hard time of it. Nothing ever came out according to the authorities with him. At last, one day, when he was around hunting up bad little boys to admonish, he found a lot of them in the old iron foundry fixing up a little joke on fourteen or fifteen dogs, which they had tied together in long procession and were going to ornament with empty nitro-glycerine cans made fast to their tails. Jacob's heart was touched. He sat down on one of those cans—for he never minded grease when duty was before him—and he took hold of the foremost dog by the collar, and turned his reproving eye upon wicked Tom Jones. But just at that moment Alderman McWelter, full of wrath, stepped in. All the bad boys ran away; but Jacob Blivens rose in conscious innocence and began one of those stately little Sunday-school-book speeches which always commence with "Oh, Sir!" in dead opposition to the fact that no boy, good or bad, ever starts a remark with "Oh, Sir!" But the Alderman never waited to hear the rest. He took Jacob Blivens by the ear and turned him around, and hit him a whack in the rear with the flat of his hand; and in an instant that good little boy shot out through the roof and soared away toward the sun, with the fragments of those fifteen dogs stringing after him like the tail of a kite. And there wasn't a sign of that Alderman or that old iron foundry left on the face of the earth; and as for young Jacob Blivens, he never got a chance to make his last dying speech after all his trouble fixing it up, unless he made it to the birds; because, although the bulk of him came down all right in a tree-top in an adjoining county, the rest of him was apportioned around among four townships, and so they had to hold five inquests on him, to find out whether he was dead or not, and how it occurred. You never saw a boy scattered so.*

Thus perished the good little boy who did the best he could, but didn't come out according to the books. Every boy who ever did as he did prospered, except him. His case is truly remarkable. It will probably never be accounted for.—*Mark Twain*

>*This catastrophe is borrowed (without the unknown but most ingenious author's permission) from a stray newspaper item, and trimmed up and altered to fit Jacob Blivens, who stood sadly in need of a doom that would send him out of the world with *eclat.*—EDITOR MEMORANDA.

April 30, 1870

Curious Dream
Containing a Moral

Night before last I had a singular dream.[184] I seemed to be sitting on a doorstep, (in no particular city, perhaps), ruminating, and the time of night appeared to be about twelve or one o'clock. The weather was balmy and delicious. There was no human sound in the air, not even a footstep. There was no sound of any kind to emphasize the dead stillness, except the occasional hollow barking of a dog in the distance and the fainter answer of a further dog. Presently up the street I heard a bony clack-clacking, and guessed it was the castanets of a serenading party. In a minute more a tall skeleton, hooded and half-clad in a tattered and mouldy shroud whose shreds were flapping about the ribby lattice-work of its person, swung by me with a stately stride, and disappeared in the gray gloom of the starlight. It had a broken and worm-eaten coffin on its shoulder and a bundle of something in its hand. I knew what the clack-clacking was, then—it was this party's joints working together, and his elbows knocking against his sides as he walked. I may say I was surprised. Before I could collect my thoughts and enter upon any speculations as to what this apparition might portend, I heard another one coming—for I recognized his clack-clack. He had two-thirds of a coffin on his shoulder, and some foot and head-boards under his arm. I mightily wanted to peer under his hood and speak to him, but when he turned and smiled upon me with his cavernous sockets and his projecting grin as he went by, I thought I would not detain him. He was hardly gone when I

heard the clacking again, and another one issued from the shadowy
half-light. This one was bending under a heavy grave stone, and dragging a shabby coffin after him by a string. When he got to me he gave
me a steady look for a moment or two, and then rounded to and
backed up to me, saying:

"Ease this down for a fellow, will you?"

I eased the grave-stone down till it rested on the ground, and in doing so noticed that it bore the name of "John Baxter Copmanhurst,"
with "May, 1839," as the date of his death. Deceased sat wearily down
by me and wiped his os frontis with his major maxillary[185]—chiefly
from former habit I judged, for I could not see that he brought away
any perspiration.

"It is too bad, too bad," said he, drawing the remnant of the shroud
about him and leaning his jaw pensively on his hand. Then he put his
left foot up on his knee and fell to scratching his ancle bone absently
with a rusty nail which he got out of his coffin.

"What is too bad, friend?"

"Oh, everything, everything. I almost wish I never had died."

"You surprise me. Why do you say this? Has anything gone wrong?
What is the matter?"

"Matter! Look at this shroud—rags. Look at this gravestone, all
battered up. Look at that disgraceful old coffin. All a man's property
going to ruin and destruction before his eyes and ask him if anything
is wrong? Fire and brimstone!"

"Calm yourself, calm yourself," I said. "It *is* too bad—it is certainly
too bad, but then I had not supposed that you would much mind such
matters, situated as you are."

"Well, my dear sir, I *do* mind them. My pride is hurt and my comfort is impaired—destroyed, I might say. I will state my case—I will
put it to you in such a way that you can comprehend it, if you will let
me," said the poor skeleton, tilting the hood of his shroud back, as if
he were clearing for action, and thus unconsciously giving himself a
jaunty and festive air very much at variance with the grave character
of his position in life—so to speak—and in prominent contrast with
his distressful mood.

"Proceed," said I.

"I reside in the shameful old grave yard a block or two above you
here, in this street—There, now, I just expected that cartilage would
let go!—Third rib from the bottom, friend, hitch the end of it to my
spine with a string, if you have got such a thing about you, though a

bit of silver wire is a deal pleasanter, and more durable and becoming, if one keeps it polished—to think of shredding out and going to pieces in this way, just on account of the indifference and neglect of one's posterity!"—and the poor ghost grated his teeth in a way that gave me a wrench and a shiver—for the effect is mightily increased by the absence of muffling flesh and cuticle. "I reside in that old graveyard, and have for these thirty years; and I tell you things are changed since I first laid this old tired frame there, and turned over and stretched out for a long sleep, with a delicious sense upon me of being *done* with bother, and grief, and anxiety, and doubt and fear, forever and ever, and listening with comfortable and increasing satisfaction to the sexton's work, from the startling clatter of his first spade-full on my coffin till it dulled away to the faint patting that shaped the roof of my new home—delicious? My! I wish you could try it to-night!" and out of my reverie deceased fetched me with a rattling slap with a bony hand.

"Yes, sir, thirty years ago I laid me down there, and was happy. For it was out in the country, then—out in the breezy, flowery, grand old woods, and the lazy winds gossiped with the leaves, and the squirrels capered over us and around us, and the creeping things visited us, and the birds filled the tranquil solitude with music. "h, it was worth ten years of a man's life to be dead then! Every thing was pleasant. I was in a good neighborhood, for all the dead people that lived near me belonged to the best families in the city. Our posterity appeared to think the world of us. They kept our graves in the very best condition; the fences were always in faultless repair, headboards were kept painted or whitewashed, and were replaced with new ones as soon as they began to look rusty or decayed; monuments were kept upright, railings intact and bright, the rosebushes and shrubbery trimmed, trained and free from blemish, the walks clean and smooth and graveled. But that day is gone by. Our descendants have forgotten us. My grandson lives in a stately house built with money made by these old hands of mine, and I sleep in a neglected grave with invading vermin that gnaw my shroud to build them nests withal! I and friends that lie with me founded and secured the prosperity of this fine city, and the stately bantling of our loves leaves us to rot in a dilapidated cemetery which neighbors curse and strangers scoff at. See the difference between the old time and this—for instance: Our graves are all caved in, now; our head-boards have rotted away and tumbled down; our railings reel this way and that, with one foot in the air, after a fashion of unseemly levity; our monuments lean wearily and our gravestones bow their heads discouraged; there be no adornments any more,—no roses, nor shrubs, nor graveled walks, nor anything that is a comfort to the eye, and even the paintless old board fence that did make a show of holding us sacred from companionship with beasts and the defilement of heedless feet, has tottered till it overhangs the street, and only advertises the presence of our dismal resting place and invites yet more derision to it. And now we cannot hide our poverty and tatters in the friendly woods, for the city has stretched its withering arms abroad and taken us in, and all that remains of the cheer of our old home is the cluster of lugubrious forest trees that stand, bored and weary of city life, with their feet in our coffins, looking into the hazy distance and not wishing they were there. I tell you it is disgraceful!

"You begin to comprehend—you begin to see how it is. While our descendants are living sumptuously on our money right around us in the city, we have to fight hard to keep skull and bones together. Bless you there isn't a grave in our cemetery that doesn't leak—not one. Every time it rains in the night we have to climb out and roost in the trees—and sometimes we are wakened suddenly by the chilly water trickling down the back of our necks. Then I tell you there is a general heaving up of old graves and kicking over of old monuments, and scampering of old skeletons for the trees! Bless me, if you had gone along there some such nights after twelve you might have seen as many as fifteen of us roosting on one limb, with our joints rattling drearily and the wind wheezing through our ribs! Many a time we have perched there for three or four dreary hours, and then come down, stiff and chilled through and drowsy, and borrowed each other's skulls to bail out our graves with—if you will glance up in my mouth, now as I tilt my head back, you can see that my head-piece is half full of old dry sediment—how top-heavy and stupid it makes me sometimes! Yes, sir, many a time if you had happened to come along just before the dawn you'd have caught us baling out the graves and hanging our shrouds on the fence to dry. Why, I had an elegant shroud stolen from there one morning—think a party by the name of Smith took it, that resides in a plebeian graveyard over yonder—I think so because the first time I ever saw him he hadn't anything on but a check shirt, and the last time I saw him, which was at a social gathering in the new cemetery, he was the best dressed corpse in the company—and it is a significant fact that he left when he saw me; and presently an old woman from here missed her coffin—she generally took it with her when she went anywhere, because she was liable to take cold and bring on the spasmodic rheumatism that originally killed her if she exposed herself to the night air much. She was named Hotchkiss—Anna Matilda Hotchkiss—you might know her? She has two upper front teeth, is tall, but a good deal inclined to stoop; one rib on the left side gone, has one shred of rusty hair hanging from the left side of her head, and one little tuft just above and a little forward of her right ear, has her under jaw wired on one side where it had worked loose, small bone of left forearm gone—lost in a fight—has a kind of swagger in her gait and a 'gallus' way of going with her arms akimbo and her nostrils in the air—has been pretty free and easy, and is all damaged and battered up till she looks like a queensware[186] crate in ruins—maybe you have met her?"

"God forbid!" I involuntarily ejaculated, for some how I was not looking for that form of question, and it caught me a little off my guard. But I hastened to make amends for my rudeness and say: "I simply meant I had not had the honor—for I would not deliberately speak discourteously of a friend of yours. You were saying that you were robbed—and it was a shame, too—but it appears by what is left of the shroud you have on that it was a costly one in its day. How did—"

A most ghastly expression began to develop among the decayed features and shriveled integuments of my guest's face, and I was beginning to grow uneasy and distressed, when he told me he was only working up a deep, sly smile, with a wink in it, to suggest that about the time he acquired his present garment a ghost in a neighboring cemetery missed one. This reassured me, but I begged him to confine himself to speech, thenceforth, because his facial expression was uncertain. Even with the most elaborate care it was liable to miss fire. Smiling should especially be avoided. What *he* might honestly consider a shining success was likely to strike me in a very different light. I said I liked to see a skeleton cheerful, even decorously playful, but I did not think smiling was a skeleton's best hold.—*Mark Twain*

[Conclusion—with the rest of the MORAL—next week.]

May 7, 1870

Curious Dream
Containing a Moral

[Concludes from Last Week's Express]

[In the chapter preceding this, was set forth how certain shrouded skeletons came mysteriously marching past my door after midnight, carrying battered tombstones, crumbling coffins, and such like property with them, and how one sat down by me to rest, (having also his tombstone with him, and dragging after him his worm-eaten coffin by a string,) and complained at great length of the discomforts of his ruinous and long-neglected graveyard. This conversation now continueth.]

"Yes, friend," said the poor skeleton, "the facts are just as I have given them to you. Two of these old graveyards—the one that I resided in and one further along—have been deliberately neglected by our descendants of to-day until there is no occupying them any longer. Aside from the osteological discomfort of it—and that is no light matter this rainy weather—the present state of things is ruinous to property. We have got to move or be content to see our effects wasted away and utterly destroyed. Now you will hardly believe it, but it is true, nevertheless, that there isn't a single coffin in good repair among all my acquaintance—now that is an absolute fact. I do not refer to people who come in a pine box mounted on an express wagon, but I am talking about your high-toned silver-mounted burial-case, monumental sort, that travel under plumes at the head of a procession and have choice of cemetery lots—I mean folks like the Jarvis's, and the Bledsoe's and the Burling's and such. They are all about ruined. The most substantial people in our set, they were. And now look at them—utterly used up and poverty-stricken. One of the Bledsoe's actually traded his monument to a late barkeeper for some fresh shavings to put under his head. I tell you it speaks volumes, for there is nothing a corpse takes so much pride in as his monument. He loves to read the inscription. He comes after awhile to believe what it says, himself, and then you may see him sitting on the fence night after night enjoying it. Epitaphs are cheap, and they do a poor chap a world of good after he is dead, especially if he

had hard luck while he was alive. I wish they were used more. Now I
don't complain, but confidentially, I *do* think it was a little shabby in
my descendants to give me nothing but this old slab of a gravestone —
and all the more that there isn't a compliment on it. It used to have

"GONE TO HIS JUST REWARD"

on it, and I was proud when I first saw it, but by and bye I noticed
that whenever an old friend of mine came along he would hook his
chin on the railing and pull a long face and read along down till he
came to that, and then he would chuckle to himself and walk off looking satisfied and comfortable. So I scratched it off to get rid of those
fools. But a dead man always takes a deal of pride in his monument.
Yonder goes a half a dozen of Jarvises, now, with the family monument
along. And Smithers and some hired spectres went by with his a while
ago. Hello, Higgins, good-bye old friend! That's Meredith Higgins—died
in '44—belongs to our set in the cemetery—fine old family—great-
grandmother was an Injun—I am on the most familiar terms with
him—he didn't hear me was the reason he didn't answer me. And I
am sorry, too, because I would have liked to introduce you. You would
admire him. He is the most disjointed, sway-backed and generally distorted old skeleton you ever saw, but he is full of fun. When he laughs
it sounds like rasping two stones together, and he always starts it off
with a cheery screech like raking a nail across a window-pane. Hey,
Jones! That is old Columbus Jones—shroud cost four hundred dollars—entire trousseau, including monument, twenty-seven hundred.
This was in the Spring of '26. It was enormous style for those days.
Dead people came all the way from the Alleghenies to see his things—
the party that occupied the grave next to mine remembers it well.
Now do you see that individual going along with a piece of a head-
board under his arm, one leg bone below his knee gone, and not a
thing in the world on? That is Barstow Dalhouse, and next to Columbus Jones, he was the most sumptuously outfitted person that ever
entered our cemetery. We are all leaving. We cannot tolerate the treatment we are receiving at the hands of our descendants. They open
new cemeteries, but they leave us to our ignominy. They mend the
streets, but they never mend anything that is about us or belongs to
us. Look at that coffin of mine—yet I tell you in its day it was a piece
of furniture that would have attracted attention in any drawing-room
in the city. You may have it if you want it—I can't afford to repair it.
Put a new bottom in her, and part of a new top, and a bit of fresh lin-

ing along the left side, and you'll find her about as comfortable as any receptacle of her species you ever tried. No thanks—no, don't mention it—you have been civil to me and I would give you all the property I have got before I would seem ungrateful. Now this winding-sheet is a kind of a sweet thing in its way, if you would like to—. No? Well, just as you say, but I wished to be fair and liberal—there's nothing mean about *me*. Good-bye, friend, I must be going. I may have a good way to go to-night—don't know. I only know one thing for certain, and that is, that I am on the emigrant trail, now, and I'll never sleep in that crazy old cemetery again. I will travel till I find respectable quarters, if I have to hoof it to New Jersey. All the boys are going. It was decided in public conclave, last night, to emigrate, and by the time the sun rises there won't be a bone left in our old habitations. Such cemeteries may suit my surviving friends but they do not suit the remains that have the honor to make these remarks. My opinion is the general opinion. If you doubt it, go and see how the departing ghosts upset things before they started. They were almost riotous in their demonstrations of distaste. Hello, here are some of the Bledsoes, and if you will give me a lift with this tombstone I guess I will join company and jog along with them—mighty respectable old family, the Bledsoes, and used to always come out in six-horse hearses, and all that sort of thing fifty years ago when I walked these streets in daylight. Good-bye, friend."

And with his gravestone on his shoulder he joined the grisly procession, dragging his damaged coffin after him, for notwithstanding he pressed it upon me so earnestly, I utterly refused his hospitality. I suppose that for as much as two hours these sad outcasts went clacking by, laden with their dismal effects, and all that time I sat pitying them. One or two of the youngest and least dilapidated among them inquired about midnight trains on the railways, but the rest seemed unacquainted with that mode of travel, and merely asked about common public roads to various towns and cities, some of which are not on the map, now, and vanished from it and from the earth as much as thirty years ago, and some few of them never had existed any where but on maps, and private ones in real estate agencies at that. And they asked about the condition of the cemeteries in these towns and cities, and about the reputation the citizens bore as to reverence for the dead.

This whole matter interested me deeply, and likewise compelled my sympathy for these homeless ones. And it all seeming real, and I not knowing it was a dream, I mentioned to one shrouded wanderer an idea that had entered my head to publish an account of this curious and very sorrowful exodus, but said also that I could not describe it truthfully, and just as it occurred, without seeming to trifle with a grave subject and exhibit an irreverence for the dead that would shock and distress their surviving friends. But this bland and stately remnant of a former citizen leaned him far over my gate and whispered in my ear, and said:

"DO NOT LET THAT DISTURB YOU. THE COMMUNITY THAT CAN STAND SUCH GRAVEYARDS AS THOSE WE ARE EMIGRATING FROM CAN STAND ANY THING A BODY CAN SAY ABOUT THE NEGLECTED AND FORSAKEN DEAD THAT LIE IN THEM."

At that very moment a cock crowed, and the weird procession vanished and left not a shred or a bone behind. I awoke, and found myself lying with my head out of the bed and "sagging" downwards considerably—a position favorable to dreaming dreams with morals in them, may be, but not poetry.—*Mark Twain*

May 7, 1870

Murder and Insanity

Governor Alcorn,[187] of Mississippi, has shrewdly devised a measure to put a stop to the prevailing confusion of distinctions between murder and insanity. In a message upon the subject to the Legislature of Mississippi he outlines an enactment which he thinks necessary to assert the principle of the distinction between the two, "with a view to the absolute restriction of inquiries into indictments for taking or attempting to take human life within the purview of the questions of fact which are made in law pertinent to trials for that class of crimes." Murder, as he says, is made to rest in law on one group of facts and insanity upon another group, and the two classes of investigation should not be allowed to blend into one. He proposes that all cases of homicide in which the plea of insanity arises shall be remitted to the Court of Chancery, which Court shall decide whether the person brought before it is sane or insane; if insane shall, "order his duress in a ward or wards to be set apart for the restraint and safe keeping of the dangerous insane in the Lunatic Asylum"; if sane shall remand him to the proper court for trial upon the charge of murder or manslaughter.

The recommendations of Governor Alcorn are sensible and timely, and ought to receive consideration not only in Mississippi but in every other State. The use of the plea of insanity on all occasions is making every murder trial a farce. It is time that it was barred out, by reference to a separate tribunal, and investigated as a distinct question, apart from the trial of the crime with which it is sought to be connected. If judged to be insane, the murderer ought, of course, to be held in custody as a dangerous lunatic and receive the treatment due to insanity; instead of which he escapes entirely by that judgment, now, and is made free to go at large. Governor Alcorn's idea is happily conceived. *[Unsigned]*

PART IV

Personal Troubles and Rumors of War

May 1870–October 1870

Personal

Ⅰn the *Galaxy* magazine for May,[188] I took Rev. T. de Witt Talmage[189] to task for saying ungracious things about bad-smelling laboring men and protesting against admitting them to the pews of his church. I took for my text a paragraph which was written by Dr. Talmage for the *Independent*[190] and afterward copied into the *Chicago Advance,* which latter paper treated it as the serious opinion of the Doctor and criticised it accordingly. [I never had seen Dr. T.'s article at all, but accepted the *Advance's* estimate of its character as being the correct one, and so *I* censured it, too.] Here is the paragraph referred to:

> "I have a good Christian friend who, if he sat in the front pew in church, and a working man should enter the door at the other end, would smell him instantly. My friend is not to blame for the sensitiveness of his nose, any more than you would flog a pointer for being keener on the scent than a stupid watch-dog. The fact is, if you had all the churches free, by reason of the mixing up of the common people with the uncommon, you would keep one-half of Christendom sick at their stomach. If you are going to kill the church thus with bad smells, I will have nothing to do with this work of evangelization."

The *Advance* criticised that, sarcastically. So did I. A few days after my article appeared, a friend told me that he had seen in some paper a remark to the effect that Rev. Dr. Talmage had been explaining through some other journal that the text I had used had been separated from its context, and its meaning exactly reversed by me, inasmuch as I had treated it seriously while in reality it was only a satire. I was just about to forward my manuscript for next month's *Galaxy,* (June,) but I delayed it till I could add a postscript asking the Doctor's pardon for my mistake, and explaining how it occurred. Presently I received a letter from one of Dr. T.'s parishioners, which I here quote:

Brooklyn, April 28.

"MARK TWAIN, *Galaxy Office, New York:*
"DEAR SIR:
    "Rev. T. de Witt Talmage is a representative democratic preacher, whom to see in a 'spike-tailed coat and kids' would astonish his friends

quite as much as does your apparent misconception of his real character
and views touching the free-church question. Will you please read his
entire article in the *Independent* from which you quote in the *Galaxy* for
May and favor your readers with such a memorandum as it may suggest, and greatly oblige,

Yours truly,

C_____ C_____,

Of Mr. Talmage's Church."

In reply, I wrote this pleasant-spoken gentleman that I had just
telegraphed to New York for the *Independent* article, so that I could
set Dr. T. right, before as many of the public as I could reach, (for it
seemed perfectly plain that I had been wronging him,) and I said I
wished to make this reparation "intelligently and immediately," without waiting a month for the *Galaxy* to issue again.

The gentleman wrote once more, expressing the entire satisfaction
of all concerned, and the next day I dropped everything else and
wrote a full explanation of how the *Advance* had defrauded me into
wronging Dr. Talmage, and along with it I stated most emphatically
that I was very sorry for having blundered into the writing of an article calculated to injure a good and innocent man.

I was just about to mail this for publication in the *Independent,* (and
had even enveloped and directed it,) when an Eastern mail brought me
Dr. Talmage's original *Independent* article in full, and I waited to read
it. Then I was sorrowfully disappointed—for alas! the most analytical
mind in the world could not tell which was the Doctor's sarcasm and
which was his "real earnest!" It was plain that the *Advance* had right
fair reason for regarding as a serious utterance a paragraph which Dr.
T. stated to be "irony." I am not questioning Dr. T.'s honesty, now. On the
contrary I am satisfied that he really looks upon his little paragraph as
irony, and very fair irony at that, but it is certainly the opaquest sarcasm that ever got into print. Any unprejudiced man who will read Dr.
T's *Independent* article and then get its author or a parishioner to explain it to him, will say that the Rev. Dr. Talmage has no business meddling with a pen. Writing is not his specialty. His barbarous grammar,
his awkward construction, his bewildering incoherence, his impenetrable "irony," and his astounding profanity, show that he is not a proper
person to be lightly turned loose upon the community with so formidable a weapon as a pen in his hand. Because, in such a case, he must infallibly hurt somebody, and it is small comfort to his friends, no doubt,

to know that the person he is most likely to hurt is himself.

Let me prove by the Rev. Mr. Talmage in person, all that I have said about his execrable literary peculiarities, and also that I spoke truly a moment ago when I said the *Advance* had right fair reason for mistaking his "irony" for serious opinion. The following is from the Doctor's original *Independent* article, and is not garbled, altered or distorted in any way. (I have simply interrupted its flow now and then with my interlarded comments.) He has been showing, in the preceding paragraphs, that men not formed by nature for extemporaneous speaking cannot so speak, and therefore they ought not to be heartbroken when they try it and fail. (The whole idea of the article seems to be, "We are as God made us—if we follow the instincts He gave us we are not blameworthy.") Then he goes on. (The italics are mine):

There are other men, to whom manuscript in a pulpit is a curse. You cannot wrap a streak of lightning in a piece of sermon-paper. It is wicked in a speaker, when a thought drops straight from the THRONE OF GOD into his heart, to say, *"That is all very well, but YOU ought to have sent that idea around to my study if YOU WANTED ME TO PREACH IT.* [Is not this clergyman on strangely familiar terms with the Deity?— M.T.] I must stick to my notes. With these ten sheets of wide-ruled paper I sink or swim, live or die, survive or perish! Before an hour passes we will have some of these people converted, if I do not lose my place and the wind does not blow my notes out of the window." Oh, there is no thrill on earth like that which comes to a man's soul when, face to face and eye to eye, [with what?—M.T.] a preacher takes up some living God's [not a dead one's—M.T.] truth and hurls it at the people, seeing it leap and bound and flame till sin is consumed and the house is ablaze with the glory of God. But let not those who can speak without manuscript consider that it was foreordained from all eternity that they should stick pins into those who cannot so speak. It matters not how gracefully the pin is stuck, if it is stuck, for a pin is a pin, save when it is a needle, and then it is not a pin.

So, also, we have opposite sentiments about churches. "Let them be free," cry many voices. "Let them not be free," say others. BOTH RIGHT. We want about five thousand free churches in this country, and we want them right away. *But do not make all churches free.* Some men enjoy the gospel more if they pay a thousand dollars for a pew and have no common people in the house. [If any of this conglomerate that I have copied, thus far, be "irony," where does the irony begin?—and if any of the following be "irony," where is the faintest sign or evidence of it discoverable?—M.T.] I have a good Christian friend, who, if he sat in the front pew in church, and a working man should enter the door at the other end, would smell him instantly. *My friend is not to blame for the sensitiveness of his nose, any more than you would flog a pointer* [There is nothing sadder than that kind of grammar, except the death of a very near and dear friend.—M.T.], *for being keener on the scent than the stupid watch-dog.* The fact is, if you had all the churches free, by reason of the mixing up of the common people with the uncommon, you would keep one-half of Christendom sick at their stomach. If you are going thus to kill the church with bad smells, I will have nothing to do with this work of evangelization. YOU CANNOT OBLITERATE THE DIFFERENCE BETWEEN CABBAGE AND CAULIFLOWER.

It will be necessary to run two trains for Heaven. The first a select car. Fare expensive, five dollars a mile. [This elephantine playfulness into which the Doctor is now drifting is probably the performance which he has been taking an innocent pleasure in regarding as "irony"—but if there is any irony in the preceding paragraph, no man that lives can prove its presence there by any evidence perceptible upon its face—nor yet by the general argument of the article in which it appears, for the spirit of that is simply "We are as God made us, and are not to blame if each of us follows his peculiar instincts."—M.T.] Patent ventilators to keep the air pure and silver spittoons in which for gentlemen to [Another dear friend gone!—M.T.] drop their quids on the way up to the Celestial City. [This is picturesque, but still it only adds testimony to the palpable fact that in Dr. Talmage's hand the pen is not mightier than the sword.—M.T.] Passengers requested to keep their feet off the damask cushions and not put their heads out of the windows. Pullman's sleeping car attached, in which the passengers may sleep through the entire route. Conductor will carry his tickets in black velvet cover, and give through tickets to Heaven by way of Princeton and Andover. [I am—and have been for some time—publishing a book of travels, and newspaper critics who had not read it invariably said in their notices that in one or two places it was marred by a little irreverence; but if any one can find anything in it remotely approaching the irreverence of this sentence just quoted from a clergyman, I well eat the book, stereotype plates and all.—M.T.] The other train is more democratic. Cheap fare. Never mind the ventilators, and the passengers to have the windows up when the accumulation of saliva demands an outlet. In this car go the plumbers, shipwrights, tailors, carpenters, masons, milkmen,—those not too liberal with chalk and water,—and indeed all classes of people who have to work for a living. It will be an accommodation train, and many annoyances may be expected. I expect that there will be many who will like neither the express train nor the accommodation, and will therefore go afoot up the same road on which John Bunyan's Pilgrim traveled.

Now I am willing to believe, and I do believe, that Dr. Talmage honestly intended that meaningless rubbish for "irony." But as I said before, his honest intent miscarried, and he made himself appear to be expressing a certain sentiment when he was really trying his best to express its very opposite. His forte in the ministry must certainly be the "extemporaneous," (which he has referred to with suggestive satisfaction.)

Let us hope so, at any rate; for it is manifest that if he were to deliberately *write* a sermon he would be as apt as any other way to send his congregation to perdition with it, when he was sincerely aiming to compass their salvation.

Rev. Dr. Talmage is not a bad man. I have credible evidence that he is a very excellent man and that his heart is really in the freeing of the churches—a thing which he would have shown in the very article I have been quoting from but for the density of his ideas and the uncertainty of his grammar. And I have evidence that he has carried his pet desire so far as to actually persuade his people to begin the erection of a church into whose pews all comers are to have welcome entrance; and I also have still higher evidence of his sincerity—and this is the last and strongest test that can be brought to bear upon a principle, viz: *the sacrificing of money to it.* He has voluntarily relinquished his salary of seven thousand dollars a year in order to help his cherished project along. Now such a man deserves well at the hands of his fellow men, and should not lightly be vilified and misrepresented by writers for the press. I, for one, am sorry I criticised him so harshly—no, not that. But I am sincerely sorry that he ever hurled that execrable column of decomposed grammar, irreverence and incipient lunacy into print and so betrayed me into unchivalrously attacking a literary cripple. He is a good man, and a well-meaning one, but he has no business meddling with a pen—let him confine himself to "banging his Bible" extemporaneously.—*Mark Twain*

P.S.—I did not mail my elaborate explanatory and apologetic letter for publication, after I got an opportunity to read Dr. Talmage's entire *Independent* article. But perhaps it was hardly necessary to mention this.

Our Precious Lunatic

N EW YORK, MAY 10—The Richardson-McFarland jury[191] has been out one hour and fifty minutes. A breathless silence brooded over court and auditory—a silence and a stillness so absolute, notwithstanding the vast multitude of human beings packed together there, that when some one far away among the throng under the north-east balcony cleared his throat with a smothered little cough it startled everybody uncomfortably, so distinctly did it grate upon the pulseless air. At that imposing moment the bang of a door was heard, then the shuffle of approaching feet, and then a sort of surging and swaying disorder among the heads near the entrance from the jury room told that the Twelve were coming. Presently all was still again, and the foreman of the jury rose and said:[192]

"YOUR HONOR AND GENTLEMEN: We, the jury charged with the duty of determining whether the prisoner at the bar, Daniel McFarland, has been guilty of murder, in taking by surprise an unarmed man and shooting him to death, or whether the said prisoner is simply afflicted with a sad but irresponsible insanity which at times can be cheered only by violent entertainment with firearms, do find as follows, namely:

That the prisoner Daniel McFarland is insane, as above described. Because:

1. His great-grandfather's step-father[193] was tainted with insanity, and frequently killed people who were distasteful to him. Hence, insanity is hereditary in the family.

2. For nine years the prisoner at the bar did not adequately support his family. Strong circumstantial evidence of insanity.

3. For nine years he made of his home, as a general thing, a poorhouse; sometimes (but very rarely,) a cheery, happy habitation; frequently the den of a beery, driveling, stupefied animal; but never, as far as ascertained, the abiding place of a gentleman. These be evidences of insanity.

4. He once took his young unmarried sister-in-law to the museum; while there his heredity insanity came upon him, and to such a degree that he hiccupped and staggered; and afterward, on the way home, even made love to the young girl he was protecting. These are the acts of a person not right in his mind.

5. For a good while his sufferings were so great that he had to submit to the inconvenience of having his wife give public readings for the family support; and at times, when he handed these shameful earnings to the barkeeper, his haughty soul was so torn with anguish that he could hardly stand without leaning up against something. At such times he has been known to shed tears into his sustenance until it was diluted to utter inefficiency. Inattention of this nature is not the act of a Democrat unafflicted in mind.

6. He never spared expense in making his wife comfortable during her occasional confinements. Her father is able to testify to this. There was always an element of unsoundness about the prisoner's generosities that is very suggestive at this time and before this court.

7. Two years ago the prisoner came fearlessly up behind Richardson in the dark, and shot him in the leg. The prisoner's brave and protracted defiance of an adversity that for years had left him little to depend upon for his support but a wife who sometimes earned scarcely any thing for weeks at a time, is evidence that he would have appeared in front of Richardson and shot him in the stomach if he had not been insane at the time of the shooting.

8. Fourteen months ago the prisoner told Archibald Smith that he was going to kill Richardson. This is insanity.

9. Twelve months ago he told Marshal P. Jones that he was going to kill Richardson. Insanity.

10. Nine months ago he was lurking about Richardson's home in New Jersey, and said he was going to kill the said Richardson. Insanity.

11. Seven months ago he showed a pistol to Seth Brown and said that that was for Richardson. He said Brown testified that at that time it seemed plain that there was something the matter with McFarland, for he crossed the street diagonally nine times in fifty yards, apparently without any settled reason for doing so, and finally fell in the gutter and went to sleep. He remarked at the time that McFarland "acted strange"—believed he was insane. Upon hearing Brown's evidence, John W. Galen,[194] M.D., affirmed at once that McFarland *was* insane.

12. Five months ago, McFarland showed his customary pistol, in his customary way, to his bed-fellow, Charles A. Dana,[195] and told him he was going to kill Richardson the first time an opportunity offered. Evidence of insanity.

13. Five months and two weeks ago McFarland asked John Morgan the time of day, *and turned and walked rapidly away without waiting*

for an answer. Almost indubitable evidence of insanity. And—

14. It is remarkable that exactly one week after this circumstance the prisoner, Daniel McFarland, confronted Albert D. Richardson suddenly and without warning and shot him dead. *This is manifest insanity.* Everything we know of the prisoner goes to show that if he had been sane at the time, he would have shot his victim from behind.

15. There is an absolutely overwhelming mass of testimony to show that *an hour before the shooting, McFarland was* ANXIOUS *And* UNEASY, *and that five minutes after it he was* EXCITED. Thus the accumulating conjectures and evidences of insanity culminate in this sublime and unimpeachable *proof* of it. Therefore—

"Your Honor and Gentlemen—We the jury pronounce the said Daniel McFarland INNOCENT OF MURDER, BUT CALAMITOUSLY INSANE."

The scene that ensued almost defies description. Hats, handkerchiefs and bonnets were frantically waved above the massed heads in the courtroom, and three tremendous cheers and a tiger told where the sympathies of court and people were. Then a hundred pursed lips were advanced to kiss the liberated prisoner, and many a hand thrust out to give him the congratulatory shake—but presto! with a maniac's own quickness and a maniac's own fury, the lunatic assassin of Richardson fell upon his friends with teeth and nails, boots and office furniture, and the amazing rapidity with which he broke heads and limbs, and rent and sundered bodies, till near a hundred citizens were reduced to mere quivering heaps of fleshy odds and ends and crimson rags, was like nothing in this world but the exultant frenzy of a plunging, tearing, roaring devil of a steam machine when it snatches a human being and spins him and whirls him till he shreds away to nothingness like a "four o'clock" before the breath of a child.

The destruction was awful. It is said that within the space of eight minutes McFarland killed and crippled some six score persons and tore down a large portion of the City Hall building, carrying away and casting into Broadway six or seven marble columns fifty-four feet long and weighing nearly two tons each. But he was finally captured and sent in chains to the lunatic asylum for life. [By late telegrams it appears that this is a mistake.—EDITOR EXPRESS.]

But the really curious part of this whole matter is yet to be told. And that is, that McFarland's most intimate friends believe that the very first time it ever occurred to him that the insanity plea was not a mere politic pretense, was when that verdict came in. They think that the startling thought burst upon him, then, that if twelve good and true men, able to comprehend all the baseness of perjury, *proclaimed under oath that he was a lunatic, there was no gain-saying such evidence, and he* UNQUESTIONABLY WAS INSANE!

Possibly that was really the way of it. It is dreadful to think that maybe the most awful calamity that can befall a man, namely, loss of reason, was precipitated upon this poor prisoner by a jury that *could* have hanged him instead, and so done him a mercy and his country a service.—*Mark Twain*

POSTSCRIPT—LATER.

MAY 11.—I do not expect anybody to believe so astounding a thing, and yet it is the solemn truth that instead of instantly sending this dangerous lunatic to the insane asylum, (which I naturally supposed they would do and so I prematurely *said* they had,) the court has actually SET HIM AT LIBERTY. Comment is unnecessary.—M. T.

May 27, 1870

Street Sprinkling

The manner in which Delaware street is sprinkled above Virginia is simply ridiculous.[196] A crippled infant with a garden-squirt could do it better. The work is done by the city government and paid for by the property owners along the street—and the pay is amply secured and the work contracted for for three years. Now one thing or the other is absolutely true, viz: Either the contractor is not paid enough to justify him in doing his work well, or else he shamefully shirks his duty. Which is it?

472 DELAWARE.

[Unsigned]

More Distinction

I have received the following notice:

THE WESTERN NEW YORK POULTRY SOCIETY,
BUFFALO, JUNE 1, 1870

MARK TWAIN, Esq.: Sir—At a recent meeting of the Executive Committee of the Western New York Poultry Society you were elected an honorary member of the Society. —E.C. Dean, Recording Secretary.

"It never rains but it pours." Neither do distinctions begin to fall upon a man in a sprinkle but very shortly they increase to a flood. Within the space of one short month I have been raised to the dignity of honorary membership in Agricultural, Horticultural and Vinicultural Societies in the States of Iowa, Indiana, California, Massachusetts, Maryland and Pennsylvania, and now, as a culminating grandeur, I have become an honorary member of the Western New York Poultry Society, and my ravenous ambition is satisfied.

Seriously, from early youth I have taken an especial interest in the subject of poultry-raising, and so this membership touches a ready sympathy in my breast. Even as a school boy, poultry-raising was a study with me, and I may say without egotism that as early as the age of seventeen I was acquainted with all the best and speediest methods of raising chickens, from raising them off a roost by burning lucifer matches under their noses, down to lifting them off a fence on a frosty night by insinuating the end of a warm board under their heels. By the time I was twenty years old, I really supposed I had raised more poultry than any one individual in all the section round about there. The very chickens came to know my talent, by and by. The youth of both sexes ceased to paw the earth for worms, and the old roosters that came to crow "remained to pray," when I passed by.

I have had so much experience in the raising of fowls that I cannot but think that a few hints from me might be useful to the Society. The two methods I have already touched upon are very simple, and are only used in the raising of the commonest clans of fowls; one is for

Summer, the other for Winter. In the one case, you start out with a friend along about eleven o'clock on a Summer's night, (not later, because in some States—especially California and Oregon—chickens always rouse up just at midnight and crow from ten to thirty minutes, according to the ease or difficulty they experience in getting the public waked up,) and your friend carries with him a sack. Arrived at the hen roost, (your neighbor's, not your own,) you light a match and hold it under first one and then another pullet's nose until they are willing to go into that bag without making any trouble about it. You then return home, either taking the bag with you or leaving it behind, according as circumstances shall dictate. N.B. I *have* seen the time when it was eligible and appropriate to leave the sack behind and walk off with considerable velocity, without ever leaving any word where to send it.

In the case of the other method mentioned for raising poultry, your friend takes along a covered vessel with a charcoal fire in it, and you carry a long slender plank. This is a frosty night, understand. Arrived at the tree or fence or other hen-roost, (your own, if you are an idiot,) you warm the end of your plank in your friend's fire vessel and then raise it aloft and ease it up gently against a slumbering chicken's feet. If the subject of your attentions is a true bird, he will infallibly return thanks with a sleepy cluck or two and step out and take up quarters on the plank, thus becoming so conspicuously accessory before the fact to his own murder as to make it a grave question in our minds, as it once was in the mind of Blackstone, whether he is not really and deliberately committing suicide in the second degree. [But you enter into a contemplation of these legal refinements subsequently, not then.]

When you wish to raise a fine, large, donkey-voiced Shanghai rooster, you do it with a lasso, just as you would a bull. It is because he must be choked, and choked effectually, too. It is the only good, certain way, for whenever he mentions a matter which he is cordially interested in, the chances are ninety-nine in a hundred that he secures somebody else's immediate attention to it, too, whether it be day or night.

The Black Spanish is an exceedingly fine bird and a costly one. Thirty-five dollars is the usual figure, and fifty a not uncommon price for a specimen. Even its eggs are worth from a dollar to a dollar and a half apiece, and yet are so unwholesome that the city physician seldom or never orders them for the work-house. Still I have once or twice procured as high as a dozen at a time for nothing, in the dark of the moon. The best way to raise the Black Spanish fowl, is to go late in the evening and raise coop and all. The reason I recommend this method, is, that the birds being so absurdly valuable, the owners do not permit them to roost around promiscuously, but put them in a coop as strong as a fire-proof safe, and keep it in the kitchen at night. The method I speak of is not always a bright and satisfying success, and yet there are so many little articles of *virtu* about a kitchen that if you fail on the coop you can generally bring away something else. I brought away a nice steel trap, one night, worth ninety cents.

But what is the use in my pouring out my whole intellect on this subject? I have shown the Western New York Poultry Society that they have taken to their bosom a party who is not a Spring chicken by any means, but a man who knows all about poultry, and is just as high up in the most efficient methods of raising it as the President of the institution himself. I thank these gentlemen right pleasantly and heartily for the honorary membership they have conferred upon me, and shall stand at all times ready and willing to testify my good feeling and my official zeal by deeds as well as by this hastily penned advice and information. Whenever they are ready to go to raising poultry, let them call for me just any evening after eleven o'clock and I shall be on hand promptly.—*Mark Twain*

P.S.—To the Recording Secretary: I know two or three good places.

June 4, 1870

How Higgins Gently Broke the News

[*Mark Twain in the* Galaxy][197]

"**Y**es, I remember that anecdote," the Sunday-school superintendent said with the old pathos in his voice and the old sad look in his eyes. "It was about a simple creature named Higgins, that used to haul rock for old Maltby. When the lamented Judge Bagley tripped and fell down the court-house stairs and broke his neck it was a great question how to break the news to Mrs. Bagley. But finally the body was put into Higgins' wagon, and he was instructed to take it to Mrs. B., but to be very guarded and discreet in his language, and not break the news to her at once, but do it gradually and gently. When Higgins got there with his sad freight he shouted till Mrs. Bagley came to the door. Then he said:

"Does the widder Bagley live here?"

"The *widow* Bagley? No, sir!"

"I'll bet she does. But have it your own way. Well, does *Judge* Bagley live here?"

"I'll bet he don't. But never mind—it ain't for me to contradict. Is the Judge in?"

"No, not at present."

"I jest expected as much. Because, you know—take hold o' suthin, mum, for I'm a going to make a little communication, and I reckon maybe it'll jar you some. There's been an accident, mum. I've got the old Judge curled up out here in the wagon—and when you see him you'll acknowledge yourself that an inquest is about the only thing that could be a comfort to *him*!" *[Unsigned]*

June 24, 1870

Buffalo Female Academy
Commencement Exercise Last Evening

The nineteenth annual commencement of the Buffalo Female Academy was held last evening at the Central Presbyterian Church. The pupils formed in procession, headed by the Principal, Rev. A. T. Chester, trustees, clergymen of the city and other gentlemen, and marched from the seminary building where the exercises commenced at half-past seven o'clock. A platform had been erected in front of the pulpit upon which were seated the trustees, clergymen and others; upon the platform was also stationed a piano, at which Prof. Carl Adam, instructor in music at the seminary, presided.

The exercises opened with singing of the hymn "O, Lord Another Year has Passed" by the young ladies of the seminary, after which prayer was offered by the Rev. Dr. Clarke.

Samuel F. Pratt, Esq., officiated as Chairman of the evening; he first announced the reading of the report of the committee appointed to attend the examinations of the Primary Department, which was read by William H. Green, Esq.

The report of the Committee on the Third Academic Department was read by Rev. Anson G. Chester.

Ray T. Spencer, Principal of the Central School, read the report on the Second Academic Department, following which the report of the First Academic Department was read by Rev. Dr. Clarke.

Rev. Mr. Dick read the report of the Collegiate Department, at the conclusion of which the exercises were varied with a chorus sung by the young ladies.

The report on the examinations in Latin, was read by Rev. Erskine N. White, the report on the examinations in French by Rev. Dr. Chester, the Principal, and the report on penmanship by Rev. P. G. Cook.

Sherman S. Rogers, Esq., read the report on music, highly complimenting the proficiency of the pupils and the course of instruction pursued by their teacher, Professor Adam.

The report on reading and recitation was read by F. Gridley, Esq., and followed by a chorus, "The Song of Spring" by the pupils.

Dr. Chester gave the report on composition for the Second Academic Department, after which the report for the First Academic Department was read by Rev. Anson G. Chester, and also the prize essay, entitled "The Blue," written by Miss Annie R. Helmer, of Lockport.

Mr. David Gray, of the *Courier,* and Mr. Samuel L. Clemens were the committee appointed to report upon composition for the Collegiate Graduating Classes. The following is their report, drawn up by Mr. Clemens and read by Mr. Gray:

> I beg leave to offer the report of the committee appointed to sit in judgment upon the compositions of the graduating and collegiate classes. We have done our work carefully and conscientiously; we have determined the degrees of literary excellence displayed, with pitiless honesty; we have experienced no sort of difficulty in selecting and agreeing upon the two first-prize compositions—and yet, after all, we feel that it is necessary to say a word or two in vindication of our verdict.
>
> *Because,* we have misgivings that our choice might not be the choice of the Academy, if the choice were left to them—nor of this assemblage—nor of a vote of the general public. Let this comfort those fair competitors whom our verdict has wronged. But we have judged these compositions by the strict rules of literary criticism, and let *this* reassure those whom our verdict has exalted.
>
> We have chosen as the two prize essays the least showy of the eighteen submitted, perhaps, but they are the least artificial, the least labored, the clearest and shapeliest, and the best carried out. The paper we have chosen for the first prize of the graduates is very much the best

literary effort in the whole collection, and yet it is almost the least ambitious among them. It relates a very simple little incident, in unpreten-
tious language, and then achieves the difficult feat of pointing it with
one of those dismal atrocities called a Moral, without devoting double
the space to it which it ought to occupy and outraging every canon of
good taste, relevancy and modesty. It is a composition which possesses,
also, the very rare merit of *stopping when it is finished*. It shows a freedom from adjectives and superlatives which is attractive, not to say
seductive—and let us remark instructively, in passing, that one can seldom run his pen through an adjective without improving his manuscript. We can say further in praise of this first-prize composition, that
there is a singular aptness of language noticeable in it—denoting a
shrewd faculty of selecting just the right word for the service needed, as
a general thing. It is a high gift. It is the talent which gives accuracy,
grace and vividness in descriptive writing.

The other first prize—the collegiate—is so simple and unpretending
that it seems a daring thing to prefer it before certain of its fellows
which we could name, but still we of the committee rigidly decree that it
is perceptibly superior to the best of them. It is nothing in the world but
just a bright and fresh little bit of fancy, told with a breezy dash, and
with nothing grand or overpowering about it. Attached to it is the in-
evitable Moral, but it is compressed into a single sentence, and is delivered with a snap that is exhilarating and an unexpectedness that is
captivating. And we are furthermore able to say, in justification of this
Moral, that the composition would not be symmetrical, keenly and
cleanly pointed and complete, without it. An application, or a "nub," or a
moral that *fits,* is a jewel of price. It is only the awkward, irrelevant and
pinchbeck moral that this committee snubs.

Now, if you have observed, we have decided that the graduates' first-
prize possessed the several merits of unpretentiousness, simplicity of
language and subject, and marked aptness and accuracy of wording—
and that the collegiate first-prize has the merits of modesty and freshness of subject and grace and excellence of treatment. But both of these
possess one other merit, or cluster of merits, which strongly attracted
us. They were instinct with *naturalness*—a most noble and excellent
feature in composition, and one which is customarily lacking in productions written for state occasions, from the Friday composition in a village school all the way up to the President's message—and you may
verify my words by critically examining any written speech that ever
was written—except this one I am reading. The two prize essays possess

naturalness, and likewise a happy freshness that marks them as the expression of the original thoughts and fancies of the minds that wrought them, and not stale and venerable platitudes and commonplaces absorbed from good but stupid books and drowsy sermons, and delivered at secondhand in the same unvarying and monotonous sequence—a sequence which they have grown so familiar with since Adam and each of his descendants in turn used them in his appointed season, that now one needs only write down the first of them and the rest fall into line without a murmur or ever a missing veteran.

We consider it a plain duty to observe that while the disposition in all school compositions to contemplate all subjects from high moral and religious altitudes would be matter for sincere praise and gratulation, if such disposition came from a strong spontaneous impulse on the part of the student, it is not matter for praise or gratulation either when that disposition is strained or forced. Nearly all the compositions submitted to us would have been right creditable specimens of literary handiwork, if the sermons had been left out of them. But, while some of these latter were the expression of a genuine impulse, the great majority of them were so manifestly dragged in and hitched on to the essay (out of pure force of habit and therefore unconsciously, we are willing to believe, but still plainly dragged in), that they sadly marred some of the compositions and entirely spoiled one or two. Religion is the highest and holiest thing on earth, and a strained or compulsory expression of it is not gracious, or commendable, or befitting its dignity.

However, we have the hardihood to say, in this place, that considering the "Standard School Readers" and the other popular and unspeakably execrable models which young people are defrauded into accepting as fine literary composition, the real wonder is, not that pupils attempt subjects which they would be afraid of at forty, and then write floridly instead of simply, and start without premises and wind up without tangible result, but that they write at all without bringing upon themselves suspicions of imbecility.

The dead weights of custom and tradition have clogged school method and discipline from a past date which we cannot name, until the present time. They have worn these dead weights so long that they unconsciously continue to wear them in these free, progressive latter days. For lingering ages, seemingly, the seminary pupil has been expected to present at stated intervals, a composition constructed upon one and the same old heart-rending plan. It is not necessary to detail this plan—it is familiar to all. This ancient model is so ingrained in the method of the schools, and has so long been allowed to pass unchallenged as being the correct idea, that it will require a considerable time to eradicate it. To the high credit of the principal and teachers of this academy, however, it can be said that they are faithfully doing what they can to destroy it and its influence and occupy their place with something new and better. But when we of the committee take into consideration that much of this atmosphere of old custom and tradition necessarily still lingers around this unquestionably excellent Female Academy, we feel that we are more than complimentary when we say that the compositions we have been examining average well indeed. When the old sapless composition model is finally cast entirely aside and the pupil learns to write straight from his heart, he will apply his own language and his own ideas to his subjects, and then the question with committees will not be which composition to select for first prize, but which one they dare reject.

We award the graduates' second place to the essay entitled "Memory," and the collegiate second prize the pleasing essay entitled "Faithful are the Wounds of a Friend." They are good. The hands that penned them are capable, with practice, of doing very acceptable work.

The third place among the graduates' compositions is awarded to the essay entitled "Boys."

Third and fourth in the collegiate list we place the papers entitled "Leaves" and "Sour Grapes." Both of these begin well, but are not entirely well sustained to the end.

At the conclusion of the report Mr. Gray read the prize essay of the Collegiate Department, written by Miss Lilly Kelsey, of Geneseo, and entitled "Little Fish," and the prize essay of the Graduating Class, "The Treasure at the End of the Bow," by Lillie W. Powell, of Fort Atkinson, Wis. *[Unsigned]*

June 25, 1870

The Editorial Office Bore

[*Mark Twain in the* Galaxy.][198]

He arrives just as regularly as the clock strikes nine in the morning. And so he even beats the editor sometimes, and the porter must leave his work and climb two or three pairs of stairs to unlock the "Sanctum" door and let him in. He lights one of the office pipes—

not reflecting, perhaps, that the editor may be one of those "stuck up" people who would as soon have a stranger defile his tooth-brush as his pipe-stem. Then he begins to loll—for a person who can consent to loaf his useless life away in ignominious indolence has not the energy to sit up straight. He stretches full length on the sofa awhile; then draws up to half length; then gets into a chair, hangs his head back and his arms abroad, and stretches his legs till the rims of his boot-heels rest upon the floor; by and by sits up and leans forward, with one leg or both over the arm of the chair. But it is still observable that with all his changes of position, he never assumes the upright or a fraudful affectation of dignity. From time to time he yawns, and stretches, and scratches himself with a tranquil, mangy enjoyment, and now and then he grunts a kind of stuffy, overfed grunt, which is full of animal contentment. At rare and long intervals, however, he sighs a sigh that is the eloquent expression of a secret confession, to whit: "I am useless and a nuisance, a cumberer of the earth."

The bore and his comrades—for there are usually from two to four on hand, day and night—mix into the conversation when men come in to see the editors for a moment on business; they hold noisy talks among themselves about politics in particular, and all other subjects in general—even warming up, after a fashion, sometimes, and seeming to take almost a real interest in what they are discussing; they ruthlessly call an editor from his work with such a remark as: "Did you see this, Smith, in the '*Gazette*'?" and proceed to read the paragraph while the sufferer reins in his impatient pen and listens; and often loll and sprawl around the office hour after hour, swapping anecdotes and relating personal experiences to each other—hairbreadth escapes, social encounters with distinguished men, election reminiscences, sketches of odd characters, etc. And through all those hours they smoke, and sweat, and sigh, and scratch, and perform such other services for their fellow-men as come within the purview of their gentle mission upon earth, and never seem to comprehend that they are robbing the editors of their time, and the public of journalistic excellence in next day's paper. At other times they drowse, or dreamily pore over exchanges, or droop limp and pensive over the chair-arms for an hour. Even this solemn silence is small respite to the editor, for the next most uncomfortable thing to having people look over his shoulder, perhaps, is to have them sit by in silence and listen to the scratching of his pen.

If a body desires to talk private business with one of the editors, he must call him outside, for no hint milder than blasting powder or nitro-glycerine would be likely to move the bores out of listening distance.

To have to sit and endure the presence of a bore day after day; to feel your cheerful spirits begin to sink as his footstep sounds on the stair, and utterly vanish away as his tiresome form enters the door; to suffer through his anecdotes and die slowly to his reminiscences; to feel always the fetters of his clogging presence; to long hopelessly for one single day's privacy; to note with a shudder, by and by, that to contemplate his funeral in fancy has ceased to soothe, to imagine him undergoing in strict and faithful detail the tortures of the ancient Inquisition has lost its power to satisfy the heart, and that even to wish him millions and millions of miles in Tophet is able to bring only a fitful gleam of joy; to have to endure all this, day after day, and week after week, and month after month, is an affliction that transcends any other that men suffer. Physical pain is pastime to it, and hanging a pleasure excursion.—*Mark Twain*

July 2, 1870

How I Edited
an Agricultural Paper

I [*From the Memoranda of Mark Twain in July* Galaxy.][199] did not take the temporary editorship of an agricultural paper without misgivings. Neither would a landsman take command of a ship without misgivings. But I was in circumstances that made the salary an object. The regular editor of the paper was going off for a holiday, and I accepted the terms he offered, and took his place.

The sensation of being at work again was luxurious, and I wrought all the week with unflagging pleasure. We went to press, and I waited a day with some solicitude to see whether my effort was going to attract any notice. As I left the office, toward sundown, a group of men and boys at the foot of the stairs dispersed with one impulse, and gave me passage-way, and I heard one of them say: "That's him!" I was naturally pleased by this incident. The next morning I found a similar group at the foot of the stairs, and scattering couples and individuals standing here and there in the street, and over the way, watching me with interest. The group separated and fell back as I approached and I heard a man say; "Look at his eye!" I pretended not to observe the notice I was attracting, but secretly I was pleased with it, and was purposing to write an account of it to my aunt. I went up the short flight of stairs, and heard cheery voices and a ringing laugh as I drew near the door, which I opened, and caught a glimpse of two young, rural-looking men, whose faces blanched and lengthened when they saw me, and then they both plunged through the window, with a great crash. I was surprised.

In about half an hour an old gentleman, with a flowing beard and a fine but rather austere face, entered, and sat down at my invitation. He seemed to have something on his mind. He took off his hat and set it on the floor, and got out of it a red silk handkerchief and a copy of our paper. He put the paper on his lap, and, while he polished his spectacles with his handkerchief, he said:

"Are you the new editor?"

I said I was.

"Have you ever edited an agricultural paper before?"

"No," I said; "this is my first attempt."

"Very likely. Have you had any experience in agriculture, practically?"

"No, I believe I have not."

"Some instinct told me so," said the old gentleman, putting on his spectacles and looking over them at me with asperity, while he folded his paper into a convenient shape. "I wish to read you what must have made me have that instinct. It was this editorial. Listen, and see if it was you that wrote it:

"Turnips should never be pulled—it injures them. It is much better to send a boy up and let him shake the tree."

"Now, what do you think of that?—for I really suppose you wrote it?"

"Think of it? Why, I think it is good. I think it is sense. I have no doubt that, every year, millions and millions of bushels of turnips are spoiled in this township alone by being pulled in a half-ripe condition, when, if they had sent a boy up to shake the tree—"

"Shake your grandmother! Turnips don't grow on trees!"

"Oh, they don't, don't they? Well, who said they did? The language was intended to be figurative, wholly figurative. Anybody, that knows anything, will know that I meant that the boy should shake the vine."

Then this old person got up and tore his paper all into small shreds, and stamped on them, and broke several things with his cane, and said I did not know as much as a cow; and then went out, and banged the door after him, and, in short, acted in such a way that I fancied he was displeased about something. But, not knowing what the trouble was, I could not be any help to him.

Pretty soon after this a long, cadaverous creature, with lanky locks hanging down to his shoulders and a week's stubble bristling from the hills and valleys of his face, darted within the door, and halted, motionless, with finger on lip, and head and body bent in listening attitude. No sound was heard. Still he listened. No sound. Then he turned the key in the door, and came elaborately tip-toeing toward me, till he was within long reaching distance of me, when he stopped, and, after scanning my face with intense interest for a while, drew a folded copy of our paper from his bosom, and said:

"There—you wrote that. Read it to me, quick! Relieve me—I suffer."

I read as follows—and as the sentences fell from my lips I could see the relief come—I could see the drawn muscles relax, and the anxiety go out of the face, and rest and peace steal over the features like the merciful moonlight over a desolate landscape:

> "The guano is a fine bird, but great care is necessary in rearing it. It should not be imported earlier than June nor later than September. In the Winter it should be kept in a warm place, where it can hatch out its young.
>
> "It is evident that we are to have a backward season for grain. Therefore, it will be well for the farmer to begin setting out his corn stalks and planting his buckwheat cakes in July instead of August.
>
> "Concerning the Pumpkin—This berry is a favorite with the natives of the interior of New England, who prefer it to the gooseberry for the making of fruit cake, and who likewise give it the preference over the raspberry for feeding cows, as being more filling and fully as satisfying. The pumpkin is the only esculent of the orange family that will thrive in the North, except the gourd and one or two varieties of the squash. But this custom of planting it in the front yard with the shrubbery is fast going out of vogue, for it is now generally conceded that the pumpkin, as a shade tree, is a failure.
>
> "Now, as the warm weather approaches, and the ganders begin to spawn—"

The excited listener sprang toward me to shake hands, and said:

"There, there—that will do! I know I am all right now, because you have read it just as I did, word for word. But, stranger, when I first read it this morning I said to myself, I never, never believed it before, notwithstanding my friends kept me under watch so strict, but now I believe I *am* crazy; and with that I fetched a howl that you might have heard two miles, and started out to kill somebody—because, you know, I knew it would come to that sooner or later, and so I might as well begin. I read one of them paragraphs over again, so as to be certain, and then I burned my house down and started. I have crippled several people, and have got one fellow up a tree, where I can get him if I want him. But I thought I would call in here as I passed along, and make the thing perfectly certain; and now it *is* certain, and I tell you it is lucky for the chap that is in the tree. I should have killed him, sure, as I went back. Good-by, sir, good-by—you have taken a great load off my mind. My reason has stood the strain of one of your agricultural articles, and I know that nothing can ever unseat it now. *Good*-by, sir."

I felt a little uncomfortable about the cripplings and arsons this person had been entertaining himself with, for I could not help feeling remotely accessory to them; but these thoughts were quickly banished, for the regular editor walked in! [I thought to myself, Now if you had gone to Egypt, as I recommended you to, I might have had a chance to get my hand in; but you wouldn't do it, and here you are. I sort of expected you.]

The editor was looking sad and perplexed, and dejected. He surveyed the wreck which that old rioter and these two young farmers had made, and then said:—

"This is a sad business—a very sad business. There is the mucilage bottle broken, and six panes of glass, and a spittoon, and two candlesticks. But that is not the worst. The reputation of the paper is injured, and permanently, I fear. True, there never was such a call for the paper before, and it never sold such a large edition or soared to such celebrity; but does one want to be famous for lunacy, and prosper upon the infirmities of his mind? My friend, as I am an honest man, the street out here is full of people, and others are roosting on the fences, waiting to get a glimpse of you, because they think you are crazy. And well they might, after reading your editorials. They are a disgrace to journalism. Why, what put it into your head that you could edit a paper of this nature? You do not seem to know the first rudiments of agriculture. You speak of a furrow and a harrow as being the same thing; you talk of the moulting season for cows; and you recommend the domestication of the pole-cat on account of its playfulness and its excellence as a ratter. Your remark that clams will lie quiet if music be played to them, was superfluous—entirely superfluous. Nothing disturbs clams. Clams *always* lie quiet. Clams care nothing whatever about music. Ah, heavens and earth, friend, if you had made the acquiring of ignorance the study of your life, you could not have graduated with higher honor than you could to-day. I never saw anything like it. Your observation that the horse-chestnut, as an article of commerce, is steadily gaining favor, is simply calculated to destroy this journal. I want you to throw up your situation and go. I want no more holiday—I could not enjoy it if I had it. Certainly not with you in my chair. I would always stand in dread of what you might be going to recommend next. It makes me lose all patience every time I think of your discussing oyster beds under the head of 'Landscape Gardening.' I want you to go. Nothing on earth could persuade me to take another holiday. Oh, why didn't you *tell* me you didn't know anything about agriculture?"

"*Tell* you, you cornstalk, you cabbage, you son of a cauliflower! It's the first time I ever heard such an unfeeling remark. I tell you I have been in the editorial business going on fourteen years, and it's the first time I ever heard of a man's having to know anything in order to edit a newspaper. You turnip! Who write the dramatic critiques for the second-rate papers? Why, a parcel of promoted shoemakers and apprentice apothecaries, who know just as much about good acting as I do about good farming, and no more. Who review the books? People who never wrote one. Who do up the heavy leaders on finance? Parties who have had the largest opportunities for knowing nothing about it. Who criticise the Indian campaigns? Gentlemen who do not know a war-whoop from a wigwam, and who never have had to run a foot race with a tomahawk or pluck arrows out of the several members of their families to build the evening camp-fire with. Who write the temperance appeals and clamor about the flowing bowl? Folks who will never draw another sober breath till they do it in the grave. Who edit the agricultural papers, you—yam? Men, as a general thing, who fail in the poetry line, yellow-covered novel line, sensation-drama line, city-editor line, and finally fall back on agriculture as temporary reprieve from the poor-house. *You* try to tell *me* anything about the newspaper business! Sir, I have been through it from Alpha to Omaha, and I tell you that the less a man knows the bigger noise he makes and higher the salary he commands. Heaven knows if I had been ignorant instead of cultivated, and impudent instead of diffident, I could have made a name for myself in this cold, selfish world. I take my leave, sir.

Since I have been treated as you have treated me, I am perfectly willing to go. But I have done my duty. I have fulfilled my contract, as far as I was permitted to do it. I said I could make your paper of interest to all classes, and I have. I said I could run your circulation up to twenty thousand copies, and if I had two more weeks I'd have done it. And I'd have given you the best class of readers that ever an agricultural paper had—not a farmer in it, nor a solitary individual who could tell a watermelon from a peach-vine to save his life. *You* are the loser by this rupture, not me, Pie-plant. Adios."

I then left.—*Mark Twain*

July 25, 1870

FIRST DAY.

THE EUROPEAN WAR!!!

NO BATTLE YET!!! HOSTILITIES IMMINENT!!!

Tremendous Excitement.

AUSTRIA ARMING

BERLIN, TUESDAY—No battle has been fought yet.[200] But hostilities may burst forth any week.

There is tremendous excitement here over news from the front to the effect that two companies of French soldiers are assembling here.

It is rumored that Austria is arming—what with, is not known.

SECOND DAY.

THE EUROPEAN WAR. NO BATTLE YET!

FIGHTING IMMINENT. AWFUL EXCITEMENT.

Russia Sides with Prussia!

ENGLAND NEUTRAL! AUSTRIA NOT ARMING.

BERLIN, WEDNESDAY—No battle has been fought yet. However, all thoughtful men feel that the land may be drenched with blood before the Summer is over.

There is an awful excitement here over the rumor from the front that two companies of Prussian troops have concentrated on the border. German confidence remains unshaken!

There is news here to the effect that Russia espouses the cause of Prussia and will bring 4,000,000 men to the field.

England proclaims strict neutrality.

The report that Austria is arming needs confirmation.

THIRD DAY.

THE EUROPEAN WAR. NO BATTLE YET!

BLOODSHED IMMINENT!

ENORMOUS EXCITEMENT!!

INVASION OF PRUSSIA!! INVASION OF FRANCE!

Russia Sides With France!!!

ENGLAND STILL NEUTRAL! FIRING HEARD!

THE EMPEROR TO TAKE COMMAND.

PARIS, THURSDAY—No battle has been fought yet. But Field Marshal McMahon telegraphs thus to the Emperor:

"If the Frinch airmy survoives intil Christmas there'll be throuble. Forninst this fact it wud be sagacious if the divil wint the rounds of his establishment to prepare for the occasion, and took the precaution to warrum up the Prussian depairtment a bit agin the day.—MIKE."

There is an enormous state of excitement here over news from the front to the effect that yesterday France and Prussia were simultaneously invaded by the two bodies of troops which lately assembled on the border. Both armies conducted their invasions secretly, and are now hunting around for each other on opposite sides of the line.

Russia espouses the cause of France. She will bring 200,000 men to the field.

England continues to remain neutral.

Firing was heard yesterday in the direction of Blucherburg, and for a while the excitement was intense. However, when the people reflected that the country in that direction is uninhabitable, and impassable by anything but birds, they became tranquil again.

The Emperor sends his troops to the field with immense enthusiasm. He will lead them in person, when they return.

FOURTH DAY.

THE EUROPEAN WAR!

NO BATTLE YET!!

THE TROOPS GROWING OLD!

But Bitter Strife Imminent!

PRODIGIOUS EXCITEMENT!

The Invasions Successfully Accomplished and the Invaders Safe!

Russia Sides with Both Sides.

ENGLAND WILL FIGHT BOTH!

LONDON, FRIDAY—No battle has been fought, thus far, but a million impetuous soldiers are gritting their teeth at each other across the border, and the most serious fears are entertained that if they do not die of old age first, there will be bloodshed in this war yet.·

The prodigious patriotic excitement goes on. In Prussia, per Prussian telegrams, though contradicted from France. In France, per French telegrams, though contradicted from Prussia.

The Prussian invasion of France was a magnificent success. The military failed to find the French, but made good their return to Prussia without the loss of a single man. The French invasion of Prussia is also demonstrated to have been a brilliant and successful achievement. The army failed to find the Prussians, but made good their return to the Vatherland without bloodshed, after having invaded as much as they wanted to.

There is glorious news from Russia to the effect that she will side with both sides.

Also, from England—she will fight both sides.

LONDON, THURSDAY EVENING—I rushed over too soon. I shall return home in Tuesday's steamer and wait till the war begins.—*Mark Twain*

August 8, 1870

Obituary
Death of Jervis Langdon of Elmira

The painful and doubtful illness suffered for so long a time past by Mr. Jervis Langdon, of Elmira, terminated, we are grieved to say, in the death of that loved and esteemed gentleman on Saturday last. We conclude that an unfavorable change in the disease of Mr. Langdon must have occurred with suddenness, and that death must have come swiftly at last, since all our later advices—as we several times mentioned them—were encouraging to the expectation of his recovery. The anxiety of the family who had watched at his bed-side with exhausting solicitude for weeks was relieved by more than hope a fortnight ago, and the crushing weight of sorrow upon them now is made heavier to bear by the terrible reaction of that spring of delusive hope.

The mourning for Mr. Langdon will be as wide spread as the circle of his acquaintance, which was very large, and not often is a man followed to the grave by grief so sincere and passing so much beyond mere outward expression. He won the hearts of all people with whom he came in contact, even in the casual relations of business and of society. In the business world he held one of the most commanding positions of any man in the State. The vast operations in which he was engaged were largely conducted in this city, and gave him an extensive personal acquaintance here. All who knew him, even by the superficial acquaintance of business, may be counted among the friends to whom the announcement of his death will give a painful shock of grief. They will all feel that a true man of the best type among men has been lost; a man of no ordinary mould, but cast in character throughout of large and impressive proportions—large in heart, large in mind, large in forceful energy, large in purpose, large in all his nature. The very wealth that he acquired, by sagacious and always scrupulously honorable enterprise, was to be recognized in his case, as it so rarely can be, among the measures of the man.

But we cannot say what demands to be said of Mr. Langdon, now that he is dead, so fittingly and so truly has it been written by our absent associate, Mr. Clemens—his son by marriage—in a brief communication that we received from him yesterday and which we here quote:[201]

> "Mr. Langdon was a great and noble man, in the best and truest acceptation of those terms. He stood always ready to help whoever needed help—wisely with advice, healthfully with cheer and encouragement, and lavishly with money. He spent more than one fortune in aiding struggling unfortunates in various ways, and chiefly to get a business foothold in the world. He had so charitable a nature that he could always find some justification for any one who injured him; and then his forgiveness freely followed. Instead of sending to prison a man whom he had pecuniarily befriended in time of need, and who, being persuaded

by an ill-adviser, defrauded his benefactor out of a great sum, he forgave him and helped his family when straightened circumstances fell to their lot again. All the impulses of Mr. Langdon's heart were good and generous. He could not comprehend the base or the little. His nature was cast in a majestic mould.

"Whatever he did, he did with his whole heart. He never was hesitating or lukewarm in anything. In business he worked with all his might; and as fast as his great gains accumulated he toiled to sow them broadcast for the good of the city, the church and the poor. In politics he showed the same decision and energy; he was an Abolitionist from the cradle, and worked openly and valiantly in that cause all through the days when to do such a thing was to ensure a man disgrace, insult, hatred and bodily peril.

"Throughout his long illness all grades of the community, from the highest to the lowest, came daily to inquire about his state; and the cheer that lit their faces when the news was good, or the sadness that fell upon them when it was ill, was touching testimony to the truth of what is here set down concerning him and to the whole community's respect and strong love for him. He was a very pure, and good, and noble Christian gentleman. All that knew him will grieve for his loss. The friendless and the forsaken will miss him."

We are not able at this time to give the facts of Mr. Langdon's biography with any completeness. His life was one of vicissitudes checquered with great misfortunes and great successes. First a merchant at Ithaca, we believe, he afterwards engaged in the lumber business in Pennsylvania, in which he experienced reverses, and finally embarked in the coal mining enterprise out of which his great fortune was acquired. Owning large interests in the Shamokin mines and elsewhere—including mines in Nova Scotia—and controlling several avenues of the coal trade, among them that by the Northern Central and New York Central Railroads to this city, he was one of the most powerful individual coal operators in the country, and was able, alone, to carry on successful competition even with such a moneyed corporation as the Delaware & Lackawana Company.

The widowed wife of Mr. Langdon survives him. He also leaves a son, Mr. Charles Langdon, a daughter, Mrs. Samuel L. Clemens, of this city, and an adopted daughter, Mrs. Crane, of Elmira.

The funeral of the deceased, as we learn from an Associated Press dispatch published elsewhere, will take place to-day at 5 P.M., when business generally in Elmira will be suspended, as a token of the great esteem in which Mr. Langdon was held by the community in which he lived. *[Unsigned]*

September 17, 1870

To the Reader

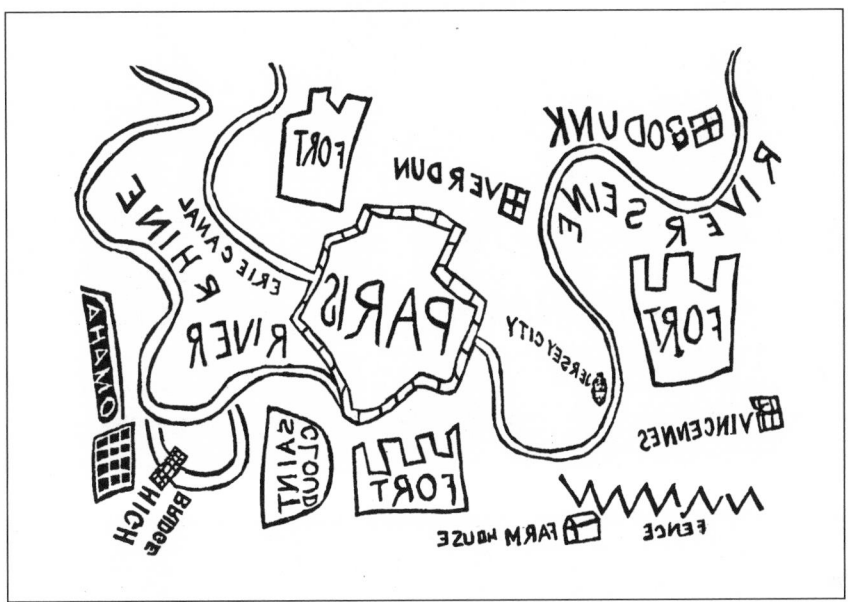

he above map explains itself.[202]

The idea of this map is not original with me, but is borrowed from the *Tribune* and the other great metropolitan journals.

I claim no other merit for this production (if I may so call it,) than that it is accurate. The main blemish of the city-paper maps of which it is an imitation, is, that in them more attention seems paid to artistic picturesqueness than geographical reliability.

Inasmuch as this is the first time I ever tried to draft and engrave a map, or attempt anything in the line of art at all, the commendations the work has received and the admiration it has excited among the people, have been very grateful to my feelings. And it is touching to reflect that by far the most enthusiastic of these praises have come from people who know nothing at all about art.

By an unimportant oversight I have engraved the map so that it reads wrong end first, except to left-handed people. I forgot that in order to make it right in print it should be drawn and engraved upside down. However, let the student who desires to contemplate the map stand on his head or hold it before her looking-glass. That will bring it right.

The reader will comprehend at a glance that that piece of river with the "High Bridge" over it got left out to one side by reason of a slip of the graving-tool which rendered it necessary to change the entire course of the river Rhine or else spoil the map. After having spent two days in digging and gouging at the map, I would have changed the course of the Atlantic Ocean before I would have lost so much work.

I never had so much trouble with anything in my life as I did with this map. I had heaps of little fortifications scattered all around Paris, at first, but every now and then my instruments would slip and fetch away whole miles of batteries and leave the vicinity as clean as if the Prussians had been there.

The reader will find it well to frame this map for future reference, so that it may aid in extending popular intelligence and dispelling the wide-spread ignorance of the day.—*Mark Twain*

OFFICIAL COMMENDATIONS

It is the only map of the kind I ever saw. —U.S. GRANT.

It places the situation in an entirely new light. —BISMARCK.

I cannot look upon it without shedding tears. —BRIGHAM YOUNG.[203]

It is very nice, large print. —NAPOLEON.

My wife was for years afflicted with freckles, and though everything was done for her relief that could be done, all was in vain. But, sir, since her first glance at your map, they have entirely left her. She has nothing but convulsions now. —J. SMITH.

If I had had this map I could have got out of Metz without any trouble. —BAZAINE.[204]

I have seen a great many maps in my time, but none that this one reminds me of. —TROCHU.[205]

It is but fair to say that in some respects it is a truly remarkable map. —W.T. SHERMAN.[206]

I said to my son Frederick William, "If you could only make a map like that, I would be perfectly willing to see you die—even anxious." —WILLIAM III.[207]

October 1, 1870

At the President's Reception

After I had drifted into the White House with the flood tide of humanity that had been washing steadily up the street for an hour, I obeyed the orders of the soldier at the door and the policeman within, and banked my hat and umbrella with a colored man, who gave me a piece of brass with a number on it, and said that that thing would reproduce the property at any time of the night.[208] I doubted it, but I was on unknown ground now, and must be content to take a good many chances.

Another person told me to drop in with the crowd and I would come to the President presently. I joined, and we drifted along till we passed a certain point, and then we thinned out to double and single file. It was a right gay scene, and a right stirring and lively one; for the whole place was brightly lighted, and all down the great hall as far as one could see, was a restless and writhing multitude of people, the women powdered, painted, jeweled, and splendidly upholstered, and many of the men gilded with the insignia of great naval, military and ambassadorial rank. It was bewildering.

Our long line kept drifting along, and by and by we came in sight of the President and Mrs. Grant. They were standing up shaking hands and trading civilities with our procession. I grew somewhat at home little by little, and then began to feel satisfied and contented. I was getting to be perfectly alive with interest by the time it came my turn to talk with the President. I took him by the hand and looked him in the eye and said:

"Well, I reckon I see you at last, General. I have said as much as a thousand times, out in Nevada, that if ever I went home to the States I would just have the private satisfaction of going and saying to you by word of mouth that *I* thought you was considerable of a soldier, anyway. Now, you know out there we—"

I turned round and said to the fellow behind me:

"Now, look here, my good friend, how the nation do you suppose I can talk with any sort of satisfaction, with you crowding me this way? I am surprised at your manners."

He was a modest-looking creature. He said:

"But you see the whole procession's stopped, and they're crowding up on me."

I said:

"Some people have got more cheek. Just suggest to the parties behind you to have some respect for the place they are in and not try to shove in on a private conversation. What the General and me are talking about ain't of the least interest to them."

Then I resumed with the President:

"Well, well, well. Now this is fine. This is what I call something *like*. Gay? Well, I should say so. And so this is what you call a Presidential reception. I'm free to say that it just lays over anything that ever *I* saw out in the sage-brush. I have been to Governor Nye's[209] Injun receptions at Honey Lake and Carson City, many and many a time—he that's Senator Nye now—*you* know him of course. I never saw a man in all my life that Jim Nye didn't know—and not only that, but he could tell him where he knew him, and all about him, family included, even if it was forty years ago. Most remarkable man, Jim Nye—remarkable. He can tell a lie with that purity of accent, and that grace of utterance, and that convincing emotion—"

I turned again and said:

"My friend, your conduct surprises me. I have come three thousand miles to have a word with the President of the United States upon subjects with which you are not even remotely connected, and by the living gee-whilikens I can't proceed with any sort of satisfaction on account of your cussed crowding. Will you please to go a little slow now and not attract so much attention by your strange conduct? If you had any eyes you could see how the bystanders are staring."

He said:

"But I tell you sir, it's the people behind. They are just growling and surging and shoving, and I wish I was in Jericho, I do."

I said:

"I wish you was, myself. You might learn some delicacy of feeling in that ancient seat of civilization, maybe. Drat if you don't need it."

And then I resumed with the President:

"Yes, sir, I've been at receptions before, plenty of them—old Nye's Injun receptions. But they warn't as starchy as this by considerable. No great long strings of high-fliers like these galoots here, you know, but old high-flavored Washoes and Pi-Utes, each one of them as powerful as a rag-factory on fire. Phew! Those were halcyon days. Yes, indeed, General, and madam, many and many's the time out in the wilds of Nevada, I've been—"

"Perhaps you had better discontinue your remarks till another time, sir, as the people behind you are growing somewhat impatient," the President said.

"Do you hear that?" I said to the fellow behind me. "I suppose you will take *that* hint, anyhow. I tell you he is milder than *I* would be. If I was President, I would waltz you people out at the back door if you came crowding a gentleman this way, that *I* was holding a private conversation with."

And then I resumed with the President:

"I think that hint of yours will start them. I never saw people act so. It is really about all I can do to hold my ground with that mob shoving up behind. But don't you worry on my account, General—don't give yourself any uneasiness about me—I can stand it as long as they can. I've been through this kind of a mill before. Why, as I was saying to you, many and many a time out in the wilds of Nevada, I have been at Governor Nye's Injun receptions—and between you and me that old man was a good deal of a Governor, take him all round. I don't know what for Senator he makes, though I think you'll admit that him and Bill Stewart and Tom Fitch take a bigger average of brains into that Capitol up yonder, by a hundred and fifty fold, than any other State in America, according to the population. Now that is so. Those three men represent only twenty or twenty-five thousand people—bless you, the least bit of a trifling ward in the city of New York casts two votes to Nevada's one—and yet those three men haven't their superiors in Congress for straight-out simon pure brains and ability. And if you could just have been at one of old Nye's Injun receptions and seen those savages—not high-fliers like these, you know, but frowsy old bummers with nothing in the world on, in the summer time, but an old battered plug hat and a pair of spectacles—I tell you it was a swell affair, was one of Governor Nye's early-day receptions. Many and many's the time

I have been to them, and seen him stand up and beam and smile on his children, as he called them in his motherly way—beam on them by the hour out of his splendid eyes, fascinate them with his handsome face, and comfort them with his persuasive tongue—seen him stand up there and tell them anecdotes and lies, and quote Watt's hymns to them until he just took all the war spirit out of them—and grim chiefs that came two hundred miles to tax the whites with whole wagonloads of blankets and things or make eternal war if they didn't get them, he has sent away bewildered with his inspired mendacity and perfectly satisfied and enriched with an old hoopskirt or two, a lot of Patent Office reports, and a few sides of condemned army bacon that they would have to chain up to a tree when they camped or the skippers would walk off with them. I tell you he is a rattling talker. Talk! It's no name for it. He—well he is bound to launch straight into close quarters and a heap of trouble hereafter, of course—we all know that—but you can rest satisfied that he will take off his hat and put out his hand and introduce himself to the King of Darkness perfectly easy and comfortable, and let on that he has seen him somewhere before; and he will remind him of the parties he used to know, and things that's slipped his memory—and he'll tell a thousand things that he can't *help* taking an interest in, and every now and then he will just gently mix in an anecdote that will fetch him if there's any laugh in him—he will, indeed—and Jim Nye will chip in and help cross question the candidates, and he will just hang round and hang around, getting more sociable all the time, and doing this, that, and the other thing in the handiest sort of way, till he has made himself perfectly indispensable—and then, the very first thing you know—"

I wheeled and said:

"My friend, your conduct grieves me to the heart. A dozen times at least your unseemly crowding has seriously interfered with the conversation I am holding with the President, and if the thing occurs again, I shall take my hat and leave the premises."

"I wish to the mischief you would! Where did you come from anyway, that you've got the unutterable cheek to spread yourself here and keep fifteen hundred people standing waiting half an hour to shake hands with the President?"

An officer touched me on the shoulder and said:

"Move along, please; you're annoying the President beyond all patience. You have blocked the procession, and the people behind you are getting furious. Come, move along, please."

Rather than have trouble, I moved along. So I had no time to do more than look back over my shoulder and say: "Yes, sir, and the first thing they would know, Jim Nye would have that place, and the salary doubled! I do reckon he is the handiest creature about making the most of his chances that ever found an all-sufficient substitute for mother's milk in politics and sin. Now that is the kind of man old Nye is—and in less than two months he would talk every—But I can't make you hear the rest, General, without hollering too loud."—*Mark Twain*

October 8, 1870

Curious Relic for Sale

"For sale, for the benefit of the Fund for the Relief of the Widows and Orphans of Deceased Firemen, a Curious Ancient Bedouin PIPE procured at the city of Endor in Palestine, and believed to have once belonged to the justly-renowned Witch of Endor.[210] Parties desiring to examine this singular relic with a view to purchasing, can do so by calling upon David S., 119 and 121 William street, New York."

As per advertisement in the "Herald." A curious old relic indeed, as I had a good personal right to know. In a single instant of time, a long drawn panorama of sights and scenes in the Holy Land flashed through my memory—town and grove, desert, camp, and caravan clattering after each other and disappearing, leaving me a little of the surprised and dizzy feeling which I have experienced at sundry times when a long express train has overtaken me at some quiet curve and gone whizzing, car by car, around the corner and out of sight. In that prolific instant I saw again all the country from the Sea of Galilee and Nazareth clear to Jerusalem, and thence over the hills of Judea and through the Vale of Sharon to Joppa, down by the ocean. Leaving out unimportant stretches of country and details of incident, I saw and experienced the following-described matters and things. Immediately three years fell away from my age, and a vanished time was restored to me—September, 1867. It was a flaming Oriental day—this one that had come up out of the past and brought along its actors, its stage-properties, and scenic effects—and our party had just ridden through

the squalid hive of human vermin which still holds the ancient Biblical name of Endor; I was bringing up the rear on my grave four-dollar
steed, who was about beginning to compose himself for his usual noon
nap. My! only fifteen minutes before, how the black, mangy, nine-
tenths naked, ten-tenths filthy, ignorant, bigoted, hungry, lazy, malignant, screeching, crowding, struggling, wailing, begging, cursing, hate- ·
ful spawn of the original Witch had swarmed out of the caves in the
rocks and holes and crevices in the earth, and blocked our horses'
way, besieged us, threw themselves in the animals' path, clung to
their manes, saddle-furniture, and tails, asking, beseeching, demanding "bucksheesh! *bucksheesh!* BUCKSHEESH!"[211] We had rained small
copper Turkish coins among them, as fugitives fling coats and hats to
pursuing wolves, and then had spurred our way through as they
stopped to scramble for the largess. I was fervently thankful when we
had gotten well up on the desolate hillside and outstripped them and
left them jawing and gesticulating in the rear. What a tempest had
seemingly gone roaring and crashing by me and left its dull thunders
pulsing in my ears!

I was in the rear, as I was saying. Our pack-mules and Arabs were
far ahead, and Dan, Jack, Moult, Davis, Denny, Church, and Birch
(these names will do as well as any to represent the boys) were following close after them. As my horse nodded to rest, I heard a sort of
panting behind me, and turned and saw that a tawny youth from the
village had overtaken me — a true remnant and representative of his
ancestress the Witch — a galvanized scurvy, wrought into the human
form and garnished with opthalamia and leprous scars — an airy creature with an invisible shirt-front that reached below the pit of his
stomach, and no other clothing to speak of except a tobacco-pouch, an
ammunition pocket, and a venerable gun, which was long enough to
club any game with that came within shooting distance, but far from
efficient as an article of dress.

I thought to myself, "Now this disease with a human heart in it is
going to shoot me." I smiled in derision at the idea of a Bedouin daring to touch off his great-grandfather's rusty gun and getting his head
blown off for his pains. But then it occurred to me, in simple school-
boy language, "Suppose he should take deliberate aim and 'haul off'
and fetch me with the butt-end of it?" There was wisdom in that view
of it, and I stopped to parley. I found he was only a friendly villain
who wanted a trifle of bucksheesh, and after begging all that he could
get in that way, was perfectly willing to trade off everything he had

for more. I believe he would have parted with his last shirt for bucksheesh if he had had one. He was smoking the "humblest" pipe I ever
saw—dingy, funnel-shaped, red-clay thing, streaked and grimed with
oil and tears of tobacco, and with all the different kinds of dirt there
are, and thirty per cent. of them peculiar and indigenous to Endor and
perdition. And rank? I never smelt anything like it. It withered a cac-
tus that stood lifting its prickly hands aloft beside the trail. It even
woke up my horse. I said I would take that. It cost me a franc, a Russ-
ian kopek, a brass button, and a slate pencil; and my spendthrift lav-
ishness so won upon the son of the desert that he passed over his
pouch of most unspeakably villainous tobacco to me as a free gift.
What a pipe it was, to be sure! It had a rude brass-wire cover to it, and
a little coarse iron chain suspended from the bowl, with an iron splin-
ter attached to loosen up the tobacco and pick your teeth with. The
stem looked like the half of a slender walking-stick with the bark on.

I felt that this pipe had belonged to the original Witch of Endor as
soon as I saw it; and as soon as I smelt it, I knew it. Moreover, I asked
the Arab cub in good English if it was not so, and he answered in good
Arabic that it was. I woke up my horse and went away, smoking. And
presently I said to myself reflectively, "If there *is* anything that could
make a man deliberately assault a dying cripple, I reckon may be an
unexpected whiff from this pipe would do it." I smoked along till I
found I was beginning to lie, and project murder, and steal my own
things out of one pocket and hide them in another; and then I put up
my treasure, took off my spurs and put them under my horse's tail,
and shortly came tearing through our caravan like a hurricane. From
that time forward, going to Jerusalem, the Dead Sea, and the Jordan,
Bethany, Bethlehem, and everywhere, I loafed contentedly in the rear
and enjoyed my infamous pipe and revelled in imaginary villainy. But
at the end of two weeks we turned our faces toward the sea and jour-
neyed over the Judean hills, and through rocky defiles, and among the
scenes that Samson knew in his youth, and by and by we touched
level ground just at night, and trotted off cheerily over the plain of
Sharon. It was perfectly jolly for three hours, and we whites crowded
along together, close after the chief Arab muleteer (all the pack-
animals and the other Arabs were miles in the rear), and we laughed,
and chatted, and argued hotly about Samson, and whether suicide
was a sin or not, since Paul speaks of Samson distinctly as being
saved and in heaven.[212] But by and by the night air, and the duski-
ness, and the weariness of eight hours in the saddle, began to tell, and

conversation flagged and finally died out utterly. The squeak-squeaking of the saddles grew very distinct; occasionally somebody sighed, or started to hum a tune and gave it up; now and then a horse sneezed. These things only emphasized the solemnity and the stillness. Everybody got so listless that for once I and my dreamer found ourselves in the lead. It was a glad, new sensation, and I longed to keep the place forevermore. Every little stir in the dingy cavalcade behind made me nervous. Davis and I were riding side by side, right after the Arab. About 11 o'clock it had become really chilly, and the dozing boys roused up and began to inquire how far it was to Ramlah yet, and to demand that the Arab hurry along faster. I gave it up then, and my heart sank within me, because of course they would come up to scold the Arab. I knew I had to take the rear again. In my sorrow I unconsciously took to my pipe, my only comfort. As I touched the match to it the whole company came lumbering up and crowding my horse's rump and flanks. A whiff of smoke drifted back over my shoulder, and—

"The suffering Moses!"

"Whew!"

"By George, who opened that graveyard?"

"Boys, that Arab's been swallowing something dead!"

Right away there was a gap behind us. Whiff after whiff sailed airily back, and each one widened the breach. Within fifteen seconds the barking, and gasping, and sneezing, and coughing of the boys, and their angry abuse of the Arab guide, had dwindled to a murmur, and Davis and I were alone with the leader. Davis did not know what the matter was, and don't to this day. Occasionally he caught a faint film of the smoke and fell to scolding at the Arab and wondering how long he had been decaying in that way. Our boys kept on dropping back further and further, till at last they were only in hearing, not in sight. And every time they started gingerly forward to reconnoitre— or shoot the Arab, as they proposed to do—I let them get within good fair range of my relic (she would carry seventy yards with wonderful precision), and then wafted a whiff among them that sent them gasping and strangling to the rear again. I kept my gun well charged and ready, and twice within the hour I decoyed the boys right up to my horse's tail, and then with one malarious blast emptied the saddles, almost. I never heard an Arab abused so in my life. He really owed his preservation to me, because for one entire hour I stood between him and certain death. The boys would have killed him if they could have got by me.

By and by, when the company were far in the rear, I put away my pipe—I was getting fearfully dry and crisp about the gills and rather blown with good diligent work—and spurred my animated trance up alongside the Arab and stopped him and asked for water. He unslung his little gourd-shaped earthenware jug, and I put it under my moustache and took a long, glorious, satisfying draught. I was going to scour the mouth of the jug a little, but I saw that I had brought the whole train together once more by my delay, and that they were all anxious to drink too—and would have been long ago if the Arab had not pretended that he was out of water. So I hastened to pass the vessel to Davis. He took a mouthful, and never said a word, but climbed off his horse and lay down calmly in the road. I felt sorry for Davis. It was too late now, though, and Dan was drinking. Dan got down too, and hunted for a soft place. I thought I heard Dan say, "That Arab's friends ought to keep him in alcohol or else take him out and bury him somewhere." All the boys took a drink and climbed down. It is not well to go into further particulars. Let us draw the curtain upon this act.

. . .

Well, now, to think that after three changing years I should hear from that curious old relic again, and see Dan advertising it for sale for the benefit of a benevolent object. Dan is not treating that present right. I gave that pipe to him for a keepsake. However, he probably finds that it keeps away custom and interferes with business. It is the most convincing inanimate object in all this part of the world, perhaps. Dan and I were room-mates in all that long "Quaker City" voyage, and whenever I desired to have a little season of privacy I used to fire up on that pipe and persuade Dan to go out; and he seldom waited to change his clothes, either. In about a quarter, or from that to three-quarters of a minute, he would be propping up the smoke-stack on the upper deck and cursing. I wonder how the faithful old relic is going to sell?—*Mark Twain*

Mark Twain
His Map and Fortifications of Paris

Mark Twain's map of the Fortifications of Paris is published in the *Galaxy* this month with the following explanatory introduction:[213]

I published my "Map of the Fortifications of Paris" in my own paper a fortnight ago, but am obliged to reproduce it in the *Galaxy*, to satisfy the extraordinary demand for it which has arisen in military circles throughout the country. General Grant's outspoken commendation originated this demand, and General Sherman's fervent endorsement added fuel to it. The result is that tons of these maps have been fed to the suffering soldiers of our land, but without avail. They hunger still. We will cast the *Galaxy* into the breach and stand by and await the effect.

The next Atlantic mail will doubtless bring news of a European frenzy for the map. It is reasonable to expect that the siege of Paris will be suspended till a German translation of it can be forwarded (it is now in preparation), and that the defence of Paris will likewise be suspended to await the reception of the French translation (now progressing under my hands, and likely to be unique.) King William's high praise of the map and Napoleon's frank enthusiasm concerning its execution will ensure its prompt adoption in Europe as the only authoritative and legitimate exposition of the present military situation. It is plain that if the Prussians cannot get into Paris with the facilities afforded by this production of mine they ought to deliver the enterprise into abler hands.

Strangers to me keep insisting that this map does *not* "explain itself." One person came to me with bloodshot eyes and a harassed look about him, and shook the map in my face and said he believed I was some new kind of idiot. I have been abused a good deal by other quick-tempered people like him, who came with similar complaints. Now, therefore, I yield willingly, and for the information of the ignorant will briefly explain the present military position as illustrated by the map. Part of the Prussian forces, under Prince Frederick William, are now boarding at the "farm-house" in the margin of the map. There is nothing between them and Vincennes but a rail fence in bad repair. Any corporal can see at a glance that they have only to burn it, pull it down, crawl under, climb over, or walk around it, just as the commander-in-chief shall elect. Another portion of the Prussian forces are at Podunk, under Von Moltke. They have nothing to do but to float down the river Seine on a raft and scale the walls of Paris. Let the worshippers of that overrated soldier believe in him still, and abide the result—for me, *I* do not believe he will ever think of a raft. At Omaha and the High Bridge are vast masses of Prussian infantry, and it is only fair to say that they are likely to *stay* there, as that figure of a window-sash between them stands for a brewery. Away up out of sight over the top of the map is the fleet of the Prussian navy, ready at any moment to come cavorting down the Erie Canal (unless some new iniquity of an unprincipled Legislature shall put up the tolls and so render it cheaper to walk). To me it looks as if Paris is a singularly close place. She was never situated before as she is in this map.—*Mark Twain*

PART V

The Last Days of Journalism

October 1870–January 1871

On Riley—Newspaper Correspondent

O ne of the best men in Washington—or elsewhere—is Riley,[214] correspondent of the great San Francisco dailies.

Riley is full of humor, and has an unfailing vein of irony which makes his conversation to the last degree entertaining (as long as the remarks are about somebody else). But notwithstanding the possession of these qualities, which should enable a man to write a happy and appetizing letter, Riley's newspaper letters often display a more than earthly solemnity, and likewise an unimaginative devotion to petrified facts, which surprise and distress all men who know him in his unofficial character. He explains this curious thing by saying that his employers sent him to Washington to write facts, not fancy, and that several times he has come near losing his situation by inserting humorous remarks which, not being looked for at headquarters and consequently not understood, were thought to be dark and bloody speeches intended to convey signals and warnings to murderous secret societies, or something of that kind, and so were scratched out with a shiver and a prayer and cast into the stove. Riley says that sometimes he is so afflicted with a yearning to write a sparkling and absorbing readable letter that he simply cannot resist it, and he goes to his den and revels in the delight of untrammelled scribbling; and then, with suffering, such as only a mother can know, he destroys the pretty children of his fancy and reduces his letter to the required dismal accuracy. Having seen Riley do this very thing more than once, I know whereof I speak. Often I have laughed with him over a happy passage and grieved to see him plough his pen through it. He would say, "I had to write that or die; and I've got to scratch it out or starve. *They* wouldn't stand it, you know."

I think Riley is about the most entertaining company I ever saw. We lodged together in many places in Washington during the Winter of '67–'8, moving comfortably from place to place, and attracting attention by paying our board—a course which cannot fail to make a person conspicuous in Washington. Riley would tell all about his trip to California in the early days by way of the Isthmus and the San Juan river; and about his baking bread in San Francisco, to gain a living, and setting up ten-pins, and practising law, and opening oysters,

and delivering lectures, and teaching French, and tending bar, and reporting for the newspapers, and keeping dancing-school, and inter-
preting Chinese in the courts—which latter was lucrative and Riley
was doing handsomely and laying up a little money when people began to find fault because his translations were too "free," a thing for
which Riley considered he ought not to be held responsible, since he
did not know a word of the Chinese tongue and only adopted inter-
preting as a means of obtaining an honest livelihood. Through the
machinations of his enemies he was removed from the position of official interpreter, and a man put in his place who was familiar with the
Chinese language but did not know any English. And Riley used to
tell about publishing a paper up in what is Alaska now, but was only
an iceberg then, with a population composed of bears, walruses, Indians, and other animals; and how the iceberg got adrift at last, and left
all his paying subscribers behind, and as soon as the commonwealth
floated out of the jurisdiction of Russia the people rose and threw off
their allegiance and ran up the English flag, calculating to hook on
and become an English colony as they drifted along down the British
Possessions; but a land breeze and a crooked current carried them by,
and they ran up the Stars and Stripes and steered for California,
missed connection again and swore allegiance to Mexico, but it wasn't
any use; the anchors came home every time, and away they went with
the northeast trades drifting off sideways toward the Sandwich Islands, whereupon they ran up the Cannibal flag and had a grand human barbecue in honor of it, in which it was noticed that the better a
man liked a friend the better he enjoyed him; and as soon as they got
fairly within the tropics the weather got so fearfully hot that the iceberg began to melt, and it got so sloppy under foot that it was almost
impossible for ladies to get about at all; and at last, just as they came
in sight of the islands, the melancholy remnant of the once majestic
iceberg canted first to one side and then to the other, and then
plunged under forever, carrying the national archives along with it,
and not only the archives and the populace, but some eligible town
lots which had increased in value as fast as they diminished in size in
the tropics, and which Riley could have sold at thirty cents a pound
and made himself rich if he could have kept the province afloat ten
hours longer and got her into port.

And so forth and so on, with all the facts of Riley's trip through
Mexico, a journey whose history his felicitous fancy can make more
interesting than any novel that ever was written. What a shame it is

to tie Riley down to the dreary mason-work of laying up solemn dead-walls of fact! He does write a plain, straightforward, and perfectly accurate and reliable correspondence, but it seems to me that I would rather have one chatty paragraph of his fancy than a whole obituary of his facts.

Riley is very methodical, untiringly accommodating, never forgets anything that is to be attended to, is a good son, a staunch friend, and a permanent, reliable enemy. He will put himself to any amount of trouble to oblige a body, and therefore always has his hands full of things to be done for the helpless and the shiftless. And he knows how to do nearly everything, too. He is a man whose native benevolence is a well-spring that never goes dry. He stands always ready to help whoever needs help, as far as he is able—and not simply with his money, for that is a cheap and common charity, but with hand and brain, and fatigue of limb and sacrifice of time. This sort of men is rare.

Riley has a ready wit, a quickness and aptness at selecting and applying quotations, and a countenance that is as solemn and as blank as the back side of a tombstone when he is delivering a particularly exasperating joke. One night a negro woman was burned to death in a house next door to us, and Riley said that our landlady would be oppressively emotional at breakfast, because she generally made use of such opportunities as offered, being of a morbidly sentimental turn, and so we would find it best to let her talk along and say nothing back—it was the only way to keep her tears out of the gravy. Riley said there never was a funeral in the neighborhood but that the gravy was watery for a week.

And sure enough, at breakfast the landlady was in the very sloughs of woe—entirely broken-hearted. Everything she looked at reminded her of that poor old negro woman, and so the buckwheat cakes made her sob, the coffee forced a groan, and when the beefsteak came on she fetched a wail that made our hair rise. Then she got to talking about the deceased, and kept up a steady drizzle till both of us were soaked through and through. Presently she took a fresh breath and said with a world of sobs:

"Ah, to think of it, only to think of it!—the poor old faithful creature. For she was *so* faithful. Would you believe it, she had been a servant in that self-same house for twenty-seven years come Christmas, and never a cross word and never a lick! And oh to think she should meet such a death at last!—a-sitting over the red-hot stove at three o'clock in the morning and went to sleep and fell on it and was actually *roasted!* not just frizzled up a bit, but literally roasted to a crisp! Poor faithful creature, how she *was* cooked! I am a poor woman, but even if I have to scrimp to do it, I will put up a tombstone over the lone sufferer's grave—and Mr. Riley, if you would have the goodness to think up a little epitaph to put on it which would sort of describe the awful way in which she met her—"

"Put it '*Well done,* good and faithful servant!'" said Riley, and never smiled.

[I have either printed that anecdote once before or told it in company so many thousand times as to carry that seeming to my mind, but it is of no consequence—it is worth printing half a dozen times.]—*Mark Twain*

October 21, 1870

The Libel Suit

The trial, which closed yesterday, of the suit for libel brought by Hon. D. S. Bennett against the proprietors of the Buffalo *Commercial Advertiser*,[215] has probably excited more interest and attracted a larger share of public attention during its progress than any case of litigation that has occurred in our courts for many years. The evidence in the case was listened to throughout by a great number of impartially interested citizens, and it has been read by a far greater number in the public prints. The just merits of the case, as it was yesterday submitted to the jury, have thus become widely understood in the community, and the verdict of the jury, since it was rendered, has therefore been subjected to more general and more intelligent discussion than a verdict often receives. We think we are safe in saying, and that it is quite proper we should say, that the announcement of the verdict in question, occasioned almost universal surprise, and that it is not the verdict which unbiased public opinion renders in its judgment upon the case. It is unquestionably a verdict which ought to satisfy the conductors of public journals, if they desire to be licensed beyond all restriction in their use of the formidable agency of public utterance that is in their hands; if they desire to have the characters of men placed wholly at their mercy; if the desire to employ their press as a deadly weapon of malice in the prosecution of personal feuds and the gratification of personal animosities, and to be made secure against all accountableness for the malignity with which it is used. If such are the desires of the conductors of public journals, the verdict rendered yesterday ought to satisfy them well; for it sanctions in the past and licenses in the future a course of conduct, in the employment of a newspaper to wreak a personal resentment and satisfy a personal enmity, on the part of those who control it, which public opinion has declared to be almost without precedent in malignity and vindictiveness. If the verdict that sanctions the malice of personal enmity with which Mr. Bennett has been pursued and traduced in public print by the men who control and conduct the Buffalo *Commercial Advertiser*—if the verdict, we say, defines correctly the rights and privileges and functions of public journalism, then we, whose happy fortune it is to command for ourselves the multiplied utterances of the press, are free to distill venom in slander at our pleasure; and woe to the people who offend us, for we pour it upon them from the walls of an unassailable fortification.

As the possessors of such a power, we might, perhaps, rejoice at the unlimited license that is given to us in the use of it. But we do not. We covet no such blasting and malignant power in our own hands, and we protest against its dangerous concession to those who are capable of the desire to possess it and capable of the disposition to use it. We desire on our own part no degradation of journalism to that personal employment in private feuds and the pursuit of private animosities, and we protest against the licensing of such degradation by other men. We protest, in fact, against the sanction to malignity in the public press that is given in yesterday's verdict; and we do so much in the name and for the sake of the true liberties of the press, which we represent as we do on account of the people whose safety of character and whose rights of protection and redress are put in peril by it. It is a verdict which dangerously emboldens the spirit of vindictive malice that has been more and more recklessly displaying itself of late in newspapers like the New York *Sun* and the journal that in the case under notice was brought into court. It ought not to stand, and we are well pleased to learn that it is to be tested by an appeal. *[Unsigned]*

A Reminiscence
of the Back Settlements

"Now that corpse [said the undertaker, patting the folded arms of the deceased approvingly] was a brick—every way you took him he was a brick.[216] He was so real accommodating, and so modest-like and simple in his last moments. Friends wanted metallic burial case—nothing else would do. *I* couldn't get it. There warn't going to be time—anybody could see that. Corpse said never mind, shake him up in some kind of a box he could stretch out in comfortable, *he* warn't particular 'bout the general style of it. Said he went more on room than style, any way, in a last final container. Friends wanted a silver door-plate on the coffin, signifying who he was and wher' he was from. Now *you* know a feller couldn't roust out such a gally thing as this in a little country town like this. What did corpse say? Corpse said, whitewash his old canoe and dob his address and general destination onto it with a blacking brush and a stencil plate, long with a verse from some likely hymn or other, and p'int him for the tomb, and mark him C.O.D., and just let him skip along. *He* warn't distressed any more than you be—on the contrary just as carm and collected as a hearse-horse; said he judged that wher' he was going to, a body would find it considerable better to attract attention by a picturesque and moral character than a natty burial case with a swell door-plate on it. Splendid man, he was. I'd druther do for a corpse like that 'n any I've tackled in seven year. There's some satisfaction in buryin' a man like that. You feel that what you're doing is appreciated. Lord bless you, so's he got planted before he sp'iled he was perfectly satisfied; said his relations meant well, *per*fectly well, but all them preparations was bound to delay the thing more or less, and he didn't wish to be kept layin' around. You never see such a clear head as what he had—and so carm and so cool. Just a hunk of brains—that is what *he* was. Perfectly awful. It was a ripping distance from one end of that man's head to t'other. Often and over again he's had brain fever a-raging in one place, and the rest of the pile didn't know anything about it—didn't affect it more than an Injun insurrection in Arizona effects the Atlantic States. Well, the relations they wanted a big funeral, but the corpse said he was down on flummery—didn't want any procession—

fill the hearse full of mourners, and get out a stern line and tow *him* behind. He *was* the most down on style of any remains I ever struck. A beautiful, simple-minded creature—it was what he was, you can depend on that. He was just set on having things the way he wanted them, and he took a solid comfort in laying in his little plans. He had me measure him and take a whole raft of instructions; then he had the minister stand up behind a long box with a table-cloth over it and read his funeral sermon, saying 'Angcore, angcore!' at the good places, and making him scratch out every piece of brag about him, and all the hifalutin; and then he made them trot out the choir so's he could help them pick out the tunes for the occasion, and he got them to sing 'Pop goes the Weasel,' because he'd always liked that tune when he was down-hearted, and solemn music made him sad; and when they sung that with tears in their eyes (because they all loved him), and his relations grieving around, he just laid there as happy as a bug, and trying to beat time and showing all over how much he enjoyed it; and presently he got worked up and excited, and tried to join in, for mind you he was pretty proud of his abilities in the singing line; but the first time he opened his mouth and was just going to spread himself, his breath took a walk. I never see a man snuffed out so sudden. Ah, it was a great loss—it was a powerful loss to this poor little one-horse town. Well, well, well, I hain't got time to be palavering along here— got to nail on the lid and mosey along with him; and if you'll just give me a lift we'll skeet him into the hearse and meander along. Relations bound to have it so—don't pay no attention to dying injunctions, minute a corpse's gone; but if I had *my* way, if I didn't respect his last wishes and tow him behind the hearse, *I'll* be cuss'd. I consider that whatever a corpse wants done for his comfort is a little enough matter, and a man hain't got no right to deceive him or take advantage of him—and whatever a corpse trusts me to *do,* you know, even if it's to stuff him and paint him yaller and keep him for a keepsake—you hear *me!*"

He cracked his whip and went lumbering away with his ancient ruin of a hearse, and I continued my walk with a valuable lesson learned—that a healthy and wholesome cheerfulness is not necessarily impossible to *any* occupation. The lesson is likely to be lasting, for it will take many months to obliterate the memory of the remarks and circumstances that impressed it.—*Mark Twain*

A General Reply

When I was sixteen or seventeen years old, a splendid idea burst upon me—a brand-new one, which had never occurred to anybody before: I would write some "pieces" and take them down to the editor of the "Republican," and ask him to give me his plain unvarnished opinion of their value![217] Now, as old and threadbare as the idea was, it was fresh and beautiful to me, and it went flaming and crashing through my system like the genuine lightning and thunder of originality. I wrote the pieces. I wrote them with that placid confidence and that happy facility which only want of practice and absence of literary experience can give. There wasn't one sentence that cost half an hour's weighing and shaping and trimming and fixing. Indeed, it is possible that there was no one sentence whose mere wording cost even one-sixth of that time. If I remember rightly, there was not one single erasure or interlineation in all that chaste manuscript. [I have since lost that large belief in my powers, and likewise that marvellous perfection of execution.] I started down to the "Republican" office with my pocket full of manuscripts, my brain full of dreams, and a grand future opening out before me. I knew perfectly well that the editor would be ravished with my pieces. But presently—

However, the particulars are of no consequence. I was only about to say that a shadowy sort of doubt just then intruded upon my exaltation. Another came, and another. Pretty soon a whole procession of them. And at last, when I stood before the "Republican" office and looked up at its tall, unsympathetic front, it seemed hardly *me* that could have "chinned" its towers ten minutes before, and was now so shrunk up and pitiful that if I dared to step on the gratings I should probably go through.

At about that crisis, the editor, the very man I had come to consult, came down stairs and halted a moment to pull at his wristbands and settle his coat to its place, and he happened to notice that I was eyeing him wistfully. He asked me what I wanted. I answered "NOTHING!" with a boy's own meekness and shame; and dropping my eyes, crept humbly round until I was fairly in the alley, and then drew a big grateful breath of relief, and picked up my heels and ran!

I was satisfied. I wanted no more. It was my first attempt to get a "plain, unvarnished opinion" out of a literary man concerning my compositions, and it has lasted until now. And in these latter days whenever I receive a bundle of MS. through the mail, with a request that I will pass judgment upon its merits, I feel like saying to the author, "If you had only taken your piece to some grim and stately newspaper office where you did not know anybody, you would not have had so fine an opinion of your production as it is easy to see you have now."

Every man who becomes and editor of a newspaper or magazine, straightway begins to receive MSS. from literary aspirants, together with requests that he will deliver judgment upon the same. And after complying in eight or ten instances, he finally takes refuge in a general sermon upon the subject, which he inserts in his publication, and always afterwards refers such correspondent to that sermon for answer. I have at last reached this station in my literary career. I now cease to reply privately to my applicants for advice, and proceed to construct my public sermon.

As all the letters of the sort I am speaking of contain the very same matter, differently worded, I offer as a fair average specimen the last one I have received:

Oct. 3.

MARK TWAIN, ESQ.

DEAR SIR: I am a youth, just out of school and ready to start in life. I have looked around, but don't see anything that suits exactly. Is a literary life easy and profitable, or is it the hard times it is generally put up for? It *must* be easier than a good many if not most of the occupations, and I feel drawn to launch out on it, make or break, sink or swim, survive or perish. Now, what are the conditions of success in literature? You need not be afraid to paint the thing just as it is. I can't do any worse than fail. Everything else offers the same. When I thought of the law—yes, and five or six other professions—I found the same thing was the case every time. viz: *all full—overrun—every profession so crammed that success is rendered impossible—too many hands and not enough work.* But I must do *something,* and so I turn at last to literature. Something tells me that that is the true bent of my genius, if I have any. I enclose some of my pieces. Will you read them over and give me your candid, unbiassed opinion of them? And now I hate to trouble you, but you have been a young man yourself, and what I want is for you to get me a job of newspaper writing to do. You know many newspaper people, and I am entirely unknown. And will you make the best terms you can for me? though I do not expect what might be called high wages at first, of course. Will you candidly say what such articles as those I enclose are worth? I have plenty of them. If you should sell those and let me know, I can send you more, as good and maybe better than these. An early reply, etc.

   Yours truly, etc.

I will answer you in good faith. Whether my remarks shall have great value or not, or my suggestions be worth following, are problems which I take great pleasure in leaving entirely to you for solution. To begin: There are several questions in your letter which only a man's life experience can eventually answer for him—not another man's words. I will simply skip those.

   1. Literature, like the ministry, medicine, the law, and *all other* occupations, is cramped and hindered for want of men to do the work, not want of work to do. When people tell you the reverse, they speak that which is not true. If you desire to test this, you need only hunt up a first-class editor, reporter, business manager, foreman of a shop, mechanic, or artist in any branch of industry, and *try to hire him.* You will find that he is already hired. He is sober, industrious, capable and reliable, and is always in demand. He cannot get a day's holiday except by the courtesy of his employer, or his city, or the general public. But if you need idlers, shirkers, half-instructed, unambitious, and comfort-seeking editors, reporters, lawyers, doctors and mechanics, apply anywhere. There are millions of them to be had at the dropping of a handkerchief.

   2. No; I must not and will not venture any opinion whatever as to the literary merit of your productions. The public is the only critic whose judgment is worth anything at all. Do not take my poor word for this, but reflect a moment and take your own. For instance, if Sylvanus Cobb or T. S. Arthur[218] had submitted their maiden MSS. to you, you would have said, with tears in your eyes, "Now, please don't write any more!" But you see yourself how popular they are. And if it had been left to you, you would have said the "Marble Faun" was tiresome, and that even "Paradise Lost" lacked cheerfulness; but you know they sell. Many wiser and better men than you pooh-poohed Shakespeare, even as late as two centuries ago; but still that old party has outlived these people. No, I will not sit in judgment upon your literature. If I honestly and conscientiously praised it, I might thus help to inflict a lingering and pitiless bore upon the public; if I honestly

and conscientiously condemned it, I might thus rob the world of an undeveloped and unsuspicious Dickens or Shakespeare.

3. I shrink from hunting up literary labor for you to do and receive pay for. Whenever your literary productions have proved for themselves that they have a real value, you will never have to go around hunting for remunerative work to do. You will require more hands than you have now, and more brains than you probably ever will have, to do even half the work that will be offered you. Now, in order to arrive at the proof of value hereinbefore spoken of, one needs only to adopt a very simple and certainly very sure process; and that is, to *write without pay until somebody offers to pay.* If nobody offers to pay within three years, the candidate may look upon this circumstance with the most implicit confidence as the sign that sawing wood is what he was intended for. If he has any wisdom at all, then, he will retire with dignity and assume his heaven-appointed vocation.

In the above remarks I have only offered a course of action which Mr. Dickens and most other successful literary men had to follow; but it is a course which will find no sympathy with my client, perhaps. The young literary aspirant is a very, very curious creature. He knows that if he wished to become a tinner, the master smith would require him to prove the possession of a good character, and would require him to promise to stay in the shop three years—possibly four— and would make him sweep out and bring water and build fires all the first year, and let him learn to black stoves in the intervals; and for these good honest services would pay him two suits of cheap clothes and his board; and next year he would begin to receive instructions in the trade, and a dollar a week would be added to his emoluments; and two dollars would be added the third year, and three the fourth; and *then,* if he had become a first-rate tinner, he would get about fifteen or twenty, or maybe thirty dollars a week, with never a possibility of getting seventy-five while he lived. If he wanted to become a mechanic of any other kind, he would have to undergo this same tedious, ill-paid apprenticeship. If he wanted to become a lawyer or a doctor, he would have fifty times worse; for he would get nothing at all during his long apprenticeship, and in addition would have to pay a large sum for tuition, and have the privilege of boarding and clothing himself. The literary aspirant knows all this, and yet he has the hardihood to present himself for reception into the literary guild and ask to share its high honors and emoluments, without a single twelve-month's apprenticeship to show in excuse for his presumption! He would smile pleasantly if he were asked to make even so simple a thing as a ten-cent tin dipper without previous instruction in the art; but, all green and ignorant, wordy, pompously assertive, ungrammatical, and with a vague, distorted knowledge of men and the world acquired in a back country village, he will serenely take up so dangerous a weapon as a pen, and attack the most formidable subject that finance, commerce, war or politics can furnish him withal. It would be laughable if it were not so sad and so pitiable. The poor fellow would not intrude upon the tin-shop without an apprenticeship, but is willing to seize and wield with unpracticed hand an instrument which is able to overthrow dynasties, change religions, and decree the weal or woe of nations.

If my correspondent will write free of charge for the newspapers of his neighborhood, it will be one of the strangest things that ever happened if he does not get all the employment he can attend to on those terms. And as soon as ever his writings are worth money, plenty of people will hasten to offer it.

And by the way of serious and well-meant encouragement, I wish to urge upon him once more the truth that acceptable writers for the press are so scarce that book and periodical publishers are seeking them constantly, and with a vigilance that never grows heedless for a moment.—*Mark Twain*

November 19, 1870

Running for Governor

A few months ago I was nominated for Governor of the great State of New York, to run against Stewart L. Woodford[219] and John T. Hoffman,[220] on an independent ticket.[221] I somehow felt that I had one prominent advantage over these gentlemen, and that was, good character. It was easy to see by the newspapers, that if ever they had known what it was to bear a good name, that time had gone by. It was plain that in these latter years they had become familiar with all manner of shameful crimes. But at the very moment that I was exalting my advantage and joying it in secret, there was a muddy undercurrent of discomfort "riling" the deeps of my happiness—and that was, the having to hear my name bandied about in familiar connection with those of such people. I grew more and more disturbed. Finally I wrote my grandmother about it. Her answer came quick and sharp. She said:

> You have never done one single thing in all your life to be ashamed of—
> not one. Look at the newspapers—look at them and comprehend what sort
> of characters Woodford and Hoffman are, and then see if you are willing to
> lower yourself to their level and enter a public canvass with them.

It was my very thought! I did not sleep a single moment that night. But after all, I could not recede. I was fully committed and must go on with the fight. As I was looking listlessly over the papers at breakfast, I came across this paragraph, and I may truly say I never was so confounded before:

> PERJURY.—Perhaps, now that Mr. Mark Twain is before the people as a
> candidate for Governor, he will condescend to explain how he came to be
> convicted of perjury by thirty-four witnesses, in Wakawak, Cochin
> China, in 1863, the intent of which perjury was to rob a poor native
> widow and her helpless family of a meagre plantain patch, their only
> stay and support in their bereavement and their desolation. Mr. Twain
> owes it to himself, as well as to the great people whose sufferages he
> asks, to clear this matter up. Will he do it?

I thought I should burst with amazement! Such a cruel, heartless charge—I never had *seen* Cochin China! I never had *heard* of Wakawak! I didn't know a plantain patch from a kangaroo! I did not know what to do. I was crazed and helpless. I let the day slip away without doing anything at all. The next morning the same paper had this—nothing more:

> SIGNIFICANT.—Mr. Twain, it will be observed, is suggestively silent
> about the Cochin China perjury.

[*Mem.*—During the rest of the campaign this paper never referred to me in any other way than as "the infamous perjurer Twain."]

Next came the "Gazette," with this:

> WANTED TO KNOW.—Will the new candidate for Governor deign to ex-
> plain to certain of his fellow-citizens (who are suffering to vote for him!)

the little circumstance of his cabin-mates in Montana losing small valu-
ables from time to time, until at last, these things having been invariably found on Mr. Twain's person or in his "trunk" (newspaper he rolled
his traps in), they felt compelled to give him a friendly admonition for
his own good, and so tarred and feathered him and rode him on a rail,
and then advised him to leave a permanent vacuum in the place he usually occupied in the camp. Will he do this?

Could anything be more deliberately malicious than that? For I
never was in Montana in my life.

[After this, this journal customarily spoke of me as "Twain, the
Montana Thief."]

I got to picking up papers apprehensively—much as one would lift
a desired blanket which he had some idea might have a rattlesnake
under it. One day this met my eye:

THE LIE NAILED!—By the sworn affidavits of Michael O'Flanagan, Esq., of
the Five Points, and Mr. Kit Burns and Mr. John Allen, of Water Street, it is
established that Mr. Mark Twain's vile statement that the lamented grandfather of our noble standard-bearer, John T. Hoffman, was hanged for highway robbery, is a brutal and gratuitous LIE, without a single shadow of
foundation in fact. It is disheartening to virtuous men to see such shameful
means resorted to to achieve political success as the attacking of the dead
in their graves and defiling their honored names with slander. When we
think of the anguish this miserable falsehood must cause the innocent relatives and friends of the deceased, we are almost driven to incite an outraged and insulted public to summary and unlawful vengeance upon the
traducer. But no—let us leave him to the agony of a lacerating conscience—
(though if passion should get the better of the public and in its blind fury
they should do the traducer bodily injury, it is but too obvious that no jury
could convict and no court punish the perpetrators of the deed).

The ingenious closing sentence had the affect of moving me out of
bed with dispatch that night, and out of the back door also, while the
"outraged and insulted public" surged in the front way, breaking furniture and windows in their righteous indignation as they came, and
taking off such property as they could carry when they went. And
yet I can lay my hand upon the Book and say that I never slandered
Governor Hoffman's grandfather. More—I had never even heard of
him or mentioned him, up to that day and date.

[I will state in passing, that the journal above quoted from, always referred to me afterwards as "Twain the Body-Snatcher."]

The next newspaper article that attracted my attention was the following:

A SWEET CANDIDATE.—Mark Twain, who was to make such a blighting speech at the mass meeting of the Independents last night, didn't come to time! A telegram from his physician stated that he had been knocked down by a runaway team and his leg broken in two places—sufferer lying in great agony, and so forth, and so forth, and a lot more bosh of the same sort. And the Independents tried hard to swallow the wretched subterfuge and pretend that they did not know what was the *real* reason of the absence of the abandoned creature whom they denominate their standard-bearer. *A certain man was seen to reel into Mr. Twain's hotel last night in a state of beastly intoxication.* It is the imperative duty of the Independents to prove that this besotted brute was not Mark Twain himself. We have them at last! This is a case that admits of no shirking. The voice of the people demands in thunderous tones: "WHO WAS THAT MAN?"

It was incredible, absolutely incredible, for a moment, that it was really my name that was coupled with this disgraceful suspicion. Three long years had passed over my head since I had tasted ale, beer, wine, or liquor of any kind.

[It shows what effect the times were having on me when I say that I saw myself confidently dubbed "Mr. Delirium Tremens Twain" in the next issue of that journal without a pang—notwithstanding I knew that with monotonous fidelity the paper would go on calling me so to the very end.]

By this time anonymous letters were getting to be an important part of my mail matter. This form was common:

How about that old woman you kiked of your premises which was beging.
Pol Pry.

And this:

There is things which you have done which is unbeknowens to anybody but me. You better trot out a few dols. to yours truly or you'll hear thro' the papers from
Handy Andy.

That is about the idea. I could continue them till the reader was surfeited, if desirable.

Shortly the principal Republican journal "convicted" me of wholesale bribery, and the leading Democratic paper "nailed" an aggravated case of blackmailing to me.

[In this way I acquired two additional names: "Twain, the Filthy Corruptionist," and "Twain, the Loathsome Embracer."]

By this time there had grown to be such a clamor for an "answer" to all the dreadful charges that were laid to me, that the editors and leaders of my party said it would be political ruin for me to remain silent any longer. As if to make their appeal the more imperative, the following appeared in one of the papers the very next day:

> BEHOLD THE MAN!—The Independent candidate still maintains silence. Because he dare not speak. Every accusation against him has been amply proved, and they have been endorsed and re-endorsed by his own eloquent silence till at this day he stands forever convicted. Look upon your candidate, Independents! Look upon the Infamous Perjurer! the Montana Thief! the Body Snatcher! Contemplate your Incarnate Delirium Tremens! your Filthy Corruptionist! your Loathsome Embracer! Gaze upon him—ponder him well—and then say if you can give your honest votes to a creature who has earned this dismal array of titles by his hideous crimes, and dares not open his mouth in denial of any one of them!

There was no possible way of getting out of it, and so, in deep humiliation I set about preparing to "answer" a mass of baseless charges and mean and wicked falsehoods. But I never finished the task, for the very next morning a paper came out with a new horror, a fresh malignity, and seriously charged me with burning a lunatic asylum with all its inmates because it obstructed a view from my house. This threw me into a sort of panic. Then came the charge of poisoning my uncle to get his property, with an imperative demand that the grave should be opened. This drove me to the verge of distraction. On top of this I was accused of employing toothless and incompetent old relatives to prepare the food for the foundling hospital when I was warden. I was wavering—wavering. And at last, as a due and fitting climax to the shameless persecution that party rancor had inflicted upon me, nine little toddling children of all shades of color and degrees of raggedness were taught to rush on the platform at a public meeting and clasp me around the legs and call me PA!

I gave up. I hauled down my colors and surrendered. I was not equal to the requirements of a Gubernatorial campaign in the State of New York, and so I sent in my withdrawal from the candidacy, and in bitterness of spirit signed it,

"Truly yours,
"*Once* a decent man, but now
"Mark Twain, I.P., M.T., B.S., D.T., F.C., and L.E."

November 26, 1870

My Watch—
An Instructive Little Tale

My beautiful new watch had run eighteen months without losing or gaining, and without breaking any part of its machinery or stopping.[222] I had come to believe it infallible in its judgments about the time of day, and to consider its constitution and its anatomy imperishable. But at last, one night, I let it run down. I grieved about it as if it were a recognized messenger and forerunner of calamity. But by and by I cheered up, set the watch by guess, and commanded my bodings and superstition to depart. Next day I stepped into the chief jeweller's to set it by the exact time, and the head of the establishment took it out of my hand and proceeded to set it for me. Then he said, "She is four minutes slow—regulator wants pushing up." I tried to stop him—tried to make him understand that the watch kept perfect time. But no; all this human cabbage could see was that the watch was four minutes slow, and the regulator *must* be pushed up a little; and so, while I danced around him in anguish and beseeched him to let the watch alone, he calmly and cruelly did the shameful deed. My watch began to gain. It gained faster and faster day by day. Within the week it sickened to a raging fever, and its pulse went up to a hundred and fifty in the shade. At the end of two months it had left all the timepieces of the town far in the rear, and was a fraction over thirteen days ahead of the almanac. It was away into November enjoying the snow, while the October leaves were still turning. It hurried up house-rent, bills payable, and such things, in such a ruinous way that I could not abide it. I took it to the watchmaker to be regulated.

He asked me if I had ever had it repaired. I said no, it had never needed any repairing. He looked a look of vicious happiness and eagerly pried the watch open, then put a small dice-box into his eye and peered into its machinery. He said it wanted cleaning and oiling, besides regulating—come in a week. After being cleaned and oiled and regulated, my watch slowed down to that degree that it ticked like a tolling bell. I began to be left by trains, I failed all appointments, I got to missing my dinner; my watch strung out three days' grace to four and let me go to protest; I gradually drifted back into yesterday, then day before, then into last week, and by and by the comprehension came upon me that all solitary and alone I was lingering along in week before last, and the world was out of sight. I seemed to detect in myself a sort of sneaking, fellow-feeling for the mummy in the museum, and a desire to swap news with him. I went to a watchmaker again. He took the watch all to pieces while I waited, and then said the barrel was "swelled." He said he could reduce it in three days. After this, the watch *averaged* well, but nothing more. For half a day it would go like the very mischief, and keep up such a barking and wheezing and whooping and sneezing and snorting, that I could not hear myself think for the disturbance; and as long as it held out, there was not a watch in the land that stood any chance against it. But the rest of the day it would keep on slowing down and fooling along until all the clocks it had left behind caught up again. So at last, at the end of twenty-four hours, it would trot up to the judges' stand all right and just on time. It would show a fair and square average, and no man could say it had done more or less than its duty. But a correct average is only a mild virtue in a watch, and I took this instrument to another watchmaker. He said the kingbolt was broken. I said I was glad it was nothing more serious. To tell the plain truth, I had no idea what the kingbolt was, but I did not choose to appear ignorant to a stranger. He repaired the kingbolt, but what the watch gained in one way it lost in another. It would run awhile and then stop awhile, and then run awhile again, and so on, using its own discretion about the intervals. And every time it went off it kicked back like a musket. I padded my breast for a few days, but finally took the watch to another watchmaker. He picked it all to pieces and turned the ruin over and over under his glass; and then he said there appeared to be something the matter with the hair-trigger. He fixed it, and gave it a fresh start. It did well now, except that always at ten minutes to ten the hands would shut together like a pair of scissors, and from that time forth they would travel together. The oldest man in the world could not make head or tail of the time of day by such a watch, and so I went again to have the thing repaired. This person said that the crystal had got bent, and that the main spring was not straight. He also remarked that part of the works needed half-soling. He made these things all right, and then my timepiece performed unexceptionably, save that now and then, after working along quietly for nearly eight hours, everything inside would let go all of a sudden and begin to buzz like a bee, and the hands would straightway begin to spin round and round so fast that their individuality was lost completely, and they simply seemed a delicate spider's web over the face of the watch. She would reel off the next twenty-four hours in six or seven minutes, and then stop with a bang. I went with a heavy heart to one more watchmaker, and looked on while he took her to pieces. Then I prepared to cross-question him rigidly, for this thing was getting serious. The watch had cost two hundred dollars originally, and I seemed to have paid out two or three thousand for repairs. While I waited and looked on, I presently recognized in this watchmaker an old acquaintance—a steamboat engineer of other days, and not a good engineer either. He examined all the parts carefully, just as the other watchmakers had done, and then delivered his verdict with the same confidence of manner.

He said:

"She makes too much steam—you want to hang the monkey-wrench on the safety-valve!"

I brained him on the spot, and had him buried at my own expense.

My uncle William (now deceased, alas!) used to say that a good horse was a good horse until it had run away once, and that a good watch was a good watch until the repairers got a chance at it. And he used to wonder what became of all the unsuccessful tinkers, and gunsmiths, and shoemakers, and blacksmiths; but nobody could ever tell him.—*Mark Twain*

An Entertaining Article

I take the following paragraph from an article in the Boston "Advertiser":223

> AN ENGLISH CRITIC ON MARK TWAIN.—Perhaps the most successful flights of the humor of Mark Twain have been descriptions of the persons who did not appreciate his humor at all. We have become familiar with the Californians who were thrilled with terror by his burlesque of a newspaper reporter's way of telling a story, and we have heard of the Pennsylvania clergyman who sadly returned his "Innocents Abroad" to the book-agent with the remark that "the man who could shed tears over the tomb of Adam must be an idiot." But Mark Twain may now add a much more glorious instance to his string of trophies. The "Saturday Review," in its number of October 8, reviews his book of travels, which has been republished in England, and reviews it seriously. We can imagine the delight of the humorist in reading this tribute to his power; and indeed it is so amusing in itself that he can hardly do better than reproduce the article in full in his next monthly Memoranda.

[Publishing the above paragraph thus, gives me a sort of authority for reproducing the "Saturday Review's" article in full in these pages. I dearly wanted to do it, for I cannot write anything half so delicious myself. If I had a cast-iron dog that could read this English criticism and preserve his austerity, I would drive him off the doorstep.—EDITOR MEMORANDA.]

[From the *London Saturday Review*.]

REVIEWS OF NEW BOOKS.

THE INNOCENTS ABROAD. A Book of Travels. By Mark Twain. London: Hotten, publisher. 1870.

Lord Macaulay died too soon. We never felt this so deeply as when we finished the last chapter of the above-named extravagant work. Macaulay died too soon—for none but he could mete out complete and comprehensive justice to the insolence, the impertinence, the presumption, the mendacity, and, above all, the majestic ignorance of this author.

To say that the "Innocents Abroad" is a curious book, would be to use the faintest language—would be to speak of the Matterhorn as a neat elevation, or of Niagara as being "nice" or "pretty." "Curious" is too tame a word wherewith to describe the imposing insanity of this work. There is no word that is large enough or long enough. Let us, therefore, photograph a passing glimpse of the book and author, and trust the rest to the reader. Let the cultivated English student of human nature picture to himself this Mark Twain as a person capable of doing the following-described things—and not only doing them, but with incredible innocence *printing them* calmly and tranquilly in a book. For instance:

He states that he entered a hair-dresser's in Paris to get shaved, and the first "rake" the barber gave with his razor it *loosened his "hide" and lifted him out of the chair.*

This is unquestionably exaggerated. In Florence he was so annoyed by beggars that he pretends to have seized and eaten on in a frantic spirit of revenge. There is of course no truth in this. He gives at full length a theatrical programme seventeen or eighteen hundred years old, which he professes to have found in the Coliseum, among the dirt and mould and rubbish. It is sufficient comment upon this statement to remark that even a cast-iron programme would not have lasted so long under such circumstances. In Greece he plainly betrays both fright and flight upon one occasion, but with frozen effrontery puts the latter in this falsely tame form: "We *sidled* toward the Piraeus." "Sidled," indeed! He does not hesitate to intimate that at Ephesus, when his mule strayed from the proper course, he got down, took him under his arm, carried him to the road again, pointed him right, remounted, and went to sleep contentedly till it was time to restore the beast to the path once more. He states that a growing youth among the ship's passengers was in the constant habit of appeasing his hunger with soap and oakum between meals. In Palestine he tells of ants that came eleven miles to spend the summer in the desert and brought their provisions with them; yet he shows by his description of the country that the feat was an impossibility. He mentions, as if it were the most commonplace of matters, that he cut a Moslem in two in broad daylight in Jerusalem, with Godfrey de Bouillon's sword, and would have shed more blood *if he had had a graveyard of his own.* These statements are unworthy a moment's attention. Mr. Twain or any other foreigner who did such a thing in Jerusalem would be mobbed, and would infallibly have lost his life. But why go on? Why repeat more of his audacious and exasperating falsehoods? Let us close fittingly with this one: he affirms that "in the mosque of St. Sophia at Constantinople I got my feet so stuck up with a complication of gums, slime, and general impurity, that *I wore out more than two thousand pair of bootjacks* getting my boots off that night, and even then some Christian hide peeled off with them." It is monstrous. Such statements are simply *lies*—there is no other name for them. Will the reader longer marvel at the brutal ignorance that pervades the American nation when we tell him that we are informed upon perfectly good authority that this extravagant compilation of falsehoods, this exhaustless mine of stupendous lies, this "Innocents Abroad," has actually been adopted by the schools and colleges of several of the States as a text-book!

But if his falsehoods are distressing, his innocence and his ignorance are enough to make one burn the book and despise the author. In one place he was so appalled at the sudden spectacle of a murdered man, unveiled by the moonlight, that he jumped out of a window, going through sash and all, and then remarks with the most childlike simplicity that he "was not scared, but was considerably agitated." It puts us out of patience to note that the simpleton is densely unconscious that Lucretia Borgia ever existed off the stage. He is vulgarly ignorant of all foreign languages, but is frank enough to criticise the Italians' use of their own tongue. He says they spell the name of their great painter "Vinci, but pronounce it Vinchy"—and then adds with a naïveté possible only to helpless ignorance, *"foreigners always spell better than they pronounce."* In another place he commits the bald absurdity of putting the phrase "tare an ouns" into an Italian's mouth. In Rome he unhesitatingly believes the legend that St. Philip Neri's heart was so inflamed with divine love that it burst his ribs—believes it wholly because an author with a learned list of university degrees strung after his name endorses it—"otherwise," says this gentle idiot, "I should have felt a curiosity to know what Philip had for dinner." Our author makes a long, fatiguing journey to the Grotto del Cane on purpose to test its poisoning powers on a dog—got elaborately ready for the experiment, and then discovered that he had no dog. A wiser person would have kept such a thing discretely to himself, but with this harmless creature everything comes out. He hurts his foot in a rut two thousand years old in exhumed Pompeii, and presently, when staring at one of the cinder-like corpses unearthed in the next square, conceives the idea that may be it is the remains of the ancient Street Commissioner, and straightway his horror softens down to a sort of chirpy contentment with the condition of things. In Damascus he visits the well of Ananias, three thousand years old, and is as surprised and delighted as a child to find that the water is "as pure and fresh as if the well had been dug yesterday." In the Holy Land he gags desperately at the hard Arabic and Hebrew Biblical names, and finally concludes to call them Baldwinsville, Williamsburg, and so on, *for convenience of spelling!*"

We have thus spoken freely of this man's stupefying simplicity and innocence, but we cannot deal similarly with his colossal ignorance. We do not know where to begin. And if we did know where to begin, we certainly would not know where to leave off. We will give one specimen, and one only. He did not know until he got to Rome, that Michael Angelo was dead! And then, instead of crawling away and hiding his shameful ignorance somewhere, he proceeds to express a pious, grateful sort of satisfaction that he is gone and out of his troubles!

No, the reader may seek out the author's exhibitions of his uncultivation for himself. The book is absolutely dangerous, considering the magnitude and variety of its misstatements, and the convincing confidence with which they are made. And yet it is a text-book in the schools of America.

The poor blunderer mouses among the sublime creations of the Old Masters, trying to acquire the elegant proficiency in art-knowledge, which he has a groping sort of comprehension is a proper sort of thing for the travelled man to be able to display. But what is the manner of his study? And what is the progress he achieves? To what extent does he familiarize himself with the great pictures of Italy, and what degree of appreciation does he arrive at? Read:

> When we see a monk going about with a lion and looking up into heaven, we know that that is St. Mark. When we see a monk with a book and pen, looking tranquilly up to heaven, trying to think of a word, we know that that is St. Matthew. When we see a monk sitting on a rock, looking tranquilly up to heaven, with a human skull beside him and without other baggage, we know that that is St. Jerome. Because we know that he always went flying light in the matter of baggage. When we see other monks looking tranquilly up to heaven, but having no trade-mark, we always ask who those parties are. We do this because we humbly wish to learn.

He then enumerates the thousands and thousands of copies of these several pictures which he has seen, and adds with accustomed simplicity that he feels encouraged to believe that when he has seen "SOME MORE" of each, and had a larger experience, he will eventually "begin to take an absorbing interest in them"—the vulgar boor.

That we have shown this to be a remarkable book, we think no one will deny. That it is a pernicious book to place in the hands of the confiding and uninformed, we think we have also shown. That the book is a deliberate and wicked creation of a diseased mind, is apparent upon every page. Having placed our judgment thus upon record, let us close with what charity we can, by remarking that even in this volume there is some good to be found; for whenever the author talks of his own country and lets Europe alone, he never fails to make himself interesting; and not only interesting, but instructive. No one can read without benefit his occasional chapters and paragraphs, about life in the gold and silver mines of California and Nevada; about the Indians of the plains and deserts of the West, and their cannibalism; about the raising of vegetables in kegs of gunpowder by the aid of two or three teaspoonfuls of guano; about the moving of small farms from place to place at night in wheelbarrows to avoid taxes; and about a sort of cows and mules that climb down the chimneys and disturb the people at night. These matters are not only new, but they are well worth knowing.* It is a pity the author did not put in more of the same kind. His book is well written and is exceedingly entertaining, and so it just barely escaped being quite valuable also.

* Yes, I calculated they were pretty new. I invented them myself. —*Mark Twain*

December 10, 1870

Dogberry in Washington

Some of the decisions of the Post Office Department are eminently luminous.[224] It has in times gone by been enacted that "author's manuscript"[225] should go through the mails for a trifling postage—newspaper postage, in fact. A calm and dispassionate mind would gather from this, that the object had in view was to facilitate and foster newspaper correspondence, magazine writing, and literature generally, by discontinuing a tax in the way of postage which had become very burdensome to gentlemen of the quill. Now by what effort of good old well-meaning, grandmotherly dullness does the reader suppose the postal authorities have rendered that wise and kindly decree utterly null and void and solemnly funny? By deciding that "author's manuscript" does not mean anything but *manuscript intended to be made into a* BOUND BOOK!"—all pamphlets, magazines, and newspapers ruled out!

Thus we are expected to believe that the original regulation was laboriously got up to save *two dollars' worth of postage to two authors in a year*—for probably not more than that number of MS. books are sent by mail to publishers each year. Such property is too precious to trust to any conveyance but the author's own carpet-sack, as a general thing.

But granting that one thousand MS. books went to the publishers in a year, and thus saved to one thousand authors a dollar apiece in postage in the twelve months, would not a law whose whole aim was to accomplish such a trifle as that be simply an irreverent pleasantry, and not proper company to thrust among grave and weighty statutes in the law-books?

The matter which suggested these remarks can be stated in a sentence. Once or twice I have sent magazine MSS. from certain cities, on newspaper rates, as "author's MS." But in Buffalo the postmaster requires full letter postage. He claims no authority for this save *decisions* of the Post Office Department. He showed me the law itself, but even the highest order of intellectual obscurity, backed by the largest cultivation (outside of a Post Office Department), could not find in it authority for the "decisions" aforementioned. And I ought to know, because I tried it myself. [I say that, not to be trivially facetious when talking in earnest, but merely to take the word out of the mouths of certain cheap witlings, who always stand ready in any company to interrupt any one whose remarks offer a chance for the exhibition of their poor wit and worse manners.]

I will not say one word about this curious decision, or utter one sarcasm or one discourteous speech about it, or the well-intending but misguided officer who rendered it; but if he were in California, he would fare far differently—very far differently—for there the wicked are not restrained by the gentle charities that prevail in Buffalo, and so they would deride him, and point the finger of scorn at him, and address him as "Old Smarty from Mud Springs." Indeed they would.

. . .

"Ouizquiz" hurls me this, under New York postmark: "I met last night on the Podunk Railroad an individual whose characteristics are best indicated by what follows:

"I handed him the *Galaxy* directing his attention to your map of Paris. He read your explanations through deliberately, and when he came to that part where you advised standing on the head or the use of a looking glass in order to see it properly, he turned to a careful consideration of the map. Holding up the sheet to the light, he looked through the *reverse side* and exclaimed "'Why, all that ain't necessary, after all! All you've got to do is to look at it the wrong way, and it makes it all right.' He read the remainder of your explanation, including certificates, and then returned to the profound study of the map. After a while he burst out:

"'Why here's a thing that's wrong, anyhow! You can't get Omaha on the west and Jersey City on the east. They're both west. I don't care who says it's right, I say.'

"I mildly suggested that Jersey City and Omaha were a long way apart, and probably the *longitude* had something to do with it: for it was impossible to suppose such military critics as General Grant and General Sherman would not have detected the blunder if it were one.

"He pondered some time. 'Ah!' he said finally, 'It must be the longitude, for you see if you go round the world one way you might get Omaha on the west; while if you went round from Jersey City the other way, you'd get that on the east. I see it; it's the longitude does it'"

. . .

The above mention of my map of Paris calls to mind that that work of art is appreciated among the learned. It is duly advertised that whoever sends a club of one hundred subscribers to the Yale College "Courant"—together with the necessary four hundred dollars—will receive as a prize a copy of my map! I am almost tempted to go canvassing myself.—*Mark Twain*

December 16, 1870

War and "Wittles"

The immense superiority of the French in the art of cookery has already been universally conceded, and if the present siege should produce for them no other national advantage it will at least have helped to place them still farther ahead of any aspiring rivals in this most useful specialty.[226] If misfortune makes a man acquainted with

strange bed-fellows on ordinary occasions, that phase of it which
arises from a state of famine none the less brings him into novel colli-
sion with strange dishes. It is now authenticated that the magnificent
collection of foreign animals which formerly adorned the Jardin des
Plantes has already been confiscated to meet the hungry needs of a
portion of a beleaguered population. That famous restaurant, the
Trois Freres, for some days had on its *carte* an extraordinary variety
of extraordinary dishes. Giraffe cutlets, rhinoceros steaks, and ragout
of kangaroo had become positively common, and many other gastro-
nomic "treats," equally novel, for a time furnished forth the fashion-
able tables. But these zoological tid-bits were only reserved for the
wealthy. Less pretentious dishes alone fell to the commonality. The
latter had to content themselves with such ordinary *plats* as horse,
mule, donkey, cats, dogs, and rats—they don't appear yet to have con-
descended to mice—and the world-renowned skill of the French *cui-
sine* appears to have created a taste for these which has reached a
positive mania. People in Paris now-a-days are said to turn up their
noses at mere beef and mutton, and the late cessation of the supply of
mule-meat seems to be regarded as something little less than a capital misfortune. It would be doing scant justice to the white-capped
and white-aproned *chefs* who preside at the presentable preparation
of these dishes to suppose them unequal to the task of preparing new
sauces piquantes equal to the occasion. We have unhappily failed to
obtain anything like a correct list of these latter gustatory attractions, but the following may be truthfully accepted as a literal copy
(translated) of a bill of fare recently presented at a "gentleman's
table" in Paris. These represent luxuries, it should be borne in mind,
that are only accessible to fellows with good long purses:

BILL OF FARE

Horse Soup, with millet.
Minced Cat, Mayonnaise Sauce.
Shoulder of Dog, Tomato Sauce.
Jugged Cat, with Mushrooms.
Dog Chops, with Peas.
Salmis of Rat, Sauce Robert.
Joint of Dog, served with young Rats, and Pepper Sauce.
Begonia, with Gravy.
Salad, etc.
English Plum Pudding, with Horse-marrow.

It is a great relief to know, from one of the *convives,* that everybody present enjoyed the feast most heartily. Perhaps they may even have offered up an unselfish sigh of regret for those absent outsiders whose hapless ignorance had so far kept them unacquainted with these culinary delights. Verily there is no accounting for tastes. *[Unsigned]*

December 17, 1870

The Facts in the Case
of George Fisher, Deceased

This is history. It is not a wild extravaganza, like "John Williamson Mackenzie's Great Beef Contract,"[227] but is a plain statement of facts and circumstances with which the Congress of the United States has interested itself from time to time during the long period of half a century.

I will not call this matter of George Fisher's[228] a great deathless and unrelenting swindle upon the Government and people of the United States—for it has never been so decided, and I hold that it is a grave and solemn wrong for a writer to cast slurs or call names when such is the case—but will simply present the evidence and let the reader deduce his own verdict. Then we shall do nobody injustice, and our consciences shall be clear.

On or about the 1st day of September, 1813, the Creek war being then in progress in Florida, the crops, herds, and houses of Mr. George Fisher, a citizen, were destroyed, either by the Indians or by the United States troops in pursuit of them. By the terms of the law, if the *Indians* destroyed the property, there was no relief for Fisher; but if the *troops* destroyed it, the Government of the United States was debtor to Fisher for the amount involved.

George Fisher must have considered that the *Indians* destroyed the property, because although he lived several years afterward, he does not appear to have ever made any claim upon the Government.

In the course of time Fisher died, and his widow married again. And by and by, nearly twenty years after that dimly-remembered raid upon Fisher's cornfields, *the widow Fisher's new husband* petitioned Congress for pay for the property, and backed up the petition with many depositions and affidavits which purported to prove that the troops, and not the Indians, destroyed the property; that the troops, for some inscrutable reason, deliberately burned down "houses" (or cabins) valued at $600, the same belonging to a peaceable private citizen, and also destroyed various other property belonging to the same citizen. But Congress declined to believe that the troops were such idiots (after overtaking and scattering a band of Indians proved to have been found destroying Fisher's property) as to calmly continue the work of destruction themselves and make a complete job of what the Indians had only commenced. So Congress denied the petition of the heirs of George Fisher in 1832, and did not pay them a cent.

We hear no more from them officially until 1848, sixteen years after their first attempt on the Treasury, and a full generation after the death of the man whose fields were destroyed. The new generation of Fisher heirs then came forward and put in a bill for damages. The Second Auditor awarded them $8,873, being half the damage sustained by Fisher. The Auditor said the testimony showed that at least half the destruction was done by the Indians *"before the troops started in pursuit,"* and of course the government was not responsible for that half.

2. That was in April, 1848. In December, 1848, the heirs of George Fisher, deceased, came forward and pleaded for a "revision" of their bill of damages. The revision was made, but nothing new could be found in their favor except an error of $100 in the former calculation. However, in order to keep up the spirits of the Fisher family, the Auditor concluded to go back and allow interest from the date of the first petition (1832) to the date when the bill of damages was awarded. This sent the Fishers home happy with sixteen years' interest on $8,873—the same amounting to $8,997.94. Total $17,870.94.

3. For an entire year the suffering Fisher family remained quiet— even satisfied, after a fashion. Then they swooped down upon government with their wrongs once more. That old patriot, Attorney-General Toucey, burrowed through the musty papers of the Fishers and discovered one more chance for the desolate orphans—interest on that original award of $8,873 from date of destruction of the property (1813) up to 1832! Result, $10,004.89 for the indigent Fishers. So now we have: First, $8,873 damages; second, interest on it from 1832 to 1848, $8,997.94, third, interest on it dated back to 1813, $10,004.89. Total, $27,875.83! What better investment for a great-grandchild than to get the Indians to burn a cornfield for him sixty or seventy years before his birth, and plausibly lay it on lunatic United States troops?

4. Strange as it may seem, the Fishers let Congress alone for five years—or, what is perhaps more likely, failed to make themselves heard by Congress for that length of time. But at last, in 1854, they

got a hearing. They persuaded Congress to pass an act requiring the Auditor to re-examine their case. But this time they stumbled on the misfortune of an honest Secretary of the Treasury (Mr. James Guthrie), and he spoiled everything. He said in very plain language that the Fishers were not only not entitled to another cent, but that those children of many sorrows and acquainted with grief *had been paid too much already.*

5. Therefore, another interval of rest and silence ensued—an interval which lasted four years, viz., till 1858. The "right man in the right place" was then Secretary of War—John B. Floyd, of peculiar renown! Here was a master intellect; here was the very man to succor the suffering heirs of dead and forgotten Fisher. They came up from Florida with a rush—a great tidal wave of Fishers freighted with the same old musty documents about the same immortal cornfields of their ancestor. They straightway got an act passed transferring the Fisher matter from the dull Auditor to the ingenious Floyd. What did Floyd do? He said "IT WAS PROVED *that the Indians destroyed everything they could before the troops entered in pursuit."* He considered, therefore, that what they destroyed must have consisted of *"the houses with all their contents, and the liquor"* (the most trifling part of the destruction, and set down at only $3,200 all told), and that the government troops then drove them off and calmly proceeded to destroy—

Two hundred and twenty acres of corn in the field, thirty-five acres of wheat, and nine hundred and eighty-six head of live stock! [What a singularly intelligent army we had in those days, according to Mr. Floyd—though not according to the Congress of 1832.]

So Mr. Floyd decided that the government was not responsible for that $3,200 worth of rubbish which the Indians destroyed, but was responsible for the property destroyed by the troops—which property consisted of (I quote from the printed U.S. Senate document)—

Corn at Bassett's Creek	$3,000
Cattle	5,000
Stock hogs	1,050
Drove hogs	1,204
Wheat	350
Hides	4,000
Corn on the Alabama River	3,500
Total	18,104

That sum, in his report, Mr. Floyd calls the *"full value* of the property destroyed by the troops." He allows that sum to the starving Fishers, TOGETHER WITH INTEREST FROM 1813. From this new sum total the amounts already paid to the Fishers were deducted, and then the cheerful remainder (a fraction under *forty thousand dollars*) was handed to them, and again they returned to Florida in a condition of temporary tranquility. Their ancestor's farm had now yielded them, altogether, nearly *sixty-seven thousand dollars* in cash.

6. Does the reader suppose that that was the end of it? Does he suppose those diffident Fishers were satisfied? Let the evidence show. The Fishers were quiet just two years. Then they came swarming up out of the fertile swamps of Florida with their same old documents, and besieged Congress once more. Congress capitulated on the first of June, 1860, and instructed Mr. Floyd to overhaul those papers again, and pay that bill. A Treasury clerk was ordered to go through those papers and report to Mr. Floyd what amount was still due to the emaciated Fishers. This clerk (I can produce him whenever he is wanted) discovered what was apparently a glaring and recent forgery in the papers, whereby a witness's testimony as to the price of corn in Florida in 1813 was made to name double the amount which the witness had originally specified as a price! The clerk not only called his superior's attention to this thing, but in making up his brief of the case called particular attention to it in writing. That part of the brief *never got before Congress,* nor has Congress ever yet had a hint of a forgery existing among the Fisher papers. Nevertheless, on the basis of the doubled prices (and totally ignoring the clerk's assertion that the figures were manifestly and unquestionably a recent forgery), Mr. Floyd remarks in his new report that "the testimony, *particularly in regard to the corn crops,* DEMANDS A MUCH HIGHER ALLOWANCE than any *heretofore* made by the Auditor or myself." So he estimates the crop at *sixty bushels* to the acre (double what Florida acres produce), and then virtuously allows pay for only half the crop, *but* allows *two dollars and a half* a bushel for that half, when there are rusty old books and documents in the Congressional library to show just what the Fisher testimony showed before the forgery, viz.: that in the Fall of 1813 corn was only worth from $1.25 to $1.50 a bushel. Having accomplished this, what does Mr. Floyd do next? Mr. Floyd ("with an earnest desire to execute truly the legislative will," as he piously remarks) goes to work and makes out an entirely new bill of Fisher damages, and in this new bill he placidly *ignores the Indians* altogether—puts no particle of the

destruction of the Fisher property upon them, but, even repenting him of charging them with burning the cabins and drinking the whisky and breaking the crockery, lays the *entire* damage at the door of the imbecile United States troops, down to the very last item! And not only that, but uses the forgery to double the loss of corn at "Bassett's creek," and uses it again to absolutely *treble* the loss of corn on the "Alabama river." This new and ably conceived and executed bill of Mr. Floyd's figures up as follows (I copy again from the printed U.S. Senate document:

The United States in account with the legal representatives of George Fisher, deceased.

1813—To 550 head of cattle, at $10	$5,500.00
To 86 head of drove hogs	1,204.00
To 350 head of stock hogs	1,750.00
To 100 ACRES OF CORN ON BASSETT'S CREEK	6,000.00
To 8 barrels of whisky	350.00
To 2 barrels of brandy	280.00
To 1 barrel of rum	70.00
To dry goods and merchandise in store	1,100.00
To 35 acres of wheat	350.00
To 2,000 hides	4,000.00
To furs and hats in store	600.00
To crockery ware in store	100.00
To smiths' and carpenters' tools	250.00
To houses burned and destroyed	600.00
To 4 dozen bottles of wine	48.00
1814—To 120 acres of corn on Alabama River	9,500.00
To crops of peas, fodder, etc	3,250.00
Total	34,952.00

To interest on $22,202,
from July, 1813, to November, 1860,
47 years and 4 months 63,053.68

To interest on $12,750,
from September, 1814 to November, 1860,
46 years and two months 35,317.50

Total $133,323.18

He puts everything in, this time. He does not even allow that the Indians destroyed the crockery or drank the four dozen bottles of (currant) wine. When it came to supernatural comprehensiveness in "gobbling," John B. Floyd was without his equal in his own or any other generation. Subtracting from the above total the $67,000 already paid to George Fisher's implacable heirs, Mr. Floyd announced that the government was still indebted to them in the sum of *sixty-six thousand five hundred and nineteen dollars and eighty-five cents,* "which," Mr. Floyd complacently remarks, "will be paid, accordingly, to the administrator of the estate of George Fisher, deceased, or to his attorney in fact."

But, sadly enough for the destitute orphans, a new President came in just at this time, Buchanan and Floyd went out, and they never got the money. The first thing Congress did in 1861 was to rescind the resolution of June 1, 1860, under which Mr. Floyd had been ciphering. Then Floyd (and doubtless the heirs of George Fisher likewise) had to give up financial business for a while and go into the Confederate army and serve their country.

Were the heirs of George Fisher killed? No. They are back now at this very time (July, 1870), beseeching Congress, through that blushing and diffident creature, Garrett Davis, to commence making payments again on their interminable and insatiable bill of damages for corn and whisky destroyed by a gang of irresponsible Indians, so long ago that even government red-tape has failed to keep consistent and intelligent track of it. (And before this number of the *Galaxy* reaches Washington, Mr. Davis will be getting ready to resurrect it once more, and alter his customary speech on finance, war, and other matters so that it will fit it.)

Now, the above are facts. They are history. Any one who doubts it can send to the Senate Document Department of the Capitol for H.R. Ex. Doc. No. 21, 36th Congress, 2d Session, and for S. Ex. Doc. No. 106, 41st Congress, 2d Session, and satisfy himself. The whole case is set forth in the first volume of the Court of Claims Reports.

It is my belief that as long as the continent of America holds together, the heirs of George Fisher, deceased, will still make pilgrimage to Washington from the swamps of Florida, to plead for just a little more cash on their bill of damages (even when they received the last of that sixty-seven thousand dollars, they said it was only *one-fourth* what the government owed them on that infernal cornfield); and as long as they choose to come, they will find Garrett Davises to drag their vampire schemes before Congress. This is not the only hereditary fraud (if fraud it is—which I have before repeatedly remarked is not proven) that is being quietly handed down from generation to generation of fathers and sons, through the persecuted Treasury of the United States.—*Mark Twain*

December 19, 1870

"Waiting for the Verdict"

Almost everybody finds himself periodically stumbling over a paragraph, with a fine flavor of antiquity about it, embodying a queer account of the manner of dispensing justice in some primitive region. The West or Southwest is generally favored by selection as the theatre where these grotesque scenes are represented as having been enacted. Many of them, however, are fine old resurrectionised Millerisms[229] which were in circulation ages ago, and long before any settlement whatever had reached the spot where, in their new shape, they are represented as having been just performed. Who is there that has not read the time-honored joke of the incriminated prisoner, more at home with a blackthorn than with Blackstone,[230] who availed himself of his privilege of "challenging the jury" by calling out the whole twelve of the "good men and true," and offering to fight the judge in the bargain? Something a good deal like it—only "rather more so"—has just actually taken place, during the present month, in the good city of San Francisco. But this new episode varies materially from the illustrious predecessor in the fact that the little unpleasantness occurred within what should have been the placid interior of the jury-chamber itself. The occasion was a murder trial, and, as is not unusual even outside of California, the twelve citizens who held the life of the arraigned in their hands could not agree on a decision. The public waited impatiently and vainly for the unconscionable period of ninety-six hours, during the whole of which the wretched dozen martyrs who formed the jury were under lock and key. The termination of four entire days found them no nearer an agreement than the commencement, and with no prospect whatever of reaching a verdict. We judge by the account of the proceedings in a leading local journal that the traditional resort to a game of cards or a "toss up," was unfortunately in this case not had. It was probably suggested, and declined, by the one obstinate juryman who held his eleven colleagues in thrall. The majority appear to have tardily recognized that the time had at length come when some energetic measures were called for to put an end to the perplexity. Patience had ceased, in their opinion, or at least one of them, to be a virtue. And the wrath-provoking juror, William Hosford, related in open court the resolve that was made for his immolation in order to relieve the impatience of his colleagues. He stated to the presiding judges that one of his coadjurors, H. C. Howard, went over to what should have been his place of repose, and threatened that if he did not immediately agree to a verdict of conviction he (Howard) would then and there incontinently shoot him (Hosford) or cut him to pieces! It must be stated for the honor of Hosford that he made this declaration less from any miserable apprehension of unpleasant bodily consequences to himself than as a convenient avenue through which he might submit to the judge a knotty legal question which he admitted had very much perplexed him. He desired to be informed what legal validity would attach to a verdict so obtained. The court proved "hisself" quite equal to the occasion, and with an admirable presence of mind told Mr. Howard that his course was not a strictly correct one, and that he ought to have known better. But the important legal issue raised by Hosford was certainly not fairly met. It may indeed be truthfully stated that it was weakly evaded. His Honor, however, requested the bloody-minded Howard at once and there and then to lay down his arms. None but Howard knows "how hard" was this command, but he "shelled out" his arsenal, consisting of a few trifles in the way of pistols and bowie-knives. The court then decided to dismiss the jury and have a new trial, and it is to be hoped that, now that Howard is again breathing the free air of heaven outside of the Court House he will allow the too conscientious Hosford to wend his way in peace, leaving to the expiation of his crime to some other murderous bullet. The self-denial should be the less difficult as he must know that, as society is at present constituted in California, he will not have to wait long. *[Unsigned]*

December 24, 1870

A Sad, Sad Business

Latterly I have received several letters, and seen a number of newspaper paragraphs, all upon a certain subject, and all of about the same tenor. I here give honest specimens. One is from a New York paper, one is from a letter from an old friend, and one is from a New

York publisher who is a stranger to me. I humbly endeavor to make these bits toothsome with the remark that the article they are praising (which appeared in the December *Galaxy,* and *pretended* to be a criticism from the London "Saturday Review" on my "Innocents Abroad") *was written by myself—every line of it:*[231]

> The "Herald" says the richest thing out is the "serious critique" in the London "Saturday Review," on Mark Twain's "Innocents Abroad." We thought before we read it that it must be "serious," as everybody said so, and were even ready to shed a few tears; but since perusing it, we are bound to confess that next to Mark Twain's "Jumping Frog" it's the finest bit of humor and sarcasm that we've come across in many a day.

[I do not get a compliment like that every day.]

> I used to think your writings were pretty good, but after reading the criticism in the *Galaxy* from the "London Review" have discovered what an ass I must have been. If suggestions are in order, mine is, that you put that article in your next edition of the "Innocents," as an extra chapter, if you are not afraid to put your own humor in competition with it. It is as rich a thing as I have ever read.

[Which is strong commendation from a book publisher.]

> The London reviewer, my friend, is not the stupid, "serious" creature he pretends to be, *I* think; but on the contrary, has a keen appreciation and enjoyment of your book. As I read his article in *The Galaxy*, I could imagine him giving vent to many a hearty laugh. But he is writing for Catholics and Established Church people, and high-toned, antiquated, conservative gentility, whom it is a delight to him to help you shock, while he pretends to shake his head with owlish density. He is a magnificent humorist himself.

[Now that is graceful and handsome. I take off my hat to my life-long friend and comrade, and with my feet together and my fingers spread over my heart, I say, in the language of Alabama, "You do me proud."]

I stand guilty of the authorship of the article, but I did not mean any harm. I saw by an item in the Boston "Advertiser" that a solemn, serious critique on the English edition of my book had appeared in the London "Saturday Review," and the idea of *such* a literary breakfast by a stolid, ponderous British ogre of the quill, was too much for a naturally weak virtue, and I went home and burlesqued it—revelled in it, I may say. I never saw a copy of the real "Saturday Review" criticism until after my burlesque was written and mailed to the printer. But when I did get hold of a copy, I found it be a vulgar, awkwardly written, ill-natured, and entirely serious and in earnest. The gentleman who wrote the newspaper paragraph above quoted had not been misled as to its character.

If any man doubts my word now, I will kill him. No, I will not kill him; I will win his money. I will bet him twenty to one, and let any New York publisher hold the stakes, that the statements I have above made as to the authorship of the article in question are entirely true. Perhaps I may get wealthy at this, for I am willing to take all the bets that offer; and if a man wants larger odds, I will give him all he requires. But he ought to find out whether I am betting on what is termed "a sure thing" or not before he ventures his money, and he can do that by going to a public library and examining the London "Saturday Review" of October 8, which contains the real critique.

Bless me, some people thought that *I* was the "sold" person!

P.S.—I cannot resist the temptation to toss in this most savory thing of all—this easy, graceful, philosophical disquisition, with its happy, chirping confidence. It is from the Cincinnati "Enquirer":

> Nothing is more uncertain than the value of a fine cigar. Nine smokers out of ten would prefer an ordinary domestic article, three for a quarter, to a fifty-cent Partaga, if kept in ignorance of the cost of the latter. The flavor of the Partaga is too delicate for palates that have been accustomed to Connecticut seed leaf. So it is with humor. The finer it is in quality, the more danger of its not being recognized at all. Even Mark Twain has been taken in by an English review of his "Innocents Abroad." Mark is by no means a coarse humorist, but the Englishman's humor is so much finer than his, that he mistakes it for solid earnest and "larfs most consumedly."

A man who cannot learn stands in his own light. Hereafter, when I write an article which I know to be good, but which I may have reason to fear will not, in some quarters, be considered to amount to much, coming from an American, I will aver that an Englishman wrote it, and that it's copied from a London journal. And then I will occupy a back seat and enjoy the cordial applause.—*Mark Twain*

Mean People

My ancient comrade, "Doesticks,"[232] in a letter from New York, quotes a printed paragraph concerning a story I used to tell to lecture audiences about a wonderfully mean man whom I used to know, and then Mr. D. throws himself into a passion and relates the following circumstance (writing on both sides of his paper, which is at least singular in a journalist, if not profane and indecent):[233]

> Now I don't think much of that. I know a better thing about old Captain Asa T. Mann of this town. You see, old Mann used to own and command a pickaninny, bull-headed, mud-turtle-shaped craft of a schooner that hailed from Perth Amboy. Old Mann used to prance out of his little cove where he kept his three-cent craft, and steal along the coast of the dangerous Kill von Kull, on the larboard side of Staten Island, to smouch oysters from unguarded beds, or pick clams off sloops where the watch had gone to bed drunk. Well, once old Mann went on a long voyage—for him. He went down to Virginia, taking his wife and little boy with him. The old rapscallion put on all sorts of airs, and pretended to keep up as strict discipline as if his craft was a man-of-war. One day his darling baby tumbled overboard. A sailor named Jones jumped over after him and after cavorting around about an hour or so, succeeded in getting the miserable little scion of a worthless sire on board again. Then old Mann got right up on his dignity—he put on all the dig he had handy—and in two minutes he had Jones into double irons, and there he kept him three weeks, in the fore hold, for *leaving the ship without orders.*

I will not resurrect my own mean man, for possibly he might not show to good advantage in the presence of this gifted sailor; but I will enter a Toledo bridegroom against the son of the salt wave, and let the winner take the money. I give the Toledo story just as it comes to me. (It, too, is written on both sides of the paper; but as this correspondent is not a journalist, the act is only wicked, not obscene.)

> In this village there lived, and continue to live, two chaps who in their bachelor days were chums. S., one of the chaps, tiring of single blessedness, took unto himself a wife and a wedding, with numerous pieces of silverware and things from congratulating friends. C., the other chap,

sent in a handsome silver ladle, costing several dollars or more. Their friendship continued. A year later C. also entered into partnership for life with one of the fair Eves; and he also had a wedding. S., being worth something less than $20,000, thought he ought to return the compliment of a wedding present, and a happy thought struck him. He took the ladle down to the jeweller from whom it was purchased by C. the year before, *and traded it off for silver salt dishes to present to C. and his bride. [Unsigned]*

January 29, 1871

The Danger of Lying in Bed

The man in the ticket office said:[234]

"Have an accident insurance ticket, also?"

"No," I said after studying the matter over a little. "No, I believe not; I am going to be travelling by rail to-day. However, to-morrow I don't travel. Give me one for to-morrow."

The man looked puzzled. He said:

"But it is for accident insurance, and if you are going to travel by rail—"

"If I am going to travel by rail, I shan't need it. Lying at home in bed is the thing *I* am afraid of."

I had been looking into this matter. Last year I travelled twenty thousand miles, almost entirely by rail; the year before, I travelled over twenty-five thousand miles, half by sea and half by rail; and in the year before that I travelled in the neighborhood of ten thousand miles, exclusively by rail. I suppose if I put in all the little odd journeys here and there, I may say I have travelled sixty thousand miles during the three years I have mentioned. *And never an accident.*

For a good while I said to myself every morning: "Now I have escaped thus far, and the chances are just that much increased that I shall catch it this time. I will be shrewd and buy an accident ticket." And to a dead moral certainty I drew a blank and went to bed that night without a joint started or a bone splintered. I got tired of that sort of daily bother, and fell to buying accident tickets that were good for a month. I said to myself, "A man *can't* buy thirty blanks in one bundle."

But I was mistaken. There was never a prize in the lot. I could read of railway accidents every day—the newspaper atmosphere was foggy with them; but somehow they never came my way. I found I had spent a good deal of money in the accident business, and had nothing to show for it. My suspicions were aroused, and I began to hunt around for somebody who had won in this lottery. I found plenty of people who had invested, but not an individual that had ever had an accident or made a cent. I stopped buying accident tickets and went to ciphering. The result was astounding. THE PERIL LAY NOT IN TRAVELLING, BUT IN STAYING AT HOME.

I hunted up statistics, and was amazed to find that after all the glaring newspaper headings concerning railroad disasters, less than *three hundred* people had really lost their lives by those disasters in the preceding twelve months. The Erie road was set down as the most murderous in the list. It had killed forty-six—or twenty-six, I do not remember exactly which, but I know the number was double that of any other road. But the fact straightway suggested itself that the Erie was an immensely long road, and did more business than any other line in the country; so the double number of killed ceased to be matter for surprise.

By further figuring, it appeared that between New York and Rochester the Erie ran eight passenger trains each way every day—sixteen altogether; and carried a daily average of 6,000 persons. That is about a million in six months—the population of New York city. Well, the Erie kills from thirteen to twenty-three persons out of *its* million in six months; and in the same time 13,000 of New York's million die in their beds! My flesh crept, my hair stood on end. "This is appalling!" I said. "The danger isn't in travelling by rail, but in trusting to those deadly beds. I will never sleep in a bed again."

I had figured on considerably less than one-half of the length of the Erie road. It was plain that the entire road must transport at least eleven or twelve thousand people every day. There are many short roads running out of Boston that do fully half as much; a great many such roads. There are a great many roads scattered about the Union that do a prodigious passenger business. Therefore it is fair to presume that an average of 2,500 passengers a day for each road in the country would be about correct. There are 846 railway lines in our country, and 846 times 2,500 are 2,115,000. So the railways of America move more than two millions of people every day; six hundred and fifty millions of people a year, without counting the Sundays. They do that, too—there is no question about it; though where they get the raw material is clear beyond the jurisdiction of my arithmetic; for I have hunted the census through and through, and I find that there are not that many people in the United States, by a matter of six hundred and ten millions at the very least. They must use some of the same people over again, likely.

San Francisco is one-eighth as populous as New York; there are 60 deaths a week in the former and 500 a week in the latter—if they have luck. That is 3,120 deaths a year in San Francisco, and eight times as many New York—say about 25,000 or 26,000. The health of the two places is the same. So we will let it stand as a fair presumption that this will hold good all over the country, and that consequently 25,000 out of every million of people we have must die every year. That amounts to one-fortieth of our total population. Out of this million ten or twelve thousand are stabbed, shot, drowned, hanged, poisoned, or meet a similarly violent death in some other popular way, such as perishing by kerosene lamp and hoop-skirt conflagrations, getting buried in coal mines, falling off housetops, breaking through church or lecture-room floors, taking patent medicines, or committing suicide in other forms. The Erie railroad kills from 23 to 46; the other 845 railroads kill an average of one-third of a man each; and the rest of that million, amounting in the aggregate to the appalling figure of nine hundred and eighty-seven thousand six hundred and thirty-one corpses die naturally in their beds!

You will excuse me from taking any more chances on those beds. The railroads are good enough for me.

And my advice to all people is, Don't stay at home any more than you can help; but when you have *got* to stay home a while, buy a package of those insurance tickets and sit up nights. You cannot be too cautious.

[One can see now why I answered that ticket agent in the manner recorded at the top of this sketch.]

The moral of this composition is, that thoughtless people grumble more than is fair about the railroad management in the United States. When we consider that every day and night in the year full fourteen thousand railway trains of various kinds, freighted with life and armed with death, go thundering over the land, the marvel is, *not* that they kill three hundred human beings in a twelvemonth, but that they do not kill three hundred times three hundred!—*Mark Twain*

Notes

1. The *Chicago Tribune* began a campaign for the Capital's removal to St. Louis on 5 July 1869. Supporters of the move called for a national convention in St. Louis on 20 October to discuss the value of the buildings and the costs of removal. Twain's figures probably come from the newspaper exchanges. The *Express* of 21 August contained a similar short editorial, written either by Twain or Larned, stating that "The question of removing the capital of the nation out in the woods somewhere comes up regularly once a year, and will continue to do so until the final judgment" (*Mark Twain's Letters* 3: 313n.4).

2. "The True Story of Lady Byron's Life," *Atlantic Monthly,* XXIV, 302 (September 1869). Mrs. Stowe wrote the article as a rebuttal of *My Recollections of Lord Byron and those of Eye-Witnesses of his Life* by Countess Theresa Guiccioli, the English edition of which was published in 1869. The story of Byron's marriage and separation had been the subject of rumor and speculation since 1816. Lady Byron maintained an official silence until the publication of Thomas Moore's *The Life, Letters, and Journals of Lord Byron* in 1830. At that time, she broke her silence only insofar as to vindicate her parents, who were accused of causing the separation. The true cause may never be known, in part due to Lady Byron's reticence but also because Moore and representatives of Augusta Leigh (Byron's sister) and Lady Byron destroyed Byron's memoirs three days after his death. By Byron's own account, the *Memoirs* contained a "very full account" of his marriage and separation and were written "to save the necessity of them being written by a friend or friends, and [I] have only to hope they will not add notes" (Lady Blessington, *Conversations of Lord Byron with the Countess of Blessington* [1834], 57).

3. Dr. Stephen Lushington was the legal counsel involved in the original separation by Lady Byron's parents. Allegedly he knew the full story and advised for the separation.

4. Artemus Ward was the pseudonym of Charles Farrar Browne (1834–1867). Twain met this humorist and lecturer when he reviewed Ward's lecture at Maguire's Opera House (18 December 1863) for the *Virginia City Evening Enterprise.* Twain and Dan De Quille (William Wright) were Ward's "hosts" during his stay in Virginia City (*Mark Twain's Letters,* 3: 269n.5).

5. Twain may have enclosed this editorial, in pencil, with a letter to Olivia Langdon of 19 August 1869 (*Mark Twain's Letters,* 3: 305).

6. Montgomery Schuyler.

7. Francis Preston Blair (1821–1875) was the Democratic vice-presidential candidate running with Horatio Seymour against the Republican ticket of Ulysses S. Grant and Schuyler Colfax. Seymour was a reluctant candidate and could not offset Blair's often inflammatory rhetoric (*Mark Twain's Letters,* 3: 462n.14).

8. A number of Buffalo residents had formed the Citizen's Mutual Coal Mining, Purchasing and Sale Company in efforts to circumvent the possible

monopoly believed responsible for the high coal prices in Buffalo at the time. The cooperative published newspaper articles that were personally critical of Jervis Langdon, who owned substantial coal interests in Buffalo. Apparently Langdon had asked to have his name kept out of any *Express* articles dealing with the coal controversy; Twain responded to this request in his letter to Olivia Langdon of 19 August 1869. Up to this point, the *Express* had been sympathetic to the citizens' cause but had refrained from publishing the criticisms.

9. John De La Fletcher Slee (1837–1901) graduated from Genesee College, Lima, N.Y. In 1866 he left a professorship of Greek and German at Fally Seminary in Fulton, N.Y., to take a position as Western Sales Manager for the Anthracite Coal Association of Buffalo. In 1869 he was Langdon's "authorized business agent," "general salesman," and "highest officer." When Langdon reorganized the company in May of 1870, Slee became a partner (*Mark Twain's Letters,* 3: 119n.4). Both Slee's letter calling for the reprinting of a *New York Evening Post* article and the article itself, "The Anthracite Coal Mines: Causes and History of the Miners Strike — The Workingmen's Benevolent Association," appeared in the 20 August edition of the *Express* with this editorial. Articles on the "coal question" virtually disappeared in the *Express* after the editorial's publication.

10. Twain probably first saw the falls in 1853 while passing through Buffalo. He again visited Niagara for three days at the end of July 1869, just prior to assuming his duties at the *Buffalo Express*. This excursion provided him with material for his first two contributions to the *Express:* "A Day at Niagara" and "English Festivities and Minor Matters," which he later revised into a single sketch, "Niagara," for inclusion in *Sketches, New and Old* (1875).

11. Uncas was a Mohegan chief who joined the English during King Philip's War in 1675.

12. Red Jacket was a Seneca chief who opposed the Euro-American takeover of Iroquois lands.

13. Louis J. Budd identifies "Hole-In-The-Day" as Ben Holladay (1819–1887), who organized mail and freight lines in the West, and was reputed to have staged Indian attacks on rival stage lines (*Mark Twain: Collected Tales, Sketches, Speeches, & Essays* [New York: Library of America, 1992] 1044n.304.27).

14. Horace Greeley (1811–1872) was an American journalist and politician who founded and edited the New York *Tribune* from 1841 until his death in 1872. Twain probably knew Greeley from the Lyceum circuit.

15. Cornelius Vanderbilt (1794–1877) was a steamboat and railroad tycoon known for his shrewd business dealings.

16. This short article also appeared as part of the "People and Things" column, a regular feature in the *Express*. Twain and Larned wrote these as a collaborative effort by Twain's own admission; however, Twain chose to republish this one in *Sketches, New and Old* (1875) under his own name. When reprinted, however, the number of years the couple was engaged was changed from 89 to 80.

17. Philip S. Foner cites "Only a Nigger" as Twain's work in *Mark Twain: Social Critic* (New York: International Publishers, 1958), 218–19, reprinting the editorial itself and discussing it in terms of Twain's view on African Americans in general and lynchings in particular. He also cites a later item from "People and Things": "Another trifling mistake by Judge Lynch: 'The negro found hanging near Dresden, Tennessee, a few years ago, and who was supposed to have been hung for committing a rape on a small girl, has proved not to be the right person." The *Express* of 8 September 1869 published an article entitled "Mob Law in Missouri," an exchange from the *St. Louis Democrat*. Clearly this stance on lynching found favor with Twain as editor. We have not been able to locate the actual Memphis exchange to which the editorial refers.

18. Charles Blondin was a pseudonym for Jean-Francois Gravelet (1824–1897), an acrobat and gymnast who gained fame by crossing Niagara Falls on a tightrope in 1859. He subsequently made many crossings, adding theatrical stunts each time, for example, blindfolded, carrying a man on his back, or trundling a man in a wheelbarrow.

19. The queen Twain refers to is Alexandrina Victoria (1819–1901), who married Prince Albert (Saxe-Coburg) in 1840 and had nine children.

20. Queen Victoria's second child, Albert Edward (1841–1910).

21. Queen Victoria's third child, later the Grand Duchess of Hesse-Darmstadt (1843–1878).

22. Queen Victoria's fourth child, Alfred (1844–1900).

23. Queen Victoria's ninth and last child, later Princess Henry of Battenburg (1857–1944).

24. All of these names are fictitious, Twain is exaggerating the size of Queen Victoria's large family.

25. The 19 October 1869 *Buffalo Express* published Twain's letter of greeting to these pioneers. The open letter was read at Delmonico's in New York.

26. In addition to other unsigned editorials included in this volume, the 21 September 1869 *Express* also published "The Byron Question," stating that Mrs. Stowe intended to give the public further proof of her allegations after Byron's friends had exhausted their defense.

27. The family solicitors, Wharton and Ford's, issued the condemnation to the London papers (Baendar, 470).

28. An actual newspaper of the time (Budd 1992, 1044n.308.2).

29. In this burlesque, Twain draws from his own experiences on Western newspapers such as the Virginia City *Territorial Enterprise* and the San Francisco *Daily Morning Call* among others. Twain himself was challenged to a duel over an article he had written for the *Enterprise*. This sketch was later republished in *Sketches, New and Old* (1875).

30. Postal laws permitted the exchange of newspapers free of charge, and columnists often quoted from "Exchange" when using material from another newspaper (Budd 1992, 1044n.308.7).

31. Used cigar or cigarette butts.

32. Samuel Nicholson (1791–1868) invented a new type of pavement consisting of wood blocks on a base of asphalt or hard-packed sand (see Budd 1992, 1045n.309.11–13). Twain probably "borrowed" this situation from Jervis Langdon's problems with a Memphis paving contract that he had underwritten to the sum of $500,000, a debt he was unable to collect. Twain used his influence to convince Whitelaw Reid of the New York *Tribune* to write an article calling for protection of Northern investments in the South at about this same time (Kaplan, 97).

33. Folk term for whiskey so strong that a person couldn't walk more than forty rods after drinking it (Budd 1992, 1044n.304.20).

34. Thomas K. Beecher was Livy's pastor at the First Congregational Church in Elmira, and both Thomas K. Beecher and Harriet Beecher Stowe were siblings of Henry Ward Beecher. He and Joseph Twitchell officiated at Clemens's marriage. In a letter to Olivia Langdon (8–9 September 1869), Twain acknowledges writing this editorial.

35. "Ishmael" is Ausburn Towner, and the excerpt of Beecher appeared in the "Friday Miscellany" column of the *Elmira Advertiser*. Beecher rebukes Towner's August column in the *Elmira Saturday Evening Review*. In the 4 September issue of the *Review* Towner acknowledges Beecher's criticism as just, but Twain probably wrote this editorial without having read the later *Review* article. An unfinished and unsent letter by Twain to Towner of 17 September salutes "Ishmael" as "My Dear Insect" and names him among "the world's unnoticed failures" (*Mark Twain's Letters,* 3: 350n.7).

36. Benjamin Franklin Butler (1818–1893) was a Civil War army officer whose harsh rule as military governor of New Orleans during May–December 1862 lead to charges of corruption and his eventual removal. After the war he became a politician.

37. Harriet Martineau (1802–1876) was an English novelist, journalist, critic and essayist. Her article, "Lady Byron" appeared in the February 1861 issue of *Atlantic Monthly*.

38. These were published opponents of Mrs. Stowe's article. Theodore Tilton wrote for the *New York Independent,* Count Johannes for the *New York Herald,* and R. Shelton MacKenzie for the *Philadelphia Press*.

39. The *Express* published the obituary of Adolphe Neil (1802–1869), Marshal of France, on 17 August 1869. The obituary, however, did not mention Neil's last words.

40. In response to an objection by Mary Fairbanks (a close, personal friend and confidant of his for thirty-two years) to his irreverent treatment of death in this sketch, Clemens wrote to her on 27 September 1869: "Well, I'll let Death alone. I will, Mother—honest—I won't bother him if he don't bother me. No, but really, I *will* be more reverential, if you want me to, though I tell you it don't jibe with my principles. There is a fascination about meddling with forbidden things."

41. Daniel Webster (1782–1852) was a well-known American politician and orator.

42. Twain "smouched" this "last word" from "The Death of Squibob," published in *Phoenixiana,* an 1855 volume by John Phoenix (George Horatio Derby). Also borrowed from "The Death of Squibob" are the "last words" of John Quincy Adams ("This is the last of earth") and of Queen Elizabeth ("Oh, I would give my kingdom for one moment more—I have forgotten my last words"). See Gladys Carmen Bellamy's "Mark Twain's Indebtedness to John Phoenix," *On Mark Twain: The Best from American Literature* (Durham: Duke University Press, 1987), 23–24.

43. John Quincy Adams (1767–1848) was the sixth president of the United States.

44. Napoleon Bonaparte (1769–1821), Emperor of France.

45. Benjamin Franklin (1706–1790) published *Poor Richard's Almanac* from 1732 to 1757.

46. Josh Billings (Henry Wheeler Shaw, 1818–1885) had been a farmer, real estate salesman, Ohio steamboat owner and auctioneer in his early life. In the 1850s he began publishing articles in newspapers in the form of sketches, short essays, and aphorisms for which he became famous as a "cracker-barrel" philosopher. These articles were later collected and published in book form (*Josh Billings' Farmer's Allminax,* 1869), and Billings was part of the Lyceum lecture circuit with Twain in the 1869 season.

47. John Dryden's "Alexander's Feast, or, The Power of Music; An Ode in Honour of St. Cecilia's Day," line 15.

48. George Gordon Byron (1788–1824), an English Romantic poet, was famous for his love affairs and unconventional lifestyle. Harriet Beecher Stowe's article, "The True Story of Lady Byron's Life," appeared in the *Atlantic Monthly* and *Macmillan's Magazine* in September of 1869. In it, she charged Byron with having an incestuous affair with his half-sister, Augusta.

49. Admiral Horatio Nelson upon his deathbed at the Battle of Trafalgar on 21 October 1805.

50. Twain appears to have had a life-long fascination with the Maid of Orleans (1412–1431). He cited her name in speeches as early as 1868, published *Personal Recollections of Joan of Arc* in 1896, and published the essay "St. Joan of Arc" in 1904. R. Kent Rasmussen (*Mark Twain A–Z,* [New York: Oxford University Press, 1995], 254) cites a story told in Paine's autobiography that a stray leaf from a history book containing information on Joan of Arc blew into Twain's hands. Paine sees this as a turning point in Twain's life, sparking an interest in history; scholars disagree on the veracity of the incident.

51. Civil War song composed by George Frederick Root (1820–1895).

52. Alexander the Great (356–323 B.C.) was King of Macedon and, at the age of 32, founded an empire that stretched from the Adriatic Sea to India. He reportedly died after drinking too much at a banquet.

53. Josephine Beauharnais (1763–1814) was Empress of France and wife of Napoleon I.

54. Cleopatra (69–30 B.C.) was an Egyptian queen famous for beauty.

55. According to tradition, this quote is attributed to Comte Pierre Jacques Etienne Cambronne (1770–1842) (Budd 1992, 1046n.317.39–40).

56. Sir Walter Raleigh (1552?–1618) was an English courtier, navigator, colonizer, and writer who was executed for treason.

57. J. C. F. Schiller, *Wilhelm Tell* (1804), act II.

58. Elizabeth I (1533–1603) was Queen of England and Ireland from 1558 to 1603.

59. Louis Napoleon Bonaparte (1808–1873) was the nephew of Napoleon I and was elected President of the Second Republic in 1848. He declared himself Emperor in 1852, but his imperialist ventures failed in the Mexican campaign of 1861–67 and the Franco-Prussian war of 1870–71, which Twain satirizes in a later sketch for the *Express*.

60. Garret Davis (1801–1872) was a Kentucky politician and noted orator.

61. "H. G." refers to Horace Greeley.

62. Henry Bergh (1811–1888) founded the American Society for the Preservation of Animals.

63. Andrew Johnson (1808–1875) was seventeenth President of the United States from 1865–69. He was a former tailor turned politician and held the posts of governor, senator, and Lincoln's vice president. Rasmussen (263) stated that Twain "mock[s] Johnson's pride in being a self-made man" in this sketch. Other references to Johnson in Twain's writing include the Appendix in *Roughing It* and the posthumously published *L'homme Qui Rit,* which was written in 1869.

64. William H. Seward (1801–1872) served as Secretary of State from 1861 to 1869.

65. Ulysses S. Grant (1822–1885) was born Hiram Ulysses Grant and became the eighteenth president of the United States. He was reported to have added the "S" to his name because he liked the sound of it.

66. Twain began his lecture tour in the fall of 1869 in Pittsburgh on 1 November and ended in Jamestown, New York, on January, 21, 1870. Twain had committed to the tour before acquiring interest in the *Express,* and his agent, James Redpath, didn't wish to cancel these appearances in light of the recent success of *The Innocents Abroad.*

67. James Redpath and George L. Fall managed the Boston Lyceum Bureau, founded in 1868, a lecture system for the Northern states and Canada. Its services included circulation of its clients, bookings, arrangement of itineraries, collection of fees, and the establishment of uniform prices. The fee for this service was ten percent, and the usual lecture fee was $100. The lecturers were farmed out in groups of six or eight, trying out new lectures in smaller, rural areas before moving them to the cities.

68. In a letter (whose correspondent is unidentified) of 7 October 1869,

Twain refers to "the Byron business": "I tried to burlesque it, & had my labor for my pains—our stove got the article." In the July 1870 issue of the *Galaxy* "Memoranda," he also refers to the "Byron Scandal" as one of a number of "unburlesquable" things. However, this editorial "sketch" survives, as does an unfinished letter from Lord Byron in Hell to be found in the manuscripts (*Mark Twain's Letters*, 3: 367n.1). Additionally, the 6 November 1869 *Express* contained an item from the *Glasgow Weekly Mail* reproducing a poem supposedly written by Byron to Harriet Beecher Stowe entitled, "Lord Byron Writing from Hades in His Own Defence."

69. This probably refers to the critic of Stowe's article in the *New York Herald* noted previously.

70. Byron was born with a club foot.

71. According to Thomas Moore's account, one of Byron's friends advised that he ought to marry and proposed for him to a lady whom Byron himself did not favor, and who rejected him. Byron himself then wrote a letter of proposal to Anne Isabelle Milbanke, who accepted (Harriet Martineau, "Lady Byron," *Atlantic Monthly*, February 1861, 7:187).

72. This doggerel verse may be a play on Butler's quote of "To Penelope" in his attack on Stowe's veracity. "Acne" was probably a euphemism for an infection or a pox—more specifically, syphilis.

73. The first two cantos of *Childe Harold* were published in March of 1812; Canto III appeared in 1816 and Canto IV in 1818. Byron's popularity skyrocketed during the period from 1811–1816.

74. *Sardanapalus* was published in 1821.

75. The site of Byron's death.

76. The San Francisco-based *Overland Monthly* was founded and edited by Bret Harte in the summer of 1866. This review reprints the substance of Harte's comments on Elizabeth Stuart Phelps's immensely popular novel, *The Gates Ajar* (1868) (*Mark Twain's Letters*, 3: 321).

77. In later years, Twain several times noted that his early version of "Captain Stormfield's Visit to Heaven," which he began writing in 1868, had turned into a satire of Phelps's novel. Twain wrote about forty thousand words and, five or six years after that, showed the manuscript to William Dean Howells, who urged him to publish it. Twain resisted his friend's urging, however, because, as he put it: "I had turned it into a burlesque of 'The Gates Ajar,' a book which had imagined a mean little ten-cent heaven about the size of Rhode Island." See Baetzhold and McCullough, eds., *The Bible According to Mark Twain* (Athens and London: The University of Georgia Press, 1995), 130–38, and Ray Browne, *Mark Twain's Quarrel with Heaven* (New Haven: College and University Press, 1970), 20–28.

78. A collection of ten works of short fiction by Phelps published in 1869.

79. Charles I (1600–1649), King of Great Britain (1625–1649), was beheaded in 1649.

80. In the Gunpowder Plot of 1605, Guy Fawkes was arrested in the cel-

lars of Parliament for attempting to blow up the House of Lords during James I's state opening of Parliament. He and his fellow conspirators were sentenced to death a year later.

81. Warren Hastings was put on trial for maladministration in India in 1788. He was acquitted of high treason in 1795.

82. The surrender at Yorktown of British forces by Charles Cornwallis (1738–1805) marked the end of the Revolutionary War.

83. Incidents mentioned recount recent sensational news items.

84. The Junius letters were a series of letters published in the *London Public Advertiser* from 21 January 1769 to 21 January 1772. Authorship was anonymous, and the letters themselves were composed of scathing attacks on George III's ministers. Over 40 persons have been posited as the author over the years, and the authorship became more important when the editor, Sampson Woodfall, was prosecuted in 1770. To the present day, authorship of these letters is still an open question.

85. A reference to Alexandre Dumas's (1802–1870) romance novel, *The Man in the Iron Mask.*

86. Probably Little Nahant, near Lynn, Massachusetts.

87. The narrative style and technique of this sketch concerning Henry Ward Beecher may have been modeled after a similar satirical sketch about Horace Greeley, entitled "Private Habits of Horace Greeley," that Twain published in the humor magazine *Spirit of the Times* in November of 1868. Beecher was a preacher, writer, alleged adulterer, and pastor of the Plymouth Church in Brooklyn. Twain's ties to the Beecher family date back to his arrival home from the *Quaker City* voyage in 1867. Isabella Beecher Hooker (Henry's half-sister) was present at Twain's first meeting with Olivia Langdon, soon to become his wife. Twain was Henry's guest on 5 January 1868, and he met Harriet Beecher Stowe and Catherine Beecher while there. His and Olivia's close ties to the Beecher family were partial reasons for the move to Hartford after Jervis Langdon's death in 1870. See Kenneth R. Andrews, 16–18.

88. Larned was part owner and political editor of the *Buffalo Express* during Twain's tenure there. Twain considered him the "model of industry and diligence" at the *Express,* wishing to emulate him during his tenure at the paper during his early days there (Steinbrink, 60).

89. George William Curtis (1824–1892) was an author, Republican journalist, and editor of *Harper's Weekly* from 1863 to 1892. His political interests included reform, an end to slavery, and women's rights. This editorial has been reprinted once by the Buffalo Historical Society in its *Publications,* 1915, 19: 338 (Fried, Martin B. "Mark Twain in Buffalo," *Niagara Frontier* 5 [Winter, 1959]: 96).

90. The article Twain refers to is also entitled "Engineer Griffin." Judge Barrett, in his address to the jury, stated: "Your verdict was against the law, and an outrage against humanity. You violated the obligations of your oath— a plain and simple obligation to render a verdict according to the evidence . . .

I trust that the spirits of the dead, dying, bleeding, and burnt victims of Mast Hope, will rebuke you as long as you live." The 29 September 1869 article "Extraordinary Verdict" stated that James Griffin's "own confession tegether with testimony elicited on the trial, showed unmistakably" that he was responsible for the Mast Hope Massacre, and attributes the jury's unconscionable verdict to Pike County's local enmity toward the Erie corporation.

91. Twain wrote this first letter from the "Around the World" series while visiting the Langdons at Elmira before the beginning of his lecture tour (1 November 1869). Although forty to fifty "Around the World" letters were envisioned, only ten were printed.

92. Mono Lake is located in the high desert country near the center of California, 300 miles north of Los Angeles. Twain visited it with Cal Higbie in August of 1862. In addition to its reference here and in other "Around the World" sketches, the lake is featured in chapters 38 and 39 of *Roughing It*.

93. Twain visited the town (Monoville) with Higbie in August of 1862. At the time he was mining in Aurora, Nevada, 25 miles east of Monoville. Monoville was the site of the first major gold strike in the Eastern Sierra.

94. Twain left Elmira the first week of October for a four-month lecture tour, and thus was unavailable to deliver this "speech" in person (Steinbrink 61).

95. The Esmeralda mining district was discovered on 26 August 1860. The camp there was unsatisfactory and was later moved to the town of Aurora, established on 25 November 1861. The population of Aurora in 1864 was 10,000; by 1869 the early bonanzas were exhausted, although the district was productive as late as 1882, long after Twain had left for the East (Francis Church Lincoln, ed., *Mining Districts and Mineral Resources of Nevada* [Las Vegas: Nevada Publications, 1982], 137).

96. The "Wide West" was established as a mine as part of the Comstock lode. Twain and Higbie purchased 200 feet of a 400 foot claim approximately 100 feet from the Wide West shaft. They named their claim "The Annipolitan." That spur was discovered (9 July 1862) to be mixed with the "Pride of Utah" claim, and the feet they purchased turned out to be worthless (George J. Williams, III, *Mark Twain: His Adventures at Aurora and Mono Lake* [Dayton, Nev.: Tree By The River Publishing, 1987], 49–54).

97. The Winnemucca mining district was discovered by a young Winnemucca Indian in 1863. It was the most important of the Humboldt district mines and credited with early production of about one million dollars worth of ore.

98. Mining activity began in this district in 1860, shortly after the discovery of the Comstock in 1859.

99. The Alba Nueva mine was part of the Humboldt district.

100. North Ophir designated both the camp and the mine located nearest the silver strike of 1859. In 1863, the site was christened "Virginia City."

101. Part of the original Comstock boom, this mine, in the form of railroad trestle and works, is still visible today.

102. Twain wrote this piece after the Cardiff Giant was discovered in

Syracuse, New York, on 16 October 1869. Reprinted in *Sketches, New and Old* in 1875, this article parallels the history of the Cardiff hoax, and bears "remarkable" similarities to Twain's own "Petrified Man" hoax published in Nevada seven years earlier. The idea of selling antiquities to the Roman government came out of his 1867 visit to Rome. At that time, the city was a papal state, and held to the policy of buying fresh discoveries at half of their assessed value. In Chapter 28 of *Innocents,* Twain comments that "when a man digs up an ancient statue in the Campagna, the Pope gives him a fortune in gold coin" (Rasmussen 59).

103. This hoax was also called the Cardiff Giant, which Twain later mentions in the sketch, "A Ghost Story." The "discovery" was current news in October of 1869: a buried piece of sculptured gypsum was claimed to be the petrified body of a giant.

104. The conflict and subsequent inflation to the Haitian economy which Twain satirizes here had been ongoing since 1794. Toussaint freed the colony's slave population and rid the island of both French and British presence in 1802. He was subsequently captured and died a prisoner in France. The rebellion remained active under Dessalines, who declared Haiti the first black republic. In 1844, the eastern two-thirds of the island declared itself the independent republic of Santo Domingo (present-day Dominican Republic). The island's history is characterized by a bitter struggle for political power between blacks and mulattoes. Soulouque, a black leader, declared himself emperor and ruled for ten years until 1859, when the mulatto Nicholas Fabre Geffard restored the republican government until 1867.

105. The name of the ship Twain sailed on during his Europe and the Holy Land tour, letters from which *Innocents* was written. Twain finished the novel just before beginning his stint as editor of the *Buffalo Express.*

106. Francisco Solano Lopez (1827–1870) was the dictator of Paraguay responsible for the Paraguayan War. The war, also known as the War of the Triple Alliance, took place 1864–1870 and was the bloodiest conflict in Latin American history.

107. The *Buffalo Express* reviewed Charles A Washburn's book, *The History of Paraguay, with Notes of Personal Observations and Reminiscences of Diplomacy under Difficulties* (Boston: Lee & Shepard, Buffalo: Breed, Lent & Co., 1870) on 14 January 1871.

108. At this time, McMahon had been replaced as Minister to Paraguay. McMahon reported Lopez to be a fine and efficient administrator, in sharp contrast to the previous Minister's (Washburne's) assessment. Lopez's stabilization plan included land grants to immigrants from the United States (*Express,* 27 October 1869). Washburne's report was published in the 5 November *New York Herald.*

109. This piece is actually a partial reprinting of "An Open Letter to the American People," published in the *New York Weekly Review* (17 February 1866, 1). Twain's immediate source is *The Celebrated Jumping Frog of Calav-*

eras County and Other Stories (New York: C. H. Webb, 1867), where the original sketch was shortened and reprinted as "A Complaint about Correspndents, Dated San Francisco." The *Express* text reproduces only the last part of the shortened sketch.

110. Twain's niece named her kitten after Henry Wagner Halleck (1815–1872), Union general in chief from 1862–64, when he was replaced by Grant.

111. The niece in question here is Annie E. Moffett (1852–1950), daughter of Pamela Ann Clemens and William Anderson Moffett (*Mark Twain's Letters*, 4: 534–35).

112. Twain here refers to temperance pamphlets popular at the time.

113. On 7 May 1868, Thomas Brown and his wife, of Hampton Falls, New Hampshire, were killed with an axe during a robbery committed by their hired hand, Josiah L. Pike. Pike's plea of insanity owing to dyspepsia was rejected, and he was sentenced to be hanged. He attracted a great deal of sympathy as his execution drew near (Budd 1992, 1046n.326.21–22). A short, untitled item (published in the "People and Things" column) in the 9 November 1869 *Express* reports that Pike was scheduled for hanging at 11:00 A.M. that day. The only witnesses were the 12 required by law, his surgeon, his spiritual advisor, and a reporter for the Associated Press. No mention is made of music in the item.

114. Twain made his first trip to San Francisco with Clement T. Rice, "the Unreliable," in early May of 1863, four months after penning his first dispatch signed "Mark Twain." He returned to San Francisco in September of the same year for a short time. He left Virginia City for San Francisco by stage on 29 May 1864 and began writing for the *Call* on 6 June. During that time he was also publishing articles in the *Golden Era* and *Californian*. Twain reported for the *Call* until October of 1864.

115. John Phoenix (George Horatio Derby, 1823–1861), was a contemporary of Twain's, humorist and lecturer. The *Philadelphia Bulletin* (8 December 1869), reprinted in *Mark Twain's Letters*, 4: 2, compares Twain favorably to this humorist: "We regard him as the very best of the humorists of his class. He is more extravagant and preposterous than John Phoenix."

116. Twain does not state the exact date of the performance he saw. He was lecturing in Boston on 10 November 1869 and could have been present for the opening night, which was Tuesday, 16 November 1869.

117. The *Transcript's* opening night review stated that the works of the scenic artist, George Heister, "show[s] the most exquisite changes of land and sea view as the fairy land drew nearer, were never approached on a Boston stage, if indeed on any stage in the country" (*Boston Evening Transcript*, 11 November and 17 November, 1869).

118. Alexander "Sandy" Baldwin (1840–69) was a member of The Third House, a group of young men who gathered after the Nevada legislative sessions to lampoon the politicians. He and Theodore Winters presented Twain with a $200 gold watch upon Twain's election as President of the Third House.

Baldwin was one of Nevada's leading attorneys, earning in excess of a million dollars representing mining companies in litigation (Williams 1993, 66–67).

119. William "Bill" Stewart was also a lawyer and member of the Third House. He and Governor James Nye became the first Nevadans elected to the Senate in 1864.

120. See note 113 above.

121. Daniel McFarland shot and wounded Albert D. Richardson, a journalist and acquaintance of Twain's, because Richardson was seeing McFarland's ex-wife. The original news story of the shooting appeared in the 29 November 1869 *Express,* entitled "Richardson-McFarland."

122. Antonio Canova (1757–1822) was best known as a sculptor, but he also did about 100 paintings.

123. Bon Marche was one of Paris's first department stores.

124. Louis Prang and Co. produced chromolithographs of famous paintings through the process Twain depicts in the sketch. Twain bought one of the newest in February of 1871 and may have owned several (*Mark Twain's Letters,* 4: 330n.1).

125. This refers to a piece that appeared in the form of a Letter to the Editor under the title "The Richardson Case" that same day. The Richardson-McFarland case appears to have instigated a discussion of divorce laws.

126. Bret (Francis) Harte (1836–1902) was a nineteenth-century American writer famous for his stories about California mining towns. Twain first met Harte in San Francisco in 1864. In early 1866, Harte proposed that the two jointly publish a book of their sketches, a project that fell through. Yet Twain considered him a mentor at this point in time, telling Thomas Aldrich Bailey in 1871 that Harte had "trimmed and trained and schooled me patiently until he changed me from an awkward utterer of grotesqueness to a writer of paragraphs and chapters that have found a certain favor in the eyes of even some of the very decentest people in the land" (Kaplan, 74).

127. The story of the Whiteman Cement Mine is a gold-rush myth based on some facts and persons who can be traced and documented. There are several versions extant, and Williams (1987, 58–59) recounts the most reliable one. Twain recycles the tale later in *Roughing It.*

128. Twain retells this tale in *Roughing It.*

129. Cuba was a Spanish colony at this time. In 1868 revolutionaries under the leadership of Manuel de Cespedes proclaimed Cuban independence, and the ensuing Ten Years War was costly for both sides.

130. Edwin M. Stanton (1814–1869) served as Secretary of War during the Civil War. His removal by Andrew Johnson and subsequent refusal to leave office precipitated Johnson's impeachment. Three days before his death he had been appointed Associate Justice; his death immediately generated speculation between the Northern and Southern state factions as to his replacement (*Express,* 28 December 1869).

131. An *Express* article of 28 December 1869 entitled "A Tribute to Stan-

ton" reprints the *Argus* article in part, prefacing the citation with "In our view, no garland can be laid upon the grave of Edwin M. Stanton which honors him more than does this spit of Copperhead venom which the Albany *Argus* has dropped upon it." The *Argus* characterized Stanton as "the unjust Judge who was about to ascend our highest tibunal to deliver his revengeful edicts, and belie the promise of peace made to the country."

132. *Hamlet*, III:i:56.

133. Thaddeus Stevens (1792–1868) was a Pennsylvania politician who led impeachment proceedings against Andrew Johnson in 1868.

134. According to Charles L. Crow, this sketch was written between the publication of *Innocents* and Twain's marriage to Olivia. Its original publication is in the *Express*, and it was later published as a separate book by Sheldon and Company in 1871. However, due to contractual conflicts with Elisha Bliss, Twain later obtained and destroyed the plates. The piece was published in a British volume of Twain's work in 1872, and it appeared under its current title, "A Medieval Romance," in *Sketches, New and Old* (1875).

135. Stowe published a second article concerning the Byron scandal (title is the same as Twain's editorial), which the *Express* published in full on this same date.

136. This is located 15 miles northeast of Carson City. Huge deposits of gold and silver were discovered there in 1860. Twain visited it and the surrounding vicinity in October of 1861 (Williams 1987, 10–11).

137. Twain tells or refers to this story in many places, including his "Greetings to the California Pioneers of 1849" and more directly in *Roughing It*.

138. Both the "Chinamen" and "Desperadoes" sections of this sketch eventually become part of *Roughing It*, which Twain began writing in July of 1870. He enlarged the "Desperadoes" sketch from *The Vigilantes of Montana* (1866) by Thomas J. Dimsdale.

139. Sam Brown was "the most feared man on the Comstock" (Norm Nielson, *Tales of Nevada*, Reno, 1989, 126–28).

140. Accounts differ about how Jack Williams, alias George Shanks, met his end. See *Lawmen & Desperadoes: A Compendium of Noted Early California Peace Officers, Badmen and Outlaws 1850–1900*, 309–11, and Roger D. McGrath, *Gunfighters, Highwaymen, and Vigilantes* (Berkeley: U. of California Press, 1984).

141. Twain also describes the first cemetery in Virginia City in chapter 48 of *Roughing It*.

142. Joseph A. (Jack) Slade (1829?–1864) was an overland stage agent and notorious desperado and murderer who was hanged on 10 March 1864 in Virginia City. Slade later becomes the central focus of Chapters 10 and 11 of *Roughing It*. Twain recalls breakfasting with the notorious agent on the ninth day of his stagecoach trip out to the territories (*Mark Twain's Letters*, 4: 196nn.2–3).

143. Twain's last contribution to the "Around the World" series. Twain's

lecture series for the 1869–70 tour was titled "Our Fellow Savages in the Sandwich Islands." He drew material for the series, and probably for this sketch, from his 1866 trip to Hawaii. The final Sandwich Islands section of *Roughing It* details this same trip, which he later recalls in *Following the Equator.* Twain had plans to write a Hawaiian novel, some portions of which remain extant in the Mark Twain Papers.

144. A Hawaiian food made of taro root corm that is cooked, pounded to a paste, and then fermented. Twain further discusses poi in detail in the Sandwich Islands chapters of *Roughing It.*

145. A utensil or container made from the dried, hollowed-out shell of the gourdlike fruit of the calabash tree, found in the tropical U. S.

146. The native Hawaiians' name for themselves.

147. Twain's spelling here is supported by *Roughing It* (Harriet Elinor Smith et al., eds., Berkeley, Los Angeles, and London: University of California Press, 1993).

148. Twain will later return to the idea of simple people performing "scientific experiments" in "Extracts from Adam's Diary" (January, 1893), "Eve's Diary" (1905), and "Autobiography of Eve" (1901–1902).

149. Polynesian for "wife."

150. Acute gastroenteritis occurring in summer and autumn and marked by severe cramps, diarrhea, and vomiting (no longer in scientific use).

151. David Ross Locke (1833–1888) was resident celebrity and part owner of the *Toledo Blade* in 1869. He began writing a series of newspaper articles in the persona of "Reverend Petroleum Vesuvius Nasby" in 1862, in which he championed liberal causes through the "violently rendered" character of the bigoted Nasby by seeming to oppose them. Twain and his wife, Olivia, attended Nasby's lecture, "The Struggles of a Conservative with the Woman Question," in Buffalo on 18 February 1870, and Twain wrote the review the following day (*Mark Twain's Letters,* 3: 56n.1, and 4: 128–29n.3).

152. This lecture was an attack on racial prejudice and injustice that Twain heard in Hartford on 9 March 1869. Reviews were mixed: the *Courant* reported that Nasby "gave great satisfaction," while the *Times* reported that "Republicans in the audience felt like changing the title of that lecture to 'Cussed be Nasby.'" Twain later described the performance for *San Francisco Alta California* readers: "It is a very unvarnished narrative of the Negro's career, from flood to the present day, and bristles with satire. . . . the lecture is a fair and logical argument against slavery, and is the pleasantest to listen to I have ever heard upon that novel and interesting subject. It is necessarily severe upon Democracy, but not more so than one would expect from Nasby." See *Mark Twain's Letters,* 3: 158–60, for more of his published comments.

153. Anson Burlingame (1820–1870) was a lawyer, statesman, Massachusetts Republican, and Ambassador to China. On 21 June 1866, an open boat arrived on the island of Hawaii containing fifteen men who had survived their vessel, the *Hornet,* having caught fire and burned forty-three days ear-

lier. Eleven of the rescued men were brought to Honolulu and placed in the hospital. Burlingame, having met Twain earlier, ordered men to haul Twain into the hospital on a stretcher so that he could interview the wounded men. As a consequence, Twain's was the first and most complete coverage of the *Hornet* disaster (Williams 1993, 110–11).

154. The Lydia Thompson Blondes were a troupe of performers who were at that time appearing in Chicago. The article concerning *Times* correspondent W. F. Storey's assault was telegraphed to the *Express* from Chicago and appeared in the 26 February edition bearing the same title as the editorial. The telegraphic report described Storey's beating by Lydia Thompson, Pauline Markham, a male confederate named Henderson, and others. The women were "lugged off to the station house," while the three male confederates escaped. A few days later (19 March 1870) the *Express*'s personal column contained this gem: "'Pauline Markham has the brain fever.' Then she must have brains!"

155. This personal notice appeared from 8 March to 11 March 1870. At the same time this proclamation of Twain's intent to remain permanently as editor of the *Express* appeared, the author was apparently drafting "A Wail," an unpublished sketch that details the author's discontent with the abuses suffered by newspapermen. This sketch resembles "Journalism in Tennessee," and scorns sappy, melodramatic "literary" material and the dreary blank verse newspapers regularly published. A second sketch written during this same time period, "A Protest," more specifically mentions the *Buffalo Express*. This sketch, too, remained unpublished. See Steinbrink, 95–100.

156. Twain also used this title for a segment of a "San Francisco Letter" on 22 December 1865, in which he made specific reference to "Solomon's wisdom" (*Mark Twain's Letters,* 4: 544n.1).

157. The actual quote, from Psalms 107:23–24, reads: "They that go down to the sea in ships, that do business in great waters; / These see the works of the Lord: and his wonders in the deep."

158. The Workingmen's Benevolent Association, organized in the Pennsylvania anthracite coal region in 1868, attempted to gain higher wages and safer working conditions for its members. It collapsed in 1875 after a disastrous strike (*Mark Twain's Letters,* 4: 544n.3).

159. The pocket pistol invented by Henry Deringer (1786–1868) was originally spelled as per its inventor's name; the incorrect spelling became established as correct (*Mark Twain's Letters,* 4: 545n.5).

160. In fact, the 3 March 1870 legislation provided for six mining inspectors for the entire anthracite region. Candidates were selected by court-appointed boards of examiners for a term of five years (*Mark Twain's Letters,* 4: 545–46n.6).

161. Jervis Langdon's firm had mines in the Shamokin region, possibly including one of those mentioned. Molly Maguires, an Irish anti-landlord organization, shouldered much of the blame for violence in the region, although

their responsibility is still disputed. The actual amount of violence declined during the period of the association's greatest strength (*Mark Twain's Letters*, 4: 546–47n.7).

162. "Pandemonium, city and proud seat / of Lucifer" (*Paradise Lost*, 10. 424–25).

163. One of Kentucky's counties, approximately 100–150 miles southwest of Louisville.

164. The Internal Revenue Department was instituted during the Civil War. Within a few days of Twain's wedding to Livy, the New York *Tribune* rumored that *Innocents* would pay the author over $100,000. The Internal Revenue Department took only a few days to send Twain a letter inquiring into his liability (there was a 5 % tax on gross income over $1,000) and sent an assessor shortly after, who dropped off a form with questions Twain found difficult to answer. The form itself, with Twain's changes and excisions in pencil and two colors of ink, resides in the Mark Twain Papers. Twain probably exaggerated the inflated figure from the *Tribune* for this sketch (Kaplan, 115–16; Steinbrink, 79).

165. *Innocents* had sold around 55,000 copies by 15 March 1870.

166. Twain actually received five percent of the retail or subscription price (Budd 1992, 1047).

167. Probably referring to the "catch-all" category: "From all sources not enumerated."

168. Actual returns were published until April of 1870 in order to prevent fraud.

169. John D. Williams and S. S. Packard, *Williams and Packard's System of Penmanship* (New York: Slote, Woodman & Company, 1868).

170. Slote is alluded to in chapters 7, 10–14, 23, 27, 30, 45, 56, and 58 of *Innocents*. After returning from the excursion, he and Twain remained friends. Slote marketed Twain's self-pasting scrapbook from Slote, Woodman and Company, and published the first book edition of *Punch, Brothers, Punch!* in 1878. He was also involved in the kaolatype process in which Twain invested heavily in 1880. When this venture failed, Twain "came to regard Slote as a crook" (Rasmussen, 432).

171. The description of Slote from chapter 35 of *Innocents* recounts Twain's borrowing of Slote's passport in order to go ashore at Sebastopol: "I had lost my passport and was traveling under my roommate's, who stayed behind in Constantinople to await our return. To read the description of him in that passport and then look at me, any man could see that I was no more like him than I am like Hercules."

172. Twain's first version of this tale appeared in the *San Francisco Daily Morning Call* on Sunday, 30 August 1863. He wrote this short version while visiting Steamboat Springs and recovering from a cold. Real names are juxtaposed "against fictional characterizations, and with geographical accuracy providing a setting for unlikely and partly unverifiable events" (Ander-

son and Branch, 2). The second version appeared in one of Twain's notebooks, kept in February of 1865. The third version (second printed one) appeared in the *Buffalo Express*. He finally extracted and refined the materials for *Roughing It* in 1872. For annotations of the persons who appear in this story, we are indebted to the copious scholarship of Frederick Anderson and Edgar M. Branch (*The Great Landslide Case: Three Versions,* Number 20, Keepsake Series, Berkeley: Friends of the Bancroft Library, 1973). Although no actual record of the trial has yet surfaced, most scholars believe that the sketch is based on an actual occurrence. Anderson and Branch offer the most detailed discussion of this possibility.

173. Anderson and Branch identify Buncombe as the then Attorney General Benjamin B. Bunker of New Hampshire.

174. Dick Sides and Isaac Roop attempted to organize a provisional Territory for Nevada out of western Utah, the Territory of New Mexico, and California. Sides was elected selectman of Carson County in 1858.

175. In the original version, this character's name was "Tom Rust." Anderson and Branch stated that "investigation has turned up nothing about him to confirm his existence."

176. It is likely that this is a thin disguise for P. H. Clayton, a well-known Carson attorney. Twain later remembers him fondly in a 24 May 1905 letter to Robert Fulton (Albert Bigelow Paine, *Mark Twain Letters,* New York: Harper & Brothers, 1917, 773). His participation in the hoax is probably characteristic, as he was also a member of the "Third House," along with Twain and several other young Nevada residents.

177. Isaac Roop (1822–1869) was elected Governor of the Provisional Territory of Nevada at the 1859 convention but did not receive authorization from either Congress or the territory's citizens. His reputation for facetiousness was earned during the final session of the Territorial Legislature, during which he announced that he "wished to offer a military salute over the graves of murdered bills" (Anderson and Branch, 16–18).

178. Ormsby House is the Carson City hotel in front of which the stagecoach dropped Sam and Orion Clemens on 14 August 1861 (Williams 1993, 11).

179. Twain's first number of "Memoranda" was to appear in the May 1870 issue of the *Galaxy*.

180. This sketch was reprinted in *Sketches, New and Old* (1875) but without mention of the McFarland case.

181. The former Harriet Sarah Moncreiffe, Lady Mordaunt, confessed to her husband that Viscount Cole was the actual father of their recently born child. Sir Charles Mordaunt filed for divorce. The woman's father counterfiled that the daughter had been insane since giving birth. Several doctors corroborated and the petition was dismissed on the grounds of insanity (Budd 1992, 1047n.353.17).

182. These are three famous murder trials, all involving the plea of insanity. General George Washington Cole (d. 1875) shot and killed his neigh-

bor, Harris Hiscock, whom he suspected of having an affair with his wife, on 4 June 1867 in Albany. His first trial ended in a hung jury (7 May 1868) and the second ended in acquittal (7 December 1868) due to insanity. Daniel E. Sickles (1819–1914) shot and killed Philip Barton Key (son of Francis Scott Key) because Key was having an affair with his wife. Sickles was acquitted on grounds of mental aberration. McFarland fatally wounded Richardson (see note 121 above) and was charged with murder. He pled temporary insanity. The highly publicized trial took place 8 April to 11 May 1870; the jury rendered a verdict of not guilty (Budd 1992, 1048n.354.19–20).

183. This sketch appeared also in the May 1870 issue of the *Galaxy*.

184. This sketch had local interest, as it was in protest of the neglect of the North Street graveyard in Buffalo ("Mark Twain in Buffalo," *Buffalo Express*, 22 April 1910).

185. Latin: forehead and jawbone.

186. Wedgewood china, cream in color.

187. General James Lusk Alcorn (1816–1894) had recently (30 November 1869) been elected governor of Mississippi. His opponent, Judge Dent, was Grant's brother-in-law ("The Mississippi Election," *Express*, 10 November 1869).

188. In the May number of the *Galaxy* this sketch appeared as "About Smells." The *Express* version was shortened.

189. Reverend Thomas DeWitt Talmage (1832–1902) was a popular minister of the Central Presbyterian Church of Brooklyn.

190. A weekly religious magazine published in New York City.

191. See notes 121 and 182 above.

192. Actually, the foreman only reported, "Not guilty" (Budd 1992, 1049n.384.15).

193. McFarland's defense cited insanity in a male, paternal first cousin.

194. A former surgeon general of the Army issued a favorable statement for the defense, but Galen was also a second-century Greek physician (Budd 1992, 1049n.386.1).

195. Charles A. Dana was the editor of the *New York Sun* who defended McFarland out of loyalty to Tammany and because of rivalry with the *Tribune*, for whom Richardson had worked.

196. This small article also appeared along with Twain's address as "signature." Kate Burr, in her *New York Times* article of 12 April 1931, "Meet Mark Twain of Delaware Avenue," quotes a Mrs. Maria Welch, who lived a few doors down Delaware: "I asked my brother Tom to form a watering can brigade of boys and girls and wet down the lawn and road in front of Mr. Clemens' house. One evening after dinner they got together and Tom led the band, each with a sprinkler, up and down in front of the house, temporarily laying the dust." Later that evening, Clemens visited the house to thank the children (all seven of them) and shake their hands.

197. This article also appeared in the June 1870 number of the *Galaxy*.

198. This sketch appeared simultaneously in the *Galaxy*'s July 1870 number.

199. Twain published this simultaneously in the July 1870 number of *Galaxy* as "How I edited an Agricultural Paper Once."

200. France declared war against Prussia on 19 July 1870, ostensibly over a dispute involving a Hohenzollern prince's right to be a candidate for the then vacant throne of Spain.

201. Twain would have sent this tribute from Elmira, as he was present at Langdon's deathbed, and arrangements were being made for the funeral at that time.

202. Twain's burlesque map appeared first in the *Express* and later in the November number of the *Galaxy* as "Mark Twain's Map of Paris." Both Bruce Michelson *(Mark Twain on the Loose)* and Kaplan recount Twain's "delight" as he carved the "map." Michelson calls it a burlesque of American journalists' "overblown treatment of foreign news, with journalistic delight in violence, with the ritualized worship of Paris as a cultural holy place, with armchair generaling by reporters and ordinary citizens, and perhaps above all with Yankee obtuseness about world geography" (11).

203. Brigham Young (1801–1877) took over leadership of the Mormon Church after the assassination of Joseph Smith. He led the Mormons from Illinois to Salt Lake City, Utah.

204. François Bazaine (1811–1888) was the French commander at Metz who surrendered a force of about 175,000 men.

205. General Louis Jules Trochu, appointed military governor of Paris on 18 August 1870, occupied the Hotel de Ville on 4 September 1870 and, at the same time, accepted the presidency of the provisional government of national defense after news reached Paris of the French defeat at Sedan and the surrender of Napoleon III.

206. William Tecumseh Sherman (1820–1891) was the American Union General in charge of the Army of the West. He captured Atlanta and mounted the destructive March to the Sea that effectively divided the Confederacy.

207. The reference is clearly to William I, King of Prussia, whom Twain also referred to as "William III, King of Prussia" in a burlesque portrait published in the January 1871 issue of the *Galaxy*.

208. This sketch appeared simultaneously in the October 1870 number of the *Galaxy* as "The Reception at the President's." According to Paine's *Autobiography* (360), Twain first met Grant in January of 1868, and the two did not meet again until 1879; therefore this sketch is Twain's own "invention." However, Kaplan (121), dates their meeting as 1870, when Twain took a quick trip to Washington in July to lobby for a judicial redistricting bill for Tennessee that affected his father-in-law's Memphis holdings and was introduced to Grant by Bill Stewart. Kaplan's contention is confirmed by Twain's 8 July 1870 letter to Livy, in which he stated: "Called on the President in a quiet way this morning. I thought it would be the neat thing to show a little embarrassment when introduced, but something occurred to make me change my deportment to calm & dignified self-possession. It was this: *The General was fearfully embarrassed himself!*" For a more detailed description of Twain's

relationship with Grant, see *Mark Twain's Letters,* 4: 168n.5.

209. James Nye was the first Territorial Governor of Nevada (1861–1864). Twain's brother, Orion, served as his secretary.

210. Appeared also in the October 1870 issue of the *Galaxy.* Fried (105) believes this material to have been saved from the *Innocents* material—a reminiscence of an imaginary episode on the *Quaker City* excursion.

211. Twain's spelling for "baksheesh," a gratuity or tip to expedite service in Near Eastern countries.

212. Samson's suicide is reported in Judges 16:28–31. Paul mentions Samson along with others being saved in Hebrews 11:32–35.

213. Seé Michelson (10–14) for a detailed discussion of Twain's humor in both the "map" and this later sketch.

214. John Henry Riley was a correspondent friend of Twain's from the Nevada days. In the fall of 1870, Twain solicited Riley's collaboration on a trip to South Africa to the diamond mines. Riley was to send back correspondence, much as D. R. Ford was to do for the "Around the World" sketches in the *Express.* Twain would then polish and publish them in book form. Riley sailed for England on 7 January 1871 and returned to London in August. Twain was at work on *Roughing It* by then and put off the Riley book several times. When Riley died in Philadelphia on 17 September 1872, his South Africa book remained unwritten. This piece appeared in the November number of the *Galaxy* as "Riley—Newspaper Correspondent."

215. The *Express* printed day three of the trial in detail on 20 October 1870. D. S. Bennett was a successful Buffalo businessman (of the firm of Bennett and Avery) and had been elected to the House of Representatives the previous fall. The *Commercial Advertiser* alleged improper dealings of the firm (using grain as collateral and moving the grain from storage elevators before the loan had been repaid) and held Bennett responsible, even though he was not a signator on the loan and had been absent campaigning during the incident. His partner, Avery, was the responsible party. Bennett attempted to sue the paper for $100,000 in damages for the libel of his reputation. The ruling found for the *Commercial Advertiser,* a verdict that evidently surprised many interested in the proceedings, including Twain.

216. Steinbrink (141) suggests that this sketch, which also appeared in the November 1870 number of the *Galaxy,* may be in particularly poor taste in light of Jervis Langdon's illness. He further suggests the sketch as Twain's experimentation with vernacular characters in preparation for writing *Roughing It.* It is reprinted in *Sketches, New and Old* (1875) as "The Undertaker's Chat."

217. This sketch also appeared in the November 1870 number of the *Galaxy* and in *Sketches, New and Old* (1875).

218. Sylvanus Cobb Jr. (1823–1887) was a New England novelist who was one of the first to undertake the wholesale production of popular fiction. He wrote over 300 novels and 1,000 short stories. Timothy Shay Arthur

(1809–1885), who produced more than 100 moral tales and tracts, is best known for *Ten Nights in the Barrow and What I Saw There* (1854).

219. Stewart L. Woodford (1835–1913) was the Republican candidate for governor of New York in 1870.

220. John T. Hoffman (1828–1888) served as Governor 1868–1872.

221. This sketch appeared first in the *Express* and then in the *Galaxy*'s December 1870 issue. It was reprinted in *Sketches, New and Old* (1875)

222. This sketch also appeared in the December 1870 issue of *Galaxy*, later in *Sketches, New and Old* (1875), and in the 1906 edition of *The $30,000 Bequest and Other Tales*. It was also used as an advertisement for the Waltham Watch Co., c.1918. Similar tales about watches and their regulation appeared in *Innocents* (1869) and *Following the Equator* (1899).

223. This sketch also appeared in the December 1870 issue of the *Galaxy*. See McElderry (149–54) for a lengthy discussion of whether Twain had read the original *Saturday Review* critique of 8 October and a reprint of that original review.

224. Dogberry was the loquacious and self-satisfied purveyor of malapropisms in Shakespeare's *Much Ado about Nothing*. The sketch also appeared in the December 1870 issue of the *Galaxy*.

225. Proof-sheets that contained material other than typographical corrections could not pass as third-class matter according to sections 159 and 166 of *The Statutes Relating to the Postal Service* (1869). First-class matter cost twelve times as much as third-class postage. Budd suggests that the direct quotation near the end of the opening paragraph may come from an oral restatement by a local postmaster (Budd 1992, 1053n.495.34).

226. This "editorial" parallels Twain's signed "European War!!!" and "Map of Paris," sketches that appeared on 25 July and 17 September 1870 respectively. During the Prussian siege Parisians ate the animals in the zoo.

227. "The Facts in the Case of the Great Beef Contract" appeared in the May 1870 issue of the *Galaxy*. Twain discusses the inspiration for the sketch in "Memoranda," *Galaxy*, September 1870.

228. The first of the three official sources Twain cites in this sketch exist, and the author's figures match to the day and the penny. The sketch was reprinted in the January 1871 number of the *Galaxy*, and in *Sketches, New and Old* (1875).

229. William Miller (1782–1849) preached that the Second Coming would take place in 1843. His followers later organized the Advent Christian Church (1860).

230. Sir Willam Blackstone (1765–1780) wrote *Commentaries on the Laws of England* (1765–1769), thought to be the most comprehensive single treatment of the body of English law.

231. See "An Entertaining Article" above.

232. "Doesticks" is the minor humorist Mortimer Neil Thomson (1831–1875), with whom Twain consulted on the potential for book publication

of the *Quaker City* voyage in 1807 (Kaplan, 37–38).

233. This article was also published in the January 1871 number of the *Galaxy*.

234. Appeared also in the February 1871 issue of the *Galaxy* and *The $30,000 Bequest and Other Tales* (1906). The sketch reveals a fascination with statistical manipulation that surfaces in Twain's earlier sketch, "The Facts in the Case of George Fisher, Deceased" and in his later Biblical works in which he discusses Creation.

Index

Adams, John Quincy, 44, 289n.43
Alba Nueva Mine, 72, 293n.99
Alexander the Great, 46, 289n.52

Baldwin, Alexander, 96–97, 295n.118
Bazaine, François, 228, 303n.204
Beecher, Henry Ward, 56–59,
    288n.34, 292n.87
Beecher, Thomas K., 37, 288n.34,
    288n.35
Bergh, Henry, 47, 290n.62
Billings, Josh. *See* Shaw, Henry
    Wheeler
Blair, Francis Preston, 10, 285n.7
Blondin, Charles, 24, 287n.18
Bonaparte, Louis Napoleon
    (Napoleon III), 47, 290n.59
Bonaparte, Napoleon (Napoleon I),
    45, 289n.44, 290n.53
Boston Lyceum Bureau, xxiii,
    290n.67
Browne, Charles Farrar (pseud.
    Artemis Ward), 9, 285n.5
Burlingame, Anson, 153–57,
    298n.153
Butler, Benjamin, 38, 288n.36
Byron, George Gordon, 46, 289n.48
Byron-Stowe Controversy, 8–9,
    19–21, 29–31, 37–43, 47–51, 120-
    30, 289n.48, 297n.135

California, 71–73, 89–93, 108–17,
    140–42
California Desperadoes (Sam Brown,
    Jack Williams, Jack Slade),
    142–44, 297n.139, 297n.140,
    297n.142

"Captain Stormfield's Visit to
    Heaven," 491n.77
Cardiff Giant, 134–39, 102n.102,
    102n.103
Charles I, 54, 291n.79
Clemens, Samuel L. (pseud. Mark
    Twain): negotiations for purchase
    of share of *Buffalo Express,*
    xiv–xx; duties and publishing at
    the *Express,* xx–xxii; authorship
    of Hy Slocum/Carl Byng pieces,
    xxiii; "Around the World"
    sketches, xxxiv–xlii; courtship of
    Olivia Langdon, xiv; marriage to
    Olivia Langdon and early per-
    sonal problems, xxiv–xxv
Cleopatra, 46, 290n.54
Cornwallis, Charles, 54, 292n.82
Cuba, 117–20, 296n.129
Curtis, George William, 59–60,
    292n.89

Davis, Garret, 47, 290n.60
Derby, George Horatio (pseud. John
    Phoenix), 91, 289n.42, 295n.115
Dick Baker's Cat, 114–17, 296n.128
Doesticks. *See* Thomson, Mortimer
    Neil

Empress Josephine Beuharnais, 46,
    290n.53
Esmerelda Mining District, 72,
    293n.95

Fairbanks, Mary Mason, xiv, 288n.40
Ford, Professor Darius R.,
    xxxv–xxxvi, 66–67

Franco-Prussian War, 222–24, 227–29, 238–39, 303n.202, 305n.226

Franklin, Benjamin, 46, 289n.45

The Gates Ajar (Phelps), 51–53, 291n.76, 291n.77

Grant, Ulysses S., 65, 228, 229–33, 285n.7, 290n.65, 303n.208

Greeley, Horace, 16, 286n.14, 292n.87

Gunpowder Plot, 54, 291n.80

Harte, Francis Bret, 108–9, 291n.76, 296n.126

Hastings, Warren, 54, 292n.81

Hayti, 78–83, 294n.104

Hole-in-the-Day, 16, 286n.13

Insanity Pleas, 177–81, 194–95, 204–7

Internal Revenue Department, 166–70, 300n.164

Joan of Arc, 46, 289n.50

Johnson, Andrew, 47, 290n.63, 296n.130

Langdon, Jervis, xix, xx, xiv, 11, 224–27, 285n.8, 285n.9, 299n.161, 303n.201

Langdon, Olivia, xix, 288n.34, 292n.87

Larned, Josephus N., xix, 59, 286n.16, 292n.88

Locke, David Ross (pseud. Petroleum Vesuvius Nasby), xix, 153, 298n.151, 298n.152

Lopez, Francisco Solano, 84–86, 294n.106, 294n.108

Lydia Thompson Blondes, 157–59, 299n.154

A Midsummer Night's Dream, 95–96

Moffett, Annie E., 87, 295n.111

Moffett, Pamela Clemens, 295n.111

Molly Maguires, 160, 299–300n.161

Mono Lake, 68–71, 293n.92

Nasby, Petroleum Vesuvius. *See* Locke, David Ross

Neil, Marshal Adolphe, 44, 288n.39

Nelson, Admiral Horatio, 289n.49

Nevada, 71–73, 130–34, 142–44

North Orphir ("Virginia City"), 72, 133, 293n.100

Nye, James, 230–33, 304n.209

Paraguayan War, 84–86, 294n.106

Phelps, Elizabeth Stuart. *See The Gates Ajar*

Phoenix, John. *See* Derby, George Horatio

Queen Alexandrina Victoria, 26, 287n.19

Queen Elizabeth I, 46, 290n.56

Raleigh, Sir Walter, 46, 290n.56

Red Jacket, 16, 46, 286n.12

Redpath, James, 47, 290n.66, 290n.67

Richardson-MacFarland Murder Case, 101–2, 107, 181, 204–7, 296n.121, 296n.125, 301n.180, 302n.182, 302n.193, 302n.194, 302n.195

Riley, John Henry, 243–46, 304n.214

Sandwich Islands (Hawaii), 144–49, 297–98n.143

Seward, William H., 47, 290n.64

Shaw, Henry Wheeler (pseud. Josh Billings), 46, 106–7, 289n.46

Sherman, William Tecumseh, 229, 303n.206

Slee, John De La Fletcher, 11, 286n.9

Slote, Daniel, 171, 300n.170, 300n.171

Stanton, Edwin M., 120–23,
    296n.130, 296-97n.131
Stevens, Thaddeus, 122, 297n.133
Stowe, Harriet Beecher, 292n.87

Talmage, Reverend Thomas DeWitt,
    199–203, 302n.189
Thomson, Mortimer Neil (pseud.
    Doesticks), 280, 305n.232
Trochu, General Louis Jules, 229,
    303n.205
Twain, Mark. *See* Clemens, Samuel L.

Uncas, 16, 286n.11

Vanderbilt, Cornelius, 18, 286n.15

Wagner, John, 21–22
Ward, Artemis. *See* Browne, Charles
    Farrar
Webster, Daniel, 44, 289n.41
Whiteman Cement Mine, 110–12,
    296n.126
William III (William I, King of Prus-
    sia), 229, 303n.207
*Williams and Packard's System of
    Penmanship,* 170–71, 300n.169
Winnemucca Mining District, 72,
    293n.97
Workingmen's Benevolent Associa-
    tion ("Miner's Union"), 159–61,
    285n.9, 299n.158

Young, Brigham, 228, 303n.203